Topics in Regulatory Economics and Policy

Series editor

Michael A. Crew, Newark, NJ, USA

More information about this series at http://www.springer.com/series/6646

Michael Crew · Pier Luigi Parcu
Timothy Brennan
Editors

The Changing Postal and Delivery Sector

Towards A Renaissance

Springer

Editors
Michael Crew
Rutgers Business School-Newark
and New Brunswick
Newark, NJ
USA

Timothy Brennan
School of Public Policy
University of Maryland, Baltimore County
Baltimore, MD
USA

Pier Luigi Parcu
Florence School of Regulation
European University Institute
San Domenico di Fiesole, Firenze
Italy

Topics in Regulatory Economics and Policy
ISBN 978-3-319-46045-1   ISBN 978-3-319-46046-8 (eBook)
DOI 10.1007/978-3-319-46046-8

Library of Congress Control Number: 2016955074

Printed on acid-free paper

This Springer imprint is published by Springer Nature
The registered company is Springer International Publishing AG
The registered company address is: Gewerbestrasse 11, 6330 Cham, Switzerland

Preface

This book is a result of the 24th Conference on Postal and Delivery Economics, which was held May 18–21, 2016 at the Robert Schuman Centre for Advanced Studies of the European University Institute in Florence, Italy. The conference was a joint effort of the Florence School of Regulation—Communications and Media (FSR C&M) at the European University Institute and the Center for Research in Regulated Industries (CRRI) at the Rutgers Business School.

It is now more than a quarter century that this conference has been held. Indeed, the conference followed all the crucial steps of the evolution in the postal sector, which is now impacted by the digital revolution.

Perhaps the major theme that emerged was the impact of the Internet and the resulting electronic competition on the postal sector. Key topics for discussion were, and are, the market change and new users' priorities, the impact on regulatory and competition dynamics and the re-thinking of the Universal Service Obligation.

The conference was made possible by the contribution of generous supporters. We would like to thank them not only for financial support. In addition, they provided helpful advice in their role on the organizing committee as well as, along with others, intellectual contributions, advice and encouragement: Mohammad Adra, Bruno Basalisco, Jody Berenblatt, Claire Borsenberger, Fabio Camerano, Steven Cape, Isabelle Carslake, Beverly Collins, João Confraria, Margaret Cigno, Peter Dunn, Colm Farrelly, Charles Fattore, Stefano Gori, Andrea Grillo, Robert Hammond, John Hearn, Paul Hodgson, George Hoopis, Adam Houck, Christian Jaag, Denis Joram, Patrick Keating, Keith Kellison, George Kuehnbaum, Martin Maegli, Meloria Meschi, Henrik Ballebye Okholm, Ted Pearsall, José María Rodríguez, Chris Rowsell, Jim Sauber, Michael Scanlon, Gennaro Scarfiglieri, Soterios Soteri, Nancy Sparks, David Stubbs, Mark van der Horst, Tim Walsh, and David Williams.

This year's conference benefited greatly from the efforts of the Conferences Unit of the Robert Schuman Centre for Advanced Studies and of the team of the FSR C&M, who were incredibly helpful during the Conference, enabling it to operate it very smoothly. They and colleagues provided both advice and assistance on numerous occasions and contributed greatly to the success of the event.

We would like to thank our distinguished dinner speaker, the President of AGCOM (the Italian National Regulatory Authority) and 2017 Chair of ERGP (European Regulators Group for Postal Services), Angelo Marcello Cardani. In his speech he focused on the impact of the digital revolution on the postal sector and the challenges it triggers and, also comparing it with other industries, he underlined the need to transform these challenges in opportunities.

In addition, we thank all authors and participants of the conference. Absent their contributions, the conference and this book would not have been possible. The usual disclaimers are applicable. In particular, the views expressed reflect the views of the authors and are not necessarily those of the editors or sponsors.

Newark, NJ, USA Michael Crew
San Domenico di Fiesole, Italy Pier Luigi Parcu
Baltimore, MD, USA Timothy Brennan

The Conference was kindly supported by:

Royal Mail
R.R. Donnelley Logistics
United Parcel Service
Pitney Bowes
Ofcom
Citizen Advice
Poste Italiane
La Poste
Copenhagen Economics
Swisspost
FedEx
Canadian Union of Postal Workers
IBM Global Business Services
GrayHair Advisors
FTI Consulting
ComReg
Frontier Economics
National Association of Letter Carriers
Cullen International
K&L Gates LLP
New Zealand Post Limited
An Post
Swiss Economics

In memory of Prof. Michael A. Crew, 1942–2016

On September 26, 2016, Michael A. Crew died peacefully at his home after a short illness, at age 74. Michael was Professor of Regulatory Economics and Director of the Center for Research in Regulated Industries (CRRI), Rutgers, The State University of New Jersey, Newark, USA. He was the founder of the series of international Conferences on Postal and Delivery Economics and co-editor of over twenty books based on proceedings from these Conferences, including this book. This book is dedicated to his memory.

Michael was born in England during World War 2. He was educated at Dudley Grammar School and the Universities of Birmingham and Bradford, where he received his PhD in 1972. Between 1964 and 1977 Michael held academic appointments in Economics and Business Studies at various British Universities and the London Graduate School of Business Studies. He was a visiting Faculty Member at Harvard University during the summer of 1975.

In January 1977 Michael moved to the USA to take up a post as Associate Professor of Business Administration at Rutgers University. In July 1984 he founded and was appointed Director of the Center for Research in Regulated Industries at the Rutgers Business School. In 1988 he founded the *Journal of Regulatory Economics* and was its editor until his untimely death. Michael's main interests were regulatory economics, peak-load pricing, and the theory of monopoly. His legacy includes a multitude of published works about public utilities and postal services, including well over 40 books, as editor or author, numerous professional papers, book reviews and testimony before the US Congress.

The late Paul R. Kleindorfer[1] was both a close friend and an academic collaborator. One of their first joint works was a professional paper "*A Note on Peak Loads and Non-Uniform Costs*" published in the *Economic Journal*, June 1970. Subsequently they worked together on the Center for Research in Regulated

[1]Former Paul Dubrule Professor of Sustainable Development, INSEAD, Fontainebleau, France and Anheuser-Busch Professor Emeritus of Management Science, The Wharton School, University of Pennsylvania, USA

Industries' program on Postal and Delivery Economics. This included conferences and corresponding edited volumes of proceedings. The first Conference was held at Coton House, Rugby, England from July 22 to 25, 1990. The partnership continued for more than 40 years until Paul Kleindorfer's sad and untimely death on August 24, 2012.

Their collaboration was focused on academic work of the highest standard, the edited volumes of Conference proceedings, 20 volumes in all, and the *Handbook of Worldwide Postal Reform*[2]. Following Paul's death, Michael worked with Professor Timothy J. Brennan, University of Maryland Baltimore County, and Professor Pier Luigi Parcu of the European University Institute at Florence to ensure the continuance of the *Postal and Delivery Economics Conferences*, and the edited volumes of proceedings. But the practical organization of the conferences, including sponsorship, selection of venues, and the minutiae of tasks necessary for a successful Conference, depended on Michael's exceptional organizational skills.

Following his retirement as the CRRI Distinguished Professor of Regulatory Economics at Rutgers Business School in 2015, Michael continued his interest in regulatory reform and the postal sector. At the 24th Annual Conference this year in Florence, Michael presented the case for reform of the US Postal Accountability and Enhancement Act of 2006 in a paper co-authored with Timothy J. Brennan, which is featured in Chap. 1 of this book.

Michael was a family man who dotted on his five grandchildren. He will be deeply missed by his wife, Hilary, and his children, Sarah and Nicholas, his grandchildren and all who knew him. He was also a supporter of the philanthropic work of *The Seeing Eye* to enhance the independence, dignity, and self-confidence of blind people through the use of *Seeing Eye®* dogs.

Michael continued to work, including his duties as editor of this book, almost until his dying day. We are all privileged to have known Michael.

John Hearn

[2]Edward Elgar 2008. The Handbook, and many of the chapters, also involved collaboration with James I. Campbell Jr.

Contents

The Postal Accountability and Enhancement Act After 10 Years—Some Proposals for Reform

Michael Crew and Timothy Brennan

1 Introduction

The Postal Accountability and Enhancement Act of 2006 (PAEA)[1] was a long time in the making, but contained features that were unsuitable for the conditions USPS faced by the time PAEA became law in December 2006. PAEA proved to be counterproductive in addressing the changed conditions that USPS faced after PAEA was enacted. As a result, USPS has some serious financial problems with no relief in sight. However, there is possibly light at the end of the tunnel in that PAEA has provisions to remedy some of the problems it has created. Section 201 requires an extensive review of "the system for regulating rates and classes for market-dominant products" after 10 years from the date of enactment by the Postal Regulatory Commission (PRC).[2] This paper provides a discussion of some of the changes that should considered in the light of the experience of the postal and delivery sector from 2007.

The problems resulting from PAEA arise from some of its provisions, the most important being the operation of the price cap formula employed, which had serious consequence for USPS because of significant and continuing annual declines in volume since 2007. Another problem that arose from declining demand involved the treatment of market power and the approach toward deregulation that was not addressed by PAEA. While this does not present an immediate threat to the financial

[1]P. L. 109–435 (Dec. 20, 2006).

[2]Id., section 201. The PRC was created by PAEA. It had previously been known as the Postal Rate Commission. The new PRC had different powers and responsibilities from that of the old PRC.

M. Crew
Rutgers University, Newark, NJ, USA

T. Brennan (✉)
University of Maryland-Baltimore County, Baltimore, MD, USA
e-mail: brennan@umbc.edu

M. Crew et al. (eds.), *The Changing Postal and Delivery Sector*,
Topics in Regulatory Economics and Policy,
DOI 10.1007/978-3-319-46046-8_1

viability of USPS, it is a matter needing to be resolved in the 10-year review. Moreover, section 701 of PAEA requires the PRC every five years to submit a report to the President and Congress with "recommendations for any legislation or other measures necessary to improve the effectiveness or efficiency of the postal laws of the United States."[3] Other issues involve quality reductions, universal service, cross-subsidy, the appropriate governance structure for USPS (e.g. privatization), and fiscal condition (including provisions on retiree healthcare coverage).

This paper will attempt to address these issues and offer possible solutions. Section 2 will address the effect of regulation on declining demand, reviewing Brennan and Crew (2014) which found that declining demand does not necessarily reduce the market power of USPS over letters delivery, but will reduce the potential profits available to meet the universal service obligation (USO). This section also discusses the fiscal problem of the price cap under seriously declining demand and describes an adjustment, summarizing Brennan and Crew (2016). Section 3 will address the remaining issues stated above. Section 4 provides concluding discussion.

2 Declining Volume: Implications for Regulation

Since PAEA was enacted, first class mail volume has declined dramatically. PAEA did not cause this decline. Rather, broad penetration of the Internet led to a substantial displacement of letter correspondence by electronic mail. Widespread use of online bill payment systems, either through the recipient's website or through the customer's bank, eliminated a significant amount of use of first-class mail. Catalogs and other forms of advertising can be delivered through the Internet, with links for ordering goods that eliminates the use of mail to make purchases from these vendors. Such purchasers have stimulated demand for parcel delivery, but since parcel delivery has a number of competitors, the USPS or national postal operators (POs) generally may not be able to make up from declining demand for letters, for which USPS has a statutory monopoly.

This declining demand has had a number of consequences for policy makers. One is whether the universal service obligation (USO) should be redefined as result of reduced revenues, e.g. fewer delivery days, use of community boxes rather than home delivery, increases in delivery time, and elimination of some post offices. A second is the extent to which POs should expand their role in unregulated and largely competitive non-postal markets, such as electronic mail, security services, and banking, also discussed below in Sect. 3.

The focus here is on the responses of regulators to declining demand. One concern is whether the migration of correspondence, bill payment, advertising, etc. to the Internet shows a level of competition that eliminates the need for regulation to protect remaining postal customers from higher rates. This migration need not justify deregulation of postal service. Whether such service should be privatized is a

[3]Id., section 701.

separate question, addressed in Crew and Brennan (2015) and discussed below in Sect. 3.

If regulation is maintained, there remains a question of how prices can be adjusted to replace lost revenues to cover the cost of postal services and subsidizing universal service.[4] Brennan and Crew (2016) proposed a mechanism for price adjustment to replace these revenues that utilizes parameters accessible to regulators, consistent with the price-cap mechanism that PAEA mandates for postal services.

Sections 2.1 and 2.2 expand on the two themes of whether Internet incursion implies sufficient competition to justify deregulation and, if not, how PAEA's price caps could be adjusted to protect USPS's ability to cover its cost of providing service.

2.1 Internet and USPS Market Power

Undoubtedly, electronic substitution has taken a large share of USPS' core business of letter mail. Thinking of this in terms of competition is reasonable in a business sense. Had the Internet not occurred, USPS and other POs in the world would have been in a stronger financial position, at least for letter mail.

It is tempting to extend the reach of the term "competition" to conclude that because USPS has faced "competition" in the business sense from electronic message delivery in the above sense of the term, that USPS operates in a market characterized by "competition" in the antitrust sense and thus requires less regulatory oversight of its prices. Brennan and Crew (2014) suggested that this temptation should be resisted. A radical new technology can take away much of the demand for an older technology; among the examples would be what cars did to the demand for bicycles, mobile phones did to the demand for landline phones, and contact lenses did to the demand for eyeglasses. But a remaining monopolist in bicycles, landline phones, or eyeglasses would likely be able to raise price over competitive levels.

The concept Brennan and Crew (2014) used to illuminate the difference between the business and antitrust senses of "competition" was the difference between "gross substitutes" and "marginal substitutes". A good or service X is a "gross substitute" for another good or service Y if X's availability reduces demand for Y. The pairs of goods above are gross substitutes, as are electronic message delivery and postal delivery—and this is the meaning of "competition" in the business sense.

For the purpose of assessing market power, for example, with market definition, however, the issue is not merely whether one good is a gross substitute for another, but whether the degree of substitution is highly sensitive to relative prices—

[4]An alternative approach is to lower service quality. For example, Houpis et al. (2015), Robinson et al. (2015) and Choain et al. (2015) examine the impact of reducing delivery frequency.

"marginal substitutes". To characterize competition in this antitrust sense of the term, X and Y have to be marginal substitutes. Regardless of the gross amount of demand X has taken from Y, X would meaningfully restrain the ability of a monopolist in Y to set price if increasing the price of Y alone would cause many buyers of Y to switch to X.

Gross substitutes are not always marginal substitutes. They may not be in the same relevant market. For example, the decision between driving and riding a bicycle is not likely to be sensitive to the price of either. Those who prefer eyeglasses to contact lenses are not likely to switch to contact lenses if the price of eyeglass were to increase 5–10 %—a level that raises concern among antitrust authorities in the U.S.

The same is true for electronic message delivery and postal services. While email has led to an enormous decline in demand for sending letters through USPS, it is far from clear that the shift from letters to email has been or would be significantly affected by the price of postage. Moreover, and perhaps counterintuitively, a reduction in demand from a gross substitute, electronic mail for example, could increase the unregulated profit-maximizing price of the incumbent product, such as postal letter delivery.

A numerical example can illustrate the possibility. Suppose that prior to the availability of electronic mail, the profit-maximizing price for a stamp was $1. (If so, regulation held price below this level.) Suppose that following widespread access to the Internet, everyone with a willingness to pay to send a letter at or below $1.50 chose to use electronic email and those willing to pay $1.50 or above would remain with postal service. Then, the profit-maximizing price would increase to $1.50.

This numerical example illustrates a broader result: With constant marginal cost, incursion by a gross substitute will increase the profit-maximizing price of the incumbent if those who turn to the gross substitute have more elastic demand for the incumbent's service than those who remain with the incumbent. Here, the profit-maximizing price would rise if those who turn to electronic mail have a more elastic demand for postal service than those left behind. The elasticity of demand for mail will be lower than it was prior to entry by the gross substitute. This reduction in demand elasticity drives increase the profit-maximizing price (holding marginal cost constant).

Two points need to be kept in mind. First, while the profit-maximizing price does not necessarily increase, electronic competition need not preclude a PO from setting the letter price significantly above cost. So, the need for regulatory oversight may remain.

Second, even if the profit-maximizing price were to increase, the profits available to a PO (or any incumbent) necessarily fall when availability of a gross substitute reduces demand. This is because when the demand curve falls, the set of price-output combinations available to the PO is smaller than it was before. Even if a PO retains market power over letters following electronic alternatives, it still potentially has less revenue at its disposal to fund the USO or any other mandate imposed by its regulator or the government. The potential of a higher price strengthens the case for regulation, but leaves the PO in a more fragile fiscal position. In that sense, the business interpretation of "competition" from email as hurting POs is valid.

2.2 Adjusting Postal Rates with Declining Demand

Under PAEA, USPS rates for market dominant services are regulated under price cap regulation (PCR).[5] Under PCR, changes over time to a regulated firm's price P are based not on its costs, but on adjustments based on the inflation rate (e.g., changes to the Consumer Price Index CPI). In addition, the regulator can prescribe ex ante reductions over time to the regulated price equal to X %. This percentage nominally reflects the amount of the expected increase in the regulated firm's productivity that would be passed on to ratepayers in the form of lower prices, although in practice it is more likely to reflect a political bargain between the regulator and the regulated firm. This adjustment is usually written as

$$\frac{\Delta P}{P} = \frac{\Delta CPI}{CPI} - X.$$

The key is that both the change in the CPI and the price reduction X factor are beyond the regulated firm's control. Productivity might be expected to increase under PCR, leading to greater returns to the regulated firm, because separating regulated rates from costs gives the regulated firm an incentive to reduce its costs. When costs fall but prices do not, the regulated firm retains the difference, whereas under conventional cost-of-service regulation the firm essentially has to return it.

As we discuss below and in the following section of the paper, the PCR analysis may be somewhat more complicated. In general, if prices are fixed by the regulator independent of the regulated firm's quality, it may have an incentive to cut quality if the savings in costs exceed the lost profits from the decrease in demand when quality falls. When a PO is state-owned, it lacks the usual residual claimants, who would gain through cost savings. So PCR may not lead to productivity increases expected for privately owned regulated firms.

Declining demand raises yet another problem with price caps. If demand is increasing, a PO (or any regulated firm) with capped prices will see its profits increase and its fiscal position improve. However, with falling demand, the reverse is true. If price is above marginal cost, as expected for typical "natural monopoly" regulated firms with high fixed costs that revenues have to cover, the firm will be less able to cover its costs. For a PO, these costs include not just the fixed costs of operation but those arising from having to meet the USO.

[5]39 U.S.C. § 3622(d), as amended by PAEA, secion 201.

Maintaining solvency therefore requires that the capped prices be adjusted. Such an adjustment has to meet three criteria. First, the adjustment factor should fit within the price cap formula above as an added term, rather than something that adopts an unfamiliar format. Second, the adjustment factor has to be based on factors that are outside the regulated firm's control; otherwise, the separation of price from actual cost that leads to the benefits of PCR could be attenuated. Third, to be practical, the adjustment factor has to be relatively simple and based on parameters that a regulator could reasonably ascertain; otherwise, it will not be adopted.

Brennan and Crew (2016) proposed such a mechanism. It is based on three parameters:

The percentage by which demand changes, Z equal to $\Delta Q/Q$, where Q is demand. With declining demand, Z is negative. This measure needs to be the change in demand independent of any change brought about by actions of the PO. In particular, if the change in demand is the result of the change in the PO's quality of service, the operator should not be rewarded by having its price go up as a result.

The elasticity of average cost, e_{AC}. This is the percentage change in average cost changes for a given change in demand and a measure of how much money the firm needs to earn to restore its solvency to what it would have been had demand not declined. Generally, for regulated firms this will be negative, in that average cost falls as demand rises. Here, this parameter gives a first approximation to how much price would have to increase to cover the increase in average cost brought about by a reduction in demand. This may seem like a difficult parameter to estimate, but Brennan and Crew (2016) show that a good approximation to e_{AC} is the negative of the ratio of fixed to total costs, when marginal costs are constant. Another approximation to e_{AC} is the ratio of marginal cost to average costs minus 1 ($MC/AC - 1$). A third way a regulator can estimate e_{AC} is to note that it is the elasticity of total cost with respect to output minus 1. The elasticity of total cost to output is the standard measure of economies of scale. So, if a regulator has some estimate of this, it has an equally acceptable alternative to derive e_{AC}.

Elasticity of demand e_D, also negative. To a first approximation, the increase in average cost brought about by a decline in demand is Ze_{AC}, the positive product of two negative numbers. However, if the regulated firm raises its price by this percentage, demand falls, measured by e_D times that percentage increase in price. To ensure that the PO maintains its fiscal position, the effect needs to be taken into account.

Putting these together, Brennan and Crew (2016) derive a declining demand price adjustment term equal to

$$\frac{\Delta P}{P} = Z\left[\frac{e_{AC}}{1 - e_{AC}e_D}\right].$$

This term can be added to $\Delta CPI/CPI - X$ in the original price cap formula. This formula meets the three criteria mentioned above.

In addition, note that if $e_{AC}e_D > 1$, the expression in the brackets is positive, meaning that the formulaic response to a fall in demand ($Z < 0$), the regulator's response would be to cut price. That would leave the PO worse off, leading to the "death spiral" about which others have expressed concern. This would make a price increase self-defeating, as it would introduce a feedback effect in which the demand reduction would require an additional price increase, bringing about an additional demand reduction. If the elasticity of demand and of average cost are sufficiently small, specifically if $e_{AC}e_D < 1$, this "death spiral" would not happen. For it to occur, we would need a substantially large elasticity of demand for postal services, that is, from the above condition, $|e_D| > 1/|e_{AC}|$. As discussed above, there need not be a high elasticity of demand for a PO's service, even if electronic message delivery has substantially reduced demand for that service.

In addition, the formula works for increases in demand as well. If demand were to increase, that is, $Z > 0$, and if $e_{AC}e_D < 1$, as we would expect, the regulator would be justified in cutting the PO's price. This would leave the PO in the same fiscal position relative to its costs as it would have been without the increase in demand. Consumers rather than the firm would get the windfall when demand goes up, just as they would be obligated to pay higher prices for postal services when demand falls.

To get an idea of the implication of this formula, Brennan and Crew applied it to reported reductions in mail volumes (not divided by class of service), using elasticities of average cost and demand of −0.3 for both, and found that under this formula, postal prices should have increased by 9.8 % from 2007 through 2013. While this estimate depends on these parameters and, importantly, ignores reductions in demand arising from changes in prices during that period, it does indicate that the effect of this adjustment for declining demand could be substantial.

3 Other Issues and Potential Reforms

The discussion in Sect. 2 provides for reform in the price cap formula to reflect the problem of declining demand and the impact on market power. It does not resolve by any means all of the problems that have occurred since 2006. Most of the additional problems arise from dramatically declining demand, and additional reforms are needed to address these problems.

3.1 Cost and Quality Reductions

Given that PCR broke the link between prices and cost by capping its rate increase exogenously at the CPI, USPS' options were to get further into the hole financially or cut costs. As discussed below, USPS did go into the hole, but it also found ways to cut costs and proposed others. It had a number of means of cutting expenditures —concessions from the unions, lowering the level of vehicle fleet and other maintenance, and reducing service quality.

The postal unions have made concessions. For example, the National Association of Letter Carriers negotiated with USPS to have a new entry level class of employee, but the terms were ultimately determined by arbitration. A non-career employee classification, City Carrier Assistant (CCA), was created. CCAs were paid an hourly rate of \$15.30 starting with annual raises for each year of the contract rising to \$15.68 and \$16.06. CCAs did not receive the pension, health benefits and COLAs that are received by career carriers. USPS, on a district by district basis, is allowed to hire a maximum of 23 % CCAs. This change will continue to result in a substantial saving in labor costs for USPS. It provides a benefit for labor in that CCA is now the sole entry point into the career. This is also a substantial benefit to USPS in that it provides a pool of trained and experienced employees.

The other source of expenditure reduction has been to lower the quality of service. In 2010 USPS made a case to eliminate Saturday delivery through an Advisory Opinion of the PRC.[6] To date this has not been achieved because of Congressional objection. In 2012 USPS again filed for an Advisory Opinion of the PRC to lower the quality of First Class Mail delivery.[7] The basic idea was to take longer to deliver mail and essentially eliminate overnight delivery. The PRC's Advisory Decision essentially accepted USPS's case to make this service reduction. In addition, major reductions in expenditure were achieved through the closure of mail processing facilities. For example, the career employee workforce was reduced by 200,000 and over 20,000 delivery routes and 360 facilities were consolidated (Brennan 2016).[8]

The requirement that USPS seek Advisory Opinions of the PRC was a provision of PAEA that limited the ability of the PRC to prevent reductions in quality induced by PCR. It has long been recognized that one way a monopolist operating under PCR may increase profit is by lowering quality (e.g. Littlechild 1986). Before regulated monopolies changed to PCR they, including USPS, were regulated by cost-of-service regulation, which normally provided incentives for high quality of service. If this level was greater than that of a profit-maximizing monopolist, then under PCR the firm would be able to increase profits by lowering service quality.[9] As a result of this it was clear that under PCR regulators needed to monitor and enforce quality standards. However, the PRC's ability to give only an Advisory Opinion seriously limits its authority. While the intent may have been to avoid micromanagement, this was a mistaken provision in PAEA. It ignored not only the academic research (e.g. Sappington 2005) but also the practice in other regulated industries, where under PCR quality is enforced by the firm's regulatory

[6]Docket No. N2010-1, Six-Day to Five-Day Carrier Delivery and Related Service Changes, 2010.

[7]Docket No. N2012-1, Mail Processing Network Rationalization Service Changes, 2012.

[8]From USPS data at https://about.usps.com/who-we-are/postal-facts/size-scope.htm, the USPS workforce at the beginning of 2016 was just under 500,000, so this represents a reduction of about 30 %.

[9]For a rigorous but readable discussion see Sappington's (2005) survey article on quality in regulated monopoly.

commission. So, Advisory Opinions should be eliminated and the PRC should have the authority to enforce standards.

3.2 USO

As noted in the above discussion of the fiscal and regulatory effects of declining demand, the ability of the USPS to fund the USO as it has been implicitly defined in the past is falling. As a consequence, the USO should be explicitly defined, with each provision justified, and its governance should be defined by statute. (In European countries, the USO is subject to formal definition.) This should include a process for modifying the USO. Almost certainly because of cost pressures additional attempts will be made to reduce the USO. The previous attempts have not struck at the core of the USO. The attempt to end Saturday delivery and the reduction in service standards did not hit at the fundamental features of the USO, namely, ubiquitous service at a uniform price.

The traditional USO had some quality difference for outlying areas, but the service had the same fundamental features of ubiquity and uniformity. If volume continues to decline, resulting in further financial pressures on USPS, some of the basic tenets of the USO may have to be rejected. It is essentially impossible that some parts of the country will be abandoned, but serious curtailments could take place. For example, some remote areas might get delivery between 1 and 3 times a week; others might get 4, 5, 6 or a few even 7 day delivery.[10] If it comes to this, binding decisions by the PRC would be required if the USO was to continue to have any meaning.

In addition to reductions in service USPS needs to be more innovative in providing means of funding the USO. One example might be postal banking, but it is problematic whether an expansion of this kind would improve postal finances. It may improve utilization of the retail network and provide a social benefit to the unbanked, who now rely on payday loans. The former might be beneficial financially but the latter would be seen as obligation, effectively expanding the USO. Moreover, expansion of regulated firms into competitive markets creates risks of cross-subsidization and discriminatory access that can inhibit efficient entry into those markets, leading to higher prices and perhaps for USPS's traditional services as well.[11] Such an expansion would be unlikely to receive the support of Congress. If it did some control would be required, such as review and binding rules set by the PRC.

---

[10]In the context of the USO under entry, Crew and Kleindorfer (2006) explore some of the implications of entry on the USO and possible strategies in response.

[11]Brennan (1987) provides a general discussion of the potential downside from letting regulated firms into unregulated markets. Brennan and Palmer (1994) examine in more detail the tradeoff between realizing economies of scope and harms from cross-subsidization.

3.3 Cross-Subsidy

The growth in package delivery has been one area where USPS has benefitted from the Internet Age. It has a ubiquitous delivery network that has proved capable of dealing with the increase in parcel volume. It has been particularly successful in providing local delivery for the major players in package delivery, UPS and FEDEX. For example, between first quarters of 2015 and 2016 Parcel Select's revenue grew a remarkable 38.1 % and volume 29.5 %. Revenue per piece was $1.88, in contrast to Priority Mail at $7.54, with volume growth of 7.7 % and revenue growth of 7.3 %. USPS is both a competitor and a supplier to UPS and FEDEX, who are themselves suppliers and competitors of USPS.

These interrelationships have not prevented UPS from filing testimony before the PRC claiming that competitive products are being cross-subsidized by market dominant products. UPS argues that the current costing system should be replaced by a fully distributed cost system, the impact of which would be to raise the amount allocated to competitive products considerably. The UPS case does not demonstrate explicitly why USPS would want to subsidize competitive products. According to Braeutigam and Panzar (1989), under PCR a firm has no incentive to cross-subsidize. However, Braeutigam and Panzar's result relies on the firm having residual claimants. USPS does not have residual claimants, so that it does not follow that this result has to hold. It could be argued that given USPS' exigent financial situation it will not add to its losses by cross-subsidy. It is possible that a public enterprise operating under PCR may have less incentive to cross-subsidize competitive products than one operating under cost-of-service regulation, the form of regulation used before PAEA. So, the argument is inconclusive and the cross-subsidy concern will remain important as long as USPS does not have residual claimants.

One approach to addressing cross-subsidy might be to reorganize USPS so that it operates more like a private business, which may make it less dependent on the costing system.[12] Instead of its hierarchical unitary form of organization, it might follow the example of many corporations with operating divisions or business units.[13] The unitary form faces a number of problems when firms get very large, including span of control of the CEO. Other issues arise including accounting and motivation. With separate business units the objectives of the individual units are clearer. USPS differs from large corporations in its over-reliance of a hierarchical structure. It still is closer to a government department than a firm. It provides services just like FEDEX and UPS but it does not have the focus on profits that

[12]Crew and Brennan (2015) voiced concerns over the USPS business model and Crew and Geddes (2014) voiced criticized the public enterprise model. The discussion that follows here is more microscopic addressing internal organization.

[13]Williamson (1970) examines the U-form versus the multi-divisional form and provides evidence for the greater efficiency of the latter.

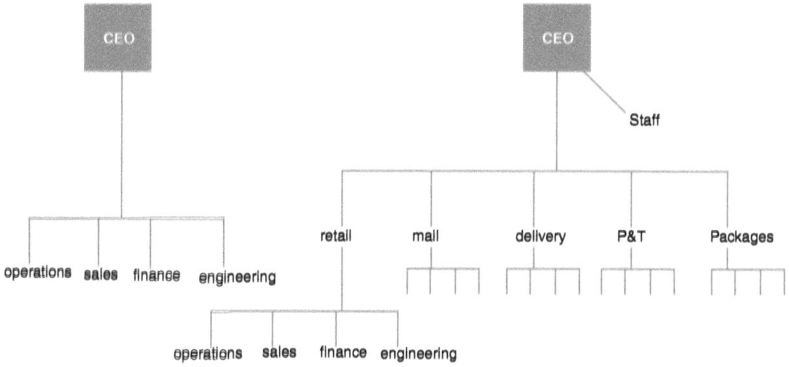

Fig. 1 A proposed organization for USPS

investor-owned companies have. USPS could be organized as business units in a number of ways.

A possible example would include the following business units: Retail, Processing and Transportation, Packages, Mail and Delivery. The organization chart contrasting with the U-form is shown in Fig. 1, which is adapted from Williamson (1970, p116).

Retail would include retail outlets, which received mail and packages for delivery by the Mail and Packages business units. It would also receive packages from especially, UPS and FEDEX for handing to Delivery. Processing and Transportation (P&T) would provide sorting and logistic services in competition with presort and logistics companies. Packages would compete with couriers for retail and commercial parcels. Mail would include retail, large mailers and would buy services from the Delivery, Retail and Processing and Transportation units. However, it could alsThis discussion of a more businesso buy these services in the market. Indeed, all business units would have the option to buy from the market. This would introduce more competition and have the potential of being cost-reducing. New business units could be added, including retail banking and financial services, which would purchase inputs from primarily Retail.

This discussion of a more business-like structure for USPS indicates a need for further research. Its intent is to highlight the importance of examining the question of reorganization. It has some potential for addressing cross-subsidy. The Packages unit would be in a position to focus directly on profits. It would, like UPS and FEDEX, have to buy its local delivery from Delivery, which would fix its rates based upon profitability. It would buy other services in the market and would not be required to buy them from internal sources. With this improved focus on profits it would be interesting to see the effect on pricing. This kind of approach may reduce concerns over inefficient preemption of entry into markets for non-dominant services.[14]

[14]Under such a structure, competitors may have a stronger case for obtaining USPS services at reasonable and non-discriminatory rates.

3.4 Privatization on the Table

Reorganization of USPS to become more businesslike is limited as long as it remains a public enterprise. Given problems faced by USPS and the record of Congressional oversight, which has mostly failed to deliver, drastic change is needed and privatization should be one of the solutions to be considered. According to perhaps the majority of postal pundits it is pointless putting privatization on the table as "it will never happen." Whether this is correct remains to be seen, but major change needs to take place. Crew and Kleindorfer (2013) examined the benefits and costs of privatization in the context of the privatization of Royal Mail, which became legally feasible as a result of the UK Postal Services Act of 2011. It concluded that the benefits exceeded the costs. Crew and Geddes (2014) concluded that the USPS business model was seriously flawed and that privatization was likely to result in a superior governance structure.

Privatization has taken place in the European Union, notably, Germany, the UK and the Netherlands, and has recently started in Italy. The EU is often criticized in the US for being socialist, but it has achieved privatization of major POs that has eluded the US. The German privatization has been mostly successful, despite its failure to enter the US market in a major way. Interestingly, it divested its banking operations.[15] The Netherlands PO has been more mixed. It divested TNT in 2011, its courier operation, with a significant loss of shareholder value. TNT was approached in 2012 by UPS with a takeover offer of $6.7 billion, which was rejected by the European Commission. In January 2016, FEDEX's proposed acquisition was approved by the EC but the price is now $4.8 billion. Royal Mail's privatization has been successful so far but it took until between 2013 and 2015 before it became fully privatized. The USO has continued after privatization, although it may be coming under increasing pressure.

Like almost everything there are benefits and costs associated with privatization. The downside may be more pressure on reducing the USO. In addition, private companies are free to make bad investment decisions. However, this freedom to make investment decisions is likely to be superior to the present situation with the USPS, whose decision making power is limited, the result of which is to stifle investment and innovation. Freeing USPS from the Congressional yoke is likely to be an improvement over the *status quo* if for no other reason than the fact that Congressional oversight has had serious negative effects. USPS can never be business-like under Congressional oversight. To take a current example, the USPS Board of Governors (BOG) has only one member remaining appointed by a President; the full complement is nine.[16] An investor-owned corporation would not be allowed to let its board drop to one member. Arguably, the BOG is an effete body as a result of the reduction in its power under PAEA, so that failure to fill the

---

[15]The German Government still owns 21 % of the stock.

[16]The President appoints 9 members. The BOG appoints the Postmaster and Deputy Postmasters General. The Presidential members have full voting rights.

seats does not have a serious impact. At minimum this calls for a redefining of the BOG's mandate. A more radical approach would be privatization, which provides the most promising means for getting Congress out of USPS' affairs.

3.5 Financial Condition

A ten-year review that took no action on the financial condition of USPS would be highly deficient, as USPS is in very bad shape financially. Its cumulative deficiency since its founding in 1971 totals $50.391 billion as of year ending September 30, 2015. The likelihood is that the deficiency will continue to grow as the loss for 2015 was $5.06 billion, including $5.7 billion that it did not pay to the retiree healthcare fund as required by PAEA. Its cash holdings are $6.634 billion, and which is inadequate liquidity for an organization of this size, and which has fully exhausted its $15 billion borrowing authority. Its pension and retiree healthcare liabilities comprised $404.7 billion, of which $337.1 billion is funded. They are off-balance sheet because the funds are held by the Office of Personnel Management (OPM), which is obligated to pay the beneficiaries. Pension funding is the one bright spot in USPS finances, comparing favorably with Fortune 500 Companies and the rest of the Federal Government.[17] The healthcare deficiency is currently $54.8 billion of which $28.1 billion is reflected on the balance sheet in the payments USPS has not made to the fund since 2012, as is required by PAEA.

Given current prices and the continuing decline in volume of First Class letters, prospects of returning to a surplus soon are poor if the business-as-usual mode continues. Indeed, there is little prospect of any immediate rate relief. USPS's Exigent Rate Increase expired on April 11, when the 49¢ stamp reverted to 47¢. The impact of the increase had been to provide USPS with approximately $2.1 billion a year.[18] Loss of this revenue will add significantly to USPS's problems. Although USPS has appealed the PRC's decision the US Court of Appeals it is unlikely that the decision will be overturned.

The Exigent Rate increase was intended to account for impact of the Great Recession. The case for its expiration relies on the notion that with the end of the recession demand would pick up. Indeed, the recession did end and demand did pick up in most sectors. However, the increase in demand eluded USPS, whose mail volumes continued to decline. The argument for continuing the Exigent Rate increase then is that the recession effectively did not end for USPS. What was not appreciated was the recession coincided with what amounted to a dramatic leap in wireless and broadband. The recession meant decisions to abandon mail for

---

[17]There are two Government pension plans funded at 89.8 and 96.7 % respectively. These compare with 80 % for Fortune 500 Companies, 30.9 % for DOD and 66 % for State Government (Brennan 2016).

[18]http://www.prc.gov/docs/93/93783/ExigSrchgRevCUMLTV%282Q14-4Q15%29.xlsx.

electronic media were made, which in many cases were irreversible. If the Exigent Rate had not expired it would have continued to provide some relief for the unrelenting decline in volume. Its effect would have been relatively small but "every little helps."

Other actions would not be immediate and would typically require a change in PAEA. The adjustment proposed in Sect. 2.2 to the price cap mechanism to reflect volume changes would presumably fall into this category. Incorporating the change would be highly contentious. As noted, according to rough data and illustrative estimates of relevant elasticities of demand and average costs, had this adjustment had been made the cumulative effect would have been that postage prices would have been 9.8 % higher by 2013 (Brennan and Crew 2016). However, arguably the exigent increase would not have been needed as the adjustment takes into account the exigency of massive volume loss. So, the actual increase would have been less than 9.8 %.

Even if the full amount were to be allowed, it would not compensate USPS for the years it did not get increases because of the absence of the adjustment. This would not abate the furor. Adjusting the price cap might be less contentious than this make-up payment, as the adjustment does contain the mitigating feature that prices would automatically be reduced if demand grew. The opponents would argue that positive growth would be slow or nonexistent. However, decline in the demand for letters also seems to have slowed, making the future impact of the adjustment much less than previously. The area where demand is growing at a brisk pace is package delivery, but this is not market dominant and therefore not subject to the adjustment.

4 Conclusions

The governance of USPS is in clear need of reform. Even if it retains market power over "market-dominant" services, its financial condition is unsound due to shrinking demand for those services. Adjustments to the price cap formula based on maintaining USPS's ability to raise revenue could bring immediate relief if applied retroactively. This would include binding decisions by the PRC on USPS' plans to lower quality and reduce the USO. Longer term much more is needed. Internal reforms may have promise—reorganization into business units—but ultimately these may not be sufficient.

Congress' record of governing USPS has been highly deficient. It has shown that this is not a way to run a businesslike and efficient operation. Congress needs to come to the realization that the rents from the postal sector are slim. Given its propensity to redistribute rents, Congress should recognize that business as usual is not going to work because of the reduced rents.

This opens up the door to privatization. The UK and other European economies have managed to bring this about. They overcame arguments that there was insufficient value in the enterprise to make privatization feasible. With a regulatory process that is sound, a private USPS could be a successful business. It has many great attributes, principally, a ubiquitous delivery network that no rival can come close to matching. Privatization should be on the table soon to stop the downward spiral that is USPS.

References

Braeutigam, R. R., & Panzar, J. C. (1989). Diversification incentives under "price-based" and "cost-based" regulation. *RAND Journal of Economics, 20*, 373–391.

Brennan, M. J. (2016). Testimony before Senate Homeland Security and Government Affairs Committee, January 21, 2016, http://about.usps.com/news/testimony/2016/pr16_pmg0121.htm, January 21, 2016.

Brennan, T. J. (1987). Why regulated firms should be kept out of unregulated markets: understanding the divestiture in *U.S. v. AT&T. Antitrust Bulletin, 32*, 741–793.

Brennan, T. J., & Palmer, K. L. (1994). Comparing the costs and benefits of diversification by regulated firms. *Journal of Regulatory Economics, 6*, 115–136.

Brennan, T. J., & Crew, M. A. (2014). Gross substitutes vs. marginal substitutes: Implications for market definition in the postal sector. In M. A. Crew & T. J. Brennan (Eds.), *The role of the postal and delivery sector in a digital age* (pp. 1–15). Cheltenham, UK: Edward Elgar.

Brennan, T. J., & Crew, M. A. (2016). Price cap regulation and declining demand. In M. A. Crew & T. J. Brennan (Eds.), *The future of the postal sector in a digital world.* New York, NY: Springer.

Choain, L., Fustier, F., & Janin, L. (2015). Potential gains and losses of (partial) lifting of home delivery optionsin. In M. A. Crew & T. J. Brennan (Eds.), *Postal and delivery innovation in the digital economy* (pp. 143–154). New York: Springer.

Crew, M. A., & Brennan, T. J. (2015). Business models: Some implication for USPS. In M. A. Crew & T. J. Brennan (Eds.), *Postal and delivery innovation in the digital economy* (pp. 1–15). New York: Springer.

Crew, M. A., & Geddes, R. R. (2014) A business model for USPS. In M. A. Crew & T. J. Brennan (Eds.), *The role of postal service in a digital age*, Edward Elgar, Cheltenham, UK.

Crew, M. A., & Kleindorfer, P. R. (2013) Privatization of postal operators: Old arguments and new realities, In *Reforming the postal sector in the face electronic competition.* Edward Elgar, Cheltenham, UK.

Crew, M. A., & Kleindorfer, P. R. (2006) The welfare effects of entry and strategies for maintaining the USO in the postal sector (with P. R. Kleindorfer). In *Progress toward liberalization of the postal and delivery sector*, edited by Springer Science+Business Media, Inc.

Houpis, G., Rodriguez, J. M., & Strobel, C. (2015). Welfare impact of changes in the scope of the USO. In M. A. Crew & T. J. Brennan (Eds.), *Postal and delivery innovation in the digital economy* (pp. 131–142). New York: Springer.

Littlechild, S. C. (1986). Regulation of British telecommunications, department of industry, London.

Robinson, M. J., Klingenberg, J. P., Haller, A., & Trinkner, U. (2015). Estimating the financial impact of discontinuing saturday delivery. In M. A. Crew & T. J. Brennan (Eds.), *Postal and delivery innovation in the digital economy* (pp. 155–168). New York: Springer.

Sappington, D. E. M. (2005). Regulating service quality: A survey. *Journal of Regulatory Economics, 27*, 123–154.

Williamson, O. E. (1970). *Corporate control and business behavior.* Englewood Cliffs, NJ: Prentice Hall.

Lessons from the Postal Sector to Telecommunications and Vice Versa

Pier Luigi Parcu and Virginia Silvestri

1 Introduction

The arrival and diffusion of the commercial Internet has been one of the main causes of change in the postal sector in the last two decades. Its impact has been rapid and it has gone straight to the core of postal operators' (POs') activities: the mail business. Electronic communications, especially email, available at zero marginal cost and relatively high quality, have quickly changed consumers' and businesses' communicating habits, leading to substitution away from traditional physical mails. Although substantial postal volumes remain, for reasons that will later be discussed, it has certainly hit the sector's volume and profitability dramatically.

At the same time, with the development of Internet services and e-commerce and the increased trust that consumers and businesses place on making economic transactions online, there has been a rising demand for parcel delivery, mostly in the Business-to-Consumer (B2C, henceforth) and Consumer-to-Consumer (C2C, henceforth) segments. This growth of demand gave an opportunity to POs to, at least partially, make up for their losses in the mail segment. Technological developments have also brought innovations within the traditional postal services, like hybrid mail, e-government, the electronic mailbox, the tracking of packages.

Besides these market changes, a concurrent challenge for the postal sector comes from evolution of the regulatory framework. The postal service has historically been provided by state-owned monopolies, mainly because of its importance to a country's national cohesion and social inclusion, translated in legal terms as the

P.L. Parcu (✉) · V. Silvestri
Florence School of Regulation Communications & Media, Florence, Italy
e-mail: pierluigi.parcu@eui.eu

V. Silvestri
e-mail: virginia.silvestri@eui.eu

M. Crew et al. (eds.), *The Changing Postal and Delivery Sector*,
Topics in Regulatory Economics and Policy,
DOI 10.1007/978-3-319-46046-8_2

Universal Service Obligation (USO) and the extensive use of price ceilings. In the last two decades, a liberalization of the postal sector has been launched in many countries around the world. There is considerable heterogeneity between countries regarding the timing and the extent to which the postal sector has been liberalized. Such a process is still at a rather early stage in most countries when compared against other, once state-owned, networked sectors, such as telecommunications.

A parallel can be drawn between the postal sector and telecommunications, since both have been heavily impacted upon by the Internet's disruptive force and both have been subject to liberalization in the last two decades. An interesting difference can be noticed among this similarity: in most cases, the Internet's disruptive effect preceded the liberalization process for the postal sector, while the process was inverted for telecommunications, where liberalization had already been achieved when the heaviest phase of Internet disruption arrived.

The following analysis will attempt to exploit this inter-temporal shift in the two sectors' epochal changes so as to derive policy and business lessons from the postal sector for telecommunications, and vice versa. Does the POs' reaction has something to teach the telecommunications operators regarding the way to react to the Internet challenge? Does telecommunications regulation have something to say about how to tackle the current regulatory issues in the postal sector? In the remainder of the paper, Sect. 2 will look at the impact of Internet diffusion; Sect. 3 will analyze liberalization as a disruptive factor for network markets. Conclusions will follow.

2 How the Internet Changed the Postal Sector and then Telecommunications

2.1 The Decline of the Core Postal Business

Around the mid '90s, the commercial Internet started its incredibly rapid growth, thanks to the HTTP protocol and HTML versatile coding language as well as improvements in computing and the speed and capacity of broadband networks. From 0.4 % of the world population in 1995, Internet penetration reached 45 % of world population in 2015, notwithstanding the profound digital divides existing between the more economically developed and the less developed countries, and within countries between rural and metropolitan areas and different socio-demographic groups.

Nowadays, the Internet offers a wide range of services, impacting upon many markets. At the start, browsing the web and exchanging emails were the main reasons why people used the Internet, affecting the postal business before many other areas. The growth of Internet adoption and the possibility of switching to electronic means of written communication had already brought about a noticeable fall in mail volumes in the US and in some European countries in the early 2000s.

In the US, where the Internet was developed, the volume of first-class mail reached its peak at 103.7 billion pieces in 2001, then began to drop. In 2015, the volume was 62 billion, same as in 1982 (USPS). The total mail volume, instead, reached its peak in 2006 with 213.1 billion pieces, then it steadily went down, getting to 154.2 billion in 2015. In Europe, the decline in mail volumes started relatively later, around 2006, but was equally strong and sustained. The total volume of domestic letter post in EU-27 reached its peak at 95.7 billion in 2006, then started to drop. In 2011 it was 82.2 billion, 9.8 % lower than 4 years before, and it has continued to decrease since then (WIK Consult 2013).

Two main motivations explain the decline in mail volumes. First is the 2008 financial crisis, which became an economic recession, and the pro-cyclical characteristic of demand for mail. The second is the negative effect that the Internet had on the letter post business.

The Internet affected letter post activity in both direct and indirect ways. The direct effect was "e-substitution": the substitution for mail of email for private and business correspondence (including online bill payment) and for advertising purposes. The indirect effect was the declining demand for delivery of magazines and newspapers, as consumers tend to read the online version of media outlets more and more frequently.

Email, in fact, constitutes an almost perfect substitute for physical mail, of higher quality in many respects, thanks to its intrinsic ubiquity; the extremely elevated speed of transmission; value-added services; and, last but not least, its essentially zero cost once one is connected to the Internet. These incontestable advantages have fostered an ever increasing level of e-substitution. The worldwide number of email accounts in 1998 was about 77 million, with a total of about 25 million emails sent per day. In 2015, the worldwide number of email accounts was about 4.3 billion, with a total of over 205 billion emails sent per day. Moreover, the growth in the number of emails sent relates mostly to the business segment, which is the most profitable for POs (The Radicati Group Inc. 2015).

Even if the current trend indicates that physical mail is in a race to the bottom, it is not easy to predict how fast mail volume will continue to decline. The speed of e-substitution is highly heterogeneous among different countries, depending on several factors: the level of broadband penetration; the degree of a society's technological openness; the perceived reliability of the online service; its convenience; and its value-added features (WIK Consult and ITA Consulting 2009). Moreover, as some have argued, physical mail also has some unrivalled advantages when compared to email, for instance, its lower level of intrusiveness, its physical interface, the fact that it is considered somewhat more formal in specific circumstances (Jaag and Trinkner 2011). These features may be sufficient for physical mail not to be doomed, but it is difficult to make exact predictions.

2.2 *Pars Construens: Increasing Parcel and Express Volumes*

While letter volumes have fallen substantially over recent years, parcel deliveries have trended upward, notwithstanding the recession. This unusual counter-cyclical tendency is due to the fast growth of e-commerce in its earlier phase of development, which impacted on the B2C/C2C segments.

The two charts below show data on parcels and express package volumes in the US and in EU27.[1] In 2008, the year when the financial crisis began, there was a drop in parcel and express volume in the US and in EU27 (WIK Consult 2013), although this latter is not included in the chart. Since 2009 there has been a sustained growth in parcel delivery.

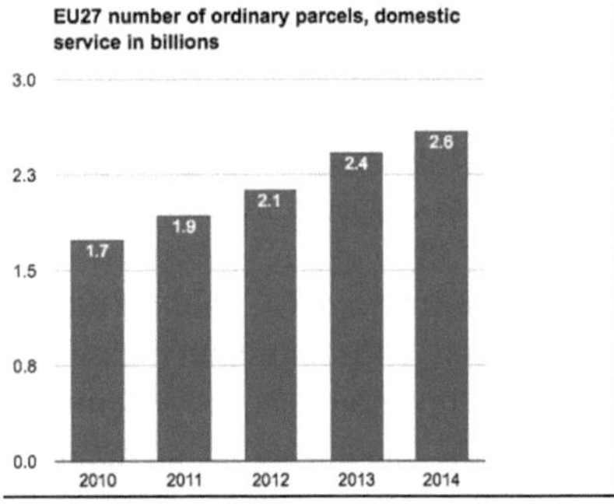

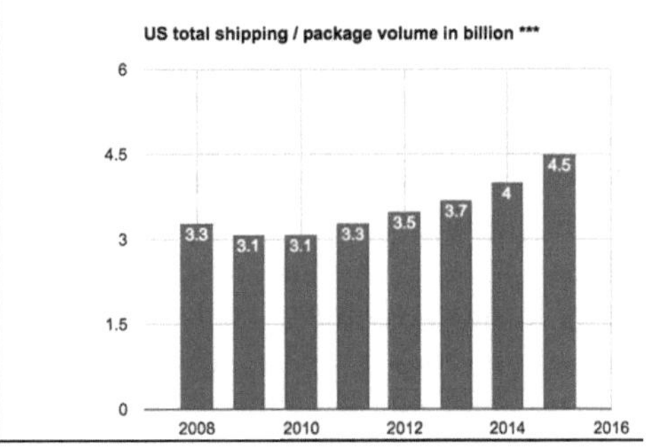

SOURCE: UPU (2014), AUTHORS' ELABORATION

SOURCE: US POSTAL SERVICE (2016), AUTHORS' ELABORATION

***Includes Priority Mail, Priority Mail Express, First-Class Packages, Package Services, Parcel Return Service and Parcel Select

According to the analysis by WIK Consult (2013), in the EU28 area, the overall economic activity of the postal service shrank from 94 billion euros to 91 billion euros between 2007 and 2011. However, the relative contributions of revenue from letter post compared to parcels and express mail together changed from a prevalence of letter post (54 % letter post, 46 % parcels and express) in 2007, to a prevalence of parcels and express mail in 2011 (48 % letter post, 52 % parcels and express). This change constitutes a structural historic turning point for the postal sector, since e-commerce continues to grow.

The Digital Agenda Scoreboard (2015a) reported that about 50 % of European citizens shopped online in 2014, a percentage that increases year by year, but in a

[1]Since there is no common definition of the parcel and express market in terms of size, weight and service characteristics, the charts shown can be used to comment on relative growth and not to compare the exact figures.

heterogeneous way in different countries. The main reasons why people shop online are: convenience, variety, value-added features, and prices.

There are also obstacles to the growth of e-commerce. Main concerns include data protection, payment security and shipment/delivery. The last can be considered to be one of the main explanations for the gap between national and cross-border e-commerce. In EU28, while 44 % of citizens shopped online nationally, only 15 % bought online from sellers across borders in 2014 (Digital Agenda Scoreboard 2015a). Consumers and smaller companies are the most worried about delivery times, costs, and uncertainty about the applicable laws for receiving and returning goods.

In the parcel and express market, which was historically more open to competition, about half of EU28 universal service providers (USP henceforth) had a market share below 20 % in 2011 (WIK Consult 2013). However, in the B2C segment, USPs have a competitive advantage due to their nationwide delivery network and possibly economies of scope in the delivery of mail and parcels in less densely populated areas. Luckily for USPs, this is the segment that has gained most from the growth of e-commerce. USPs have also benefited from a shift from B2B to B2C as producers increasingly sell directly to consumers, bypassing wholesalers and retailers. Several commercial B2B operators are planning to enter the B2C business (WIK Consult 2013).

2.3 *How the Postal Sector Reinvented Itself*

Faced with structural changes in demand due to the Internet, increasing competition due to liberalization, and adverse general economic trends, POs had to add a few strings to their bows by readapting their core business and opening new businesses. The response from POs in different countries has been highly heterogeneous, mainly owing to the different regulatory frameworks.

2.3.1 Innovation and Digitalization in Traditional Postal Services

One of the main reactions from the POs has been innovation of their core activities, including improvements in service reliability, more customer orientation, rationalization of existing assets and procedures, investment in more efficient sorting and delivery operations (e.g., more automation), and the adoption of technologically advanced retail services. In the letter post and the parcel segments, POs have made increasing use of digitalization and Internet-based applications at several points of the value chain. In the letter post segment, POs have created electronic delivery services, such as electronic mailboxes and so-called hybrid mail. In the parcel and express market, many USPs have adopted technological innovations in order to retain and reinforce their advantageous market position in B2C parcel delivery. Such innovations include tracking and tracing techniques, notification services about the status of shipments, flexible delivery points, parcel lockers, expansion toward logistics with all-in-one solutions. Many national POs are also trying to facilitate the return of parcels, particularly with regard to cross-border B2C parcels, where the returns procedure is known to be a major worry for online shoppers.

An additional area in which advanced technologies that are coupled with POs' expertise became an opportunity for innovation is cyber-security. Given the long history of the experience of POs in protecting information transmission, some have identified cyber-security as an important and future-proof route for development through research.

Several of the incumbent POs have tried to decrease costs by developing their post office network in various potential directions. One method is decreasing the number of post offices, where this is unrestricted by the USO. Another is replacing some post offices with postal agencies, where basic postal services are outsourced to third parties (e.g., retail outlets, grocery stores). In some cases, instead, the densely distributed postal infrastructure has been used as a competitive advantage with which to enter new markets.

2.3.2 Business Diversification

Aside from innovating in their core postal activities, several USPs have chosen to diversify their businesses by leveraging existing assets, such as infrastructure, customer base, reputation and distinctive competencies. USP business expansion has taken different directions, mostly going towards retail financial services, but also to telecommunications services (e.g., entering the mobile market as virtual network operators) and logistics.

Different USPs can be grouped into 3 main categories of business model according to their level of diversification: postal-postal; postal-financial; postal-hybrid. The chart below shows the frequency of each of the 3 categories (plus a residual one, "other business models") across 20 different USPs worldwide.

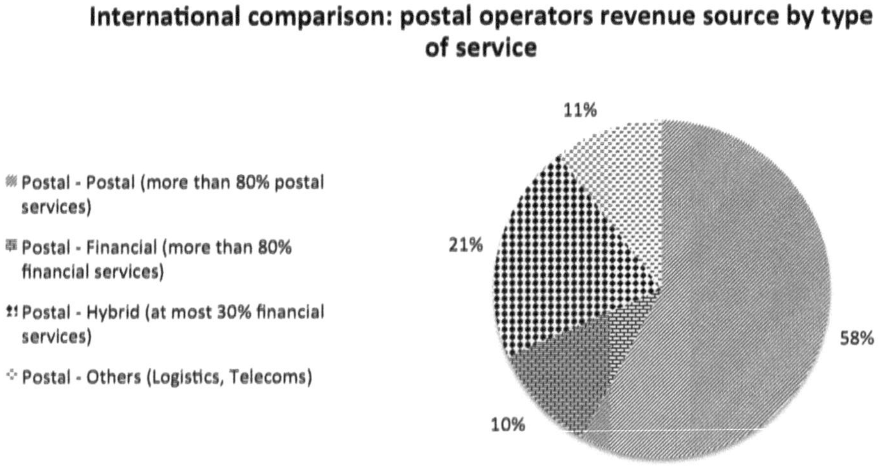

Postal–Postal
The majority of USPs did not enter new markets, but remained exclusively active in traditional postal business, with over 80 % of their total revenues, representing 57.9 % of the total industry's revenues coming from mail and parcel services. Half of this group's USPs earn 100 % of their revenues from postal services (Australia, Austria, Canada, UK, Norway). Belgium and Portugal have been included in this category even though they have diversified their business a little, earning less than 10 % of their revenue from financial services. A further distinction into national operators that are active exclusively (Ireland), or almost exclusively (Spain, US, Netherlands, Belgium, Portugal), in the mail business, earning at least 75 % of revenues from the mail segment, and those earning similar revenue shares from parcel and mail (UK, Norway, Austria, Canada, Australia) can be made.

Postal–Financial
The red slice of the pie chart represents the Italian and the Japanese USPs which earn over 80 % of their revenues from financial services, like retail banking, life insurance, pension funds, investment plans, and mortgages. Core postal services have become a minor economic activity for them. These operators used assets such as ubiquity across the national territory, economies of scope with other financial services (e.g., paying bills), the trust that people place on POs due to their historical obligation to offer reliable and convenient services and their State support, ICT competencies in managing sensible information and large databases, as leverage.

Postal–Hybrid
This third category includes USPs that have diversified their business by expanding into retail financial services, but not to a large degree. This group includes France, Russia, Switzerland and New Zealand. Financial services range from 22 % (France) to 35 % (Russia, New Zealand, Switzerland) of the total USP's revenue, the remainder comes from traditional postal services.

Other Business Models
Germany and Luxembourg are outliers in this group of 20. In Germany, the USP is particularly strong in the logistics segment, earning 50 % of its revenue there and 30 % from parcel and express. In Luxembourg, the USP instead earns 75 % of its revenue from telecommunications services, and the rest from mail services.

Another reaction from several USPs was to increase letter post prices. This has been made possible by the weak level of competition and the recent deregulation of USO obligations. The following chart shows a comparison between the percentage change in the prices of postal services, telecommunications equipment, communications, and newspapers and periodicals, in EU28 as a whole and in a few selected European countries, between 2000 and 2015. From this comparison is interesting to derive insights on the relationship between the degree of competition in these sectors and their price reaction, in a phase of crisis due to the Internet and the recession.

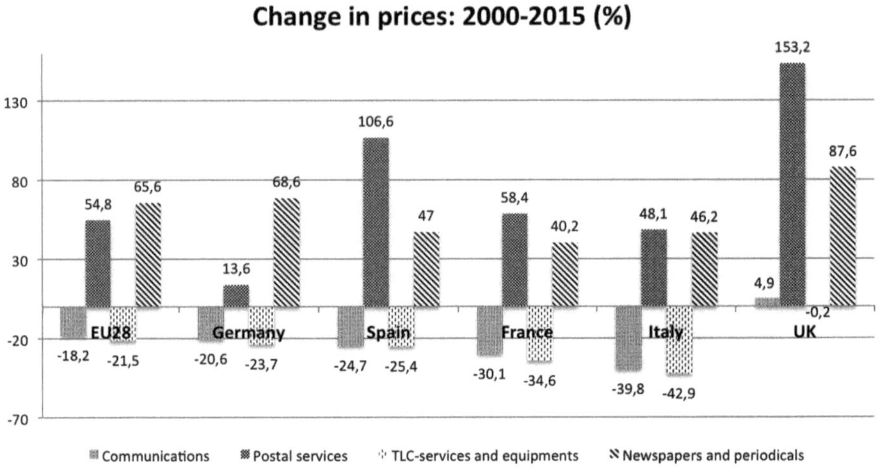

In more competitive regulated sectors such as the telecommunications, prices declined substantially.[2] In the newspapers sector, prices went up as result of rather inelastic demand and specific business strategies (aside from the consolidation process). Prices for postal services have increased as well. There is a considerable heterogeneity in the increases in the prices of postal services. On average, they increased by 54.8 % in EU28 over this time period. Compared to the other countries, the UK and Spain have had a relatively larger increase in the price of postal services. Both countries are in the postal-postal category, with Spain relying heavily on mail.

There seems to be a positive correlation between countries with a postal–postal business model and a higher growth in postal service prices, together with a decrease in the frequency of delivery and a decrease in the number of post offices and/or their substitution by postal agencies. In other words, when POs did not diversify, as a result of an autonomous business choice or, as is more likely of a regulatory imposition, they had to overcome the decrease in mail volume and the related revenue within the core postal business by cutting costs, decreasing quality standards and increasing the prices for their service. To avoid additional e-substitution that might follow, USPs have added technological and online features, as mentioned in the previous paragraph, to their core postal services. POs' revenue in this category have remained either stable or decreased from 2000 to 2006 (Jaag et al. 2015). Those relying strongly on letter mail have performed relatively worse.

In countries where POs have been able to diversify their business, the infrastructure network has, in most cases, been maintained and used along with other new

[2]The UK telecommunications' prices appear to decline less than in other EU countries only because the liberalization process was started before, therefore a part of the price decline happened before the year 2000.

services (financial, telecommunications, logistics). POs that focus their strategic efforts more on financial services risk leaving the core postal service behind. Both Japan and Italy haven't been able to keep up with the opportunity coming from the increasing demand for B2C parcels, which is mostly served by other commercial parcel operators. The revenue of postal-financial and postal-hybrid operators has, though, increased more of compared with operators in the postal-postal category (Jaag et al. 2015).

2.4 *Lessons for the Telecommunications Industry*

The postal business has been the first network industry to be heavily impacted upon by the Internet. Since then, POs have been competing in intermodal competition with rival services that are offered through the Internet by the so-called Over-The-Top operators (OTT henceforth).

OTT operators have developed several services which are similar to those offered by other network operators, but that can be supplied over the web without a specific physical infrastructure. Sending an email, sending a text message via instant messaging applications, making a VoIP call, are all examples of products offered by OTTs that, in part, substitute for those offered by traditional network operators in their respective areas.

Traditional telephone companies (telcos henceforth) have seen revenues from voice and SMS decline due to Internet-based services competition. At the same time, the telecoms network has become the main infrastructure used to offer dial-up and broadband Internet connection, so the increase in Internet penetration and adoption has raised their revenues from Internet connection subscriptions. As with the postal sector, telcos have been deprived of the safe harbor part of their revenues, but they have also gained in other areas.

In telecommunications, the Internet's disruptive impact arrived at a point when the market had already been largely liberalized (and privatized) and years of pro-competitive regulation had succeeded in reaching a good level of competition. This marks a difference from the postal sector, where the Internet wave arrived prior to, if not along with, with deregulation and liberalization, which is still in process, particularly in the mail segment. A general fear that is expressed by most incumbent telcos is that they will become mere commodities. Their role seems to move from one of being the suppliers of retail services to one of being network owners whose main activity is selling Internet access, with not much to say about the content that is offered over it.

In part, this may happen also to POs as the liberalization expands. POs may be required to give access to their network to rival operators, under fair and non-discriminatory conditions. However, POs may find providing network access attractive because of very high scale economies in those networks that might otherwise be lost due to the decline in demand for their own services. Secondly, their market shares in the mail and parcel segment must become comparable to those of rival operators (even those that are active on other technological platforms). In that hypothetical case, even POs may risk becoming mere providers of access products.

Telecoms operators' have reacted to the growth of the Internet. Their core business reaction has consisted of developing new offers that encompass the tendency towards the convergence of different communications platforms, such as triple-play offers that include Internet, TV and voice. They are expanding into adjacent markets, in particular, the content market, such as Telefonica in Spain or Vivendi with Mediaset in Italy. They are also calling for the ability to compete under the same conditions as OTTs and a deregulation of their role as Internet Service Providers (ISP henceforth).

The lesson for the postal sector is that successful reaction strategies are primarily based on exploiting and re-adapting existing strong assets. Telecoms operators can count on several distinctive valuable assets including infrastructures, a large customer base, the availability of big data; and, technological know-how. Similarly to the USPs that must ride on the e-commerce wave by strengthening their advantageous position in B2C delivery, it is essential for telcos to maintain their prominent role as ISPs, which is threatened by other competing technological platforms (e.g., cable) and by other network companies that are interested in investing in new fiber-networks (e.g., the energy incumbent in Italy). Investments in existing network upgrades and in rolling-out new fiber-networks are thus essential. Entry into the adjacent content market also seems to be a natural route to take for telecommunications providers, just as POs have with financial and telecommunications services. Some telecommunications operators did indeed enter the audio-visual content industry, for instance, by offering their own TV channels (e.g., Telefonica in Spain).

3 How Liberalization Changed the Telecommunications and then the Postal Sector

3.1 *Liberalization as Disruption*

The table below lists the main regulatory challenges in liberalized network markets. The focus of the analysis will be on the first three that appear the most important with reference to the postal sector.

Universal service obligation For universal service sectors, less profitable areas may not be served without public subsidies, which, however, may distort competition if not properly defined
Access regulation Access to the incumbent operator's network must be guaranteed under fair, cost-based and non-discriminatory conditions

(continued)

(continued)

Technological neutrality Regulation should follow the principle of the same regulation for similar services offered across different technological platforms
Termination regulation In case of two-way access and competitive bottlenecks, termination charges for interconnection must be kept at a cost-based level

Notice that termination regulation is more typical of the telecommunications industries, where those who make and those who receive a phone call are customers of different operators. This is not an issue for railways, energy and gas, and only partially relates to the postal service in the case of cross-border roaming, so it will not be further analyzed here

Liberalization disrupts the industries involved. The equilibrium created by public monopolies is replaced with open competition, more often than not by means of sectorial pro-competitive regulation. One important change facing both telecommunications and postal services is the need to compete with rivals who are not necessarily active on exactly the same technological platform. This evolution may lead to deregulating services for which there are several alternatives or regulating in the same way similar services that are offered via different technological platforms.

3.1.1 The Scope of the USO

Postal infrastructures are somewhat different from other network infrastructures in that much of the transmission is made up of common means of transportation, with no dedicated physical infrastructure. For this reason, the risk of market failure due to the presence of an essential facility, and the consequent need for access regulation in order to make competition viable, is less serious. At the same time, though, it is more costly to deliver the service in respect to other network industries, where a dedicated grid reaches every customer's home at a negligible marginal cost. This makes the universal service obligation more stringent in respect to other liberalized network industries.

While the concept of universal service has always existed as a duty of legacy monopolists, it has been maintained but became a complex regulatory issue after liberalization (Finger and Finon 2011). A USO of sorts has been defined for telecommunications, electricity, railways and postal services. In each of these sectors the obligation takes different forms, but is always inspired by two aims: ubiquity, meaning that the service has to be available to everyone regardless of location; and affordability with equality of treatment, meaning that everyone should pay the same affordable price regardless of the cost of serving them. In the postal sector, the USO is defined around three main dimensions: the range of products covered, the number of postal offices, their price (with price caps and price uniformity obligation), and quality in terms of number of postal offices and the frequency of delivery.

The USO is designed to be a flexible concept, periodically modifiable to account for evolving social, economic and technological contexts. If a market failure no longer exists because alternative services are available, there is no reason to impose restrictions relating to the way a certain service is offered. In that case, the USO should be softened by including alternative services, possibly from other technological platforms also, or by simply restricting its scope, liberating the relative services from obligation. In the context of a liberalized service, the USO should be implemented in a way that does not privilege or penalize the historical operator over the new entrants. Cross-subsidization that is internal to incumbent operators between more profitable and less profitable services should no longer be allowed.

One of the major current debates regards whether the scope of the USO in the postal sector should be updated in view of the market dynamics (Crew and Kleindorfer 2004). As similar alternative services become available to more and more consumers, thanks to the Internet, the USO on traditional postal services becomes less important. The Internet is not yet truly ubiquitous, so it will not be enough to satisfy the USO, but, nonetheless, the USO standards could be updated to encompass the role of ICTs. As more households use the Internet rather than postal services for their communications, a technologically neutral USO should include Internet access.

The same can be said for telecommunications, where the USO has gradually lost its importance because it was defined on voice services only, and particularly on fixed telephony. As alternative services have become more prominent, broadband Internet should be included in the scope of the telecommunications USO. The EU and Member countries' financial efforts to provide all European citizens with a broadband connection is not openly labeled as being a USO issue, but has such a flavor. A few countries have already expanded the telecommunications USO to include broadband service obligation: Switzerland (600 Kbits), Spain, Finland (both 1 Mbit) and the UK (10 Mbits to be reached in 2020). It would be advisable to define a unified technologically neutral USO for communications, encompassing telecommunications, postal services and Internet access.

In the EU, there is a widespread VAT exemption in favor of USPs. This should be maintained only when insufficient commercial alternatives are available to customers. In a survey carried out by WIK Consult (2013), there was a general consensus between 16 European NRAs that a VAT exemption can be justified only when the provision of the universal service cannot rely on market forces. In all European countries, except for Norway, Sweden and Switzerland, though, a VAT exemption is present for basic letter and parcel posts. For other services, such as bulk letters, bulk parcels, direct mail and non-priority letter post, the VAT exemption is present only in a few countries. This may cause an unjustified barrier to entry for new operators, which would have to undercut the incumbent operator's price by the amount of the VAT.

3.1.2 Access Regulation

Post-liberalization regulation is mostly asymmetric. Incumbent operators, due to network ownership, face obligations that new entrants do not face. Most salient is the obligation to offer access to the network at cost-oriented prices. Given the inefficient duplication of the high fixed costs entailed in building a new network, access regulation is an essential tool for opening up the sector to competition.

In the areas of parcel and express mail, which were liberalized early on in Europe in the late '90s, the market functions on a normal competitive basis. In the mail segment, though, opening up to competition is proving to be a slow process, with a tendency to delay adoption of the necessary measures and evidence of anti-competitive behavior on behalf of some USP's (European Commission 2015b). Furthermore, the disruptive impact of liberalization reinforces that of the Internet, with further erosion of the incumbent PO's revenue, making the universal service mission more difficult. Also, there may be an incentive to delay the implementation of the necessary access regulation provisions since PO's still in the process to be privatized would lose market value.

The Third Postal Directive identifies several elements of the postal network that should be subject to access obligations: postcodes, an address database, post office boxes, delivery boxes, and redirection and return services. According to latest comprehensive study on the developments of the implementation of the Third Postal Directive in the EU, WIK Consult (2013), by 2012 only a few European countries had made decisive steps in providing access to the listed elements of the USP's infrastructure, while the majority had ensured access to only a few of the elements indicated in the Directive. In the most recent years the economic crisis and, in some case, the intention to privatize more profitable companies appear to have further slowed down the process.

3.2 *Lesson from Telecommunications Regulation*

As a consequence of radical changes in technology, the telecommunications sector felt the wave of liberalizations earlier than did other network sectors. By the late '90s, the EU had taken decisive steps were made in this direction, with the liberalization of voice and telephony in the EU in 1998, coming shortly after the Telecommunications Act in the US in 1996. In the EU electricity and gas markets the liberalization process started in 1996 culminating with the second liberalization directive in 2003 and the railways' liberalization process started with the First Railway Package in 2001. Postal services' liberalization was gradually introduced with the 2002 and 2008 amendments to the first 1997 postal directive. Still today, in many European countries, the state plays a major role in the operation of incumbent energy, gas and postal service providers, even after they were transformed into private companies. The telecommunications sector, instead, has been fully privatized and the State no longer holds shares in incumbent operators' companies.

The regulation of telecommunications is a success story (Parcu and Silvestri 2014). The main regulatory provision at the European level for telecommunications is the so-called "Telecommunications Framework Directive", adopted in 2002 (2002/21/EC). Eighteen markets were identified that needed ex-ante regulation due to a lack of workable competition. Successive revisions in 2007 and in 2014 cut this number to seven and then to four, as those areas that were once raising competitive concerns have been judged to be sufficiently competitive.

It is possible to derive some lessons for the postal sector from telecommunications regulation. One difference is that liberalization greatly affected the services that are covered by the USO. This did not really happen with telecommunications, where the services under its USO were surpassed by other newer services, making the USO less important. This is only true, however, to the extent that the USO is not updated to include those services that can also substitute for traditional public services (i.e., email for mail, VoIP for calls).

A general lesson from the telecommunications experience is that the regulatory framework should have an economic-oriented rationale. Even when there appear to be other important targets (e.g., social inclusion, redistribution), the question for regulation should always be whether there exists a market failure. Therefore, regulatory rules should not be designed to provide rigid normative pictures of the market, but rather they should be applied when necessary and according to a case-by-case economic analysis. The prominent example of this kind of approach is the Significant Market Power (SMP) analysis, which is inspired by the antitrust legal concept of dominant position. The SMP analysis implies that a certain regulatory rule should be applied to a certain service, depending on whether its provider has a significant market power. Access regulation in postal services should be based on a similar concept.

The USO definition should also be made more flexible so it can be aligned with the economic context in which a certain service is offered. Just as fixed telephony was eventually completely lifted from ex-ante regulatory intervention in telecommunication regulation, universal postal services that no longer require a single USP should be provided under equal conditions by all market operators. This is the only way to reap all the benefits from increased competition. Moreover, having an incumbent continue to be the only firm that has to fund and meet the USO speeds up the path of e-substitution in a vicious circle.

As for telecommunications after liberalization, access regulation makes the incumbent operator the provider of a facility (the network), essentially a commodity, aside from a retail service supplier. It is most important in this phase that, instead of being attached to the past, incumbent operators recognize their comparative advantage as network owners. For USPs, delivery seems to be the area of true comparative advantage in respect of new entrants. Ensuring access for new entrants to the delivery network at fair prices can be an optimal strategy for POs so that they can sustain their declining revenues in the mail segment by increasing the volumes handled. Mail delivery does have a high cost, if compared to the delivery of electricity or the delivery of a phone call, and therefore reaching adequate economies of scale is of strategic importance to POs.

Furthermore, POs should consider big postal data as an opportunity. Uncovering customer needs with the analysis of big postal data could empower POs with new services and innovative ideas. Another area connected with the use of data, that potentially overlaps both the telecommunications and postal sectors, is cyber-security. The postal sector has a competitive advantage in respect of data security. These sectors are in a position to invest in developing research programs and cutting-edge encryption techniques for the future of digital communications and financial transactions.

4 Conclusions

The postal and telecommunications sectors have been affected by principally by two disruptive forces in the last two decades: the Internet and market liberalization. Liberalization of the postal sector started after the structural market changes caused by the Internet and is still ongoing in several of its aspects. For the telecommunications industry, the most dramatic impact of the Internet came after the markets were already fully privatized and had been subject to years of pro-competitive regulation. Exploiting this difference, the postal sector can teach something to telecommunications in relation to how to react to the Internet challenge. At the same time, it can draw several lessons from telecommunications' regulatory experience to solve typical post-liberalization competitive issues.

The postal sector reacted to the Internet challenge by adopting different business models that can be grouped into 3 different types: postal–postal, postal–financial, postal–hybrid. Due to regulatory restrictions, most historic POs are in the postal–postal group, with a business model that is almost exclusively based on traditional postal services. Those who were able to diversify their business did it in different ways and to different degrees. In the postal–financial group, there are POs who are now earning more than 80 % of their revenue from financial services. In the postal–hybrid group, there are POs who earn comparable revenue shares from traditional postal and financial services. Two outliers, Germany and Luxembourg, mainly rely on logistics and telecommunications, respectively. Operators belonging to the first group have had more difficulties in countering the decline in mail revenue by innovating the core services and rationalizing operations. On the other hand, operators who have diversified their businesses have been able to successfully increase their revenue to a noticeable extent, even if sometimes at the expense of traditional postal services' importance in their business plans.

Telecommunications operators are living a phase of challenge due to the replacement of analog voice and SMS services by Internet delivered services, just as with the e-substitution of mail by email. The lesson to take away from POs' experience is to try to innovate core services and, more importantly, to enhance the existing valuable assets. Successful business reactions are those that are able to identify and exploit comparative advantages in a creative way.

For traditional telephone operators, this implies not only to expanding into an adjacent market (e.g., content), but also by retaining their prominent position as ISPs, as companies coming from other network industries (e.g., the incumbent electricity company in Italy) or rival operators from other technological platforms (e.g., cable) may try to gain greater shares in the market for Internet connection. It is important to invest in the network so that it does not become obsolete. Becoming a commodity may seem to be a step backwards in respect of the past, but it cannot be dismissed as a fundamental opportunity.

The same can be said about incumbent POs in respect of their duty to give access to postal network facilities and information resources. POs should recognize their advantageous position in the delivery of mail and parcels and offer rival operators convenient access conditions in order to continue to enjoy economies of scale.

As regards postal sector regulation, a general lesson that can be learned from the telecommunications success story is that regulation should be economically-oriented and not rigidly defined. In this respect, it would be necessary to update the USO definition so as to align it with the economic context and to include Internet services, if they are close substitute services under USO. The USP should not be assigned privileges, such as VAT exemption, when the satisfaction of the USO can rely on market forces. Furthermore, the increasing convergence between postal services and OTT applications calls for a co-evolution of postal and telecommunications regulation. It would be advisable in the future to define a unified technologically neutral USO for communications, encompassing telecommunications, postal services and Internet access.

References

Autorità per le Garanzie nelle Comunicazioni (AGCOM). (2016). *Communications markets monitoring system n. 1/2016*. Available at http://www.agcom.it/documents/10179/4304099/Allegato+6-4-2016/e17e2d92-160d-4b77-9202-9469cc990d14?version=1.1 as of May 2016.

Crew, M. A., & Kleindorfer, P. R. (2004). Access and the USO for letters and parcels. In *Competitive transformation of the postal and delivery sector*, Topics in Regulatory Economics and Policy Series (Vol. 46, pp 3–41).

ERGP. (2014). ERGP Report on indicators on the postal market. ERGP (13) 33 Rev. 1.

European Commission. (2015a). Digital agenda scoreboard. Available at http://ec.europa.eu/digital-agenda/en/digital-agenda-scoreboard

European Commission. (2015b). Report from the commission to the European parliament and the council of 17.11.2015 on the application of the postal services directive (Directive 97/67/EC as amended by Directive 2002/39/EC and 2008/6/EC), COM(2015) 568 final. Available at http://eur-lex.europa.eu/legal-content/EN/TXT/HTML/?uri=CELEX:52015DC0568&from=EN

Finger, M., & Finon, D. (2011). From the "public service" model to the "universal service" obligation. In M. Finger & W. Kunneke (Eds.), *Handbook of liberalised infrastructure sectors*. London: Edward Elgar Publisher.

Jaag, C., Trinkner, U., & Moyano, J. P. (2015). Postal strategies in a digital age. Swiss Economics Working Paper, Zurich, Switzerland.

Jaag, C., & Trinkner, U. (2011). The future of the USO—Economic rationale for universal services and implications for a future-oriented USO. Swiss Economics Working Paper, Zurich, Switzerland.

Parcu, P. L., & Silvestri, V. (2014). Electronic communications regulation in Europe: An overview of past and future problems. *Utilities Policy, 31*, 246–255.

The Radicati Group Inc. (2015). Email statistics report 2015–2019. Available at http://www.radicati.com/wp/wp-content/uploads/2015/02/Email-Statistics-Report-2015-2019-Executive-Summary.pdf as of May 2016.

Universal Postal Union (UPU). (2014). Development of postal services in 2014. Available at http://www.upu.int/en/resources/postal-statistics/2014-results.html as of May 2016.
US Postal Service (USPS). (2016). First-class mail volume since 1926. Available at https://about.usps.com/who-we-are/postal-history/first-class-mail-since-1926.htm as of May 2016.
WIK Consult. (2013). Study for the European commission, directorate general for internal market and services. Main developments in the postal sector (2010–2013).
WIK Consult and ITA Consulting. (2009). Study for the European commission, directorate general for internal market and services. The evolution of the European postal market since 1997.

E-Substitution and the Demand for Business Mail in the UK: Trends and Prospects

Frank Rodriguez, Soterios Soteri and Stefan Tobias

1 Introduction

In recent years there has been a significant reduction in the volume of addressed letter mail in most developed countries including the UK (PwC 2013). Much of this decline has arisen from the substitution of letter mail by electronic modes of communication. Econometric estimates for the UK using methods outlined in Veruete-Mckay et al. (2011) indicate that in recent years this process has been advancing rapidly although other factors such as increases in GDP have mitigated some of this negative impact on letter mail volumes. Prospects for addressed letter mail will depend fundamentally on the future course of e-substitution, whose impact on the demand for mail varies across different content categories. For example, its impact on social or advertising mail may differ from that on business (or transactional) mail both in scale and process (PwC 2013; USPS 2010).

This chapter focuses on addressed business to consumer (B2C) business mail which constitutes a little under a half of all addressed inland mail in the UK and around three quarters of addressed business mail in total. Evidence is outlined on past trends in the e-substitution of this type of mail in the UK and the prospects for its further erosion to electronic substitutes considered over the long term. A theme

The views expressed in this paper are those of the authors and do not necessarily reflect those of the organizations to which they are affiliated.

F. Rodriguez
Oxera Consulting LLP, Oxford, UK

S. Soteri (✉)
Royal Mail Group, London, UK
e-mail: soterios.soteri@royalmail.com

S. Tobias
CER, Brussels, Belgium

M. Crew et al. (eds.), *The Changing Postal and Delivery Sector*,
Topics in Regulatory Economics and Policy,
DOI 10.1007/978-3-319-46046-8_3

emphasized is that whether addressed mail is sent often depends not only on decisions of senders but also on the ability and willingness of recipients to accept communications electronically instead of by letter mail (Nikali 2008; De Donder et al. 2015). A framework is developed to assess the prospects for the e-substitution of business mail which takes account of the role of both senders and recipients and the possible extent of e-substitution is considered using scenario analysis. One dimension of particular interest is that of differences in mail received by age group of recipients, an area previously explored in Jimenez et al. (2006).

This chapter is structured as follows. Section 2 reports estimates of key trends in the e-substitution of business mail in the UK. The approach to the modeling of scenarios on possible future paths of e-substitution of B2C business mail is outlined in Sect. 3 and 4 reports some indicative values for two hypothetical scenarios in the years up to 2025. Section 5 concludes.

2 Trends in the E-Substitution of Business Mail

The extent of e-substitution is measured using an index, E_t, defined as (1− the proportionate loss of mail to e-substitution) where $(0 < E_t \leq 1)$ and $E_t = 1$ represents a year t when there had been no overall net impact on mail volumes from e-substitution. A value of E_t of 0.8 in year t indicates that mail volumes were only 80 % of the level they would have reached in that year if there had been no impact on volumes from e-substitution. Estimates of E_t for addressed business mail in aggregate were derived from an econometric model of the demand for mail reported in Veruete-McKay et al. (2011). The methodology and derivation of the e-substitution index, E_t, which use the estimated coefficients from an updated equation of that model, were set out in Rodriguez et al. (2016).

Figure 1 reports estimates of E_t for business mail overall and by recipient age groups. These include also a relatively small impact of prices on volumes estimated by that model. From Veruete-McKay et al. (2011), the first year for which e-substitution is estimated to have had a discernible net impact on business mail volumes in the UK is 2002 implying that $E_t = 1$ in the years up to 2001. The development of e-substitution from the early 2000s is coincident with a sharp rise in the number of households with access to the Internet and the spread of broadband access.[1] The impact of e-substitution on business mail volumes in the UK accelerated from about 2010. It seems likely that the great recession of 2008–09 led firms to place even greater emphasis on lowering cost levels, increasing their use of electronic communication as part of that process. Industrial action at Royal Mail towards the end of the 2000s may have further contributed to the worsening trend of

[1] The percentage of households with access to the Internet in the UK rose from 13 % in 1999 to 25 % in 2000, 36 % in 2001 and 42 % in 2002 (Office for National Statistics 2015a). Broadband access rose from virtually 0 % of households in 2001 to 11 % by the end of 2003 and 50 % by the start of 2007 (Ofcom 2005, 2014).

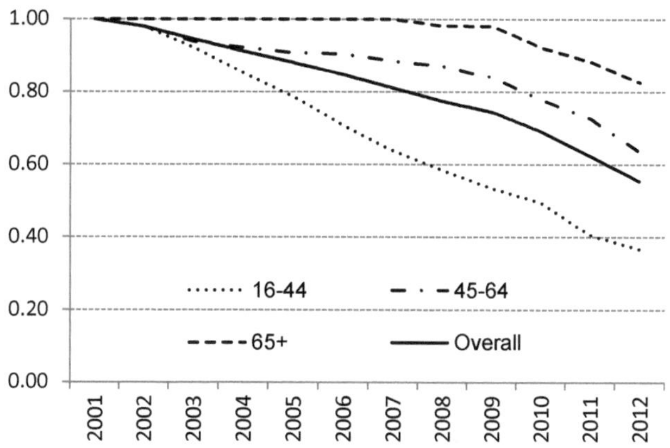

Fig. 1 Estimates of E-substitution Index, E_t, for business mail overall and by age group of recipients (2001 = 1). *Source* Royal Mail Group and author calculations. E_t equals (1− proportionate loss to e-substitution) where $E_t = 1$ implies no overall e-substitution (last such year estimated as 2001) and $E_t = 0$ implies complete loss of all mail

business mail traffic from about 2010. From Fig. 1, while the average decline in business mail volumes due to e-substitution (including price effects) is estimated to have been a little under 4 % per annum from 2002 to 2009, from 2010 this decline is estimated to have accelerated to about 9 % per annum with the index, E_t, at 0.55 in 2012. More recently, business mail volumes in the UK have declined broadly in line with the post-2010 historical trend suggesting a continuation of e-substitution at this higher rate.

Rodriguez et al. (2016) also report estimates of e-substitution of B2C business mail by: content type (for example, financial statements and business letters); sender group (for example, banks and government); and age group of recipient. These estimates were derived by combining estimates of E_t with a time-series of data collected through a continuing internal business survey of individuals and their use and receipt of mail. Data from the survey were used to prepare estimates of volume shares of segments of B2C business mail and were available up to 2012. A number of assumptions were also made in deriving these disaggregated estimates of e-substitution.[2] Given these and that the data for the disaggregated estimates were from a sample survey, the estimates of e-substitution at a disaggregated level are best viewed as indicative of trends over time and subject to some element of noise and uncertainty.

Figure 1 shows estimates disaggregated by three age groups of recipients which suggest that there are substantial differences in the extent of e-substitution by age group with the greatest impact up to 2012 on the youngest of the age groups (who

[2]These included the use of estimates of E_t as a proxy for the equivalent index for B2C business mail as a whole and that the elasticities of demand for each segment of traffic with respect to variables such as GDP and population were equal.

Table 1 Percentage estimates of access by individuals in the UK to the Internet by age group

	Age group							
	16–24	25–34	35–44	45–54	55–64	65–74	75+	All
2012 Q3	98	97	95	90	80	58	26	82
2015 Q1	99	99	97	94	87	71	33	86

Source Office for National Statistics (2013a, 2015b). Percentage of individuals using the Internet by any device in the preceding 3 months

in 2012 received about a quarter of all B2C business mail) and the least on the oldest (who also received about a quarter of such mail in 2012). In part these differences reflect the higher level of access to the Internet of the younger groups reported in Table 1 but these differences are estimated to be less than the extent of e-substitution between the three age groups in Fig. 1. For example, in 2012 about 85 % of those in the UK aged 45–64 had used the Internet in the preceding three months compared with about 97 % for those under the age of 45. But, from Fig. 1, the E-indices for the two age groups were estimated to be 0.63 and 0.37 respectively and the difference between these indices is over twice that in rates of access to the Internet. In addition to differences in the ability to receive e-communication, a second factor impacting on the extent of e-substitution is likely to be the willingness of individuals to receive communication electronically even where they have access to the Internet.

3 Methodology for Modeling Scenarios of Future Paths of Business Mail E-Substitution

(i) Decomposition of the e-substitution index. The starting point for modeling possible future losses of addressed B2C business mail to e-substitution is a decomposition of the e-substitution index, E_t. The potential effects of decisions regarding e-substitution by senders and recipients of mail are considered separately while, for both, a distinction is drawn between the ability to send or receive an electronic substitute in place of business mail and the willingness to do so.

On the sender side, the proportionate reduction of mail that senders would wish to achieve can be considered as the product of their ability to send e-communications (θ_s) (defined as the proportion of communications from senders in time period t that could be mailed (and would have been mailed prior to the development of e-substitution) for which senders have the technology to communicate electronically ($0 \leq \theta_s < 1$)) and their willingness to do so (π_s) (the proportion of communications from senders in time period t that could be mailed for which senders have the technology to communicate electronically and, in fact, wish to send in this way and so displace letter mail ($0 \leq \pi_s < 1$)). For example, if in time period t senders were able to send electronically a proportion θ_s of a particular segment of communication that could be mailed while, of this volume, senders wished to send a proportion π_s electronically rather than by letter mail then the overall proportionate loss in mail to e-substitution that senders of that segment of communication would wish to achieve would be the product of these two parameters, $\theta_s\pi_s$, assuming that the ability and willingness of senders to substitute electronic communication for letter mail are independently distributed. Where senders are able "unilaterally" to communicate electronically without the agreement of recipients, $\theta_s\pi_s$ would also represent the proportionate loss in mail that could be achieved by senders. For example, some bank statements could be sent quarterly rather than monthly without a recipient being required to enable such a change.

However, whether senders are able to substitute out of business mail sometimes depends also on recipients' ability and willingness to receive communications electronically that currently they receive as mail. For example, bills and invoices can be settled through on-line payment but this requires the recipient to have both the ability to settle an invoice in this way and the willingness to do so. Where e-substitution of business mail by senders requires the explicit involvement of recipients, such mail can be described as "bilateral" or "actionable". This potential involvement by recipients can be viewed also as being the product of two factors: the ability of recipients to accept e-communications (θ_r) (the proportion of communications that could be mailed (and would have been mailed prior to the development of e-substitution) which is received by individuals who have the technology to accept e-communications ($0 \leq \theta_r < 1$)) and their willingness to do so (π_r) (the proportion of communications that could be mailed which is received by individuals who have the technology to receive e-communications and wish to accept an e-communication instead of letter mail ($0 \leq \pi_r < 1$)). The overall proportionate loss of mail to electronic communication that recipients would wish to accept would then be $\theta_r\pi_r$. Bringing together these two sides, senders in period t would wish to send electronically a proportion $\theta_s\pi_s$ of communication that could be mailed but if all of that communication were bilateral then recipients either through a lack of ability to accept e-communication or a lack of willingness to do so would only wish to accept $\theta_r\pi_r$ of such a displacement. In the bilateral case then the proportionate loss of mail to e-substitution would be the product of $\theta_s\pi_s\theta_r\pi_r$ (again assuming that the mail that senders wish to displace with e-communication is distributed across potential recipients independently of the distribution of recipients that are able and wish to have mail displaced by an electronic substitute and those that are either unable or do not wish to accept this) and the e-substitution index in period t, E_t, can be written as:

$$E_t = 1 - (\theta_s * \pi_s * \theta_r * \pi_r) \quad (1)$$

For unilateral mail, Eq. (1) simplifies the proportionate loss of mail to e-substitution to $\theta_s\pi_s$. Mail prices also affect e-substitution of B2C business mail in various ways and, although the model set out here does not incorporate such linkages explicitly, in general, an increase in the relative price of mail will lead to an increase in one or more of the parameters in the model and hence in e-substitution.[3] Note also that the parameters on the right hand side of (1) are assumed to have an upper bound at less than 1. Those maxima are of importance as they directly affect the potential minimum value of E_t for B2C business mail overall over the very long term.

(ii) Calibration of 2012 base. The approach used to model future e-substitution of B2C business mail was based on (1). Data were available segmented by content type i (6), sender group j (6) and age group k (6) or a total of 216 segments. The model was calibrated at this level of disaggregation for 2012. For each of these segments an estimate was made of the corresponding e-substitution index using information on volume shares of these disaggregations and a number of constraints to ensure model consistency. For θ_s and π_s some evidence was provided by internal surveys of senders of mail. In the case of θ_r, ONS data on access to the Internet represent a proxy for individuals' ability to receive electronic communications and use was made of the estimates reported in Table 1 for 2012Q3. There was no direct information to calibrate the parameter, π_r. However, with estimates or assumptions for the other elements in (1), rearrangement and solution of that equation provided an initial estimate of π_r and a procedure was then applied to ensure that the condition that $\pi_r < 1$ was satisfied in the few cases where an initial estimate violated that constraint.

Information on the calibration values of these parameters is reported in Table 2. The upper part of the table records qualitative indicators for the largest ij pairs of traffic by volume (for example, "Bills and invoices" sent by Utilities) which together constituted well over a half of all B2C business mail traffic in 2012. On a five-level scale from "Low" to "High", the first column provides an indication of the assessed sender ability and willingness to communicate electronically from the calibration of θ_s and π_s and hence $\theta_s\pi_s$. In nearly all the segments these indicators are either "High"[4] or "Medium to High" based on the numerical values applied in the model. The second column reports equivalent indicators for recipients' ability and willingness to receive e-communications from the calibration of θ_r and π_r and hence $\theta_r\pi_r$. In all of the segments these indicators range from "Low" to "Medium". The final column of Table 2 reports qualitative indicators of the extent of e-substitution estimated to have occurred in each of these segments by 2012 measured through e-substitution indices, E_t. Segments where e-substitution is estimated to have advanced most by that time include "Bills and invoices" sent by Utilities[5] and "Statements" sent by Retailers. The extent of e-substitution is

[3]For example, if the prices of business mail increase, senders will tend to send less mail where they can (unilateral mail) either by introducing technology to do so or, where they have this, potentially increasing its use (that is, θ_s, π_s increase with the price of mail so that E_t declines). More generally, similar effects arise where other costs of sending mail increase or the price of substitutes falls for it is relative prices that matter.

[4]From the key to Table 2, for "High": $0.90 \leq \theta_s\pi_s < 1$.

[5]From the key to Table 2, for "Medium to High": $0.25 \leq E_t < 0.50$.

Table 2 Calibration of sender and recipient ability and willingness to send and receive e-communications, 2012 base

Content by sender	Sender ability and willingness	Recipient ability and willingness	Extent of E-substitution
1. Bills and invoices sent by:			
Utilities	High	Medium	Medium to High
2. Business letters sent by:			
Banks	Medium to High	Low to Medium	Medium
Government	Medium	Low to Medium	Low to Medium
Insurance companies	Medium to High	Low	Low
Other Businesses	Medium	Medium	Medium
3. Insurance, legal, financial documents sent by:			
Insurance companies	High	Low to Medium	Medium
4. Statements sent by:			
Banks	Medium to High	Low to Medium	Low to Medium
Retailers	High	Medium	Medium to High
5. Other financial correspondence sent by:			
Banks	Medium to High	Low to Medium	Medium
Government	Medium	Low	Low to Medium
Insurance companies	Medium to High	Low to Medium	Low to Medium
6. Other B2C Business Mail sent by:			
Banks	High	Medium	Medium to High
Age group of recipient			
16-34	Medium to High	Medium to High	Medium to High
35-44	Medium to High	Medium to High	Medium to High
45-54	Medium to High	Low to Medium	Medium
55-64	Medium to High	Low	Low to Medium
65-74	Medium to High	Low	Low to Medium
75 and over	Medium to High	Low	Low

Keys:	Sender and recipient columns:	E-substitution column:
	0.90 ≤ High < 1	High < 0.25
	0.75 ≤ Medium to High < 0.90	0.25 ≤ Medium to High < 0.50
	0.60 ≤ Medium < 0.75	0.50 ≤ Medium < 0.60
	0.45 ≤ Low to Medium < 0.60	0.60 ≤ Low to Medium < 0.85
	Low < 0.45	Low ≥ 0.85

Source Royal Mail Group and author calculations

estimated to have been lower for content types "Business letters" and "Other financial correspondence" and for B2C business mail originating from Insurance companies and Government.

The lower part of Table 2 reports equivalent information by age group of recipient. As the content types and sender groups sending mail vary little across age groups, sender ability and willingness to send electronic communications in place of letter mail are assessed to be at the overall average for B2C business mail in 2012 of "Medium to High". However, from Fig. 1, there are significant differences by age group estimated in the extent of e-substitution which are reflected in the final column of Table 2. Underlying these differences then are even more marked variations across age groups in the ability and willingness of recipients to receive electronic communication.

(iii) Modeling of parameters for scenarios. From the base developed for 2012 it is possible to explore a number of long term hypothetical scenarios and two are considered for the period up to 2025 by modeling possible levels of e-substitution in three years: 2015, 2020 and 2025. For 2015 use was made of three main sources. The first of these was extrapolation and sensitivities around these of recent trends in overall e-substitution of B2C business mail from econometric estimates of E_t. Second, survey data were available on the expectations of businesses for the e-substitution of B2C business mail. Third, use was made of ONS information on trends in access to the Internet as a way to inform prospective movements in the parameter θ_r by age group of recipients. Additionally, it was necessary to make assumptions regarding other parameters in the model at a disaggregated level set within the envelope determined by the information outlined above.

However, for 2020 and 2025, it was more difficult to obtain useful information from surveys of senders and recipients as the timescale extends outside of respondents' range of likely knowledge. Similarly, extrapolations from an econometric model estimated on historical data become less informative over the very long term as further structural change may occur. Indeed, it is the possibility of exploring such developments that makes scenario analysis useful. So scenarios for 2020 and 2025 were developed directly from assumptions for the parameters on the right hand side of (1) implying changes in the mix of B2C business mail over time. As shown in Table 2, the values for the sender parameters were for many disaggregations already high by 2012 and the main factors affecting the future path of e-substitution of B2C business mail are likely to be on the recipient side.

Two separate factors influence the path of each of these parameters, outlined here in the case of θ_r. First, a population cohort born in period l may increase, over time, the proportion of communication it receives which can be accessed via the Internet (an "accessibility effect"). Second, younger and middle aged groups have greater access to the Internet currently than older groups and, over time, as they age and themselves enter older age groups the access to the Internet of that older group will reflect that higher level of access being carried forward by the younger cohort (an "ageing effect"). Indeed, this effect may be enhanced as this younger cohort itself may increase the proportion of communication which it can access through the Internet.

To separate these effects groups were defined by their year of birth (which do not change over time) rather than their age (which do). The proportion of a segment of communication received by individuals in age group k with the ability to receive e-communications in year $t = (2015 + m)$ is given by:

$$\theta_{rk} = \sum_{l \in k} \theta_{rl} \cdot \left(\frac{P_{l \in k}}{P_k} \right) \tag{2}$$

where m is the number of years after 2015; θ_{rl} is the proportion of a segment of communication that could be mailed (and would have been mailed prior to the development of e-substitution) received by individuals born in period l with the ability to receive e-communications in year $t = (2015 + m)$; $P_{l \in k}$ is the population born during period l which is within age group k in year $t = (2015 + m)$; and P_k is the population of age group k in year $t = (2015 + m)$. The summation is over all population cohorts born during periods l which are contained in age group k in year $t = (2015 + m)$. In applying this approach use was made of population projections for the UK by cohort from the ONS (2013b) and these were combined with assumptions for ability to receive e-communications by cohorts defined by age in 2015, θ_{rl}. A similar approach and equivalent expression to (2) was used for modeling the future path of π_r. In that case, in addition to the ageing effect outlined above, in place of an accessibility effect there is an "acceptance effect".

4 Hypothetical Scenarios

(i) Outline of hypothetical scenarios. Given the high degree of uncertainty about the future course of the e-substitution of B2C business mail, two hypothetical scenarios were evaluated using the framework set out in Sect. 3. In both, e-substitution advances significantly further than the estimates for 2012 leading to a very high level of e-substitution overall and are referred to as the "Lower rate of advance of e-substitution" scenario (LES) and "Higher rate of advance of e-substitution" scenario (HES). The path of e-substitution in these scenarios depends on two proximate factors. The first of these is the extent to which either the ability or willingness of senders and recipients of B2C business mail to substitute or accept e-communications in place of letter mail turns out to be less than complete (that is, the extent to which the maximum values of θ_s, π_s, θ_r and π_r prove to be less than 1). These assumptions underpin the scenarios on the overall extent of e-substitution over the very long term. The second factor is the pace of approach to these maxima.

Each of the parameters in the model is likely to reach a maximum value close to but below unity. From the sender side, while all firms effectively have the means to communicate electronically, other factors potentially limit the ability of senders to substitute out of letter mail (θ_s). These include mail where a physical signature is required; items that cannot be sent electronically (for example, bank cards); and where there is a regulatory or legal requirement for delivery through letter mail. In both scenarios it is assumed that such types of communication represent only a very small constraint on the ability of senders to substitute out of letter mail (a maximum of $\theta_s = 0.99$).

With regard to senders' willingness to substitute e-communications (π_s), again there are reasons for senders to be likely to wish to maintain some communication by letter mail. These include: concerns with respect to security and proof of identification when dealing remotely with new customers (for example, applying for a credit card); increasing levels of high value actionable activity (for example, notification of hospital appointments and reminders to attend expensive publicly funded treatment or procedures); legal requirements or precautionary communications that protect large businesses from accusations of taking advantage of customers (for example, when changes are proposed to banking provided services); and where senders wish to maintain and develop a relationship with recipients (for example, when offering new customers welcome packs and, in the absence of having a physical local presence, maintaining some limited contact via letter mail to encourage cross-selling or renewing existing contracts at a future date). In both scenarios values of π_s are assumed to be extremely high and at 0.99 by 2025 in HES and lower than this but above 0.90 in LES for reasons outlined above, except in the case of government senders where slightly lower values are assumed in both scenarios.[6] In terms of the scaling and segmentation reported in Table 2, on the sender side, sender ability and willingness to substitute e-communications for letter mail are assumed in 2025 to be at "High" in nearly all *ij* pairs of traffic in both scenarios so that the differences that arise between the scenarios are principally from assumptions regarding recipients.

As indicated in Table 1, by 2015 accessibility to the Internet was already close to its maximum level for younger individuals. However, these rates were well below saturation for groups aged over 65. For the ability to receive e-communications, θ_r, to increase further requires access to the Internet among these older age groups to rise. As discussed, this can be expected to occur through the combination of rising access to the Internet for a population born during a given period and the ageing over time of younger cohorts with higher access into older age groups. By 2025, both scenarios assume that such access will rise from an average of about 86 % in 2015 to the mid-90s percent but with the oldest groups still having access to the Internet below younger groups. Further, fast broadband services may not be

[6]While some Government digitization programmes are achieving significant online penetration (such as annual tax self-assessment returns) others are not expected to e-substitute at all (PwC 2013).

available even in completely developed networks in all locations so also restricting the maximum potential value of θ_r.

Perhaps the greatest uncertainty regarding the future path of e-substitution of business mail relates to the extent to which recipients will be willing to accept e-communication as a substitute for letter mail. There are a number of reasons for expecting this parameter in the model, π_r, to reach a maximum level below unity. These include recipients wishing to receive paper copies for records or confirmation of address; being less comfortable or effective in the use of electronic means of communication and so preferring letter mail; pre-empting the digital clutter that often develops once communication takes place electronically; and having concerns about and limiting the use of electronic media on grounds of security or privacy, particularly, for example, in the cases of high value business transactions and legal documents. A number of these factors are based on "deep, scientifically established, psychological instincts" and emotional effects which result, on average, with people valuing physical letter communications more highly than electronic mail (Royal Mail Group 2015).[7] It is likely that such factors will persist and change slowly over time amongst older recipients of mail suggesting lower values for π_r for these groups. The two hypothetical scenarios differ most in the extent to which they differentiate assumptions on π_r. In LES, the maximum values assumed for π_r are lower and the pace at which they are approached less rapid than in HES.

Assumptions on recipient ability and willingness to receive e-communications in place of letter mail in LES are one or two levels higher on the scale used than the base year values reported in Table 2 (for example, scalings of "Low to Medium" in 2012 rise to either "Medium" or "Medium to High" in 2025). The assumptions in HES are generally two or three levels higher reflecting both higher long term maxima for π_r and a more rapid pace of approach to these higher values. The implications of these assumptions on sender and recipient willingness for the modeled extent of e-substitution in 2025 are that even in LES, all *ij* pairs of traffic in Table 2 have e-substitution which is assumed to rise to "Medium to High" while in HES this is so to the scale of "High" for nearly all of the segments. This is also the case by age group *k* except for those aged 75 and over.

(ii) E-substitution and B2C business mail volumes. Figure 2 plots E-indices for both scenarios up to 2025. The values for 2015 and 2020 have been calculated using the approach outlined in Sect. 3 and summarized in this section for 2025 with values for other years interpolated. The E-index for 2025 under LES is 0.25 compared with an estimate of 0.55 in 2012; that is, while in 2012 B2C business mail is estimated to have been just over a half of the level it would have reached if there had been no impact from e-substitution, by 2025 under LES that fraction would have dropped to a quarter. Under HES the E-index is 0.11. Compared with the post-2010 historical trend of a decline in B2C business mail from e-substitution

[7]For example, Royal Mail Group (2015) shows that the "value" of paper communications is higher than via email in terms of recipients taking the communication more seriously, imparting a better impression of the sender and making the recipient feel more valued.

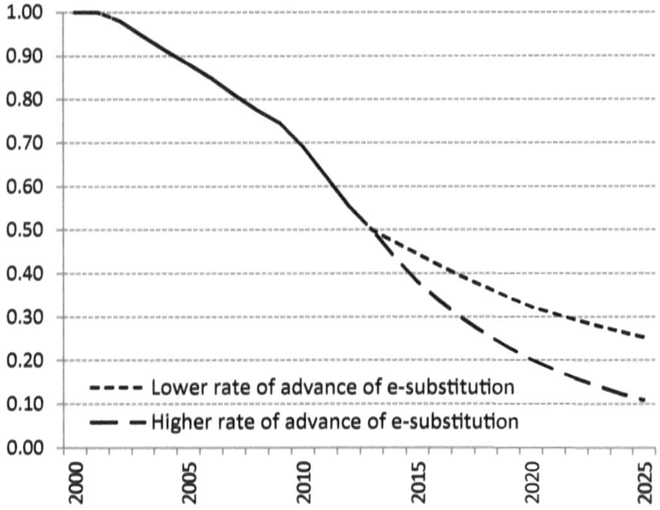

Fig. 2 Estimates of E-substitution index, E_t, to 2012 and two hypothetical scenarios to 2025 (2001 = 1). *Source* Historical estimates from Royal Mail Group and author calculations; hypothetical scenarios constructed by authors

of about 9 % per annum, under LES this rate reduces to about 6 % per annum between 2015 and 2020 and under 5 % between 2020 and 2025. By contrast, under HES the impact of e-substitution accelerates to between 11 and 12 % per annum up to 2025. The two scenarios also differ in that under LES the share of these reduced volumes received by younger and middle aged groups, although contracting compared with estimates for 2012, remains higher than under HES.

The econometric model set out in Veruete-McKay et al. (2011), which underpins the e-substitution framework developed in this chapter also identifies positive impacts on mail volumes from economic and demographic growth which partially offset the negative impact from e-substitution. Using the updated elasticities for these variables reported in Rodriguez et al. (2016) (mail volumes with respect to GDP and population[8] respectively of 0.9 and 1) it is possible to produce estimates for B2C business mail volumes under the two hypothetical scenarios. Applying these elasticities, the cumulated impact on mail volumes from population (using population projections from the ONS) and GDP (assuming trend growth in GDP of a little over 2 % per annum) would imply mail volume growth of just under 50 % between 2012 and 2025 or about 3 % per annum. The E-indices from the two hypothetical scenarios can be used to factor these trend extrapolations. Using this

[8]The demographic variable in Veruete-McKay et al. (2011) is number of households rather than population but the latter is used here as a proxy. A demographic variable is introduced separately into that model and reflects approximately delivery point growth and its additional effect on demand for mail rather than the direct impact of demography on total economic activity which is captured by the GDP term.

approach, under LES the volume of B2C business mail in 2025 would be around two thirds of its level in 2012. Under HES the volume of mail implied would be barely a third. In terms of growth rates, under LES volumes would decline by about 3 % per annum between 2015 and 2020 and slow down to less than 2 % per annum between 2020 and 2025; that is, by about 3 % less than the decline due to the effects of e-substitution from the positive effects of population and GDP growth. Under HES, however, despite the mitigating effects of these factors, B2C business mail volumes would decline by between 8 and 9 % per annum.

5 Conclusions

This chapter has presented estimates of reductions in the volume of business (or transactional) mail in the UK as a result of electronic substitution. These estimates have been derived from econometric modeling of the demand for business mail (and include also a relatively small impact on prices estimated by that model) and indicate that e-substitution impacted negatively on business mail volumes from about 2002. By 2012 (the last observation available at the time of modeling) business mail volumes were estimated to be only a little over a half of the level they might have been expected to reach based on the impact of other factors affecting these volumes such as GDP and demography after excluding the estimated impact of e-substitution.

The chapter considers the prospects only for B2C business mail in the UK. The framework for assessing these focuses not only on the ability and willingness of senders to communicate on-line rather than by letter mail but also, for many types of business mail, on the ability and willingness of recipients to accept e-communications in place of letter mail. For example, bills and invoices can be settled through on-line payment but this requires the recipient to have both the ability to settle a bill in this way and, importantly, be willing to do so even when such access is in place. Estimates (from the ONS) indicate that access to the Internet among older individuals in the UK is less than complete and (from modeling) that there has been a lower level of e-substitution to date for older individuals, even allowing for this lower ability to receive e-communications.

Given the high level of uncertainty regarding the prospects for e-substitution over the long term, the modeling framework developed in this chapter is used to consider the possible path of the e-substitution of B2C business mail volumes up to 2025 through two hypothetical scenarios. The scenarios are distinguished primarily by differences in the extent to which senders wish to substitute e-communication for letter mail and the willingness of recipients to accept such changes.

Econometric estimates of the demand for business mail indicate that GDP and demography continue to exert positive impacts on these volumes so it is likely to be the combination of these two opposing sets of factors which will determine the future path of business mail volumes overall. Compared with recent rates of decline of 5 to 6 %, the two hypothetical scenarios point to a wide possible range for business mail volume decline with prospects over the next decade being highly dependent on the extent and pace with which recipients of paper communications are able and willing to replace them with electronic alternatives. The less able and more reluctant mail recipients are, especially older individuals, the more likely a significant slowdown in the rate of letter decline, perhaps nearing broadly flat levels of volumes in the UK within the next decade. By contrast, if older individuals engage more actively with Internet related technologies and their willingness to adopt e-communications increases substantially there is a risk that the rate of business mail volume decline in the UK will be considerably higher and could approach near double digit rates of decline, as is the case today in some Scandinavian countries.

Ultimately the long term prospects for business mail will depend on sender and recipient choices and how these are impacted by technological developments, postal policy and attitudes to the use of mail relative to electronic substitutes. These factors are, however, inherently highly uncertain. Scenario analysis using a sender-recipient framework can be used by postal operators to explore some of these uncertainties in more depth, as well as examining opportunities to implement strategies to dampen the decline in letter mail in specific sender-recipient segments. An extension of the framework outlined in this chapter for future research could be a more explicit treatment of the impact of prices on senders' willingness and recipients' acceptance to substitute mail for electronic communications and the impact this could have on the long term rate of decline in letter traffic.

References

De Donder, P., Cremer, H., Rodriguez, F., Soteri, S., & Tobias, S. (2015). Analyzing the prospects for transactional mail using a sender-recipient framework. In M. A. Crew & T. J. Brennan (Eds.), *Postal and delivery innovation in the digital economy*. Berlin: Springer.

Jimenez, L., Owsiany, A., & Szeto, C. (2006). Scenarios of mail recipient patterns across generations. In M. A. Crew & P. R. Kleindorfer (Eds.), *Liberalization of the postal and delivery sector*. Broadheath: Edward Elgar.

Nikali, H. (2008). Substitution of letter mail for different sender-receiver segments. In M. A. Crew & P. R. Kleindorfer (Eds.), *Competition and regulation in the postal and delivery sector*. Broadheath: Edward Elgar.

Ofcom (2005, 2014). *Communication Market Report 2005* (2014).

Office for National Statistics. (2013a). *Internet quarterly update, Q1 2013*.

Office for National Statistics. (2013b). *2012-based population projections by single year of age and sex. United Kingdom. Projection type: Principal assumptions.*

Office for National Statistics. (2015a). *Internet access—households and individuals, 2015*.

Office for National Statistics. (2015b). *Internet users, 2015*.

PwC. (2013). *The outlook for UK mail volumes to 2023*. http://www.royalmailgroup.com/sites/default/files/The20%Outlook20%for20%UK20%mail20%volumes20%to20%2023.pdf

Rodriguez, F., Soteri, S., & Tobias, S. (2016). *The impact of e-substitution on the demand for mail: Some results from the UK*. Paper presented to 9th Postal Economics Conference on E-commerce, Digital Economy and Delivery Services, University of Toulouse, March 31, 2016 available at

http://idei.fr/conferences/2016-ninth-biannual-postal-economics-conference-e-commerce-digital-economy-and-delivery-services?page=1
Royal Mail Group. (2015). *The private life of mail*. http://www.mailmen.co.uk/reports
USPS. (2010). *Projecting US mail volumes to 2020: Compendium*, available at http://www.prc.gov
Veruete-McKay, L., Soteri, S., Nankervis, J., & Rodriguez, F. (2011). Letter traffic demand in the UK: An analysis by product and envelope content type. *Review of Network Economics, 10*(3).

An Examination of the Links Between Postal Price Constraints, Efficiency, Competition and Public Welfare

Philippe De Donder, Frank Rodriguez and Soterios Soteri

1 Introduction

Mail volumes in developed countries are in decline while universal service obligations (USOs) and uniform pricing constraints on some mail products remain in place. Within this environment and with the EU promoting competitive entry into the postal sector there are strong pressures on universal service providers (USPs) to raise efficiency and reduce fixed costs. Lower costs and prices help to maintain profitability and protect USPs from potential losses to electronic (e-)substitution and postal market competitors. However, the drive to increase efficiency is not without risks in a labor intensive and highly unionized industry, for the greater the targeted gain in efficiency, and hence job losses and/or changes in working practices, the greater the possibility of strike action to resist such changes.

The objective of this chapter is to examine the trade-offs faced by a USP when considering pricing and efficiency decisions in a world of decreasing mail volumes with continuing USOs and competitive entry. The chapter extends the literature on optimal pricing with USO and regulatory constraints in a competitive environment (in particular De Donder et al. 2006) to take account of the impact of a USP

The views expressed in this paper are those of the authors and do not necessarily reflect those of the organizations to which they are affiliated.

P. De Donder
Toulouse School of Economics, CNRS, University of Toulouse Capitole, Toulouse, France

F. Rodriguez
Oxera Consulting LLP, Oxford, UK

S. Soteri (✉)
Royal Mail Group, London, UK
e-mail: soterios.soteri@royalmail.com

M. Crew et al. (eds.), *The Changing Postal and Delivery Sector*,
Topics in Regulatory Economics and Policy,
DOI 10.1007/978-3-319-46046-8_4

targeting different levels of efficiency and the potential risk of industrial action.[1] A two-period model is developed where mail volumes decline significantly between one period and the next and competition takes place through entrants accessing the USP delivery network or bypassing it. The chapter focuses on decisions the USP makes on efficiency targets in the first period while cost reductions take place in the second. The USP is assumed to choose profit-maximizing prices subject to regulatory constraints.

Section 2 outlines the model. Section 3 applies a calibrated version of the model to consider trade-offs between USP efficiency and profitability. Section 4 reports sensitivities for cases of unexpectedly larger and smaller declines in mail volumes and Sect. 5 concludes. The Appendix provides further detail on the model and its calibration.

2 The Model

2.1 *Operators, Zones and Goods*

The structure of the model, in terms of operators, goods and delivery areas, is an extension of De Donder et al. (2006) to three delivery zones. The model is set out formally in the Appendix and an overview of its main components and assumptions is outlined below. The model assumes two postal operators: the incumbent USP, indexed by *I*, and entrants, indexed by *E*. Operators are active in three zones: urban high (delivery) cost, *UH*; urban, low (delivery) cost, *UL*; and rural, high (delivery) cost, *R*. There are three postal products: single-piece (SP) mail, bulk mail (BM) and an access service. As part of the USO, the USP is required to offer SP mail at a uniform price across all zones. By assumption, entrants do not find it profitable to offer such a service, principally because of the high cost of delivery in some areas, and choose not to enter this market. As a result the USP has a de facto monopoly over SP mail.

The USP faces competition from entrants in the bulk mail market. Competition can either be end-to-end (E2E), where entrants perform upstream (collection, sortation, transport) and downstream (delivery) activities, or through access to the USP delivery network, in which case entrants only perform upstream activities and pay a unit access charge per item of BM that the USP delivers on their behalf. The entrants compare the access charge in zone *i* with their own unit downstream cost, and choose the cheaper method. The delivery method does not affect consumers' desirability of the entrants' good. Both the USP and entrants practice zonal pricing

[1]While there is an extended empirical literature on the impact of strikes and trade unions on efficiency (Dickerson et al 1997; Doucouliagos and Laroche 2003; Maki 1983), to the best of our knowledge we are the first to model analytically how the possibility of industrial action impacts efficiency choices of a regulated firm.

for BM, including access charges. The BM goods are imperfect substitutes, so that an increase in the price set by one operator increases the quantity sold by the other, and are independent across zones. Furthermore, SP mail and BM are independent products and there is no substitution of one product by the other.[2] Entrants charge an exogenous mark-up m_i over variable costs, including the access charge where they access the USP delivery network in zone i. This mark-up reflects the intensity of competition and depends on whether competition takes the form of access or bypass. Postal market entry via access is assumed to be easier than by bypass, so there is more competition in zones with access, resulting in a lower value of m_i where access occurs, compared to bypass.

All operators face constant unit variable costs for upstream and downstream activities. Beyond uniformity of SP mail prices across zones, the USO also requires the USP to maintain a given level of quality of service in the provision of its services. Additionally, the USP has a network of collection points, processing centres and delivery offices to allow delivery of mail to all addresses in all zones at the required quality of service. This aspect of the USO translates into a fixed cost F for the USP. Entrants are not subject to the USO and do not face a corresponding fixed cost.

2.2 *Timing, Constraints, Decisions, Efficiency and Strikes*

This chapter extends De Donder et al. (2006) by adding an efficiency dimension and two time periods, P_1 and P_2. The model assumes firms announce prices for period 1 at the beginning of the period. The USP's objective is to maximize profit in P_1, subject to several constraints.[3] First, SP mail is regulated through a price-cap: the uniform SP mail price p cannot be larger than $\bar{p}$, which is set exogenously in the model (constraint C1). The cap is determined by the regulator to protect the affordability of SP mail and allow break-even for the overall economic profit the USP can be expected to achieve. Second, the difference between the SP mail price and the USP's bulk mail price in zone i cannot be smaller than the difference in their upstream costs (constraint C2) (otherwise, there would be no demand for BM). Third, there is a margin squeeze constraint on access prices in each zone i: the difference between the USP's BM price and access charge cannot be smaller than the USP's BM upstream cost (constraint C3). The regulator introduces this constraint to promote competition and prevent anti-competitive behavior. The USP sets all prices to maximize profit in P_1, subject to these constraints. Entrants observe the access charges posted by the USP, compare them with their own delivery costs and

[2]This assumption is a good approximation provided the price difference between the two goods is not too small. See constraint C2 in the Appendix for a precise mathematical statement.

[3]See the end of this section for a precise definition of first-period profit and the Appendix for a mathematical statement of these constraints, labeled C1 to C3.

choose access or bypass delivery operations in each zone, posting a mark-up m_i over their costs.

The regulator then announces the price constraints it will set during the next regulatory cycle, which is assumed to last five years, based on its assessment of prospects for mail demand and efficiency improvements. The regulator assesses the value of e, which is the yearly percentage reduction in (both variable and fixed) costs the USP could be expected to attain and sets the price cap $\bar{p}$ and the margin squeeze constraint. Reductions in costs may arise from improvements in productive efficiency or lower wage costs or a mix of both factors. The value of e is assumed to be obtained from a rigorous efficiency review process undertaken in P_1 that yields a challenging yet achievable estimate in P_2. The USP then announces efficiency targets to be achieved during that regulatory cycle, P_2, but the value of e it chooses need not equal that used by the regulator to set its price constraint $\bar{p}$. The announcement of efficiency targets by the USP is associated with risks of industrial action. If a strike occurs, this is assumed to result in a decrease of γ percent in the size of the postal market in P_1 which affects both the USP and entrants, and the USP is assumed not to adapt its prices in P_1.[4] P_{1S} (respectively, P_{1NS}) denotes the first-period when a strike does (respectively, does not) occur and it is assumed the regulator does not take into account the possibility of a strike when assessing its value of e.

The model assumes the USP efficiency targets announced in P_1 are achieved in P_2 whether or not a strike occurred in P_1 and, with a regulatory cycle of five years, its costs decrease by $5e$ by the end of P_2. For simplicity, entrants' costs are assumed to be the same as in P_1, such that e can be interpreted as the amount by which the USP lowers or improves its costs each year relative to competitors.[5] Mail market volumes are assumed to trend downwards for all operators due to e-substitution, independent of postal prices. The total reduction in postal market volumes is given by the parameter λ so that, for any given prices, mail volumes are λ % lower in P_2 than in P_1. To this downward trend, a further loss of γ % occurs in P_1 and subsequent years if a strike materialised in P_1 due to increased e-substitution.[6] P_{2S} (respectively, P_{2NS}) denotes the second-period when a strike did (respectively, did not) occur in P_1. The USP then chooses prices for P_2 to maximize profit in P_2, subject to the three price constraints, its costs (given its choice of e) and market demand during P_2. The USP of course knows whether a strike occurred in P_1, and can charge different prices accordingly. Entrants decide whether to access or bypass the USP delivery network and post their prices for P_2 simultaneously.

The USP's profit is denoted by π_{ab} in period $a = \{1, 2\}$ whether a strike occurred in P_1 (b = S) or not (b = NS). Observe that the same set of USP prices

[4] As explained at the end of this section, it would not wish to change them anyway.

[5] This is broadly equivalent in the model to positing absolute changes in efficiency for both types of operator separately and then considering the difference between these two rates (relative efficiency).

[6] See the Appendix for an analytical statement of volumes in P_2, and in P_{1S}.

maximize π_{aS} and π_{aNS} in the model because the impact of a strike is to scale down volumes by γ %, and prices which maximize a specific function also maximize (1-γ) times this function. So, prices will not differ between P_{2S} and P_{2NS}, and it does not matter whether first-period prices maximize π_{1S}, π_{1NS} or any linear combination of the two. Note that prices in P_1 do not affect profit levels in P_2 (since they do not affect the strike outcome), so the assumption that prices in period $a = \{1,2\}$ maximize profit in the same period a is innocuous, since the same sets of prices also maximize any weighted combination of profits in the two periods. The Appendix explains how the USP weighs the two periods to evaluate overall discounted profit when setting the value of e in period 1. The weights placed on profit in P_1 and P_2 are denoted respectively by w_1 and w_2 and discounted profit when a strike occurs is denoted by:

$$\pi_S = w_1\pi_{1S} + w_2\pi_{2S}, \tag{1}$$

while the discounted profit where a strike does not occur is:

$$\pi_{NS} = w_1\pi_{1NS} + w_2\pi_{2NS}. \tag{2}$$

3 Base Case Results

The model outlined in Sect. 2 was calibrated using parameter values based on published information or broadly based assumptions reflecting in general terms key aspects of liberalized postal markets in Europe. Details of the calibration referenced below are reported in the Appendix. Insights from the calibrated model were obtained from two base case variants which differ only in the constraints placed on the access prices charged by the USP. In the first, the only constraint in place on access prices is that for margin squeeze through which the regulator constrains access prices being raised to deter entry by competitors through access. In the second variant, the regulator limits access prices to low levels to promote entry by competitors on favorable terms and underpin demand from business customers by ensuring low prices for BM. In both cases entry through bypass is available to entrants.

3.1 *Bypass in Urban Areas and Access in Rural Areas*

The results of the first base case variant are recorded in Table 1. The first two columns report results attained in the first period. The value of $\bar{p}$ in P_1 had been set by the regulator at 1.015 (a 1.5 % mark-up over fully allocated costs of 1 per uniformly priced SP mail item), which corresponds to the USP breaking even in P_{1NS} when setting profit-maximizing prices in the BM market. At $\bar{p} = 1.015$, the constraint C1 is binding so that $p = \bar{p} = 1.015$. Equilibrium volumes, consumer surplus and contributions to profit in the three zones then reflect their relative sizes.

Table 1 Prices, volumes and welfare under alternative industrial action scenarios: entry through bypass and access under central case assumptions[a,b]

	P_1		P_2 with 2 % efficiency		$P_2$with 3 % efficiency	
Prices, Euro	No strike	Strike	No strike	Strike	No strike	Strike
USP, single piece	1.015		1.015		1.015	
USP, bulk mail urban low cost	0.552		0.539		0.533	
USP, bulk mail urban high cost	0.598		0.582		0.574	
USP, bulk mail rural	0.715		0.745		0.760	
USP, access rural	0.615		0.655		0.675	
Entrant bulk mail urban low cost, bypass	0.396		0.396		0.396	
Entrant bulk mail urban high cost, bypass	0.440		0.440		0.440	
Entrant bulk mail rural, access	0.689		0.729		0.750	
Volumes, billion items	**9.64**	**8.68**	**7.72**	**6.76**	**7.73**	**6.76**
USP total	7.18	6.46	5.89	5.16	5.97	5.22
USP, single piece	1.99	1.79	1.60	1.40	1.60	1.40
USP, bulk mail urban low cost	3.05	2.75	2.55	2.23	2.61	2.28
USP, bulk mail urban high cost	0.97	0.87	0.82	0.72	0.84	0.74
USP, bulk mail rural	1.17	1.05	0.93	0.81	0.93	0.81
Entrant total	2.46	2.22	1.83	1.60	1.76	1.54
Entrant bulk mail urban low cost, bypass	1.72	1.55	1.30	1.14	1.26	1.10
Entrant bulk mail urban high cost, bypass	0.56	0.51	0.42	0.37	0.40	0.35
Entrant bulk mail rural, access	0.18	0.16	0.11	0.10	0.10	0.08
Entrant share of bulk mail	32 %	32 %	30 %	30 %	29 %	29 %
Entrant share of total mail	26 %	26 %	24 %	24 %	23 %	23 %
USP economic profit net of fixed costs[c]	**0.00**	**−0.24**	**0.01**	**−0.26**	**0.26**	**−0.03**
USP efficiency target ("e") per annum set in P_1 and achieved in P_2[d]	–	–	2%	2%	3%	3%
Total welfare	**12.00**	**10.79**	**9.86**	**8.62**	**9.98**	**8.74**
USP contribution to profit[e]	2.40	2.16	2.17	1.90	2.30	2.01
Entrant contribution to profit	0.09	0.08	0.07	0.06	0.06	0.06
Net consumer surplus	9.51	8.55	7.62	6.66	7.62	6.67

Notes

[a]Further details on demand, cost and entrant pricing are contained in the Appendix

[b]Entry through bypass in urban areas and access in rural. Values for P_1 and P_2 are year 5 of five year regulatory cycles

[c]USP Profit = Revenue − (variable + fixed) costs. For example, fixed cost in P_1 = 2.4 billion €

[d]2 % pa efficiency implies fixed and variable costs lower 10 % in year 5 of P_2 than P_1

[e]Before fixed cost

The total contribution of SP mail to the USP profit is slightly over a third of the USP fixed costs of 2.4 billion €.

In the BM market a mark-up on costs for entrants is assumed of 2 % for access and 10 % for bypass. Entrants in this scenario bypass the USP in both urban zones, as entrants' delivery costs are lower than the USP's access prices, but require access in zone *R*. There, two pricing constraints are binding at equilibrium: the minimum price difference between SP and USP's BM prices (C2), and the margin squeeze constraint (C3) for access. Taken together, these constraints identify the USP's BM price and access charge. The entrants' price in zone *R* is obtained via a 2 % mark-up over its variable cost. Price constraints C2 and C3 are not binding in urban areas, where bypass occurs and the USP sets profit-maximizing prices, which are intuitively higher in the high cost urban zone than in the low cost one. Both USP and entrants' prices are significantly lower in the urban, compared to the rural, areas and entrants' BM market share is significantly higher at around 36 % and of total mail about 32 %. The total contribution to USP profit of BM is slightly below two thirds of the fixed costs, and the USP breaks even by construction. In the strike case, P_{1S}, all prices are the same as in P_{1NS} so volumes sold decrease by $\gamma = 10\,\%$ (compared to P_{1NS}), as do consumer surplus and contributions to profit. Market shares remain unchanged. The USP then ends up with a loss of γ of its fixed cost (0.24 billion €).

In P_2 the model calibration assumes the regulator expects the overall market to contract by $\lambda = 20\,\%$ against base volumes with no strike in P_1, and the USP would need to improve efficiency by about 2 % per annum to break-even with the price cap it set in P_1 ($\bar{p} = 1.015$) remaining unchanged in P_2. This improvement effectively is relative to competitors as their costs are assumed unchanged in P_2. The resulting profit-maximizing USP prices follow the same pattern of binding price constraints in the SP and BM markets as in P_1. Even though the USP observes whether a strike occurred in P_1 when setting its prices in P_2, the same prices maximize profit, for the reasons explained above. However, these prices depend on the value of *e*, since *e* affects costs. Table 1 reports the price levels corresponding to the value of *e* of about 2 %, such that the USP breaks even in P_{2NS}. In the SP mail market, these conditions result in USP prices in P_2 equal to P_1 (as a result of the price cap constraint), so that volumes decrease by 20 % (compared to P_{1NS}) and costs decrease by $5e$ = 10 % by P_2. For bulk mail, the results follow the same pattern of access (in zone *R*) and bypass (in the two urban zones), and of binding price constraints as in P_1. From Table 1, the USP lowers its costs by 2 % allowing it to decrease prices in the urban zones but it does so by less than 10 % (its reduction in costs) so enabling it to increase both its market share and its margins. The volume effect is larger than the cost effect, so that contributions to profit (and overall welfare levels) decrease, compared to P_1.[7] As for P_{2S}, lower volumes ($\lambda + \gamma = 30\,\%$ compared to P_{1NS}) with same prices and costs as in P_{2NS} result in a loss for the USP.

[7]As explained in the Appendix modelling a decrease in volumes demanded requires decreasing the surplus that consumers obtain from consuming any given quantity of mail. Recall that the fixed cost also decreases by 10 % in P_2 compared to P_1, so that the USP breaks even in P_{2NS} even though the contributions to profits are lower.

As stressed above, the USP need not choose the same value of e as the one on which the regulator based its computation of $\bar{p}$. The last two columns of Table 1 report results when the USP sets a value of e equal to 3 %, so that its costs are 15 % lower by the end of P_2 than the end of P_1. In the SP market, prices and volumes are the same as in the case where $e = 2$ %. In the urban BM market, lower costs (compared to $e = 2$ %) allow the USP to further decrease prices while increasing volumes at the expense of entrants. The contributions to profit of the USP increase in all markets (compared to $e = 2$ %) which, together with a lower fixed cost, mean the USP now makes a positive economic profit in P_{2NS}, and a smaller loss in P_{2S}.

3.2 Low Access Prices and Access in All Areas

In the second variant of the base case, access prices are assumed to be limited by the regulator to low levels such that the USP sets access prices which incorporate only a 10 % margin over its downstream FAC. Results are reported in Table 2. The main impact of lower access prices in P_{1NS} is that delivery costs for competitor services using access are below entrants' bypass prices and result in entrants offering service by access in all zones. Entrants' prices are lower than in the mixed bypass/access case as they incorporate not only lower delivery costs but also only a 2 % mark-up.

The price constraints C2 and C3 affecting the USP are not binding in the low access price base case and the USP sets prices at their profit-maximizing level given the prices chosen by entrants. The USP's profit-maximizing BM prices are below its prices in the mixed case but, despite this, the USP has a lower market share in the BM market because of low access charges feeding into entrant prices. Lower prices and market share lead to the USP's BM services producing a smaller contribution to fixed costs than in the mixed case and for break-even it is necessary for the SP price cap set by the regulator to be higher at 1.25€ (compared with 1.015€). Moving to P_{1S}, volumes and consumer surplus decrease by $\gamma = 10\,\%$, with unchanged prices, compared to P_{1NS} and the USP makes a loss of approximately γF—(that is, 0.24 billion € as in the mixed bypass/access case).

The results in Table 2, as in Sect. 3.1, assume the regulator bases its calculation of the break-even value of $\bar{p}$ on the assumption that the USP can achieve 2 % yearly reduction in costs. Given that entrants' prices are lower than in the mixed bypass/access case, the USP's profitability in the BM market is also lower. This then requires the regulator to increase its SP cap in the second period to 1.34 to allow the USP to offset this reduction in profitability by increasing profitability in SP mail. Although in the BM market the USP's prices and market shares are lower than in the mixed case, there are also similarities. For example, the USP makes use of its lower costs in P_2 to decrease BM prices, but by a lesser amount than its costs, so that it has slightly higher margins and market shares in all delivery zones. However, with the same prices but lower volumes in P_{2S}, the USP makes a loss. The results of the USP choosing $e = 3$ % while the price cap remains at $\bar{p} = 1.34$ show the USP using its lower costs to decrease its (retail and access) BM prices, resulting in higher volumes

Table 2 Prices, volumes and welfare under alternative industrial action scenarios: entry through access in all areas under central case assumptions[a,b]

	P_1		P_2 with 2 % efficiency		P_2 with 3 % efficiency	
Prices, Euro	No strike	Strike	No strike	Strike	No strike	Strike
USP, single piece	1.250		1.340		1.340	
USP, bulk mail urban low cost	0.520		0.499		0.488	
USP, bulk mail urban high cost	0.576		0.549		0.535	
USP, bulk mail rural	0.651		0.616		0.599	
USP, access urban low cost	0.220		0.198		0.187	
USP, access urban high cost	0.286		0.257		0.243	
USP, access rural high cost	0.374		0.337		0.318	
Entrant bulk mail urban low cost	0.286		0.263		0.252	
Entrant bulk mail urban high cost	0.353		0.324		0.309	
Entrant bulk mail rural	0.443		0.405		0.385	
Volumes, billion items	**9.91**	**8.92**	**8.04**	**7.03**	**8.10**	**7.09**
USP total	6.09	5.48	4.93	4.32	4.98	4.36
USP, single piece	1.90	1.71	1.49	1.30	1.49	1.30
USP, bulk mail urban low cost	2.58	2.32	2.11	1.85	2.13	1.87
USP, bulk mail urban high cost	0.83	0.75	0.68	0.60	0.69	0.60
USP, bulk mail rural	0.79	0.71	0.65	0.57	0.66	0.58
Entrant total	3.82	3.44	3.10	2.71	3.12	2.73
Entrant bulk mail urban low cost	2.39	2.15	1.93	1.69	1.94	1.70
Entrant bulk mail urban high cost	0.75	0.67	0.61	0.53	0.61	0.54
Entrant bulk mail rural	0.69	0.62	0.56	0.49	0.57	0.50
Entrant share of bulk mail	48 %	48 %	47 %	47 %	47 %	47 %
Entrant share of total mail	39 %	39 %	39 %	39 %	39 %	39 %
USP economic profit net of fixed costs[c]	**0.01**	**−0.23**	**0.00**	**−0.27**	**0.18**	**−0.09**
USP efficiency target ("e") per annum set in P_1 and achieved in P_2^d	–	–	2 %	2 %	3 %	3 %
Total welfare	**12.04**	**10.84**	**9.90**	**8.66**	**10.05**	**8.79**
USP contribution to profit[e]	2.41	2.17	2.16	1.89	2.22	1.95
Entrant contribution to profit	0.02	0.02	0.02	0.02	0.02	0.02
Net consumer surplus	9.61	8.65	7.72	6.75	7.80	6.83

Notes
[a]Further details on demand, cost and entrant pricing are contained in the Appendix
[b]Entry through access in all areas. Values for P_1 and P_2 are year 5 of five year regulatory cycles
[c]USP Profit = Revenue − (variable + fixed) costs. For example, fixed cost in P_1 = 2.4 billion €
[d]2 % pa efficiency implies fixed and variable costs lower by 10 % in year 5 of P_2 than P_1
[e]Before fixed cost

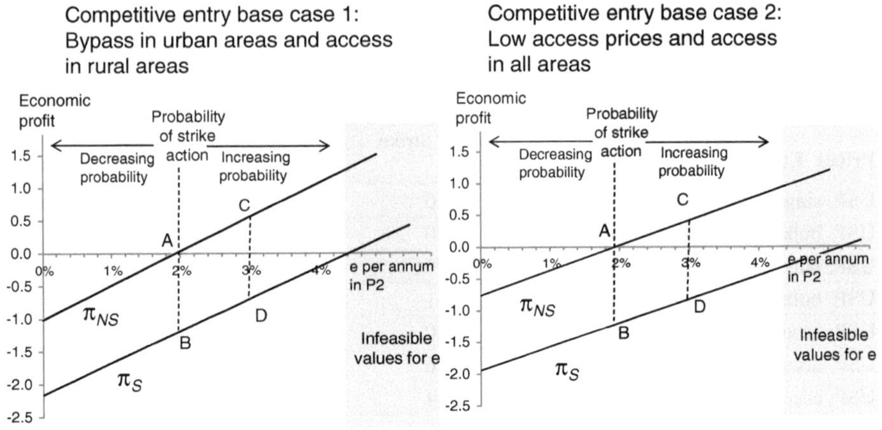

Fig. 1 USP's economic profit and efficiency trade-off options

for the USP and entrants, while market shares remain similar to their level when $e = 2$ %. As in Sect. 3.1, the USP makes a positive profit in P_{2NS}, and a loss in P_{2S}.

3.3 *Profit and Efficiency Trade-Off Options*

For both the mixed bypass/access and access only cases, Fig. 1 depicts how USP profits vary with the value of e when a strike does and does not occur[8] and shows that π_S and π_{NS} increase with e.[9] Recall from (2) that π_{NS} is the (appropriately weighted) sum of profits in periods 1 and 2 when a strike does not occur, and the model is calibrated in both scenarios to yield zero overall economic profit ($\pi_{NS} = \pi_{2NS} = 0$) when $e = 2$ % as shown in Fig. 1. However, raising the target level of efficiency may increase the probability of a strike. In addition, it is likely that raising efficiency above some maximum level may not be feasible (and for illustrative purposes only this is shown by the shaded areas in Fig. 1). In the case of a strike, discounted profit across the two time periods, π_S (defined by (1)), is lower than the no strike case, π_{NS}, for all values of e (since $\pi_{1S} < \pi_{1NS}$ and $\pi_{2S} < \pi_{2NS}$). The value of e such that $\pi_S = 0$ may lie inside or outside the feasible range (the latter being the case in both scenarios illustrated in Fig. 1).

Points A in Fig. 1 represent the value of e consistent with zero economic profit in P_2 for the USP in both base case scenarios. As noted previously, the model framework assumes this value is obtained from an efficiency review and is a challenging value for the USP to achieve. The risk of industrial action occurring

[8]The results reported in Tables 1 and 2 are profit-maximizing prices, volumes and welfare outcomes for just two points on each of these schedules, at e = 2 and 3 %.

[9]The linearity of demand functions explains why profit is close to being linear in *e*.

around this value is therefore assumed to be material, with values of e to the left of point A associated with a lower chance of a strike taking place and a higher risk of a strike taking place for values to the right of point A. The USP could choose to target an efficiency rate in P_2 that is higher or lower than that consistent with points A in Fig. 1 and its decision will depend on a number of factors. Two important ones are: how does the USP value a higher level of e translating into a higher profit (or a lower loss), when a strike is avoided (moving from point A to C) or occurs (moving from B to D); and secondly how does the USP value a higher level of e translating into a higher probability of a strike occurring (with the probability of ending up at D rather than at C if $e = 3\ \%$ is greater than the probability of ending up at B rather than at A if $e = 2\ \%$). An analysis of the USP's preferred range of options is worthy of further examination in future research. However, consider briefly the specific case where the USP is a publicly owned limited company that is subject to significant shareholder pressure to deliver an economic rate of return of at least zero. Here, the USP will try its utmost to avoid a strike, as all points on the strike curves contained in Fig. 1 assumed to be feasible yield negative economic profit. Similarly, the USP will be under substantial pressure to avoid being to the left of point A on the no strike curves, as again all points result in negative economic profits. The only range of outcomes where the USP could meet market expectations lie on the right hand side of point A on the no strike curves. However, to achieve this a profit maximizing USP would need to deliver efficiency gains that are in line, or higher, than those consistent with the regulatory price constraints.

Note also that in Fig. 1, the π_S and π_{NS} curves in the low access price case are somewhat flatter than the mixed bypass/access case and the difference between the schedules greater even though in both the USP adopts profit-maximizing prices. This difference implies that the change in losses to the left of A (moving to lower values of e) and the change in positive profits (moving to higher values of e) are smaller than in the mixed bypass/access case. More generally, the price constraints set by the regulator impact not only on which of the mixed bypass/access and access only cases result but also the trade-off between efficiency and USP profitability under conditions both where a strike occurs or does not occur in P_1.

4 Comparative Statics for Higher and Lower Volumes

Letter volumes are declining in developed countries, primarily due to e-substitution. The extent and pace of this fall is uncertain and challenging for postal sector USPs that have to contend with diseconomies of scale and manage highly unionized workforces (Rodriguez et al. 2017). In order to provide insight into this issue comparative static exercises using the calibrated model have been run to examine the impact of mail volume outcomes differing to those assumed by the regulator and USP. For simplicity, the cases examined assume the USP targets efficiency levels consistent with the outcome of the regulatory review performed in P_1 (that is, $e = 2\ \%$ per annum) and both the regulator and USP expect volumes to decline by

Table 3 USP comparative statics for low, central and high volume scenarios. Economic profit, €billion

	Bypass and access		Low access price	
	No strike profit	Strike profit	No strike profit	Strike profit
Low volume (λ = 0.3)	−0.5	−1.8	−0.6	−2.0
Central case (λ = 0.2)	0.0	−1.2	0.0	−1.4
High volume (λ = 0.1)	0.6	−0.6	0.6	−0.9

All scenarios evaluated for case where e = 2 %

20 % in the absence of a strike (λ = 0.2). The model is solved to optimize prices under different assumptions for the realized level of mail decline between P_1 and P_2 and whether a strike occurs or not. In particular, scenarios where mail volumes decline by 30 % (λ = 0.3) and 10 % (λ = 0.1) are considered. The results for the USP level of economic profit are reported in Table 3.

In both the strike and no strike cases the results suggest the USP's economic profit deteriorates considerably when volume outcomes are 10 % lower and improve substantially when they are 10 % higher (with the difference between the two cases being almost equal and opposite in size) than the central case (λ = 0.2). In the majority of cases, including all the strike cases, economic profits are negative and the only scenario where that yields a higher level of economic profit than the central case scenario is where mail volume declines are 10 % less (that is, λ = 0.1) and the USP avoids a strike.

5 Conclusions

This chapter developed and calibrated a two-period model to examine the challenges faced by a USP aiming to deliver efficiency gains in the future but which may lead to costly strike action in advance of these being achieved. In particular, it examined the profit maximizing decisions of a USP operating in a competitive environment and explored trade-offs between achieving efficiency gains and economic profit versus the risk of strike action. The model structure and assumptions consist of four important elements. First, mail volumes are in structural decline due to competition from electronic media. Second, there is a requirement for the USP to meet a pre-specified USO but entrants are not required to do so and can enter the postal market by choosing access only or a mixture of bypass/access services in different areas. Third, the USP is subject to price controls. Fourth, fixed costs are inherent in meeting the USO and require efficiency gains to offset the impact of volume declines.

The calibrated model considered two competitive entry base-case scenarios which differed only in the constraint placed on the access prices charged by the USP. In the first, the only constraint on access prices is a margin squeeze constraint and in the second, access prices are constrained to low levels. In the first case bypass competition emerges in urban low cost and high cost areas and access competition emerges in rural areas. In the second case, competition is via access only in all areas and the entrants' volume market share is considerably higher. In both cases, competition leads to significant differences in prices between single-piece and bulk mail traffic and among the latter by zone. Furthermore, competition via bypass and access results in lower social welfare than via access alone.

The USP is assumed to operate within a price control structure that requires a specific rate of efficiency to be achieved to maintain a normal rate of return during the next price control period if no strike takes place. In such an environment the USP is assumed to be able to achieve higher/lower efficiency than this specific level but runs an increasing/decreasing risk of industrial action. In the event of a strike being avoided the calibration results indicate the USP's profit could increase considerably if it were to target higher efficiency rates. However, the calibration results also suggest that if a strike occurs the USP could suffer significant losses and the level of efficiency required to generate an economic profit may not be feasible. An analysis of the USP's preferred range of options when it is required to meet specific objective criteria is worthy of further examination in future research. However, in the case where the USP is a publicly owned limited company and subject to significant shareholder pressure to deliver a normal market rate of return, it would need to deliver efficiency gains that are in line, or higher than those consistent with regulatory price constraints. The analysis indicates that there are complex trade-offs for the USP to evaluate between improving efficiency, seeking higher levels of profit and reducing the risk of industrial action and these are affected by regulatory constraints.

The chapter ends with an analysis, using the calibrated model, of the impact of volume uncertainty. In both the strike and no strike cases examined the results suggested the USP's profit level would deteriorate considerably if volumes were 10 % lower over a five-year price control period and improve substantially if they were 10 % higher over the same period. However, in the strike case all profits were negative and suggested the risks related to volume uncertainty and strike action could potentially err on the downside.

Appendix

(1) **Analytical model**.

The net utility that consumers in zone $i \in \{UH, UL, R\}$ obtain from consuming quantity x of SP mail at unit price p is denoted by $u_i(x) - px$. (3)

The demand function for good x in zone i is obtained by maximizing utility with respect to x, and is denoted by $x_i(p)$. Utility is quadratic in quantities, so that the demand function is linear and of the form $x(p) = \alpha - \beta p$.

The utility function $u_i(x)$ is calibrated and used to obtain the demand function in P_{1NS}. In P_{1S}, volumes are lower by γ % compared to P_{1NS}. The utility function is modified to $u_i(x, \gamma)$, and the maximization of (3) where $u_i(x)$ is replaced by $u_i(x, \gamma)$ gives the demand function $x(p, \gamma) = (1 - \gamma)x(p)$.[10] A similar process is followed for P_{2NS} (where γ is replaced by λ) and for P_{2S} (where γ is replaced by $\gamma + \lambda$).

For costs, the unit variable cost for SP mail is denoted by c_i. The contribution to USP profit of SP mail in zone i is then $(p - c_i)x_i(p)$.

The net utility obtained by consumers in zone i from consuming BM is $v_i(y_i^I, y_i^E) - q_i^I y_i^I - q_i^E y_i^E$, where q_i^j denotes the consumer price operator $j \in \{I, E\}$ posts in zone i, and y_i^j the quantity consumed of that good. The demand for goods in each zone is obtained by maximizing the consumers' utility, and is denoted by $y_i^I(q_i^I, q_i^E)$ and $y_i^E(q_i^I, q_i^E)$. Note that both operators' prices influence demand for both goods, because the function v_i is non separable in y_i^I and y_i^E. The utility function $v_i(.)$ is quadratic in quantities, so that BM demand functions are linear in prices. The process followed for SP mail is used to calibrate utility and demand functions for BM in P_{1S} and then to scale them down by, respectively γ, λ and $(\gamma + \lambda)$ % for periods P_{1S}, P_{2NS} and P_{2S}, respectively.

For BM costs, d_i^j denotes operator j's (constant) marginal delivery cost in zone i, and c_i^j operator j's total (upstream and downstream) constant unit cost in zone i. In urban zones, entrants decide whether to deliver themselves by comparing their delivery cost, d_i^E, and the access charge a_i, adopting the cheapest method. The volume of BM that the entrants deliver themselves in zone i is b_i^E, and z_i^E the amount of access taking place in zone i so that $b_I^E = y_I^E$ and $z_i^E = 0$ if $a_i \geq d_i^E$, and $b_I^E = 0$ and $z_i^E = y_I^E$ if $a_i < d_i^E$.

When setting the value of its access charges, the USP assumes entrants do not bypass its delivery network. A profit-maximizing level of the access charge larger than the entrant's delivery cost results in bypass. Limit pricing by the USP, where it would set access charge at the highest level compatible with access (just below entrants' delivery cost) is not allowed even if this is more profitable to the USP than bypass as it is assumed that limit pricing would be ruled out by competition authorities.

[10]Precise analytical statements are available upon request to the authors.

The entrants' profit in zone i is obtained as $(q_i^E - a_i - (c_i^E - d_i^E))z_i^E(q_i^I, q_i^E) + (q_i^E - c_i^E)b_i^E(q_i^I, q_i^E)$, as entrants do not meet the USO and so incur no fixed costs. Their prices are given by $q_i^E = (1+m)c_i^E$ if bypass occurs in zone i, and $q_i^E = (1+m)(c_i^E - d_i^E + a_i)$ if access occurs in zone i, with a higher mark-up m in case of bypass than access. The contribution to USP's profit of BM in zone i is equal to $(a_i - d_i^I)z_i^E(q_i^I, q_i^E) + (q_i^I - c_i^I)y_i^I(q_i^I, q_i^E)$. The incumbent also faces a fixed cost F, due to being required to meet the USO.

The USP is assumed to face three price constraints set by the regulator. The first is a simple cap on the SP mail price $p \leq \bar{p}$. (C1)

The second constraint is that the difference between the (higher) SP mail price and the (lower) BM price, in each zone, cannot be lower than the difference in USP upstream costs between the two types of mail. Anticipating the calibration assumption that unit downstream costs in any given zone i are the same for SP mail and BM, this constraint can be written as $q_i^j \leq p - \left(c_i - c_i^I\right)$, (C2), $i \in \{UL, UH, R\}$ and $j \in \{I, E\}$.

The third constraint is a margin squeeze constraint: the difference between the USP's BM price and access charge, in any zone i, must be at least equal to the fully allocated upstream cost of the USP in that zone: $q_i^I - a_i \geq \left(c_i^I - d_i^I\right)(1+\phi)$, (C3) where ϕ is the fully allocated cost (FAC) factor.

(2) **Weighting of the two periods.**

P_1 and P_2 are both the last year of a five year regulatory cycle. In the case where a strike does occur in P_1, the USP's profit levels in P_1 and P_2 are, respectively, π_{1S} and π_{2S}. A linear progression is assumed from the final year of P_1 to P_2, and a yearly discount factor $\delta = 0.91$. The discounted value of the USP's profit over six years, evaluated in P_1, is given by

$$\pi_{1S} + \sum_{i=1}^{5} \delta^i \left(\pi_{1S} + i\frac{\pi_{2S} - \pi_{1S}}{5}\right) = w_1\pi_{1S} + w_2\pi_{2S}$$

where

$$w_1 = \frac{5 + 4\delta + 3\delta^2 + 2\delta^3 + \delta^4}{5}, w_2 = \frac{1 + 2\delta + 3\delta^2 + 4\delta^3 + 5\delta^4}{5}.$$

(3) **Calibration.**

(A) *Demand.* In both SP mail and BM markets, when the price of the good is the same in all zones, the *UL* zone represents 60 % of total volumes, and zones *UH* and *R* each represent 20 %. SP mail: at a price of 1, price elasticity is −0.2 (all zones) and total volume 2 billion items. BM market, hypothetical monopoly setting: at price of 0.5, demand price elasticity of −0.4 (in all zones), and total volume of 8 billion items. With competition, displacement ratio $-\left[\partial y_i^I(q_i^I, q_i^E)/\partial q_i^E\right] / \left[\partial y_i^E(q_i^I, q_i^E)/\partial q_i^E\right]$ of 0.9. Market share of 10 % for entrants when $q_i^I = q_i^E = 0.5$ and of 50 % when $q_i^I = 0.5$ and $q_i^E = 0.25$.

(B) *Costs.* SP mail market: same upstream cost of 0.36 in all three zones with $c_{UL} = 0.7$, (hence, for example, downstream cost in *UL* is 0.2); $c_{UH} = 0.62$; and $c_R = 0.7$. BM market, USP: same upstream cost of 0.06 in all three zones, and same downstream cost in zone *i* as for the SP mail product with $c_{UL}^I = 0.26$, $d_{UL}^I = 0.2$; $c_{UH}^I = 0.32$, $d_{UH}^I = 0.26$; and $c_R^I = 0.4$, $d_R^I = 0.34$. BM market, entrants: same upstream cost of 0.06 in all three zones and $c_{UL}^E = 0.36$, $d_{UL}^E = 0.3$; $c_{UH}^E = 0.4$, $d_{UH}^E = 0.34$; and $c_R^E = 0.8$, $d_R^E = 0.74$. USP: fixed cost of $F = 2.4$; and FAC factor ϕ of 2/3.

(C) *Entrant mark-ups.* Access: $m = 0.02$; bypass: $m = 0.1$.

References

De Donder, P., Cremer, H., Dudley, P., & Rodriguez, F. (2006). A welfare analysis of price controls with end-to-end mail and access services. In: M. A. Crew & P. R. Kleindorfer (Eds.), *Liberalization of the postal and delivery sector* (pp. 53–72). Cheltenham: Edward Edgar.

Dickerson, A. P., Geroski, P.A., & Knight, K. G. (1997). Productivity, efficiency and strike activity. *International Review of Applied Economics, 11*(1), 119–134.

Doucouliagos, C., & Laroche, P. (2003). What do unions do to productivity? A meta-analysis. *Industrial Relations, 42*(4), 650–691.

Maki, D. R. (1983). The effects of unions and strikes on the rate of growth of total factor productivity in Canada. *Applied Economics, 15*(1), 29–41.

Rodriguez, F., Soteri, S., & Tobias, S. (2017). E-substitution and the demand for business mail in the UK: Trends and prospects. In M. A. Crew, P. L. Parcu, & T. J. Brennan (Eds.), *The changing postal and delivery sector—towards a renaissance.* Berlin: Springer.

The Personalization and Volume Trade-Off: A Future Without Saturation Mail?

Michael D. Bradley and Adam C. Houck

1 Introduction

High density, saturation advertising mail is a significant revenue source for the United States Postal Service (USPS), totaling $3.03 billion in Fiscal Year 2015. However, the revenue generated by these saturation products is at risk as they run contrary to the contemporary and cutting-edge marketing techniques that use analytics to send highly targeted messages to granular segments of individuals to maximize response rates per mail piece. Indeed, the future might demand quite a significant evolution from the imprecise, carpet-bombing approach of traditional saturation mailings.

Changes in the nature of advertising suggest that maintaining and increasing the value of physical mail within multi-channel marketing campaigns will increasingly rely on highly targeted advertising mail pieces that increase individual response rates. However, as marketers become more adept at precisely targeting consumers, they may very well be able to send fewer advertising mail pieces and achieve the same response rates. While this is of potential benefit to the marketer, it could have significant volume and financial impacts to postal operators (POs) including USPS.

Therefore, USPS should evaluate scenarios in which these saturation volumes decline significantly and estimate the corresponding effects on revenues, costs, and thus profits. If these volumes indeed disappear, what new products could replace

The views expressed are those of the authors and do not necessarily represent those of the George Washington University or IBM Global Business Services.

M.D. Bradley
George Washington University, Washington, D.C, USA

A.C. Houck (✉)
IBM Global Business Services, Richmond, VA, USA
e-mail: ahouck@us.ibm.com

M. Crew et al. (eds.), *The Changing Postal and Delivery Sector*,
Topics in Regulatory Economics and Policy,
DOI 10.1007/978-3-319-46046-8_5

these volumes and what product attributes would be required in order to do so? This paper examines these questions in an analytical framework based upon Bradley et al. (2015) and De Donder et al. (2011). In the next section, we explore the background of advertising mail, some of the disruptive technology trends in direct mail and advertising that are most directly applicable to POs, and previous research. Section 3 presents the method and results, and conclusions are presented in Sect. 4.

2 Direct Mail Marketing and Advertising: Background

The first signs of modern direct mail in the U.S. point to Ben Franklin in 1744 with the invention of the mail order catalog ‘A Catalog of Choice and Valuable Books’. However, the concept of direct marketing dates back millennia to 1000 BC Egypt, with landowners scribing advertisements on papyrus offering rewards of gold for the return of a runaway slaves. Ancient merchants in Babylon also carved messages into stone tablets to advertise products when visiting nearby towns. It was not until 1440 with Gutenberg’s invention of the printing press that direct marketing took a significant step forward, paving the way for the proliferation of mass-produced advertising messages being distributed to wide audiences.

The mail order process was refined by American entrepreneurs Aaron Montgomery Ward and Richard Warren Sears in the late 19th century. They mailed pamphlets and flyers to customers to sell a variety of products, revolutionizing how people purchase goods and redefining the engagement model between retailer and potential customer. This new model, however, was not universally viewed as an improvement in the use of the mail system. In an 1864 letter to the editor of the Times, a gentleman provided his thoughts on receiving a late night direct mail piece from a local dentistry practice regarding the hours of operation: “I have never had any dealings with Messrs. Gabriel (dentistry practice) and beg to ask by what right do they disturb me by a telegram which is evidently simply the medium of advertisement? A word from you would, I feel sure, put a stop to this intolerable nuisance” (The Economist 2007, online).

Bulk mail, especially advertising mail, has grown tremendously in volume to becoming a significant contributor to the net financial position of POs, especially USPS. Indeed, these direct mail products play an important role in the future sustainability of USPS; roughly 85 % of the total 150.2 billion pieces of market dominant mail in Fiscal Year 2015 had a one-to-many relationship, with a single mailer sending volume to countless receivers. As the composition of the mail mix continues to change in the U.S. to reflect fewer First Class letters, more Standard Mail products and more parcels, advertising mail can potentially play an even more significant role in the years ahead.

There are two main categories within direct mail: transactional mail and advertising mail. De Donder et al. (2010) said, “Through transactional mail the sender is able to meet its obligation of providing information to the recipient (examples include bank statements and utilities’ invoices. Through advertising mail, the sender is able to provide information to the recipient to encourage a response or purchase." Interestingly, similar to television advertising, the purchaser of the advertising mail piece is not the true customer, yet recipients determine the ultimate value. Value in this context is defined by the quality of the advertising message a recipient receives that provokes a response that benefits the sender.

In an age defined by the conversion of many advertising messages from physical to digital, evidence confirms why retailers and other firms continue to spend so much on direct mail; it works. Retailer Williams Sonoma spends half its total marketing budget on catalog production and postage (Holmes 2014). Response rates quantify and confirm these direct advertising messages are indeed effective. A 2015 report from the Direct Marketing Association (DMA) (2015) showed direct mail achieves a 3.7 % overall response rate; according to the study, oversized envelopes have the best response rate at 5.0 %, followed by postcards at 4.25 %, catalogs 3.9 %, and letter-sized envelopes 3.5 %. These response rates have remained consistent, if even increased, as the same DMA report from 2010 confirmed a 3.42 % overall response rate. By comparison, all digital channels combined to only achieve a 0.62 % response rate, significantly less than their analog counterparts.

In this digital age, firms are sending more email advertisements than ever before, evidenced by a recent IPC report. In 2013, an estimated 507 billion emails were sent, 81 % of which were spam (IPC 2011, p. 45). However, the vast majority of these messages are being ignored; "the latest survey from Goo Technologies shows that more than 80 % of Americans flat-out ignore the digital ads to which they are exposed" (Mobilestorm 2014, online, no page number).

Indeed, more accurate monitoring, via digital breadcrumbs and tracking cookies, of how an individual interacts with a digital advertisement, combined with intense competition for advertising dollars, has likely pushed firms to shift to more digital messages. However, research confirms just how valuable physical advertising messages remain compared to digital. A 2015 report from the USPS Office of Inspector General (OIG) working with the Temple University Center for Neural Decision Making explored survey questionnaires, eye tracking, core biometrics, and neuroimaging to assess the differences in how people respond to physical versus digital media to understand when mail is more valuable to recipients "and as a result, effective for senders, ultimately elevating the entire mail value chain" (USPS OIG 2015, p. 4). They found that while participants grasped an identical amount of information from both physical and digital media, physical advertisements had a longer lasting impact compared to digital and that "although participants stated similar preferences and willingness to pay for an item regardless of whether they saw the ad in a physical or digital format, their brain activity indicated greater subconscious value for products or services advertised in physical format", a strong predictor of purchases made (USPS OIG 2015, p. 8).

Better targeting has become increasingly important in recent political elections, most notably in the United Kingdom (UK) and the U.S. In the 2015 British general election, the Labour Party employed the cheaper option of Royal Mail door drops (i.e. saturation direct mail to specific post codes) as opposed to better targeted direct mail advertisements. "There is a tradeoff between cost and the ability to segment accurately… (and) the result was that the Conservatives were able to target their message more precisely, and for longer, on potential swing voters" (Cowley and Kavanagh 2016, online). In the U.S., the Democratic Party won election in 2012 in large part due to the predictive analytical models employed to determine key micro-segments of voters to target with direct advertising messages. Instead of simply sending saturated direct mail messages to large geographic areas, the Obama campaign sought to understand who could be susceptible to influence; precisely, "who could be convinced to vote Obama if (and only if) contacted?" (Siegel 2013, online). The campaign more precisely defined swing voters into micro-segments of the population who could be influenced. Instead of predicting an individual's behavior to purchase a good or click through an advertisement, they predicted the ability to persuade and as a result of better targeting, fewer pieces of advertising mail were sent, better response rates were achieved, and the Democrats won victory in 2012.

Previous research on direct mail advertising has focused on key elements including the benefits of increasing targeting strength and how the mode of letter delivery affects response rates. Bradley et al. (2015) used the Bergemann and Boratti (2011) framework to model demand for direct mail as a function of targeting strength and found "the effect of targeting on profit is unambiguously positive" (p. 74). Despite a significantly higher price ratio relative to marginal cost (36 % for targeted mail vs. 12 % for saturation mail), targeted mail was still more profitable for the PO which suggests "an optimal targeting level, for any given distribution of consumers across product markets, would maximize the contribution from ad mail to the PO bottom line" (p. 75). Additionally, Bradley et al. (1999) explored the importance of mode of delivery in how recipients interact with direct mail advertising. Analyzing survey data they found "cluster box recipients reported significantly lower read and respond rates than door recipients for all types of advertising mail. In a number of instances, the cluster box read-and-respond rates were half of those for door recipients" (p. 228). This suggests the quality of the advertising message includes an element of how recipients first experience the message, and the closer a retailer or firm can get the advertising message to the door or curbside, the greater chance of success.

Overall advertising market expenditure in the U.S. has fallen 20 % in the last 8 years to $190B. Since 1995 total spent on Internet advertising increased from 0 to 30 % while newspapers' share declined from 31 to 7 %, yet the share of advertising expenditure on mail remained nearly constant, falling from 12 to 11 % (USPS OIG 2016, p. 9). Maintaining this share perhaps confirms the value of advertising mail products as elements of multi-channel advertising campaigns, but as suggested by recent evidence in election direct mail targeting and confirmed by Bradley et al. (2015), the effect on profit of greater targeting in advertising mail is "unambiguously positive" (p. 74). Therefore, for advertising mail to maintain its value as an advertising broadcast medium into the future, the targeting ability within advertising mail must increase.

This does not mean that saturation mailings will not play an important role in niche marketplace uses for select firms. "Up to 85 % of (a) business's customers come from the five-mile radius surrounding it" (Nice Branding 2015, no page number, online). Evidenced by the successful introduction and growth of the Every Door Direct Mail (EDDM) product by USPS, saturation advertising mail can still work.[1] However, the value of the advertising mail broadcasting channel cannot be rooted in a carpet-bombing approach and must seek to drive greater targeting and greater value for recipients in the years ahead. Parti (2014, online, no page number) observed, "in today's day and age, you can have five-to-seven screens in your house, but you still only have one mailbox." It is therefore important to examine the scenarios of a future where these myriad effects combine to decrease the total volumes of traditional saturation mail and their corresponding effects on the net financial position of USPS.

3 Methodology and Results

To assess the potential impact of losing saturation-style advertising on USPS, this analysis estimates the lost profit caused by this market shift; it then investigates the prices and approximate volumes of a targeted advertising mail product needed to replace that lost profit.

A first requirement in assessing the impact in the loss of saturation mail is defining its current volume. USPS describes its products by their physical characteristics and service standards, not by their use. Thus, it is not possible to examine USPS volume figures and immediately identify the amount of saturation advertising mail. USPS products are initially broken into two broad categories, market dominant products and competitive products. Market dominant products are subject to a price cap whereas competitive products can be priced to market as long as the prices exceed unit costs. Competitive products include competitive package and expedited services, so our analysis of saturation advertising will focus on market dominant products.

As Table 1 shows, First Class Mail and Standard Mail generate nearly all the market dominant volumes, accounting for approximately 96 % of the volume.

First Class Mail includes communications mail, bill presentment and payment and some advertising. However, because of the cost of First Class mail, that advertising tends to be targeted, not saturation and we will assume there is no saturation advertising in First Class Mail. Thus, this analysis focuses attention on Standard Mail.

All Standard Mail prices are bulk prices, and each mailing must meet a minimum quantity of 200 pieces or 50 lb of mail. Standard mail consists of flyers and other advertising pieces. Within the product line, there are different individual products based upon the nature of mail preparation and address coverage. Carrier Route mail must be sorted to the individual carrier's route, prepared in sequence order and must

[1]EDDM generated $452 m in revenue from approximately 2.8 billion pieces in 2015 (USPS OIG 2016, p. 14).

Table 1 Postal service market dominant volumes—Fiscal year 2015

Product line	Volume (billions of pieces)	Proportion (%)
First class	63.1	42.2
Standard	80.1	53.5
Periodicals	5.8	3.9
Package services	0.6	0.4

Table 2 Standard mail products—Fiscal year 2015

Product	Volume (billions of pieces)	Proportion (%)
High density and saturation	17.7	22.1
Carrier route	8.3	10.4
Standard regular	53.0	66.2
Other	1.1	1.3
Total	80.1	100.0

include at least 10 pieces per carrier route. High Density mail must also be sorted to carrier route and sequenced but must have a route minimum that ranges from 125 to 300 pieces. Saturation mail has similar make up requirements as high density but must cover 90 % of residential addresses if addressed and 100 % of addresses if unaddressed (Table 2).[2]

Because the definition of saturation advertising mail is a bit ambiguous, this analysis takes a three-way approach. The narrowest definition is probably the least controversial and defines saturation advertising mail to be equal to the 17.7 billion pieces of High Density and Saturation Mail USPS handled in Fiscal Year 2015. The middle definition adds the 8.3 billion pieces of Carrier Route mail to produce a total of 26 billion pieces. Finally, the broadest measure adds 40 % of Standard Regular mail under the assumption that the remaining 60 % is made up of targeted advertising.[3,4]

The profit or "contribution" that USPS would lose if it lost saturation advertising mail is the difference between the mail's total revenue and total cost. Total revenue can be obtained directly from USPS's Cost and Revenue Analysis (CRA) report, which explicitly lists the revenue earned by each market dominant product. Total product cost is more difficult to obtain. USPS's CRA presents each product's "attributable" cost, which is equal to the product's volume multiplied by the marginal cost of the last piece delivered along with its marginal cost. Although

[2]"Other" standard mail includes Every Day Direct Mail and Standard Mail negotiated service agreements.

[3]Standard Regular mail includes a small amount of parcels. They are excluded from our analysis.

[4]A 2008 IBM study for the value of the USPS monopoly found that 40 % of Standard Mail would be lost to entrants; assuming that entrants would take the high density mail, we use this figure for our 'saturation' proportion in the scenario.

useful for setting prices, this measure understates the total cost caused by each product because USPS experiences economies of scale, density, and scope. Consequently, each product's marginal cost rises as its volume decreases. In a multiproduct firm like USPS, the total cost of any individual product or group of products is measured by its incremental cost. Incremental cost is the total cost that would disappear if a product or group of products were not produced, which is exactly the cost measurement needed to analyze what would happen to USPS's financial position if saturation advertising mail disappeared.

Conceptually, the incremental cost for a product (or group of products) can be calculated by comparing USPS's total cost before the product is added to the mix with USPS's total cost after the product is added to the mix. In theory then, for Product "A", the incremental cost is given by:

$$IC_A = TC(V_i) - TC(V_i - V_A).$$

However, in practice, USPS calculates marginal costs by calculating each product's marginal cost across a series of cost segments. Each segment represents a different activity like mail processing, city carrier delivery, or transportation. Moreover, the costs in these activities are caused by variations in an intermediate output, known as a "cost driver." For example, in highway transportation, the cost driver is the cubic foot-miles of transportation required. This means that the actual calculation of incremental cost must account for the fact that different products make different uses of the cost drivers in each segment. Consequently, our calculation of incremental cost proceeds at the cost segment level. The total costs in any segment, C_j, can be expressed as function of the cost driver (D_j) for that segment.[5]

$$C_j = \gamma_j(D_j).$$

The amount of the cost driver, D_j, is determined by the amount of volume, V_j.

$$D_j = \delta_j(V_i).$$

As mentioned above, different products will require different amounts of the cost driver in each segment. The amount of the driver required for Product A, introduced above, is the difference between the amount of the driver used before Product A was provided and the amount of driver required when all products are provided:

$$D_{jA} = \delta_j(V_i) - \delta_j(V_i - V_A).$$

The incremental cost for Product A in that segment is the sum of any product specific cost for the product (in that segment) and the additional variable cost caused by providing the product.

[5]The equations in this section is derived from Bradley et al. (1997).

$$IC_{jA} = \gamma_j(D_j) - \gamma_j(D_j - D_A).$$

The overall product incremental cost is just the sum of the segment incremental costs. Finally, to facilitate the computation of the relevant incremental costs, the analysis uses a constant elasticity approximation to the individual segment cost functions[6]:

$$C_j = \alpha_j D_j^{\varepsilon_j},$$

where

$$\varepsilon_j = \frac{\partial C_j}{\partial D_j}\frac{D_j}{C_j}.$$

With this approximation, our estimate for Product A's incremental cost in Segment j is given by:

$$IC_{jA} = \alpha_j D_j^{\varepsilon_j} - \alpha_j(D_j - D_{jA})^{\varepsilon_j}.$$

The impact on USPS's financial position arising from the loss of saturation advertising mail can now be approximated. Before those approximate effects are presented some caveats are in order. First, in each scenario, it is assumed that all saturation mail, as defined in that scenario, disappears. Second, mitigating cost savings associate with network realignment are not allowed. To the extent USPS can realign its network, it can possibly save additional institutional costs. Nevertheless, these figures provide insight into the financial effects.

Table 3 shows that the losses are substantial. The revenue loss ranges from about \$3 billion to about \$10 billion depending upon the specific definition of saturation mail. These revenue losses are associated with material profit declines ranging from a low of \$1.2 billion to a high of \$3.3 billion. Given USPS's current financial situation and the limitations on its borrowing, profit losses of this size might potentially call into question it ongoing financial viability. Cleary, saturation advertising mail is currently an important product for USPS.

One way of mitigating the lost profit from eroding saturation advertising mail would be to introduce a targeted advertising mail product. Such a product would be more expensive to handle than saturation mail because of its lower density. However, as demonstrated by Bradley, Colvin and Perkins, USPS would be able to charge a higher price for targeted advertising mail because it provides a higher value to advertisers. Targeted mail has much higher response rates than saturation mail and thus provides a higher value on a per piece basis.

It is beyond the scope of this chapter to estimate what the actual cost and price for a targeted advertising product would be. However, the amount of targeted mail

[6]For an analysis of this approximation, see Bradley et al. (1997).

Table 3 Approximate financial effects of lost saturation advertising mail

Scenario	Lost revenue	Incremental cost	Lost profit
One	$3028	$1758	$1271
Two	$5265	$3554	$1711
Three	$10,117	$6807	$3310

USPS would need to restore its profits can be approximated using rough cost and price estimates. To approximate the cost and price the best available proxy is First Class Mail. By definition, communications mail is "targeted" as well as bill presentment. Thus, it makes sense to use First Class as a proxy. What is not clear, however, if targeted advertising mail would be more like First Class Single Piece mail or First Class Presort mail. Because of this uncertainty a range of three different costs and prices is examined. On the cost side, it is assumed the range varies from the marginal cost of First Class Presort ($0.124) to the marginal cost of single piece First Class Mail ($0.269). To complete the range an intermediate value is used that is the average of the two marginal costs. The same approach is used for prices, using a low of $0.394, the average revenue per piece for presort, to a high of $0.505, the average revenue per piece for single piece, and the average of the two.

For each of the three scenarios, nine possible combinations of prices and costs are constructed. This provides a range of unit contributions for the targeted mail and provides insight into the range of demands required to make USPS financially whole. For example, when the price is relatively high and cost is relatively low, the estimated contribution per piece for targeted mail will be high. In contrast, the lowest estimate contribution per piece occurs when price is its lowest and cost is its highest. Table 4 presents the nine price/cost combinations and the resulting contributions per piece for targeted mail. The table helps assess the required characteristics of targeted mail.

Most favorable for USPS would be if a targeted mail piece was like First Class single piece in revenue and First Class presort in cost; then it would provide a unit contribution of 38.1 cents. This is less than the current unit contribution for First Class flats which is 47.8 cents, but well above the average contribution for First Class of 26.1 cents. The more that targeted mail takes on the cost profile of single piece mail but USPS can only charge rates similar to current presort mail the less attractive it would be. In the worst case, the targeted mail would have to be handled like single piece incurring high operation costs but would generate under 40 cents

Table 4 Alternative approximate profits per piece for targeted mail

		Marginal cost of targeted mail		
		$0.269	**$0.196**	**$0.124**
Price of targeted mail	**$0.505**	$0.236	$0.308	$0.381
	$0.449	$0.181	$0.253	$0.326
	$0.394	$0.125	$0.198	$0.270

per piece. In this case, the unit contribution is similar to that for current standard mail letters.

These unit contributions are then used to calculate the volumes necessary for USPS to earn enough from a new targeted product to exactly compensate for the losses created by the disappearance of saturation mail. This is a somewhat artificial goal, but it is an appropriate benchmark for beginning the assessment of if, and how, USPS could pursue a targeted mail product to replace eroding saturation volume. This calculation is performed for each of the three scenarios reflecting various degrees of saturation mail erosion.

To provide perspective on the calculated volumes it is noted that USPS loses 17.7 billion pieces of saturation mail in Scenario 1, 26.0 billion pieces in Scenario 2 and 47.2 billon pieces in Scenario 3.

Table 5 presents the calculated volumes (in millions of pieces) for each of the three scenarios. In general, the results suggest that USPS would need relatively modest volumes of targeted mail to offset the loss of saturation mail. This is because the calculated unit contribution for targeted mail is larger than the current unit contributions for saturation mail. For example, in Scenario 1 in which USPS loses solely its high density and saturation advertising mail, it would need new targeted mail volumes in the 5 billion-piece range, which is similar to its current Periodicals volume, which is a relatively small volume product.

As USPS loses more saturation mail, the volume demands for targeted mail increase. In Scenario 2, in which USPS also loses is carrier route mail, the required targeted volume rises to 6–7 billion-piece range. Finally, when USPS also loses

Table 5 Targeted volume required to restore lost saturation mail profit

		Scenario 1		
		Marginal cost of targeted mail		
		$0.269	**$0.196**	**$0.124**
Price of targeted mail	**$0.505**	5389.1	4121.8	3337.1
	$0.449	7035.3	5020.3	3902.5
	$0.394	10,129.4	6419.6	4698.7
		Scenario 2		
		Marginal cost of targeted mail		
		$0.269	**$0.196**	**$0.124**
Price of targeted mail	**$0.505**	7255.9	5549.6	4493.0
	$0.449	9472.2	6759.2	5254.3
	$0.394	13,638.1	8643.2	6326.3
		Scenario 3		
		Marginal cost of targeted mail		
		$0.269	**$0.196**	**$0.124**
Price of targeted mail	**$0.505**	14,038.6	10,737.3	8693.1
	$0.449	18,326.8	13,077.7	10,166.0
	$0.394	26,387.0	16,722.8	12,240.0

40 % of its regular standard mail volume, the required targeted volumes climb to the range of 13–16 billion pieces.

4 Conclusion

High density, saturation advertising mail continues to be a significant revenue source for USPS. However, evidence suggests the market for advertising is going the way of technology, micro customer segmentation, and highly granular targeting. As these more refined targeting abilities exist for advertisers, there is little reason to believe they will not attempt to acquire deeper targeting capabilities as have been seen in recent political election direct mail advertising campaigns. This evolution contributes to the need for POs to adjust to this new paradigm and offer higher targeted advertising products to replace the potential lost saturation volumes that were not targeted.

This analysis suggests that replacing saturation mail with a more targeted product would allow USPS to move closer to a net break even financial position, even at lower volumes than they currently deliver today. This could imply USPS can continue with its network rationalization efforts of downsizing its supply chain network and still deliver outstanding value in this critical channel. It is possible that after most non-targeted volumes disappear, saturation volumes that are still micro-targeted by geography like Every Door Direct Mail can provide value in this localized advertising channel.

The analysis also suggests that targeted mail has the potential to provide greater value per piece to USPS compared to pure saturation mail in terms of both revenue and contribution. As the share of saturation volume with respect to total USPS mail volume is relatively low, this implies USPS can likely survive and endure even if these volumes disappear; however, that does not imply the existing advertising volumes do not have to evolve with the changing nature of targeted advertising into the future.

References

Bradley, M. D., Colvin, J., & Panzar, J. C. (1997). Issues in measuring incremental cost in a multi-function enterprise. In M. Crew & P. Kleindorfer (Eds.), *Managing change in the postal and delivery industries* (pp. 3–21). Dordrecht: Kluwer Academic Publishers.

Bradley, M. D., Colvin, J., & Panzar, J. C. (1999, July). On setting prices and testing cross-subsidy with accounting data. *Journal of Regulatory Economics, 16*(1), 83–100.

Bradley, M., Colvin, J. & Perkins, M. (2015). Targeting versus saturation: Derived demand for direct mail. In M. A. Crew & T. J. Brennan (Eds.), *Postal and delivery innovation in the digital economy*. Berlin: Springer.

Cowley, P., & Kavanagh D. (2016). The British general election of 2015. Houndsmills, Basingstoke, Hampshire, UK: Palgrave Macmillan Publishers Limited.

De Donder, P., Cremer, H., Dudley, P., & Rodriguez, F. (2011). Welfare and pricing of mail in a communications market. *Review of Network Economics, 10*(3).

Direct Marketing Association. (2015). DMA response rate report 2015. Web. March 21, 2016.

Holmes, E. (2014, April, 16). Why online retailers like Bonobos, Boden, Athleta mail so many catalogs. Web. April 18, 2014.

International Postal Corporation. (2011). Strategic perspectives on the postal market 2011. March 2, 2016.

Mobile Marketer. (2014, February 5). Report: Most digital ads aren't cutting it. The digital marketing blog. Web. March 15, 2016.

Nice Branding Agency. (2015, February 26). Direct mail campaigns: Targeted mailing lists vs. every door direct mail. Web. March 28, 2016.

Parti, T. (2014, August 3). A throwback ploy survives the digital age. Web. June 5, 2016.

Siegel, E. (2013, January 22). Team Obama mastered the science of mass persuasion—And won. Web. June 6, 2016.

The Economist. (2007). Getting the message, at Last. Web. March 24, 2016.

USPS Office of Inspector General with Temple University Center for Neural Decision Making. (2015). Enhancing the value of mail: The human response. https://www.uspsoig.gov/sites/default/files/document-library-files/2015/rarc-wp-15-012.pdf

USPS Office of Inspector General. (2016). Advertising mail: Past and present. https://www.uspsoig.gov/sites/default/files/document-library-files/2016/RARC-WP-16-006.pdf

An Economic Perspective on Terminal Dues

Henrik Ballebye Okholm, Bruno Basalisco, Jimmy Gårdebrink and Anna Möller Boivie

1 Introduction

The Universal Postal Union (UPU) is an international organization and a global forum for cooperation between postal sector players, originally founded in 1874. Today, 220 countries and territories are part of the UPU. The UPU's activities relate to many aspects of international mail including making the rules for international mail exchanges between designated postal operators in its member countries. An essential part of this work concerns intergovernmental agreements governing *terminal dues*—payments between designated postal operators for the transport, sorting, and delivery of cross-border letter post items (terminal dues apply to "small letters" (P), "large letters" (G), sometimes referred to as "flats", and "bulky letter", sometimes referred to as "small packets" (E))[1] in the destination country. Several researches are looking at effects from these agreed terminal dues defined by UPU (see for instance Campbell 2015) and its implications with EU competition law (see Geradin 2012; Wojtek 2015).

[1]They are defined by a set of minimum and maximum dimensions and weights. **Small letters (P)** are defined by the characteristics; Minimum dimensions: 90 × 140 mm, Maximum dimensions: 165 × 245 mm, Maximum weight: 100 g, Maximum thickness: 5 mm. **Large letters (G)** are characterized as items that cannot be classified as small letters; Minimum dimensions: 90 × 140 mm, Maximum dimensions: 165 × 245 mm, Maximum weight: 100 g, Maximum thickness: 5 mm. **Bulky letters or small packets (E)** (a non-standard envelope or parcel up to 2 kg) are characterized as items classified neither as small letters nor as large letters; Minimum dimensions: 90 × 140 mm, Maximum dimensions: 900 mm length, width and depth combined, with the greatest dimension not exceeding 900 mm, Maximum weight: 2 kg (5 kg for items containing books or pamphlets), cf. UPU (2015).

H.B. Okholm (✉) · B. Basalisco · J. Gårdebrink · A.M. Boivie
Copenhagen Economics, Copenhagen, Denmark
e-mail: hbo@copenhageneconomics.com

M. Crew et al. (eds.), *The Changing Postal and Delivery Sector*,
Topics in Regulatory Economics and Policy,
DOI 10.1007/978-3-319-46046-8_6

In 2013, 3.5 billion cross-border letter post items were sent globally, corresponds to 1 % of total letter post traffic world wide (UPU 2014d at 2). Terminal dues affect all cross-border deliveries of letter mail (either directly or indirectly)[2] and thus, these payments are very important for designated postal operators. As some cross-border letter post traffic grows, spurred by the positive development in e-commerce, the importance of terminal dues increases.[3] The volume of cross-border letter post sent to and from its country influences the degree to which terminal dues affect an individual postal operator.

Data on global letter post flows within and between regions demonstrates that the main flows of cross-border letter post are between industrialized countries.[4] This suggests that designated operators in these countries, and their competitors, would be most affected by any changes to the current level of terminal dues. However, with an increasing share of citizens in Western Europe and North America shopping at online marketplaces in Asia, the flow of cross-border letter mail from Asia to Western Europe and North America is increasing. As a result, designated operators in these countries will also be significantly affected by any changes to the current terminal dues system.

The current UPU system for terminal dues consists of a target system and a transitional system. (The latter concerns only developing countries, and is not at issue in this chapter).[5] For the target system, the rates are based on domestic tariffs, although subject to caps and floors. The level of the caps and floors depend on a group classification.

The UPU has proposed an update of the regulation of the terminal dues rates. The update is a continuation of the current system, but with a few adjustments (see UPU 2016a). There are two alternatives outlined by the Postal Operations Council (POC), the technical and operational body of the UPU. However, one option has been adopted by the POC and is the one expected to be approved in Istanbul in September 2016. If so, it will be effective from first of January 2018. Perhaps most noticeably, the new regulation will separate terminal dues charges for the different post letter formats.

While the purpose of terminal dues system is to compensate the destination country for the cost associated with the handling, transport and delivery of letter post items from the foreign country, the amount of compensation for each bilateral mail

[2]For letter post flows where postal operators have negotiated bilateral agreements, terminal dues are still relevant as they work as a fall-back option in the negotiations. I.e. the bilaterally negotiated rates are usually not very different from the terminal dues. Terminal dues under the REIMS V agreement are not publicly available, but under REIMS II, terminal dues were set at 80 % of the domestic price for a single-piece priority letter, i.e. not very different from the uncapped UPU rates.

[3]E-commerce deliveries are to a large extent sent by letter post (as “bulky letters” or “small packets”) see for example UPU (2013, p. 17, 2014c).

[4]According to UPU (2014b, p. 196), 43 % of total international letter post flows (measured in kg) were intra Western Europe and 15 % were between Western Europe and North America.

[5]The transitional system concerns only developing countries. It represents a fixed rate by UPU. We took this into account in our estimation but did not detail it as it has only a marginal impact. For more explanations on the current UPU system, ie, transitional system and target system, see UPU (2015) and Campbell (2016, pp. 4–10).

flow is not a direct translation of the costs, nor the price of equivalent domestic services. If the regulated compensation differs significantly from the value of the services conducted, this results in a market distortion in the international mail market. There is an extensive literature underlying distortions from terminal dues (see for example, Campbell et al. 2011; Geradin 2012; Haller et al. 2012; WIK Consult 2013; United States Postal Service Office of Inspector General 2014b; Campbell 2015).

Two reports by Copenhagen Economics (2014, 2016) introduced a model of such distortions and developed an empirical method for quantifying the effects of the current terminal dues system in monetary terms. Three types of market distortions were identified. Firstly, there is a distortion of competition for last-mile handling and first-mile handling of cross-border letter post items—consistently with past literature which stated that the anticompetitive effects implied by these distortions cannot be "seriously contested" (Campbell 2015, p. 329). Secondly, there is a distortion of demand for delivery within and outside the terminal dues system, for domestic versus cross-border delivery as well as for cross-border delivery originating in transition versus target countries. Thirdly, and the focus of the current paper, we observe a distortion effect through financial transfers between postal operators.

For the remainder of this paper the outlay will be as follows: Section 2 defines the model of distortion as used in the paper. Section 3 summarizes the methodology. Section 4 presents the results and Sect. 5 provides a summary and implications.

2 Model of Distortion—The Concept of Financial Transfers

Financial transfers between designated postal operators occur in cases where (compared to a counterfactual situation with non-distortionary terminal dues) the sending postal operator today overpays or underpays for delivery in the destination country. An underpayment for delivery implies a net financial transfer from the receiving postal operator to the sending one. Similarly, an overpayment for delivery implies a net financial transfer from the sending postal operator to the receiving one. Looking closer into the dynamics of the financial transfers provides an indication of how these market distortions could develop in the future.

The terminal dues rates influence the financial position of postal operators, given their bilateral mail flows, via two channels: inbound cross-border flows (import volumes) and outbound cross-border flows (export volumes). On the inbound side, the effect (for a specific postal operator and a specific bilateral mail flow) equals the difference between the terminal dues charged and a counterfactual rate (defined in the following section[6]), times the amount of inbound letter post items. If the

[6]We define the counterfactual rate as 70 % of the domestic postage rates for end-to-end delivery of single-piece letters of three formats (small letters, large letters, and small packets), see appendix for more explanations.

terminal dues rate is below the counterfactual rate, this implies a negative financial transfer for the receiving operator. On the outbound side, the effect (for a specific postal operator and a specific bilateral mail flow) equals the difference between the terminal dues paid and the counterfactual rate in the destination country times the amount of outbound letter post items. If the current terminal dues rate charged by the destination country is below the counterfactual rate in the destination country, this implies a positive financial transfer for the sending operator.

3 Our Analysis

3.1 Scenario of Increased e-Commerce

There is an ongoing trend in international postal markets. The widely spread growth in e-commerce is calling for more small packets to be sent. Many of these packets are sent via bulky letters from exporting countries in Asia to importing countries in Europe and North America. In this paper, we model a simplified scenario, which takes departure in the estimated flows for 2014, and assume that some flows of bulky letters, i.e. the E-format, will grow in the coming years. We select a set of exporting countries, namely China, Hong Kong, India, Singapore and Malaysia. We then scale up all the flows of the E-format going from these countries to a selected 41 countries consisting of OECD, EU-28 Brazil and Russia, by an annual growth rate of 50 %.[7] To trace the effects in a simple manner, we have decided to leave all other mail flows unaltered.[8]

3.2 A Model for Estimating Financial Transfers

In order to estimate the financial transfers created by the terminal dues system, a model is created that compares the terminal dues received/paid by designated postal operators worldwide in two situations: (i) the actual situation with the set of terminal dues reflecting the framework of the UPU and (ii) a counterfactual situation with an alternative set of non-distortionary terminal dues. The model follows our

[7]This growth rate is based on aggregate estimates of bulky letters from the UPU's IPK studies and a study made by the OIG specifically on the growth of e-letters from Asia into the US. See UPU (2014d) and Office of Inspector General (2014a).

[8]This will lead to different estimate depending on the scenario considered for the development of the letter post after 2014. Campbell (2015, p. 320) made a set of additional assumptions, including (i) letters decline from 59 to 49 %; (ii) an increase in worldwide small packets from 25 to 37 %; (iii) an increase of 50 % per year of small packets from the whole of Asia; (iv) a 15 % increase in small packets from industrialized countries; (v) a 20 % increase in flats (large letters) from the whole of Asia; (vi) a 5 % decrease for letters and 3 % for flats in industrialized countries.

methodology from our previous report (Copenhagen Economics 2016) to estimate financial transfer of international postal flows with the current regulation and move on to a situation with increased e-commerce and the new regulatory framework.[9] We assume for this exercise that all countries follow the terminal dues system in place.

An important part of the analysis is to state an appropriate counterfactual situation. The counterfactual terminal dues could, for example, be defined by the prices of similar domestic delivery services. However, since these tariffs are not always available in the public domain, previous studies have often used a set of counterfactual terminal dues rates set, as noted above, at a percentage (typically 70–80 %) of the domestic postage rates for end-to-end delivery of single-piece letters of three formats (small letters, large letters, and small packets).[10] Since the UPU also bases its analysis on 70 % of domestic tariffs, it is a good starting point. Our counterfactual differs from the rates set by the UPU as we are using more granular information and we are not imposing any caps or floors.

3.3 Elements in the Model and Data Collection

The model consists of three main elements, bilateral mail flows, actual terminal dues rates, and counterfactual terminal dues rates. While complete primary data are not available in the public domain, multiple sources can be used as inputs to construct reliable estimates for each element. Most of the inputs are provided by the UPU.[11] Our data strategy is described in detail in the Appendix 1.

3.4 Bilateral Flows of Letter Mail up to 2 kg Between All Designated Postal Operators

The *total* inbound and outbound mail flow (in terms of number of items) for individual countries is provided by UPU and NRAs. This results in a data set of inbound and outbound volumes (in number of items) for 182 countries and territories. We assume that the inbound and outbound flows for each designated postal operator are proportional to the inter-regional mail flows to and from for the region where the postal operator is located, that is, proportional regional participation (see

[9] However, datasets differ between this paper and our previous report. Despite these different datasets, our estimates remain close for year 2014 financial transfers.

[10] 70 % of the domestic postage rates is also used by the UPU as the benchmark when calculating terminal dues before adjusting for caps and floors and by Campbell (2015, p. 324) to estimate distortions from terminal dues.

[11] Much of our data is collected from documents, publications, and databases from the Universal Postal Union, for example UPU (2015).

Appendix 1). Using this assumption, we estimate each bilateral mail flow as a percentage of the global cross-border mail flow in 2014. These ratios are then multiplied with the global volume of international mail in order to get each flow measured in items. Using data on regional distribution of letter format, we are able to split each bilateral mail flow according to the different letter formats. We further assume that the distribution of P, G and E items in a specific bilateral mail flow between two regions is the same as the distribution of P, G, and E items in the total inter-regional mail flow between the same two regions. Each bilateral flow is broken down into weight and formats using data on average weight for each product type.

For the new scenario (i.e. the proposed UPU's regulation and the increase in E-format), we simply scale up the targeted mail flows of the E-format by 50 % annually. Figure 1 illustrates systematically how we estimate the mail flows.

Actual terminal dues rates for each bilateral mail flow

Actual terminal dues rates are calculated directly based on the UPU method set out in the 25th UPU congress for the period of 2014 through 2017 (UPU 2012). For the proposed scenario, we base our terminal dues rates on the proposal for the UPU terminal dues system for the 2018–2021 cycle, as outlined by the UPU (2016a). The new regulatory system builds on the current one, but adds in particular a separate calculation for the small packets. In both systems, for each bilateral mail flow the effective rate will depend on (i) the group to which a postal operator belongs, (ii) from which country the inbound mail flow is coming, and (iii) whether or not the terminal dues for the bilateral flow in question is subject to a cap or floor.

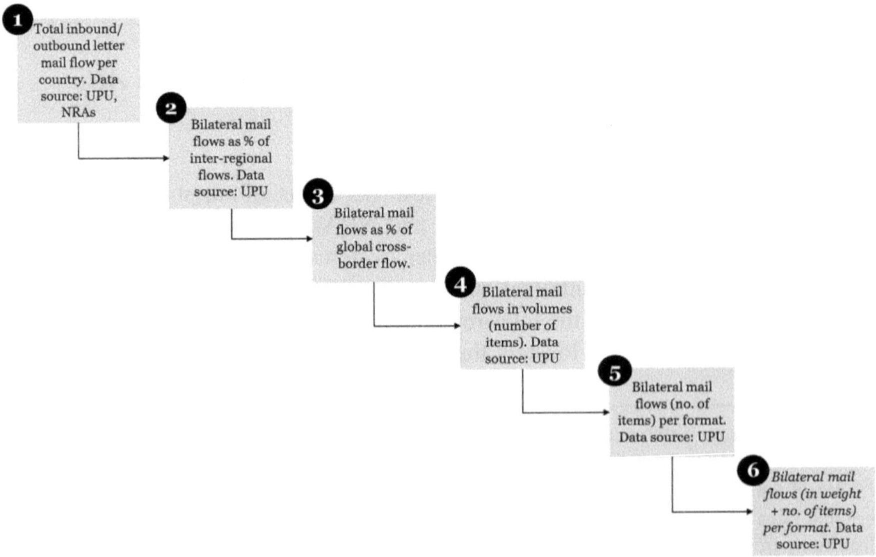

Fig. 1 Process map for estimating postal flows (*Source* Copenhagen Economics)

Counterfactual terminal dues rates for each bilateral mail flow
The counterfactual terminal dues rates should ideally reflect (for each country) the price for handling of bulk cross-border letter post items that a private customer (i.e. not affiliated with the UPU) would pay for delivery of similar domestic letters. We depart from the domestic, end-to-end postage rates for single-piece items of the three different formats (P, G, E) and several different weight steps within each format. This is combined with information on the distribution of weight steps and the average weights to estimate the average price for each format in each country. The counterfactual terminal dues are calculated as 70 % of the domestic rates, following Campbell's method (2016, p. 324).

4 Results

The starting point for the quantification of financial transfers in the model is 2014, where the current system is in place.

4.1 The Total Value of Financial Transfers

In 2014, the total value of the net financial transfers is estimated to 940 million SDR, approximately 1.168 million EUR,[12] For the forecasted scenario with the new proposed system, the total value of the net financial transfers is estimated to 1.851 million SDR, approximately 2.301 million EUR. This is an increase by 97 %.

For increased flows, if the current system of terminal dues remained, the total net financial transfers would be an estimated 2.008 million SDR, approximately 2.496 million EUR.[13] This is 8 % higher than our estimate under the new system because of a decreased distortion effect; see Fig. 2. Hence, the new system reduces the financial transfers by roughly 8 %.

The total net financial transfer caused by small letters (P) and flats (G) are essentially the same with and without the change in system, whereas the distortion from the small packets (E) are smaller with the new system. The small packets accounts for 90 % of the total value of financial transfers in our forecasted scenario with the new proposed system.

[12]SDRs or Special Drawing Rights, is a monetary unit defined by the International Monetary Fund. One SDR is equal to approximately 1.24 EUR. See IMF (2016, April 29th).

[13]Details on the numerical estimation are available from the authors.

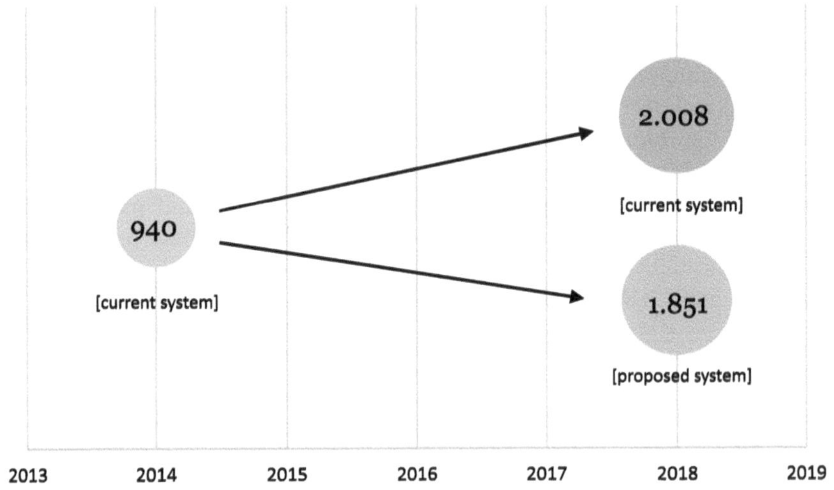

Fig. 2 Total value of net financial transfers (Million SDR) (*Source* Copenhagen Economics based on model data)

4.2 *Patterns of Change*

Even though the discount given (i.e. the difference between the terminal due charge and the equivalent domestic postage) is smaller for many bilateral flows with the new system the total net effect is larger compared to 2014 since the volumes of the important format, the small packets (E) increase. The postal operators that have significant negative financial transfers with the selected exporters of e-commerce packets will have an increased negative effect in the forecasted scenario, compared to 2014. For one group of postal operators, that already had a negative effect in 2014, there is an even larger negative effect in our future scenario, see Fig. 3. For example, Canada would see a negative effect of 526 million SDR in 2018 under the proposed system.[14] This is equivalent to approximately 654 million EUR.

Another group of postal operators that had a positive net transfer in 2014, would see a shift from positive towards negative effect in 2018. These countries had a positive net effect from the small letters (P) and flats (G) in 2014 that outweighed the negative effect from the small packets (E). In the forecasted scenario, the increase in small packets from Asia make the total effect smaller or negative. In the case of United States and Great Britain the shift goes from a significant positive to a large negative effect in 2018, see Figs. 4 and 5. The effect for the United States is

[14]Estimated impacts for each country are available from authors.

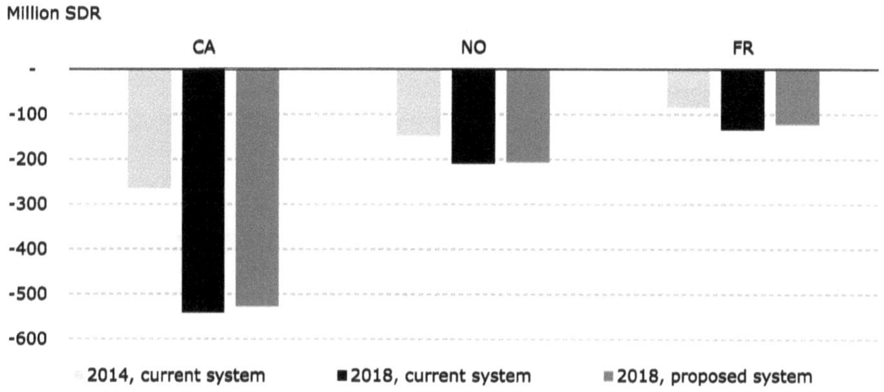

Fig. 3 Countries with larger negative effect (*Source* Copenhagen Economics based on model data)

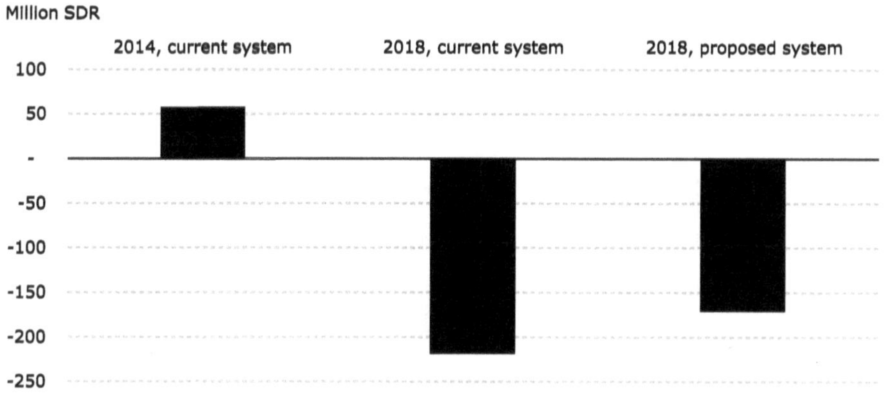

Fig. 4 Countries with effect going negative: United States (*Source* Copenhagen Economics based on model data)

estimated to be negative, at 170 million SDR, approximately 212 million EUR. We can see, however, that the effect would be slightly larger, if the current system remained in 2018.

For the selected exporting countries we can see that the effect increase from 2014. This is of course not surprising since the volumes that had the largest effect in 2014 increase substantially in our new scenario. Figure 6 shows the net financial transfers for three selected countries with positive net effect in the new scenario: Hong Kong, China and Singapore.

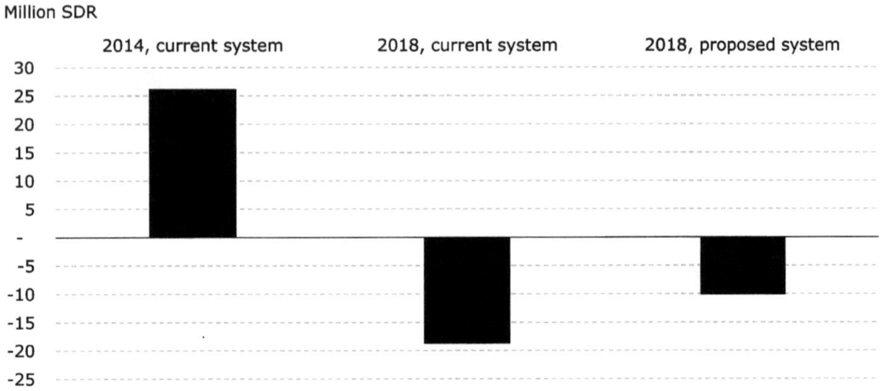

Fig. 5 Countries with effect going negative: Great Britain (*Source* Copenhagen Economics based on model data)

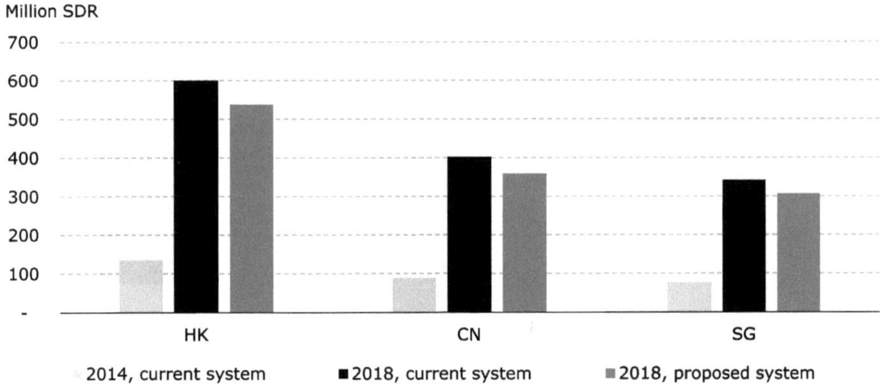

Fig. 6 Countries with larger positive effect (*Source* Copenhagen Economics based on model data)

4.3 The Financial Effect from the Small Packet (E) Delivery

For those postal operators that see a shift from positive towards negative, the impact of the growing e-commerce is very clear. The net effect from the small letters (P) and flats (G) are still positive in the future scenario. However, the large distortionary effect from the small packets (E) projects them towards a negative effect, see Figs. 7 and 8.

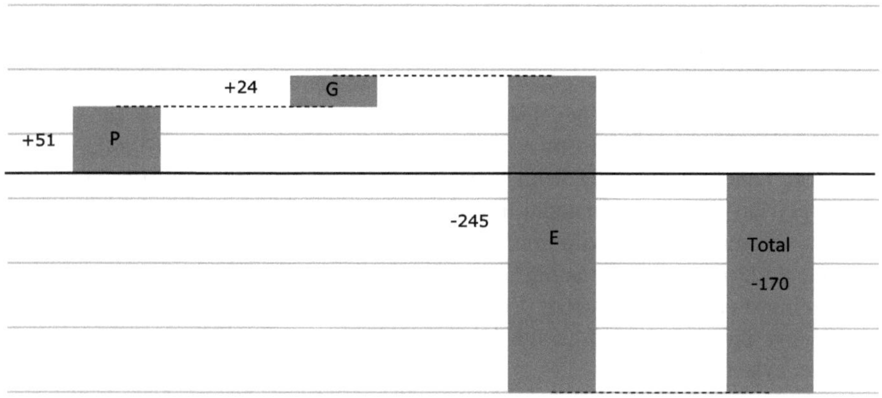

Fig. 7 The net effect by letter format for the United States (*Note* The graph shows the forecasted net effect for the United States postal operator in 2018 with the proposed new system. *Source* Copenhagen Economics based on model data)

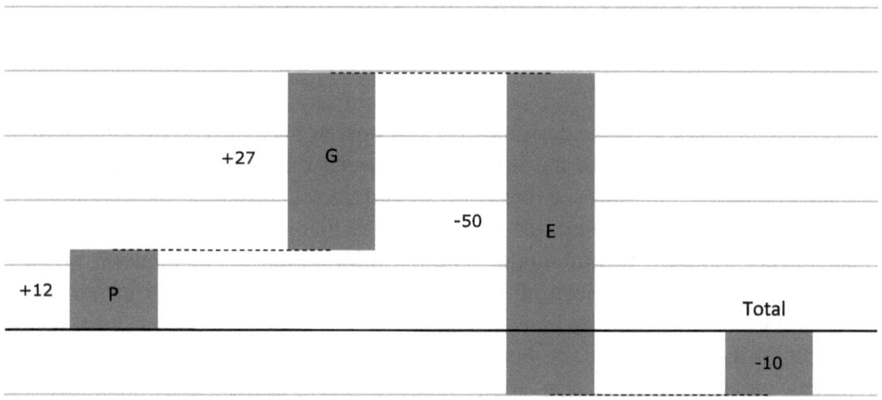

Fig. 8 The net effect by letter format for Great Britain (*Note* The graph shows the forecasted net effect for the British postal operator in 2018 with the proposed new system. *Source* Copenhagen Economics based on model data)

5 Implications

This paper has estimated the distortionary financial transfers that arise from the terminal dues system in 2014 and for a forecasted scenario in 2018. Our results indicate that with a significant increase in small packets, due to e-commerce, the total value of financial transfers is likely to increase in the future. The new regulatory system proposed by the UPU shows a very small mitigating effect on the financial transfers, without altering significantly neither the pattern nor the magnitude. As a result, the countries that showed the largest negative effect in 2014 see an even larger negative effect going forward.

Our results indicate that some countries that today do not suffer losses from the system are likely to experience a shift towards a negative effect, due to the growing volumes of small packets from Asia. Further, our results show that the key postal operators benefiting already from subsidies from other countries will continue to have very large positive financial transfers. The distortionary effect from the small packets (E) remains the main source for the financial transfers in the global mail market. Indeed, our forecasting analysis shows the significant effect that the expected growth in e-commerce driven shipments of small packets (E) will have on amplifying the cross-operator subsidies arising due to the Terminal Dues remuneration system.

Appendix 1—Supplementary Description of Methodology

Description of Data Collection and Calculations

Bilateral mail flows
Bilateral mail flows between designated postal operators are an essential input in the model. In combination with the difference between the actual terminal dues rates and the counterfactual ones (i.e. the equivalent domestic postage), the magnitude of bilateral mail flows will determine the size of the financial transfers. Estimation of financial net transfers in our model requires information about bilateral flows of letter mail up to 2 kg between all designated postal operators (both in number of items and in weight), split by letter format (P, G, E). This information is not readily available in the public domain, but the data can be constructed our own data set. Whereas we have information about flows of cross-border letter post between regions, we do not know how the cross-border volume to/from each region is disaggregated among the countries in the region. Moreover, we do not have information about the product mix (i.e., letter formats) in the volumes. For this reason, we use a number of proxies to approximate mail flows subject to UPU terminal dues.

As a first step, we create estimates of the total inbound and outbound mail flow (in terms of number of items) for individual countries. The starting point for this is readily available data for total inbound and outbound mail flows from the UPU (see UPU 2015) measured in number of items. Since 2011 is the year in the UPU statistics for which we have the broadest coverage of data (139 countries and territories covered), we use this as a reference. If we cannot find information for a specific country or territory in the UPU dataset from 2011, we turn to UPU statistics from other years. This adds data points for another 31 countries. When neither of these sources can provide us with an estimate, we turn to domestic sources such as the national regulatory authorities. This adds data points for another five countries.

For seven additional countries with data for domestic (but not cross-border) letter volumes, we are able to construct our own estimate of cross-border volumes by using a reasonable ratio of cross-border to domestic letter mail volumes.[15] This results in a data set of inbound and outbound volumes (in number of items) for 182 countries and territories.

As a second step, we set the estimates of inbound and outbound flows in 2011 for each designated postal operator relative to the 2011 inter-regional mail flows to and from for the region where the postal operator is located.[16] This provides us with a ratio (for each designated operator) of (i) the inbound flow relative to the total inbound flow to the region and (ii) the outbound flow relative to the total outbound flow from the region.

As a third step, we make an important assumption about proportional regional participation, where we depart from the ratios from step two and apply them to inter-regional mail flows from 2014. By applying this assumption, we are able to estimate data points for each bilateral mail flow as a percentage of the global cross-border mail flow in 2014. While this methodology fails to take into account factors such as distance and international relations,[17] it is the best available approximation of bilateral flows and does not suffer from further data gaps.

Assumption of proportional regional participation

The assumption about proportional regional participation allows us to estimate the percentage of the world's mail flow that goes from a country *i* in region A to a country *j* in region B based on the following information:

(i) The percentage of region A's outbound flow originates in country i,
(ii) The percentage of region B's inbound letter mail flow that is delivered to country j
(iii) The share of the global total cross border mail flow that goes from region A to region B

[15]The ratios used are based on information from previous years regarding the relationship between domestic and cross-border mail volumes. Where this information is not available, a ratio is constructed based on assumptions regarding the similarity of countries (i.e. countries of similar size can be expected to have the same ratio between domestic and cross-border flows).

[16]Data for inter-regional mail flows are available in UPU (2014b).

[17]Factors such as distance, international relations, and a common language can be important for the mail exchange between certain countries. With respect to the growing share of cross-border e-commerce, for example, we often observe larger online trade between countries that share a common language or culture (e.g., Germany and Austria, the United States and Canada). For the case of the United States, we have tried to compensate for this by adjusting bilateral flows between the US and Canada based on publicly available information about cross-border mail flows between these countries.

For each mail stream that goes *between countries from different regions*, we apply the following calculation:

$$X_{ij} = \frac{O_i}{O_A} \times \frac{I_j}{I_B} \times X_{AB} \quad (1)$$

For each mail stream that goes between countries within the same region, we apply the following calculation:

$$X_{ij} = \frac{O_i}{O_A} \times \frac{I_j}{I_A \times \left(1 - \left(\frac{I_i}{I_A}\right)\right)} \times X_{AA} \quad (2)$$

X_{ij} percentage of world's mail flow that goes from country i to country j
X_{AB} percentage of world's mail flow that goes from region A to region B
X_{AA} percentage of world's mail flow that goes within region A
O_i total outbound mail flow from country i
O_A total outbound mail flow from region A
I_j total inbound mail flow to country j
I_B total inbound mail flow to region B

The assumption in (1) and (2) is essentially the same but the calculations differ in the relative inbound. The difference is due to the fact that the total inbound flow to region A also includes mail destined for country i. This is a pragmatic solution to solve a mechanical problem in the model because we do not want to include domestic mail.

As a fourth step, we convert each bilateral flow (until now measured as a percentage of the global flow of international mail) into an estimate in terms of volumes (number of items). We do this by multiplying it with the global volume of international mail.[18]

As a fifth step, we split each bilateral mail flow according to the different letter formats (P, G, and E). In order to do this, we use a UPU (2014d) survey among 49 designated postal operators that contain regional estimates for the distribution of formats (in percentage of number of items and weight). This study also provides estimates of the average weights per format. By assuming that the distribution of P, G and E items in a specific bilateral mail flow between two regions is the same as the distribution of P, G, and E items in the total inter-regional mail flow between the same two regions, this provides us with a per-format estimate of letter mail volumes for each bilateral mail stream.

[18]Information about global cross-border letter post volumes is available in UPU (2014a).

As a sixth step, we apply the average weight for each product type (from the UPU survey referred to above) in order to get the bilateral flows measured in kilograms instead of number of items.

Based on this, we are able to estimate bilateral cross-border flows of letter post items between 183 countries and territories worldwide. Depending on the size and structure of bilateral mail flows, the current design of the terminal dues system will affect designated operators differently. For example, large outbound flows of cross-border mail may imply that designated postal operators experience large positive transfers on the outbound side. Similarly, in combination with a negative difference between actual terminal dues received and the equivalent domestic postage rate, large inbound may imply that designated postal operators experience large negative transfers on the inbound side. Understanding the structure of bilateral mail flows will thus be very helpful when trying to understand the structure of net financial transfers created by the current terminal due system.

Lastly, for the new scenario of growing e-commerce we select the set of exporting countries, namely China, Hong Kong, India, Singapore and Malaysia. We then scale up all the flows of the E-format going from these countries to any EU-28 or OECD country by an annual growth rate of 50 % from 2014 to 2018 (United States Postal Service Office of Inspector General 2014a).

Terminal dues rates

Actual terminal dues rates are directly based on the UPU method set out in the 25th UPU congress for the period of 2014 through 2017.[19] For the proposed scenario, we base our terminal dues rates on the proposal for the UPU terminal dues system for the 2018–2021 cycle, as outlined by the UPU (see UPU 2016a). In the target system the terminal dues charges consists of a per-item rate and a per-kilogram rate. Before the application of any caps and floors the rates are calculated based on two reference tariffs, a 20 g small letter and a 175 g large letter.[20] A linear relationship between these two are drawn and evaluated at the weight of an average item. If the revenue from an average package are above the cap revenue, the cap rates are applied. Equivalently, if it is below the floor revenue, the floor rates are applied. If the average revenue is between the cap and floor a target rate is applied.

The target rates per kilogram are calculated as:

$$R_w = 70\ \% \times \frac{M \times \left(W_{avg} - 0.01\right) + DP_1}{R_{wfl} \times W_{avg} + R_{Ifl}} \times R_{wfl} \tag{3}$$

and the target rates per item are calculated as:

$$R_I = 70\ \% \times \frac{M \times \left(W_{avg} - 0.01\right) + DP_1}{R_{wfl} \times W_{avg} + R_{Ifl}} \times R_{Ifl} \tag{4}$$

[19]See UPU (2012) for a complete description of the methodology.

[20]The data are provided by UPU (2016b).

Table 1 Parameters for the two cycles

	Current system	Proposed system
Average weight P/G/E	81.8 g	91.9 g
Average weight P/G	n/a	37.6 g
Average weight E	n/a	375 g
Item-to-kilo ratio P/G/E	0.128	0.128
Item-to-kilo ratio P/G	n/a	0.128
Item-to-kilo ratio E	n/a	0.445

Source UPU (2012); UPU, Approval of draft Congress–Doc 40 (2016a)

where,

M	*Constant rate of change = (DP2–DP1)/(0.175–0.01)*
DP_1 and DP_2	*Domestic postage rates without VAT for 0–20 g P and 100–250 g G*
W_{avg}	*The average weight of an letter post item, set to 81 g in the current system*
R_{wfl}	*Floor rate per kilogram*
R_{Ifl}	*Floor rate per item*

The methodology of the proposed regulatory system is a continuation of the current system. The main difference is a separation of the E-format letters. Whereas the P and G format can be calculated in the same way as before, the E letters now get slightly different parameters. The revenue of a letter of average weight, i.e. the numerator in Eqs. (3) and (4), is based on the average weight of an E-letter letter (375 g) and the item and weight rates from the current system. The cap and floor rates are also different for the E-format. In particular, the ratio between the per-item floor rate and the per-kilo floor rate (this is the so-called item-to-kilo ratio) is higher. Although often expressed as a percentage by the UPU, it is in practice better described as a weight. It is the weight for which, an item of a specific weight and at a specific kilogram rate, is equivalent to the item charge. A higher item-to-kilo means the structure of the rates is "flatter", something that is intended to better reflect the price structure of the small packets (UPU 2016a) (Table 1).

Counterfactual terminal dues rates

As a proxy for the counterfactual terminal dues rates, we depart from the domestic (end-to-end) postage rates for single-piece items of three different formats (P, G, E) and weights. This means that we use more granular data than what the UPU uses to calculate terminal dues. In particular, the terminal dues does not use prices for items of E format. In order to reflect the price charged for delivery of domestic letter mail, we apply an adjustment factor of 70 %.[21]

[21]This adjustment factor is the same as used by the UPU for the calculation of uncapped terminal dues for operators in the target system. According to the 25th congress document describing the base for the current terminal dues system, "Domestic tariffs, exclusive of VAT and other taxes, will be used as a reference for calculating TD rates. The percentage of domestic tariffs retained for use

Instead of making a simple linear relationship between two tariffs, we use information about different weight-steps for three products. Our methodology uses three weight steps for small letters, five weight steps for large letters and seven weight steps for small packets. This allows us to calculate equivalent domestic postage rates that mirror the actual situation better than what would have been the case if only two prices would have been used. We collapse the data on domestic postage rates to a level that fits our counterfactual purposes. In order to calculate an average postage rate per item, we thus need to make assumptions about the distribution of weights. These assumptions are primarily based on a UPU study (see UPU 2014d) containing estimated distributions on different weight steps for each product type P, G and E. Since we also have information of average weights of mail flows we can vary the distributions based on average weight. Once the weight distribution for each format is established, it is straightforward to calculate a domestic rate per item for each product type.

For industrialized countries and all European countries, data on domestic postage rates mainly comes from a survey conducted by WIK consulting, containing a comprehensive overview of domestic postage rates in 2013 (see WIK 2013). For other countries domestic postage rates are collected from a UPU database with 2008 priority domestic rates by product type and weight step.[22] These rates are adjusted based on inflation to create an estimate of tariff levels in 2014 and subsequently 2018. Our data set contains domestic postage rates for 164 countries and territories. Combined with the data set of bilateral mail flows (consisting of 182 countries and territories), this leaves us with a set of 155 designated operators (for which we have estimates of all necessary parameters) to include in the analysis.

Calculations for net transfers

For each bilateral country pair we estimate:

$$\pi_{ij}^{I} = X_{ji}(TD_{ij} - EDP_{ij})$$
$$\pi_{ij}^{O} = X_{ij}(TD_{ji} - EDP_{ji})$$
$$NT_{i} = \pi_{ij}^{I} - \pi_{ij}^{O}$$

where π_{ij}^{I} is country i's loss (gain) on inbound letter mail from country j expressed as the difference between what country i gets in terms of terminal dues from country j today and what it would get in the counterfactual scenario. X_{ji} is the letter mail flow subject to terminal dues going from country j to country i, TD_{ij} is the actual terminal dues rate that country i receives as revenue from country j and EDP_{ij} is the equivalent domestic postage (i.e. the counterfactual terminal dues rate).

(Footnote 21 continued)

is 70 %. This figure results from the inbound mail handling cost, calculated based on information from the cost study" UPU (2012).

[22]The database from 2008 is the most recent source available containing such a comprehensive and granular overview of domestic tariffs.

Equivalently, π_{ij}^{O} is country *i*'s gain (loss) on outbound letter mail to country *j* expressed as the difference between what country *i* pays in terms of terminal dues to country *j* today and what it would pay in the counterfactual scenario.

NT_i is thus the net transfer for country *i* related to its bilateral cross border exchange of mail with country *j*. In order to get the total net transfer for country *i*, one has to conduct the same analysis for all bilateral mail flows to and from country *i*.

References

Campbell, J., et al. (2011). Terminal dues: Winners, losers, and the path to reform. In *Presentation at the 19th Conference on Postal and Delivery Economics, CRRI.*

Campbell, J. (2015). Quantifying the distortive effects of UPU terminal dues. In: M. A. Crew & T. J. Brennan (Eds.), *The future of the postal sector in a digital world* (pp 313–330).

Campbell, J. (2016). *A terminal dues model.* Available at: http://jcampbell.com/TDM/20160309TDM9/Reports/TDM_paper.pdf

Copenhagen Economics. (2014). *The economics of terminal dues.*

Copenhagen Economics. (2016). *Quantification of financial transfers caused by Universal Postal Union terminal dues.*

Geradin, D. (2012). *Legal opinion on the compatibility of the proposed target system for terminal dues with EU law.*

Haller, A., et al. (2012). *Termination charges in the international parcel market, Working Paper.*

IMF. (2016). *SDRs per currency unit and currency units per SDR.* https://www.imf.org/external/np/fin/data/rms_five.aspx. Accessed on April 29, 2016.

United States Postal Service Office of Inspector General. (2014a). *Inbound China ePacket costing methodology.*

United States Postal Service Office of Inspector General. (2014b). *International terminal dues white paper.* Office of Inspector General, United States Postal Service.

UPU. (2012). *UPU terminal dues system for the period 2014–2017.* Joint Council of Administration and Postal Operations Council report, Congress-Doc. 20b.

UPU. (2013). Union Postale no. 4.

UPU. (2014a). *Development of Postal Services in 2013.*

UPU. (2014b). *Development strategies for the postal sector: An economic perspective.* Chapter 8: Global postal connectedness.

UPU. (2014c). *Fulfilling the global e-commerce promise.*

UPU. (2014d). *Results of the items per kilogramme (IPK) study.* POC C3 LPRG 2014. 2 Doc 4a.

UPU. (2015). *Statistics and accounting guide.*

UPU. (2016a). *Proposal for the UPU terminal dues system for the 2018–2021 period.* Joint Council of Administration and Postal Operations Council proposal. POC 2016. 1-Doc 12h.

UPU. (2016b). *Impact tool, version 1 of the 2018–2021 cycle.*

WIK Consult. (2013). *Main developments in the postal sector (2010–2013).*

Wojtek, R. (2015). UPU compensation rates for packages under EU competition law: Are there lessons to be learned from other international fee arrangements. In: M. A. Crew & T. J. Brennan (Eds.), *The future of the postal sector in a digital world* (pp 331–345).

A Case Study of Density of Retail Outlets in Portugal: Regulation and Politics in Postal Markets

João Confraria, Vítor Miguel Ribeiro, Agostinho Franco and Frederico Pereira

1 Introduction

Under the Postal Services Directive[1] (henceforth, Directive), and in the framework of the universal service obligation (USO), European Union's (EU) Member States (MS) shall take steps to ensure that the density of points of contact and of access points takes into account users' needs.

In the EU, most Governments and National Regulatory Authorities (NRAs) have imposed network density objectives to make sure that a minimum number of retail access points (henceforth, outlets) is available to end users.

This paper examines the Portuguese experience in setting network density objectives, highlighting two related issues: definition of Government and NRA roles, and public interest objectives to be pursued. Changes in political objectives and NRA behavior are discussed as well as their relation to market outcomes.

Section 2 reviews briefly the literature on postal network density. Section 3 reviews current regulatory options in the EU. It provides a brief overview on the evolution of the regulatory framework and decision making process used in addressing the issue of the opening and closing of outlets in Portugal. It presents ANACOM's decision of August 2014 setting the network density objectives in place until the end of September 2017. Section 4 concludes. It is argued that

The views in this paper are those of the authors and do not reflect the view of ANACOM, neither UCP.

[1]Directive 97/67/EC, amended by Directive 2002//39/EC and by Directive 2008/6/EC.

J. Confraria (✉) · V.M. Ribeiro · A. Franco · F. Pereira
ANACOM—The Portuguese National Communications Authority, Lisbon, Portugal
e-mail: joao.confraria@anacom.pt

J. Confraria
UCP—Universidade Católica Portuguesa, Lisbon, Portugal

M. Crew et al. (eds.), *The Changing Postal and Delivery Sector*,
Topics in Regulatory Economics and Policy,
DOI 10.1007/978-3-319-46046-8_7

network density objectives may be understood as a political concern and not necessarily as a response to market failures.

2 Literature Review

Few studies in economic literature focus on the optimization of postal network density. Panzar and Waterson (1991) concluded that if the postal sector is a natural monopoly, then competition should be carefully introduced. The trade-off should be addressed by an adequate intervention on network density.

Regulated postal retail networks simultaneously embrace public and business objectives. According to some views, this leads to oversized postal retail networks as compared to the ones that would be sustained in purely commercial basis (Cohen et al. 2008). The authors compare the number of post offices in relation to the number of banks in Italian rural areas, and in relation to the number of pharmacies in rural areas of the United States of America (USA). These constitute two purely commercial services, however, arguably as important to the average citizen as post offices. In both analyses, there is evidence of an excessive number of post offices. A reduction of post offices should be, thus, expected or, at least, their transfer to franchisees, if the postal network was run on a purely commercial basis

A larger number of outlets can be justified on the basis of positive spillovers (Boldron et al. 2008). The authors analyze the accessibility to postal network as compared to other industries in France. It is argued that "*[t]here are differences between the accessibility of public services and the accessibility of commercial services between constrained and unconstrained networks. Broadly speaking, commercial services networks tend to be more concentrated in urban areas and tend to offer a much better accessibility in urban areas than in rural areas. This is in line with the economic geography theory which accesses that there exists an economic movement of concentration.*" Notwithstanding, they showed that the territorial presence of post offices, particularly, in rural areas creates positive spillovers that may enhance social welfare.

Borsenberger et al. (2011) provide cross-country analysis of postal network accessibility relying on two dimensions. From a demographic coverage point of view, Borsenberger et al. (2011, pp. 126) find that the "*highest number of post offices is found in Ireland, Switzerland and France (...) while the lowest number of post offices is found in Spain*". In turn, from a geographical coverage point of view, Borsenberger et al. (2011, pp. 125) conclude that the "*highest number of post offices is found in Malta, Netherlands and Switzerland (...) while the lowest number of post offices is found in Finland, Sweden and Spain.* Moreover, political and legal constraints influencing the establishment of an adequate postal network density are identified. For instance, as claimed in Borsenberger et al. (2011, pp. 130), "*postal operators providing banking services seem to have larger networks and these are often own-managed (...) due to the legal obligation to have a skilled and well-trained staff to offer banking services*".

Recently, it has been considered that regulatory authorities setting postal network density criteria should not jeopardize the digitalization trend of post services. In particular, Borsenberger (2014) argued that virtual access relaxes the need of physical access points. Partnerships between postal operators and local retailers constitute feasible option to meet the USO without necessarily addressing accessibility with standalone offices.

3 Regulatory Framework

According to Article 3, no. 1 and 2 of the Directive, EU MS shall ensure that users enjoy the right to a universal service involving the permanent provision of a postal service of specified quality at all points in their territory at affordable prices for all users. To this end, EU MS shall take steps to ensure that the density of points of contact and of access points takes into account users' needs.

Most EU MS seem to consider that network density rules are necessary to prevent the Universal Service Provider (USP) from holding an excessively small postal access network because, otherwise, the number of access points would be below the desired level. The main regulatory trends may be summarized as follows: (see Appendix)[2]:

(a) Most EU MS impose a minimum density of outlets;
(b) CZ, IE, NL and UK do not have obligations related to minimum number of outlets;
(c) PL does not have distance related obligations (to outlets and/or to letterboxes). AT, IE and PT have a maximum absolute distance obligation that guarantees that no one is located more than a certain distance from the nearest outlet;
(d) BE, CZ, DK, EE, HU, IT, LT, PL, PT, and SI have obligations related to minimum number of letterboxes;
(e) AT, CZ, EE, HU, IE, IT, PT and SI have obligations related to minimum services provided at postal outlets.

In most EU MS, network density has been a political decision made by the Government. In others, like SI, the NRA is empowered to set network density objectives. In Portugal both cases happened.

In any case, Governments and regulators have substantial discretion to define adequate network density criteria. The Directive does not make clear which market failures require correction by network density rules neither the appropriate regulatory measures to be adopted. Economic literature also appears to lack sufficient and adequate content to support regulatory decision making. The size of current regulated postal networks is arguably larger than the size of postal networks

[2]Network density has been defined by EU MS including other variables not considered here, as for example minimum operating hours.

if left unregulated. However, there seems to be no obvious decision rule to achieve an economically efficient outcome comparable, for instance, with decision rules applied to monopoly price regulation, e.g. imposition of cost oriented prices.

The evolution of the legal framework and changes in network density regulation in Portugal help to highlight some of the problems involved in public decision making.

Before 2000, when the universal service concession contract between the Portuguese State and CTT was signed,[3] the USP had the flexibility to open and close outlets and to define the range of postal services provided, contingent on the social and economic requirement of holding sufficiently high level of population served, and to determine opening hours bearing in mind service requirements and demand levels. By then, CTT was a state company committed to guidelines issued by the Government.

Under the universal service concession contract, ANACOM was assigned the power to regulate CTT's outlets. In particular, the open or closure of outlets became dependent on prior favorable opinion of ANACOM.[4] This was done on a case-by-case approach through the submission, by CTT, of a specific request to open/close a given outlet. ANACOM's position was not subject to legal constraints. Arguably, it was expected from ANACOM to have adequate information about consumer's preferences, as well as about the costs of different network density options, thereby being able to find an appropriate balance between the interests of the parties involved.[5] However, NRA's capabilities were overestimated. Actually, the informational problem was solved by asking local authorities their position about closing/opening a given outlet belonging to the respective jurisdiction area. Moreover, ANACOM followed local authorities' declared position.

Local authorities, trying to avoid social dissent, were expected to defend users' interests. However, this created a free riding problem. In each local area, local authorities opposed any type of closure, thereby not bearing the full cost of this policy because, under uniform pricing, eventual losses would be spread over all consumers. Accordingly, from 2000 to 2003, the number of outlets in Portugal increased, since closures were not allowed and new outlets were open to satisfy changes in urbanization rates and population distribution (Fig. 1). Traffic and revenues per outlet remained relatively constant (Figs. 2 and 3).

---

[3]Currently the concession contract includes: (1) the provision of the universal postal, including the registered mail service used in court and administrative proceedings; (2) the issue and sale of stamps, stamped post cards and other stamped items bearing the word "Portugal"; (3) the sitting of letterboxes on the public highway intended for the deposit of postal items by users; (4) the provision of postal money orders and (5) the provision of the electronic mailbox public service. The concession also includes the maintenance, development and operation of the postal network allocated to the concession.

[4]And changes in opening hours as well.

[5]In theoretical welfare economics this would amount to designing an appropriate (limited) social welfare function.

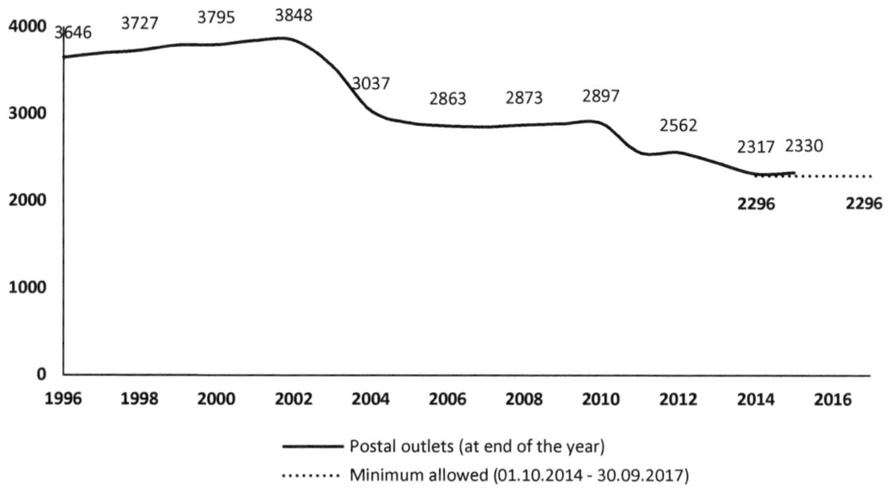

Fig. 1 Evolution in the number of outlets (1996–2015) and minimum targets (2014–2017)

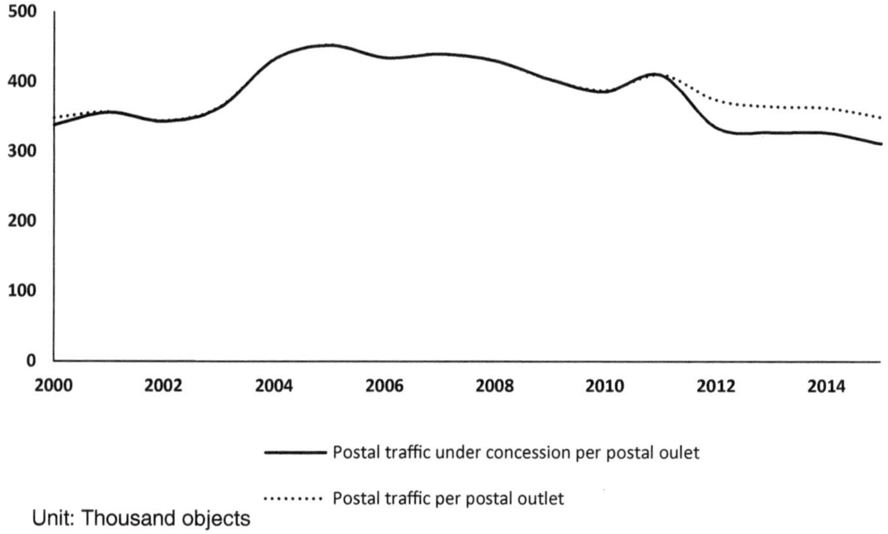

Fig. 2 Evolution of the postal traffic per outlet (2000–2015)

By 2003, this situation became a source of concern, as data began to suggest traffic stagnation and decline of CTT's net profit (Figs. 4 and 5). By then, there was an increasing focus on CTT's financial returns. This happened due to the Government's concern with state finances and because state budget was used to

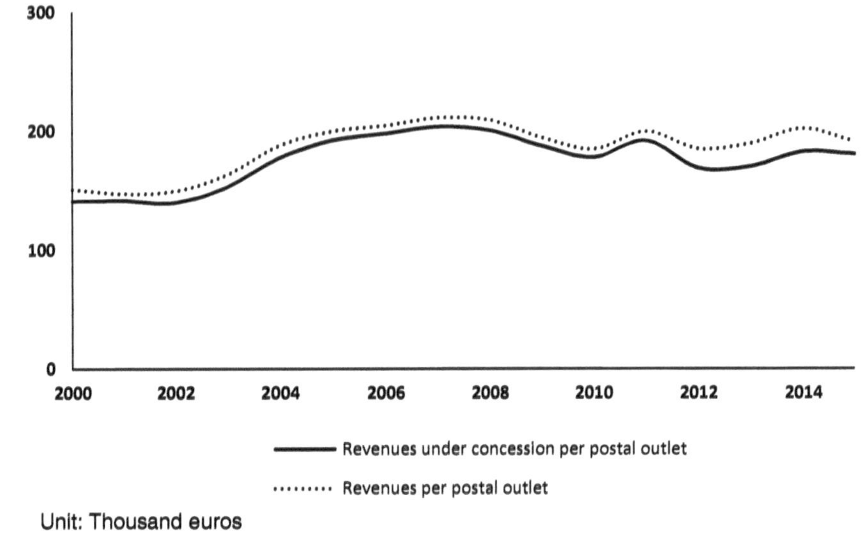

Fig. 3 Evolution of the postal revenues per outlet (2000–2015)

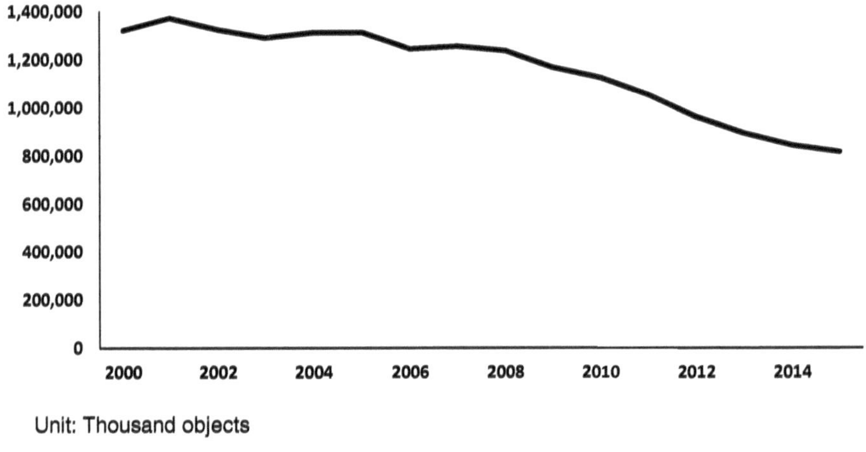

Fig. 4 Evolution of the USP's postal volumes (2000–2015)

solve the deficit in CTT's pensions fund[6] putting, thereby, fierce public emphasis on obtaining returns from the invested capital (Fig. 5).

These facts suggest an explanation for the change in the legal framework introduced in 2003.[7] More autonomy was given to CTT on opening/closing outlets.

[6]Decree-Law no 246/2003.

[7]Decree-Law no. 116/2003.

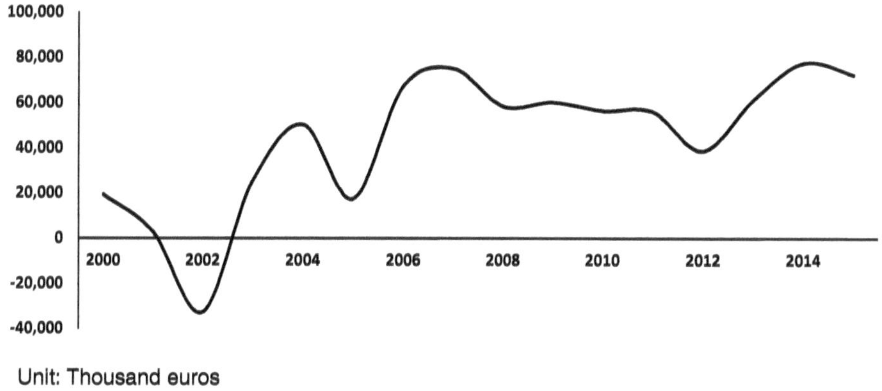

Fig. 5 CTT net profits (2000–2015)

ANACOM was only empowered to oppose decisions related to the closure of outlets directly operated by CTT (*estações*).[8] ANACOM's decision would have to be based on service needs, demand levels and fulfillment of users' needs. CTT were, since then, free to open and close outlets operated under contract by local retailers or in local authorities' premises (*postos*). These correspond to the outlets most frequently observed in rural areas. Furthermore, ANACOM's capacity to regulate the closing of *estações* was eliminated in 2006 (under a new amendment made to the concession contract by way of Decree-Law no. 112/2006). Since then, CTT enjoyed full autonomy on opening/closure decisions. As expected, the number of outlets declined substantially. Apparently, eventual concerns on political costs of closing outlets were overridden by concerns on financial sustainability of postal operations. These were also important given the new political objective of ensuring CTT's privatization. Improving CTT's efficiency before privatization was seen as essential to increase privatization revenues. The final result was the increase in traffic and revenues per outlet, despite the decrease in total traffic (Figs. 2, 3 and 4). Given the focus on efficiency, the Government, as CTT's shareholder could not avoid the political cost of closures, independently of ANACOM's role.

With privatization, the Government decided not to be involved in further discussions relative to postal network density. In 2013, by the end of a period of pre privatization fast restructuring and under a new legal framework characterized by full market opening, ANACOM was empowered to evaluate, at countrywide level, the network density objectives proposed by CTT and, then, accept them or impose own objectives. ANACOM's discretion was slightly limited by law. The law stated that network density objectives should be set taking into account the distribution of the population, the distance between access points, the urban or rural nature of areas covered and traffic and demand evolution. ANACOM was also required to take into

[8]Or reduction of the opening hours of *estações*.

account the objective of ensuring the existence, availability, accessibility and quality of the universal service provision, as well as the objective of ensuring the economic and financial sustainability and viability of the universal service provision. Meanwhile, CTT was given flexibility to open and close any specific outlet. However, any decision in this regard should respect the general network density objectives accepted or imposed by ANACOM.[9]

Implementing this new legal framework, by 2014 CTT submitted to ANACOM a proposal for the density of outlets and other points of access (letterboxes),[10] minimum services and operating hours.

ANACOM considered that the objectives and rules presented by CTT failed to meet users' needs, thereby forcing CTT's presentation of a revised proposal.[11] Having considered that CTT's revised proposal still failed to meet users' needs, ANACOM issued a draft decision with objectives and rules on postal network density and availability of minimum postal services. These were, then, submitted to the prior hearing of CTT and consultation of users, as specified by legal framework. The final decision was adopted on August 2014, with network density objectives set for a period of 3 years.

The objectives defined concerned to density of outlets, services provided, operating hours of outlets and density of letterboxes.[12]

Regarding the number of outlets, ANACOM's decision did not imply major changes relative to the current market situation. The number of outlets was set close to the level verified at the end of 2013 (Fig. 1). The same happened with other network density objectives, as in the case of defining maximum distances, expressed in meters travelled by population, to reach the nearest outlet from the place of residence. It seems fair to say that ANACOM considered that, by the end of 2013, the network guaranteed the satisfaction of users' needs. This idea is consistent with surveys and studies related to users' satisfaction.[13] Information on

---

[9]Base XV and Base XX, no 3, of the universal service concession, as amended by Decree-Law no. 160/2013.

[10]Infrastructures provided for the public, where postal items may be deposited in the postal network by users.

[11]Base XV, no 5, of the universal service concession, as amended by Decree-Law no. 160/2013.

[12]Please refer to the Appendix for the list of objectives. For more details, please refer to the decision of ANACOM of 28 August 2014, available at www.anacom.pt.

[13]ANACOM (2012). According to this survey, the level of satisfaction of users in relation to the postal network was very positive, with "Location" of the outlets giving rise to highest levels of satisfaction among users of outlets during 2012 [average evaluation of 8.5 points in a scale ranging from 1 (not important) to 10 (very important)]. "Accessibility for people with special needs" and "waiting time" generated lowest levels of satisfaction (average evaluation of 7.5 and 7.8 respectively), in both cases still a very positive evaluation by users. The average level of satisfaction with "Opening hours" was 8.2. Users of outlets mostly used branches located in their area of residence (75.1 %).

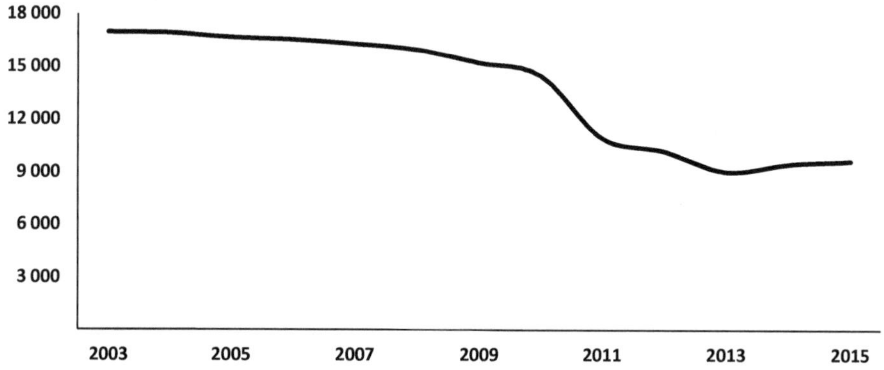

Fig. 6 Evolution in the number of letterboxes

consumer satisfaction at local level was not widely available.[14] ANACOM's role seems to be consistent with a form of adaptive behavior to customer satisfaction since no network density optimization process was actually done. The number of outlets was considered acceptable, being consistent with relatively high level of consumer satisfaction, measured at countrywide level.[15]

An exception was the letterboxes. At the time of ANACOM's decision, there were parishes[16] without any letterbox and the USP significantly reduced the number of letterboxes by 40.7 % between 2009 and 2013 (Fig. 6). ANACOM considered that, in order to ensure the existence, availability, access and quality in the provision of the universal service, the number of geographic points where letterboxes were located should be increased and better distributed along the Portuguese territory. This decision was based on a qualitative assessment, ordered by ANACOM, whereby it was analyzed how the reduction in the number of letterboxes was affecting the accessibility to the universal service. Moreover, regulator's action may be explained by the consideration that the increase in the number of letterboxes would not imply significant increase in USO's cost compared to users' benefit. Given the imposition of additional number of letterboxes, a staged implementation was set, to be implemented until the second quarter of 2015. As expected the number of letterboxes increased since ANACOM's decision (Fig. 6).

---

[14]The survey conducted in 2012 (ANACOM 2012) did not capture relevant differences in the level of satisfaction across different areas (NUTS II) of Portugal. Occasional press reports suggested that, in areas where *estações (outlets strictly operated by CTT)* had been replaced by *postos (operated by local retailers)*, satisfaction levels recovered after initial surge of complaints.

[15]Apparently CTT managed to change network density from 2004 to 2013, maintaining relatively high level of consumer satisfaction at country level. This suggests some management capabilities to deal with the problem. However the decline in traffic also helped, of course, reducing demand for access to postal outlets.

[16]The smallest administrative territorial jurisdiction.

4 Conclusions

The Directive gives substantial discretion to EU MS to solve on the matter of the density of outlets what may be either a market failure or a political objective. Eventually, postal network density may be seen as a political concern rather than an economic efficiency issue. Equality of access and balanced regional distribution of public services may be considered by public decision makers as more important than economic efficiency. Network density is an important component of the USO and of the corresponding cost. Although network density might play a vital role for social cohesion, USPs currently deal with new competitive concerns, e.g. electronic substitution. Therefore, USPs attempt to align postal network density vis-à-vis changes in users' needs. With decreasing demand for traditional postal services, a lack of focus on economic efficiency may impose an increasing burden on the sustainability of the USO.

In practice, it may be very difficult for politicians and regulators to manage this trade-off. If outlets close, political opposition increases, sharpened by the popular circular argument: outlet closures may be the result of low demand levels, and low demand levels are also influenced by weak local economic activity, but closures will accelerate decline in local economic activity, postal services demand and local labor market helping, thus, to create a vicious cycle of economic decline and poverty. If, based on efficiency arguments, hundreds of outlets should be closed over a relatively short period of time, e.g. one or two years, and if local complaints are subject to daily discussion in media, the political cost of network density rules strictly based on economic efficiency arguments increases.

Any principle in favor of USO's realignment should be consumer-oriented. Most of users' needs might be satisfied by plausible alternatives, e.g., electronic means. However, the assumption that consumers are totally open to accept drastic innovations may be dubious. Notwithstanding, the USO may incorporate gradual flexibility to reduce the respective cost.

Future research should provide additional theoretical or empirical support to postal regulators on the definition of postal network density, according to efficiency objectives or to different sets of political objectives. Another interesting topic that future research should not jeopardize is to anticipate market trends likely to hold in future. Depending on the specificities of EU MS, USPs may pursue distinct business strategies. In an extreme side, USPs may strictly provide postal services, eventually fostering digital access. In the opposite standpoint, USPs may follow a multi-integrated business strategy through portfolio diversification, for instance including banking services, whereby traditional services are complemented with high value services. In the case of Portugal, it seems that CTT may move towards the increased provision of high value services.

Appendix

Network density objectives in the EU Outlet's obligations

	Minimum number obligations	Traveling distance obligations	Minimum services obligations (including operating hours)
Austria (AT)	The minimum number of outlets must be equal to 1650.	In towns with more than 10,000 inhabitants and in every capital of district there should be an outlet within 2 km. Outside these areas de distance should be no more than 10 km.	Outlets should open at least 5 working days a week for no less than 20 weekly hours, with the exception of outlets managed by municipalities which must be open at least 3 days a week for no less than 15 weekly hours. Postal service points shall also include third party-operated postal service points which are opened fewer than 20 h per week or 5 working days per week, or do not offer all of the relevant services, or those which are third party-operated by a municipal office open fewer than 20 h per week or 5 working days per week. The total number of postal service points under these conditions shall not exceed 165.
Belgium (BE)	1300 postal service points with a minimum of 650 postal offices, of which at least one in every municipality	At least 95 % of the population should have access to a postal service point offering the basic assortment within a 5 km distance and at least 98 % within a 10 km' distance (by road).	N/A

(continued)

(continued)

	Minimum number obligations	Traveling distance obligations	Minimum services obligations (including operating hours)
Czech Republic (CZ)	N/A	The population should be able to reach a postal establishment using public transportation. When that is not possible, the maximum distance to a postal establishment should not exceed 2 km.	One outlet should be open: (a) on Saturdays in residential areas with more than 10,000 inhabitants; (b) on Sundays in residential areas with more than 100,000 inhabitants and in each metropolitan area; (c) every day until midnight in residential areas with more than 250,000 inhabitants;
Denmark (DK)	There is to be a minimum of one outlet in each municipality and cities with more than 5000 inhabitants. In cities between 2000 and 5000 inhabitants the USP cannot close an outlet unless it is replaced by another one.	In small cities and villages outlets cannot be closed if the traveling distance to the nearest outlet increases by 10 km in a straight line.	N/A
Estonia (EE)	One outlet per municipality and parish. In cities with more than 20,000 inhabitants there should be an outlet for every additional 20,000 inhabitants. In parishes with more than 2500 inhabitants there should be an additional outlet.	N/A	Outlets must be open at least 2 h per day between 8 a.m. and 6 p.m.
Finland (FI)	One outlet per municipality	(a) 82 % of the population should be at a maximum of 3 km of the nearest outlet; (b) The maximum distance from the inhabitants' permanent resident may exceed 10 km only for a maximum of 3 % of population. (c) The service points must be located such that the users of universal are within a reasonable distance.	N/A

(continued)

(continued)

	Minimum number obligations	Traveling distance obligations	Minimum services obligations (including operating hours)
France (FR)	All municipalities with more than 10,000 inhabitants must have at least one contact point every 20,000 inhabitants.	At least 99 % of the population at the national level and 95 % in each province should have an outlet within 10 km.	N/A
Germany (DE)	At least 12,000 fixed outlets. Every municipality with more than 2000 inhabitants should have at least one outlet and each administrative district should have one outlet per 80 km^2.	In contiguous building areas with more than 4000 inhabitants the maximum traveling distance must be, in principle, no more than 2 km in a straight line.	N/A
Hungary (HU)	An outlet in every town. In towns with more than 20,000 inhabitants the USP should provide an outlet per 20,000 inhabitants.	In towns with more than 20,000 inhabitants the USP should provide an outlet per 20,000 inhabitants from which the inhabitants cannot be further than 3 km in a straight line. Also, the distance between postal offices cannot exceed 6 km.	Outlets managed by the USP should function for at least 2 h a day between 7 a.m. and 8 p.m. In towns with more than 15,000 inhabitants there should be at least one outlet open every working day for at least 6 h in which one of the 6 h must be before 8 a.m. and after 5 p.m.
Ireland (IE)	N/A	N/A	There should be a facility to buy postage stamps at a retail outlet in the vicinity of every pillar/wall box in town areas.
Italy (IT)	An outlet must be present in at least 96 % of the municipalities. The closure of the outlets is forbidden in municipalities with only one outlet. Also, the closure of outlets in rural municipalities is prohibited unless an alternative is provided and should be previously communicated to the town mayors.	The USO must ensure an outlet: i. Within 3 km for 75 % of inhabitants; ii. Within 5 km for 92.5 % of inhabitants; iii. Within 6 km for 97.5 % of inhabitants.	(a) Outlets must open at least three days and 18 h hours per week. (b) If there is one outlet in a municipality with fewer than 500 inhabitants (and no other outlet within 3 km which is open for at least three days per week), it cannot be open for less than two days and 12 h per week.

(continued)

(continued)

	Minimum number obligations	Traveling distance obligations	Minimum services obligations (including operating hours)
Lithuania (LT)	In rural areas there should be at least an outlet.	In urban areas, users cannot be at more than 3 km of an outlet.	N/A
Poland (PL)	At least 8240 points of access throughout the country located taking into account the demand in a particular area. A point of access should cover, in average: (a) 7000 inhabitants in urban areas; (b) an area of 85 km^2 in rural areas; At least one point of access should exist in each parish. The areas of parishes with more than 5000 inhabitants are allowed to be covered by a neighbor area or by a mobile point of access as long as the point of access guarantees a more efficient service to customers residing in the area provided by this point of access.	N/A	N/A
Portugal (PT)	The average number of inhabitants per outlet is lower than or equal to 4600 inhabitants. In parishes with more than 20,000 inhabitants, the USP must ensure at least one outlet providing the full range of concessionary services and an additional outlet, providing the same range of services, for each additional 20,000 inhabitants. In parishes where the number of inhabitants	The maximum distance to an outlet shall be: (a) At national level, 6000 meters for 95 % of the population. (b) In urban areas, 4000 meters for 95 % of the population. (c) In rural areas, 11,000 meters for 95 % of the population. The maximum distance to an outlet providing the full range of concessionary services intended for the	The USP must ensure the provision of a delivery service for the blind. The provision of the full range of concessionary services must be ensured at least by one outlet per municipality. The percentage of outlets that provide the full range of concessionary services intended for the occasional user, in the total of outlets, must be at least 75 %. In rural areas, where the residing population is

(continued)

(continued)

	Minimum number obligations	Traveling distance obligations	Minimum services obligations (including operating hours)
	exceeds 10,000 and is lower than or equal to 20,000 inhabitants, the USP must ensure at least one outlet providing the full range of concessionary services.	occasional segment shall be: (a) At national level: 8500 meters for 97.5 % of the population; (b) In urban areas: 5500 meters for 97.5 % of the population; (c) In rural areas: 15,500 meters for 97.5 % of the population. The maximum distance to an outlet providing the full range of concessionary services must be inferior to 30,000 meters.	from a distance exceeding 10,000 meters to the nearest outlet, postmen shall also perform itinerant customer service operations; The percentage of outlets providing the service of judicial mail must be at least 50 %. Minimum operating times: (a) The number of outlets opened to the public less than 5 working days and/or 15 h per week must not exceed 1.5 % of all outlets; (b) The number of outlets opened to the public less than 5 working days and/or 15 h per week must not exceed 20 % of outlets in each municipality.
Slovenia (SI)	The USP shall provide an outlet in each municipality.	95 % of the population must be within 4.5 km of the nearest outlet, by direct line.	Outlets must be open 5 working days a week for at least two consecutive hours.
The Netherlands (NL)	N/A	The spread of outlets should at the national level result in one service point: (a) with a full offer of services within 5 km of at least 95 % of population; (b) with a full offer of services outside of residential areas with more than 5000 inhabitants within a radius of 2.5 km for at least 85 % of the inhabitants involved.	N/A

(continued)

(continued)

	Minimum number obligations	Traveling distance obligations	Minimum services obligations (including operating hours)
United Kingdom (UK)	N/A	The distribution of outlets capable is such that: (a) 95 % of users of postal services are within 5 km of such an outlet; (b) in all postcode areas the premises of not less than 95 % of users of postal services are within 10 km of such an outlet, and such outlets are available to the public in accordance with conveniently published schedules.	N/A

Sources Legislation, NRAs' decisions and/or ERGP

Letterboxes' obligations

	Minimum number obligations	Traveling distance obligations
Austria (AT)	N/A	In highly populated residential areas the distance to a letter box should not exceed 1 km.
Belgium (BE)	At least one mailbox in every municipality. Last collection must be set at 5 p.m., and at 7 p.m. in those municipalities where this is justified.	N/A
Czech Republic (CZ)	In resident areas with higher mail demand, the USP should increase the number of letter boxes.	N/A
Denmark (DK)	The USP is obliged to provide an adequate number.	N/A
Estonia (EE)	At least two letter boxes per municipality.	In cities the maximum distance to a letter box should be 0.5 km and in parishes the maximum distance should be 2 km.
Finland (FI)	N/A	N/A
France (FR)	N/A	N/A
Germany (DE)	N/A	In contiguous building areas with more than 4000 inhabitants the maximum distance should be no more than 1 km also in straight line.
Hungary (HU)	At least a letter box in every town.	Less than 1 km and the distance between letter boxes can't exceed 2 km.

(continued)

(continued)

	Minimum number obligations	Traveling distance obligations
Ireland (IE)	N/A	No one has to travel more than 1 km within the town area to post a letter and more than 3 km to postal a letter in rural areas.
Italy (IT)	(a) At least one letter box in municipalities with up to 1000 inhabitants; (b) There must be three letter boxes in municipalities with between 1000 and 5000 inhabitants; (c) A letter box in every outlet.	N/A
Lithuania (LT)	In rural areas with more than 200 addresses there should be at least one letter box.	In urban areas letter boxes should be at least at no more than 2 km in straight line.
Poland (PL)	The number of letter boxes should be adjusted to the local needs.	N/A
Portugal (PT)	The number of inhabitants per geographic point of access to a letterbox is lower than or equal to: (a) 1160 by the 4th quarter 2014; (b) 1140 by the 1st quarter 2015; (c) 1100 by the 2nd quarter 2015 and subsequently. The number of inhabitants per point of access to a letterbox is lower than or equal to: (a) Predominantly urban area: 1767 inhabitants per letterbox; (b) Moderately urban area: 881 inhabitants per letterbox; (c) Predominantly rural area: 492 inhabitants per letterbox. The percentage of parishes with at least one letterbox shall be: (a) 92.5 % by the 4th quarter 2014; (b) 95.0 % by the 1st quarter 2015; (c) 100 % by the 2nd quarter 2015 and subsequently.	N/A
Slovenia (SI)	At least a letter box, in cities: (a) with less than 5000 inhabitants for every 400 inhabitants; (b) between 5001 and 25,000 inhabitants for every 700 inhabitants; (c) between 25,001 and 80,000 inhabitants per 1000 inhabitants; (d) between 80,001 and 250,000 inhabitants for every 1300 inhabitants; (e) with over 250,000 inhabitants per 1500 inhabitants.	N/A

(continued)

(continued)

	Minimum number obligations	Traveling distance obligations
The Netherlands (NL)	N/A	Residential areas with more than 5000 inhabitants should have a collect letter box within a 1 km radius. Outside this areas collect letter boxes should be within a 2.5 km radius.
United Kingdom (UK)	N/A	A letter box within half a mile of the premises of not less than 98 % of users of postal services In the case of any users of postal services whose premises are not within half a mile of a letter box or other outlet, the USP shall provide access to the universal service in a manner which sufficiently meets the reasonable needs of such users.

Sources Legislation, NRAs' decisions and/or ERGP

References

ANACOM. (2012). Survey on the use of postal services—residential population in December 2012.

ANACOM. (2014). Approval of the objectives and rules governing density of the postal network and minimum services of CTT, August 28, 2014.

Boldron, F., Dewulf, K., Joram, D., Panet, C., Roy, B., & Vialaneix, O. (2008). Accessibility of the postal retail network, social cohesion and economic development. In M. A. Crew & P. R. Kleindorfer (Eds.), *Competition and regulation in the postal and delivery sector* (pp. 47–61). Cheltenham, UK and Northampton, US: Edward Elgar.

Borsenberger, C., Joram, D., & Roy, B. (2011). How many outlets if the USP does not face any USO? A cross-country comparison. In M. A. Crew & P. R. Kleindorfer (Eds.), *Reinventing the postal sector in an electronic age* (pp. 123–141). Cheltenham, UK and Northampton MA, US: Edward Elgar.

Borsenberger, C. (2014). Accessibility/proximity in the digital age: What does it mean for postal networks and postal services? In M. A. Crew & T. J. Brennan (Eds.), *The role of the postal and delivery sector in a digital age* (pp. 267–279). Cheltenham, UK and Lyme, US: Edward Elgar.

Cohen, R., Di Paola, L., Sheehy, R., & Comandini, V. V. (2008). The distribution of post offices in Italy and the United States. In M. A. Crew & P. R. Kleindorfer (Eds.), *Competition and regulation in the postal and delivery sector* (pp. 36–46). Cheltenham, UK and Lyme, US: Edward Elgar.

Panzar, J. C., & Waterson, M. (1991). Is postal service a natural monopoly? Comments. In M. A. Crew & P. R. Kleindorfer (Eds.), *Competition and innovation in postal services* (pp. 219–231). Boston, US: Springer.

Minimum Wages in the Award of Public Contracts After *RegioPost*

Alessandra Fratini

1 Introduction

This paper discusses the judgment of the Court of Justice of the EU (the 'CJEU') in the *RegioPost* case[1] and its bearing on minimum wage obligations in the context of the award of public contracts for postal services. The case concerned the decision by a municipality in the Rhineland-Palatinate Land (Germany) to exclude RegioPost from an EU-wide call for tender relating to postal services in that municipality. The municipality had excluded RegioPost for not having undertaken, at the time of submitting the tender, to pay its staff the minimum wage set by the Law of the Land for public contract awards. The CJEU ruled that the Law of the Land is compatible with Article 26 of the Public Procurement Directive (2004/18/EC),[2] which provides that contracting authorities may lay down special conditions relating to the performance of a contract concerning social considerations. The judgment seems to deviate from the restrictive interpretation of the rules on minimum wages given by the CJEU in previous similar cases, which generally restrained the imposition of national or regional labor standards in the presence of a cross-border dimension in a procurement process. As such, the judgment is of interest for the labour market in the postal sector, where providers of postal services are increasingly relying on "non-standard" employment contracts.

[1]Judgement of the CJEU of 17 November 2015, Case C-115/14, *RegioPost GmbH & Co. KG v Stadt Landau in der Pfalz*, EU:C:2015:760.

[2]Directive 2004/18/EC of 31 March 2004 on the coordination of procedures for the award of public works contracts, public supply contracts and public service contracts (OJ 2004 L 134, p. 114, and corrigendum OJ 2004 L 351, p. 44), as amended by Commission Regulation (EU) No 1251/2011 of 30 November 2011 (OJ 2011 L 319, p. 43).

A. Fratini (✉)
FratiniVergano—European Lawyers, Brussels, Belgium
e-mail: a.fratini@fratinivergano.eu

M. Crew et al. (eds.), *The Changing Postal and Delivery Sector*,
Topics in Regulatory Economics and Policy,
DOI 10.1007/978-3-319-46046-8_8

After a brief description in Sect. 2 of the rules and previous case law that the case is set against, Sect. 3 turns to the legal reasoning of the CJEU, in particular where it moves away from that case law by relying on the characteristics of the measure at issue, in order to determine to what extent *RegioPost* restricts the effects of the previous line of cases in this area. Section 4 reviews the impact of the judgment in the light of the new Procurement Directive 2014/24/EU,[3] as the CJEU's reasoning is equally applicable to the new Directive under its Article 70. Section 5 concludes with an examination of whether *RegioPost* can be suitably relied upon by contracting authorities tendering out postal services, to enforce "social considerations" in the postal and transport sectors.

2 *RegioPost* in Context: The Applicable Rules and Precedents

Before examining the reasoning of the CJEU, it is necessary to set the *RegioPost* judgment within the complex system of EU rules governing public procurement and social policy objectives. The relevant rules and precedents the case draws on are Article 56 of the Treaty on the Functioning of the EU ('TFEU') on the free movement of services, the Directive on the posting of workers in the framework of the provision of services (Directive 96/71/EC),[4] the 2004 Public Procurement Directive (Directive 2004/18/EC); and previous case law in this area, particularly the *Rüffert* and *Bundesdruckerei* judgments.[5]

Article 56 TFEU prohibits restrictions on "freedom to provide services" with respect to parties that are established in a State other than that of the intended recipients of those services. Any discrimination based on nationality is prohibited. A restriction can be justified, however, if it satisfies one of a number of exemptions in the Treaty, including if it is necessary for the protection of workers' rights.

The Directive on the Posting of Workers ('PWD') provides that workers who are temporarily "posted" from one EU Member State to another by their employers are entitled to enjoy the same minimum employment rights as those available to workers permanently located in the host Member State (Article 3). These employment rights are limited to terms and conditions laid down by "law,

[3]Directive 2014/24/EU of 26 February 2014 on public procurement repealing Directive 2004/18/EC (OJ 2014 L 94, p. 65).

[4]Directive 96/71/EC of 16 December 1996 concerning the posting of workers in the framework of the provision of services (OJ 1997 L 18, p. 1).

[5]Judgment of the CJEU of 3 April 2008, Cases C-346/06, *Rechtsanwalt Dr. Dirk Rüffert, in his capacity as liquidator of Objekt und Bauregie GmbH & Co. KG v Land Niedersachsen* (*Rüffert*), EU:C:2008:189; Judgment of the CJEU of 18 September 2014, Case C-549/13, *Bundesdruckerei GmbH v Stadt Dortmund*, EU:C:2014:2235.

regulation or administrative provision" or collective agreements or arbitration awards that have been declared "universally applicable", i.e., "which must be observed by all undertakings in the geographical area and in the profession or industry concerned" (Article 3(8)).

The 2004 Public Procurement Directive ('PPD') provides that contracting authorities are entitled to lay down "special conditions relating to the performance of a contract" concerning social and environmental considerations, provided that these conditions are not directly or indirectly discriminatory, are otherwise compatible with general EU law, and are indicated in the contract notice or in the specifications (Article 26).

The 2006 *Rüffert* case concerned a regional law of Lower Saxony that required public authorities to obtain a written undertaking from bidders and subcontractors tendering for a public services contract to pay their employees the minimum remuneration set by a collective wage agreement when performing that contract. The CJEU held that the collective wage agreement which the regional law sought to impose on subcontractors could not be imposed under the PWD in respect of Polish workers "posted" to Germany to carry out the contract at issue (in the construction sector), as it was neither a "law" nor a universally applicable collective agreement within the meaning of its Article 3(8). In addition, the CJEU noted that the wage agreement applied to workers in relation only to public contracts but not private contracts. Following Article 56 TFEU, the CJEU further held that the regional law constituted a restriction on free movement of services and that it could not be justified by reference to the objective of protecting workers' rights, as there was no information to suggest that workers who were employed under a public service contract, as opposed to those under a private contract, needed such enhanced protection.

Conversely, the 2014 *Bundesdruckerei* case concerned the obligation to guarantee the payment of a minimum wage to the employees of subcontractors of tenderers, provided for by the regional law of North Rhine-Westphalia, even when the subcontractor is established in another Member State and all of the services relating to the performance of the contract are to be carried out in that other Member State (Poland in that case). As there was no issue of "posted" Polish workers to Germany in the case, the CJEU held that the PWD was not applicable and assessed the regional law's compatibility with EU law from the perspective of the TFEU.

Consistent with *Rüffert*, the CJEU held that the minimum wage requirement was capable of constituting a restriction within the meaning of Article 56 TFEU, as it constituted an additional economic burden for subcontractors that could prohibit, impede or render less attractive the provision of their services in the host Member State. Such a restriction could not be justified by reference to the objective of ensuring that employees are paid a reasonable wage in order to avoid both social dumping and the penalization of competing undertakings that grant a reasonable wage to their employees. The CJEU determined that the measure was not "universally applicable", as it applied only to public contracts. In addition, as it bore no relation to the cost of living in Poland, it was disproportionate.

3 The Reasoning of the CJEU in *RegioPost*

In *RegioPost* the CJEU was asked, once again by a German court, to rule on the compatibility of the minimum wage requirement after RegioPost challenged its exclusion from the municipality of Landau's postal services procurement process on the grounds that it had not declared that it would pay any staff providing the services a minimum wage. Both the contract notice and the specifications referred to the Law of the Land for public contract awards,[6] which required those providing services under public contracts to pay their staff no less than a gross minimum hourly wage of EUR 8.70. At the time of the facts that gave rise to the case, there was no federal law or collective agreement setting a mandatory minimum wage for postal workers in Germany more generally. RegioPost argued that the condition breached EU law as it infringed its freedom to provide services within the EU.

Although RegioPost submitted its tender before the deadline, it did not include the minimum wage compliance declaration required by the contract notice. The local authority wrote to RegioPost, allowing 14 days to remedy the omission. In the absence of the requested declaration, RegioPost was excluded from the procurement procedure. It challenged this exclusion before the German Public Procurement Board, which dismissed the application for review. The Higher Regional Court of Koblenz found that the outcome of the proceedings turned on whether it was required to disapply the contested provision of the Law of the Land on the grounds that it was incompatible with EU law.

It thus referred two questions to the CJEU, the most relevant here being whether Article 56 TFEU—in conjunction with the PWD—precludes a national provision which makes it mandatory for a contracting authority to award contracts only to tenderers which undertake (and whose subcontractors undertake) in writing to pay their employees performing the contract work a minimum wage fixed by the State for public contracts (but not for private ones), where there is neither a general statutory minimum wage nor a universally binding collective agreement that binds potential contractors and possible subcontractors.[7]

[6]The Law of the Land on guaranteeing compliance with collective agreements and minimum wages in public contract awards of 1 December 2010 required tenderers and subcontractors to undertake to pay a minimum wage to staff performing the services covered by a public contract. Currently, the "*Minimum Wage Act*" of 11 August 2014 (BGBl. 2014 I, p. 1348) provides, in principle, that all workers are entitled to a minimum wage of EUR 8.50 gross per hour from 1 January 2015.

[7]By the second question, the referring court asked whether the exclusion from participation in the award procedure of tenderers who refused to submit in writing the undertaking above complied with the PPD (Article 26), given that the latter does not provide for grounds for exclusion for infringement of special conditions. In addition, the undertakings required from tenderers are of a declaratory nature only and issues of compliance with the special condition they undertook to comply with only arise after the award of the contract to an operator. As such, in the referring court's opinion, it is not a qualitative selection criterion that might justify the exclusion of a tenderer (see § 40 of the Judgement).

The case offered the CJEU the opportunity to step once again in the debate about whether the EU internal market is a social market and to either confirm or mitigate its previous case law[8] on this point (criticized by some, e.g., Monti Report 2010).[9] If the solution finally adopted by the CJEU mitigates its existing strict approach, it does so with some interesting turns based on the specific characteristics of the case without openly overturning its precedents. These turns concern three issues in particular: the application of the PWD to a situation which entailed no posting of workers from another Member State, via a re-formulation of the first preliminary question; the compatibility of the minimum wage requirement with the PWD even where applicable to public contracts alone; and the compatibility of the requirement with primary EU law (Article 56 TFEU).

3.1 Re-Formulation of 1st Question and Application of PWD to a Situation with no Posting of Workers

To answer these questions, the CJEU engaged in a step-by-step analysis. First, in assessing the admissibility of the first question, the CJEU noted that the PPD was applicable to the main proceedings, as the value of the contract for postal services at stake clearly exceeded the relevant threshold for the application of that directive (at the time set at 200,000 EUR). The contract was thus to be regarded as having "a certain cross-border interest".[10] Undertakings established in Member States other than Germany might have been interested in the contract even if, ultimately, they decided not to participate because of the minimum wage obligation, particularly those in Member States where the cost of living and the applicable minimum pay were significantly lower than those in the Land of Rhineland-Palatinate. Therefore, a question relating to the interpretation of one of its provisions, namely Article 26, was admissible even though it was raised in the context of a dispute where all the elements were confined within a single Member State. Moreover, the CJEU has jurisdiction to rule on Article 56 TFEU to the extent that the degree of

---

[8]Besides *Rüffert*, *Viking*, judgment of the CJEU of 11 December 2007, case C-438/05, EU: C:2007:772; and *Laval*, judgment of the CJEU of 18 December 2007, Case C-341/05, EU: C:2007:809.

[9]The Report argues that that line of case law has revived the divide between advocates of greater market integration and those who feel that the call for economic freedoms and for breaking up regulatory barriers is code for dismantling social rights protected at national level. See Monti Report, p. 68: "The revival of this divide has the potential to alienate from the Single Market and the EU a segment of public opinion, workers' movements and trade unions, which has been over time a key supporter of economic integration".

[10]*RegioPost*, cit., § 51.

harmonization envisaged in that directive so permits.[11] The first question was thus re-formulated as in the first place concerning the interpretation of Article 26 of the PPD.

Moving on to the substance, the CJEU admitted that the minimum wage requirement under the Law of the Land was a "special condition" within the meaning of Article 26 and acknowledged that it had been appropriately set out in the contract and was not discriminatory. However, under Article 26, special conditions are allowed "provided that these are compatible with Community law". With an unpredicted turn, to determine to what extent such requirement could be assessed under EU law, the CJEU analyzed it first against the PWD instead of the Treaty. Despite having stated that the minimum wage requirement was to be assessed in light of EU primary law, consistent with the CJEU's settled case law and given that the PPD had not exhaustively harmonized EU law in this area, the CJEU examined the requirement against the PWD (which would qualify as secondary, rather than primary law).[12] On this point, the CJEU deviated from the view of Advocate General Mengozzi, who stated that in a situation such as the one in *RegioPost*, the *renvoi* made to EU law by Article 26 of the PPD related exclusively to Article 56 TFEU and the PWD was not applicable, as also found in *Bundesdruckerei*.[13]

Without declaring that the PWD applied based on the facts of the case, the CJEU relied on a reference to it in recital 34 of the Procurement Directive. The PPD says that "in cross-border situations in which workers from one Member State provide services in another Member State for the purpose of performing a public contract", it is necessary to determine whether the minimum conditions laid down in the PWD are observed.[14] While this may be justified by the preliminary question being framed in terms of the interpretation of Article 56 TFEU "in conjunction with" the PWD, it can be reasonably expected that the latter be always applicable to situations falling within the scope of application of the PPD, even where these do not directly involve the posting of workers. At the same time, that leaves the door open for future cases that explicitly involve a cross-border element to be covered by the judgment.

[11] *Ibidem*, §§49–50.

[12] It has been argued that, had the Court assessed the compatibility of the requirement with the Treaty, it would have most probably come to the same conclusions as in *Bundesdruckerei*, i.e. that it constituted a restrictive measure that could not be justified by the objective of protecting workers, absent evidence of the need to grant greater protection under public contracts than in private contracts (Norton Rose Fulbright 2016).

[13] Opinion of AG Mengozzi, delivered on 9 September 2015, in *RegioPost*, cit. §§ 51–60.

[14] *RegioPost*, cit., §§ 66–77.

3.2 *Compatibility of Minimum Wage Requirements with the PWD, When Applicable Solely to Public Contracts*

Framing its analysis in terms of the PWD, the CJEU confirmed that the measure at issue in *RegioPost* was to be regarded as a "law", for the purposes of Article 3(1) of the PWD, laying down a "minimum rate of pay". In that respect, it distinguished it from the measure that gave rise to the judgment in *Rüffert* on two grounds. In *RegioPost*, it is the law itself that laid down the minimum rate of pay, while in *Rüffert* the law referred to the minimum wage set out by a collective labor agreement that was not declared to be generally binding by a legislative measure. In addition, at the time of the facts in the main proceedings, Germany had not established a lower minimum wage for the postal services sector.[15] In other words, the finding in *Rüffert* that the measure in question could not be justified by the objective of protecting workers was not relevant in this case. *Rüffert* related to a collective agreement applicable in the construction sector that had not been declared universally applicable and to a minimum wage set at a level higher than under the federal law applicable to cross-border service provision.

The CJEU further clarified that the measure in question was compatible with EU law more generally, despite only applying to public contracts, since the condition regarding the universal application, as defined in Article 3(8) of the PWD, only applies to collective agreements or arbitration awards. In addition, since the national measure at issue falls within the scope of Article 26 of the PPD which allows, subject to certain conditions, the imposition of a minimum wage in public contracts, "that measure cannot be required to extend beyond that specific field by applying generally to all contracts, including private contracts."[16] In fact, the "limitation of the scope of the national measure to public contracts is the simple consequence of the fact that there are rules of EU law specific to that field, in this case, those laid down" in the PPD.[17]

On this point, the Advocate General had clearly said that the implications of *Rüffert* in the *RegioPost* case were to be reconsidered in the light of Article 26 of the PPD, which he defined as "an entirely new provision in EU public procurement law which was not applicable at the time of the facts giving rise to that judgment."[18] He had explicitly stated that Article 26 of the PPD would be denied its practical effect. He added that its "special conditions" would cease to be special if Member States

[15]*Ibidem,* § 62.

[16]*Ibidem,* § 64.

[17]*Ibidem,* § 65.

[18]Opinion of AG Mengozzi in *RegioPost,* § 70. It is worth recalling that, at the time of *Rüffert*, AG Bot concluded in favour of compatibility, noting that the "*possibility of integrating social requirements into public procurement contracts has already been recognised by the Court and is now enshrined in Directive 2004/18*" (Case C-346/06, cit., Opinion of AG Bot, delivered on 20 September 2007, § 133).

were not permitted to adopt laws and regulations applicable only to public contracts.[19]

Based on the above, the CJEU concluded that Article 26 of the PPD, read together with the PWD, allows a contracting authority to require tenderers to comply with a special condition relating to minimum hourly wages for work under public contracts, where that special condition is based on a "law" within the meaning of the PWD and, arguably, a collective agreement of universal application. In fact, as raised by the referring court,[20] it would be illogical to interpret Article 3 (1) of the PWD as it requires collective agreements setting a minimum wage to cover those employed in the performance of public contracts or private contracts, while minimum legislative provisions can be limited only to those workers assigned to the performance of public contracts. If *Rüffert* could be overcome on this point, the CJEU could temper its interpretation of the level of universality required of minimum wages based on collective agreements for the purpose of their application to posted workers (Dumont 2016).

3.3 Compatibility of Minimum Wage Requirement with Article 56 TFUE (Necessity Test)

The aforementioned interpretation of Article 26 of the PPD, according to the CJEU, is further confirmed by a reading of it in the light of Article 56 TFEU, since that article seeks to bring about the freedom to provide services, a fundamental freedom guaranteed by the Treaty. Consistently with *Bundesdruckerei*,[21] the measure may impose an additional economic burden and constitute a restriction within the meaning of Article 56 TFEU, yet it may, in principle, be justified by the objective of protecting workers.[22] In *Rüffert*, the CJEU had considered that the national measure imposing a minimum wage could not be justified under that objective. There was no evidence in the file to show that such protection was necessary for workers in the context of a public contract and not in private contracts. In addition, the minimum wage rate set by the collective agreement exceeded that provided by national law.

To justify its divergent reading in this case, the CJEU underlined that it had "based that conclusion on certain characteristics specific to that measure, which clearly distinguish that measure from the national measure at issue in the main proceedings." Contrary to the *Rüffert* case, the national measure at issue was laid down in a legislative provision that, as a mandatory rule for minimum protection, in principle applies generally to the award of any public contract in the Land of Rhineland-Palatinate. With regard to postal workers, that legislative provision

[19]*Ibidem*, §§ 71–73.

[20]*RegioPost*, cit., § 38.

[21]*Bundesdruckerei*, cit. § 30.

[22]*RegioPost*, cit., §§ 70–73.

conferred a minimum social protection since, at the time of the facts in the main proceedings, no other national legislation set a lower minimum wage for the postal services sector.[23]

There are conflicting views as to whether the facts at stake were sufficiently different to justify a different decision. At any rate, the reasoning of the CJEU here appears somewhat rushed when compared to the traditional compatibility test run by the CJEU when assessing national measures restricting the freedom to provide services. That test typically involves an analysis of whether the measure can be justified by overriding reasons of general interest, such as protection of workers, and whether the measure is necessary and proportionate to achieving that objective. In *Rüffert*, the CJEU found that the measure was not necessary to the protection of workers as it concerned public procurements alone and provided for a minimum wage rate higher than that provided at the national level. In *RegioPost*, the CJEU barely hinted at the necessity of the measure in its reference to the "minimum social protection" that it provided workers.

On other occasions, the CJEU had the opportunity to clarify that in order to justify a measure restricting freedom to provide services as a means of protecting workers, it needed to confer a genuine and significant benefit on the workers concerned.[24] In *RegioPost*, without addressing whether a measure that only applies to public contracts may be regarded as necessary for the protection of workers, the CJEU merely stated that the measure provided minimum protection, as at the time of the facts there was no national regulation setting lower minimum wage rates. Yet, as commented above, the Advocate General had clearly put forward a different view with regard to the entry into force of the PPD after *Rüffert* and, in particular, its Article 26, which allows Member States to impose special conditions on public procurement contractors. For the Advocate General, imposing an extension of special working conditions, such as minimum wage rates, to the performance of private contracts "would ultimately have the effect of compelling the Member States to introduce a universal minimum rate of pay applicable in some or all parts of their respective territories, which they are currently in no way obliged to do under EU law".[25]

A clarification by the CJEU would have been welcome, especially in the light of *Bundesdruckerei,* where the CJEU had unambiguously stated that, to the extent it did not apply to private contracts, the national measure at issue was not appropriate for achieving the objective of protecting workers.[26] That was the case even if the measure, as in *RegioPost*, was a law that itself set the minimum wage (rather than a collective agreement that had not been declared universally applicable).

[23] *Ibidem,* §§ 74–76.

[24] Judgment of the CJEU of 24 January 2002, Case C-164/99, *Portugaia Construções Lda*, EU: C:2002:40, § 29.

[25] Opinion of AG Mengozzi in *RegioPost,* § 73.

[26] *Ibidem,* § 32.

It has been argued (Dumont 2016) that it will require a new court decision or legislative revision of the PWD[27] to clarify when a national measure (law, administrative provision or collective agreement) concerning public procurement alone may require that service providers comply with a minimum wage. However, as explained in the next section, the implementation of the 2014 Public Procurement Directive, which will be applicable in 2018, will most likely play a significant role in limiting the impact of *RegioPost*.

4 The 2014 Public Procurement Directive

The 2004 PPD has been replaced by Directive 2014/24/EU (the '2014 Public Procurement Directive'). In the new Directive, Article 70 largely mirrors the language of Article 26 of the 2004 PPD and similarly allows contracting authorities to lay down special conditions for the performance of contracts, including "social or employment-related considerations". That provision shall be read in light of recital 37 of the 2014 Directive, which explains that Member States and contracting authorities shall take relevant measures to ensure compliance with social and labor law obligations that apply where the services are provided and result from both national and Union laws and regulations, as well as from collective agreements, provided that such rules, and their application, comply with EU law. Article 70 shall be also read against recital 98 of the new Directive, which states that "… award criteria or contract performance conditions concerning social aspects (…) should be applied in accordance with Directive 96/71/EC, as interpreted by the Court (…) and should not be chosen or applied in a way that discriminates directly or indirectly against economic operators from other Member States (…)".

Thus, requirements concerning the basic working conditions regulated in Directive 96/71/EC, such as minimum rates of pay, should remain at the level set by national legislation or by collective agreements applied in accordance with Union law in the context of that Directive. Article 71 of the new Directive further provides that contracting authorities may require that subcontractors comply with applicable labor and social laws and collective agreements and require tenderers to replace any subcontractors that do not comply.[28] The above implies that the ability to exclude a tenderer or subcontractor based on non-compliance with minimum wage requirements is limited to those that are set out in EU or national law and collective agreements,[29] thus limiting the effect of *RegioPost*. However, it will be now very

[27]Following the Work Programme 2016 and the commitment to submit a labour mobility package comprising a targeted revision of the PWD, on 8 March 2016 the Commission presented a proposal for revision of the PWD (COM (2016) 128 final).

[28]In that respect, the Directive affords an expanded ability to evaluate the supply-chain management measures that a tenderer has in place at the selection stage (Article 60(1) and Annex XII, Part II (d)).

[29]Or the international conventions listed in Annex X of the new Public Procurement Directive.

difficult for an excluded tenderer to claim that such requirements are not compatible with EU law because they apply only to public contracts and not to private ones.

5 Conclusions

Employment-related social conditions in public contracts raise a whole series of complex legal questions. *RegioPost* was welcome as striking a balance between the economic freedom to provide cross-border services and the respect for workers' social rights within the EU. The judgment has a broad significance, at least when it comes to public tenders that fall under the Public Procurement Directives, for the labor market in the postal sector, where providers are increasingly relying on "non-standard" employment contracts, outside collective agreements (flexible and temporary employment, outsourcing, self-employed delivery staff) to improve their competitiveness.

Following *RegioPost*, it is clear that any employment-related conditions, while allowed under the Public Procurement Directives, must comply with the PWD if they are applicable (even just hypothetically) to workers sent from another Member State for the provision of a service. It follows that, to comply with EU law, a contractual condition to pay a minimum wage shall be set by law (or by a collective agreement which is made universally applicable by law) and not at a higher level than the generally applicable minimum wage. Otherwise, it is unlikely to meet the requirement not to go beyond the mandatory protection provided for by the PWD.[30] Similarly, there may be grounds for a tenderer to refuse to comply with employment-related conditions in the host Member State if these exceed those applicable in its country of establishment, even if it intends to carry out the public contract entirely in its Member State or subcontract the public contract entirely to an entity based outside the adjudicating entity's Member State. But it is very unlikely that such circumstances (no worker physically located in the host Member State during the performance of the contract) would arise in practice in connection with the provision of postal services.

RegioPost confirms that public procurement is a powerful instrument that can usefully support other public and social policies. However, in declining to enforce the non-discrimination requirement regarding public contracts vs. private contracts, the Court has left the door open for the dissimilar treatment of workers carrying out the same activity within the same company or in different companies, depending on whether it is a under public contract or a private contract.

---

[30]The Scottish Government, for example, obtained clarification from the Commission to the effect that contracting authorities are unable to make payment of the "Living Wage" a mandatory requirement as part of a competitive procurement process, where the "Living Wage" is greater than any minimum wage set by law. See letter of Commissioner Barnier of 8 May 2014, available at: http://www.gov.scot/Resource/0045/00456861.pdf (lastly visited on 11 July 2016).

In the short term, it remains to be seen whether the judgment, and the newly established balance between the economic freedom to provide cross-border services and the protection of workers' social rights, will affect the outcome of the pending infringement procedures concerning the systematic application of the minimum wage legislation by France and Germany to all transport operations which touch their respective territories.[31] The Commission has raised doubts in that respect in relation to the PWD, the freedom to provide services and freedom of movement of goods, and the principle of proportionality,[32] as it considered that more proportionate measures than the minimum wage are available to safeguard the social protection of workers and to ensure fair competition, whilst allowing for free movement of goods and services.[33] The two new letters of formal notice having been sent after *RegioPost*, it appears that the Commission remains convinced that the application of the minimum wage to certain international transport operations "*having only a marginal link to the territory of the host Member State*"[34] cannot be justified, as it creates disproportionate administrative barriers, which prevent the internal market from functioning properly.

References

Dumont, L. (2016, January 28). *L'imposition d'un salaire minima aux adjudicataires de marchés publics devant la CJUE: continuité apparente ou assouplissement déguisé?*, CDRE. http://www.gdr-elsj.eu/2016/01/28/liberte-de-circulation/limposition-dun-salaire-minima-aux-adjudicataires-de-marches-publics-devant-la-cjue-continuite-apparente-ou-assouplissement-deguise/ (lastly visited on 12 July 2016).

Monti Report. (2010, May 2). *A new strategy for the single market*. http://ec.europa.eu/internal_market/strategy/docs/monti_report_final_10_05_2010_en.pdf (lastly visited on 12 July 2016).

Norton Rose Fulbright. (2016, February). Minimum wage special conditions in public procurement tender processes: Regiopost v Stadt Landau (Case C-115/14). http://www.nortonrosefulbright.com/knowledge/publications/136611/minimum-wage-special-conditions-in-public-procurement-tender-processes-regiopost-v-stadt-landau-case-c-1151 (lastly visited on 12 July 2016).

[31]On 19 May 2015, while "*fully supporting the introduction of a minimum wage in Germany*", the Commission opened an infringement procedure against Germany (see IP/15/5003). On 16 June 2016, a supplementary letter of formal notice was sent to Germany and a similar infringement procedure was opened against France, in connection with the law on the application of French minimum wage to the transport sector (see IP/16/2101).

[32]The Commission considers that "the application of the Minimum Wage Act to all transport operations which touch German territory restricts the freedom to provide services and the free movement of goods in a disproportionate manner" (see IP/15/5003).

[33]Commission's press release of 19 May 2015, IP/15/5003.

[34]Commission's press release of 16 June 2016, IP/16/2101.

Protecting Consumers Using Postal and E-Commerce Delivery Services in Competitive European Markets

John Hearn

1 Introduction

Consumer protection in two separate, but related, markets is considered in this paper. The two markets are the traditional postal services, generally focused on letters and small packets, and e-commerce delivery services focused on the delivery of goods purchased on the internet and other electronic media. State-owned, or recently privatized, companies, designated as USP's (Universal Service Providers), remain the dominant providers of the traditional postal services. On the other hand e-commerce delivery services are provided by a wide range of companies in competition with each other and the USP's. Prior to the adoption of the EU's Postal Directive (1997), consumers using postal services had few rights to reimbursement and/or compensation in the event of loss, theft or damage to items they had sent or which they expected to receive. The reasons for this are described in Sect. 2.

Section 3 describes how from the 1970s onwards there was a transition to a more commercial customer focused approach. The CJEU (European Court of Justice), in the "Corbeau" case, distinguished between the traditional postal services and the more innovative and customer focused products that were emerging, and noted the greater consumer rights offered by the latter services. Section 4 tells how, following this judgment, the Postal Directive (1997) required countries to draw up transparent, simple and inexpensive procedures to deal with postal users' complaints, and to enable disputes to be settled fairly and promptly with provision for a system of reimbursement and/or compensation.

This paper represents the personal views of the authors and should not be taken to represent the policy of ComReg, CERP, or any other organization.

J. Hearn (✉)
Formerly vice-chair CERP and Project Manager Postal Regulation, ComReg, Dublin, Ireland
e-mail: john@john-hearn.eu

M. Crew et al. (eds.), *The Changing Postal and Delivery Sector*, Topics in Regulatory Economics and Policy,
DOI 10.1007/978-3-319-46046-8_9

Changes in the technical, economic and social environment have been significant since the Postal Directive was enacted almost 20 years ago. Consumer use of postal services to send and receive letters of importance to them is no longer significant. Furthermore, many of the postal service providers now offer services well beyond the scope of the traditional postal services. The changes are described in Sect. 5, which concludes that the consumer protection measures introduced by the Postal Directive (1997) are sufficient to protect the interests of users of the traditional postal services, although there is scope for greater harmonization. Issues such as the provision and scope of the universal service may however become a problem in the coming years.

As noted in Hearn (2016), e-commerce is evolving very rapidly and the boundaries between the various sales channels are becoming blurred. Postal and other home delivery options are no longer the automatic preference of consumers. For many the ability to collect the goods from a local store or from a parcel locker accessible 24/7 is more desirable. The use of big data to personalize and localize the offers of retailers blurs the distinction between domestic and international markets. There is a variety of players active in B2C delivery and this presents many challenges regarding consumer protection.

As a consequence of the Consumer Rights Directive (2011), consumers contract exclusively with the seller (the e-retailer), and title to the goods purchased only passes when the goods are received by the consumer. This has significant implications for consumer protection in the context of e-commerce delivery. The liability of service providers is exclusively to the e-retailer, and inevitably prices and service specifications are the subject of commercial negotiations between these parties. Section 6 concludes with the view that there is a need to establish an information campaign to inform consumers about the implications of these changes and to inform e-retailers and delivery service providers of their mutual obligations.

2 20th Century Consumers Had Few Rights. WHY?

Since the introduction of postage stamps in the middle of the 19th century, postal services were generally provided on the basis of a state monopoly. Until relatively recently this invariably was under the supervision of a government minister. The legal doctrine of "Sovereign immunity", or "crown immunity" (under which the state is immune from civil suit or criminal prosecution) therefore applied to the provision of postal services. The terms and conditions for using the postal services were normally set out in primary and/or secondary legislation. The costs incurred in provision were a charge on the national treasury. The charge for use of the services was a tax, "postage", which often bore no relation to the costs of service provision. Such services were focused primarily on the delivery of written communications, including books and newspapers.

This doctrine was also extended to international postal services. The UPU (Universal Postal Union) was established in 1874 as an inter-governmental organization to ensure the provision of international postal services and its regulations exclude liability to senders and receivers of postal items—see Table 1.

Table 1 The universal postal union convention

Article 23 *Liability of designated operators. Indemnities* Designated operators shall not be liable for items other than registered items, ordinary parcels and insured items
Article 24 *Non-liability of member countries and designated operators* Member countries and designated operators shall not be liable in cases of force majeure, when loss or damage has been caused by the fault or negligence of the sender or arises from the nature of the contents; when the sender's actions may be suspected of fraudulent intent, aimed at receiving compensation, etc.
Article 25 *Sender's liability* The sender of an item not acceptable for conveyance shall be liable for injuries and damage to postal officials, equipment and other postal items
Article 19 *Inquiries* Must be made within six months
Article 26 *Payment of indemnity* Indemnity shall be paid by designated operator of origin or destination, to sender or if agreed by sender to the addressee
Article RL 163 *Period for payment of indemnity* Normally within 3 months

Both sender and addressee had an interest in a postal item and therefore the postal service was an intermediary between the sender and the addressee. There are two different sets of rules that apply to this unusual legal status.

Under international law, the postal service is an agent of the sender of a postal item. Article 5.1 of the Universal Postal Convention provides that "A postal item shall remain the property of the sender until it is delivered to the rightful owner" and Article 5.2 provides that "The sender of a postal item may have it withdrawn from the post or have its address altered or corrected". Therefore if a postal item is lost/stolen or damaged in the course of transmission by post it was the sender that bore any financial or consequential loss. In cases of dispute between sender and addressee the sender had to prove that the postal item was received by the addressee, which necessitated the provision of "registered post" services. Most countries observe these rules in their national legislation.

However, forty-eight countries, principally common law jurisdictions including the UK and Ireland, have signed a protocol to the UPU Convention stating that the principles of international law do not apply in their jurisdictions. Under the common law the postal service providers in these countries which accept items for transmission by post become irrevocably the agent of the addressee immediately upon the posting of the item, and the postal item must be delivered to the addressee. If a postal item was lost, stolen or damaged in the course of transmission by post it was the addressee that bore any financial or consequential loss. In cases of dispute the sender only had to prove that a letter/notice was posted and the courts would assume that the postal item was received by the addressee "in due course of post".

All these characteristics—the postal monopoly; state provision; the lack of a legal contract between the postal service and its users; the distinction between both users' interest in the delivery of a postal item and its legal ownership; and the role of the postal service as an agent or intermediary—meant that consumers using such services had few rights to reimbursement and/or compensation in the event of loss, theft or damage to items they had sent or which they expected to receive. These very restricted rights are still enshrined in the Universal Postal Union Convention.

For so long as the postal services provided high quality services which met the needs of users these restrictive rights were not challenged. However the Treaty of Rome (1957) restricted the scope of the postal monopoly and opened up the prospect of competition and better consumer protection.[1]

3 Emerging Competition

Significant competition began to emerge towards the end of the 20th century. The telephone became the preferred method of personal communication. In response to the decline in the volume of letters posted the Posts transformed themselves into an advertising medium. Of more significance was the emergence, during the 1970s and 1980s, of the Courier and Express Industry to meet the needs of businesses for fast international communication.

In response to the challenges this posed to the traditional state owned operators from the 1970s onwards the traditional model of postal service provision began to transition to a commercial customer focused approach with the provision of postal services increasingly transferred from government agencies to state-owned companies or public corporations. As early as 1967 the British Government created a government corporation, "the Post Office", to provide postal services. Also the Posts began to compete with each other internationally, based on arbitrage of the terminal dues system of inter-state remuneration, which lead to the emergence of "Remail".

There was also structural separation of Post and Electronic Communication and explicit restrictions on the postal monopoly. For example the British Telecommunications Act 1981 removed to a certain extent the exemption from

[1]Article 90 of the Treaty of Rome of 1957 required that:

2. Undertakings entrusted with the operation of services of general economic interest or having the character of a revenue-producing monopoly shall be subject to the rules contained in this Treaty, in particular to the rules on competition, in so far as the application of such rules does not obstruct the performance, in law or in fact, of the particular tasks assigned to them. The development of trade must not be affected to such an extent as would be contrary to the interests of the Community.

liability to users of postal services (section 70) and made provision for the suspension of the monopoly in certain circumstances (section 69).

The provisions of the Treaty of Rome ensured that the emerging competitors were allowed to continue as independent operators rather than being subject to the state monopoly, as had happened in the past. The defining judgment of the European Court of Justice, in the "Corbeau" case,[2] was that the Belgian Post Office had a "dominant position in a substantial part of the common market within the meaning of Article 86 of the Treaty" and that:

> 23. (2) The provisions of Article 90(1) of the Treaty, in conjunction with Article 86, prevent a Member State from applying the statutory monopoly established for the basic postal service also to rapid delivery services such as those at issue in the main proceedings, which present an actual added value as compared with the operations of collection and delivery of correspondence effected by the basic postal service.

So far as consumer protection is concerned the Court observed that "the service gives rise to a direct fiduciary relationship between the defendant and his customers".

The foundations were now in place to give consumers significant rights. Legislation was necessary to give full effect to the Court's decision.

4 European Postal Directive (1997)

The Corbeau judgment came at about the same time as the European Commission published its Green Paper on postal services in 1993, and four years later the Postal Directive (1997) was adopted. The legal purpose of this Directive was to protect incumbents from the full rigor of the provisions of the Treaty of Rome for a transitional period of 'gradual and controlled liberalization of the market'.[3]

Countries were required to guarantee the provision of certain basic postal services (the "universal service").[4] They have the flexibility to decide what exactly constitutes the universal service to fit their domestic circumstances. The specification of the universal service is important from the consumers' point of view not just because of its guaranteed provision but also because of other obligations imposed by the Postal Directive (1997), including transparent, cost-orientated and affordable prices and measurable quality of service standards apply only to the universal service.

Article 19 of the Postal Directive (1997) effectively ended the sovereign immunity which postal services had enjoyed for so long.[5] It required countries to

---

[2]European Court of Justice Case C-320/91 Paul Corbeau 19 May 1993, [1993] ECR 1-2563.

[3]Directive 97/67, Recital 8.

[4]Directive 97/67, Article 3.

[5]although by then the doctrine of sovereign immunity was no longer enforceable in some countries —see for example Byrne v Ireland, [1972] 1 IR 241.

Table 2 Scope of universal service

No of countries	Scope
9	Single piece only
7	Single piece and bulk letters
11	All

draw up transparent, simple and inexpensive procedures to deal with postal users' complaints, particularly in cases involving loss, theft, damage or non-compliance with service quality standards, about items they had sent or which they expected to receive. These should 'enable disputes to be settled fairly and promptly with provision, where warranted, for a system of reimbursement and/or compensation'. Users who do not get satisfaction from the USP can appeal to a 'competent national authority'.

The changes mandated by the Postal Directive (1997) in terms of compensation payable and access to simple and inexpensive complaints procedures have not been implemented in a harmonized manner. There are also significant differences from one country to another concerning the scope of the universal service. Many commonly used postal services are not part of it, even where they are provided by the universal service provider, particularly value-added services like track and trace or delivery by a specified time. The European Commission (2015) summarizes the current scope of the universal service as shown in Table 2.

The position with regard to compensation is more positive. ERGP (2015) reports that mandatory compensation schemes for consumers are now required in 22 European countries and in 10 other countries compensation is covered by general terms and conditions and by civil law. According to WiK (2013) in 16 countries both the NRA (National Regulatory Authority) and NCPA (National Consumer Protection Authority) have power to enforce these user protections measures, in 13 countries it is the sole prerogative of the NRA and in one country it is the sole prerogative of the NCPA.

Recital 34 to the Postal Directive (1997) also confirmed that Council Directive 93/13/EEC of 5 April 1993 on unfair terms in consumer contracts applies to the postal services.

5 Traditional Postal Services

Since the Postal Directive was enacted almost 20 years ago, changes in the technical, economic and social environment have been significant. For example, the use of the post to receive and pay utility bills is much reduced. Email, Skype, Facebook and other social media have replaced the mail as the preferred means of personal correspondence, especially cross-borders. The receipt of advertising material through the letterbox is more targeted. Overall 'letter post' volumes are much reduced and expected to fall further.

Consumer correspondence (C2B and C2C) is now a very small percentage of the total number of letters. ITA/WiK (2009) reported that the importance of private correspondence (C2B and C2C) has declined in many countries and that, overall, more than 85 % of letters were sent by businesses. Given the decline in volumes since then the percentage of private correspondence has almost certainly declined further. Also with changes in the type of letters sent by businesses, the interest of addressees in receiving the mail is most probably much reduced. There is obviously less interest in receiving bills or advertising material than receiving a letter containing a check or travel tickets, both of which have been more prone to e-substitution.

Sovereign immunity, in terms of legal restrictions on access to the courts, lives on. See for example section 26 of Ireland's Communications Regulation (Postal Services) Act 2011. It is not surprising that there is no access to the Courts given the low cost of using the post and the high cost of legal proceedings, which, of course, is why the Postal Directive (1997) mandates the use of simple and inexpensive complaints procedures and encourages the use of ADR (Alternative Dispute Resolution).

The conflict between European and International law in the case of cross-border mail is a cause for concern. For example, the terms and conditions of the UK universal service provider states that Royal Mail "will only accept liability, where the loss or damage is due to any wrongful act done, or any neglect or default committed by a member of staff or agent of Royal Mail …". This means that if loss or damage is incurred in another country or while being transported by an airline, compensation might be refused.

But there is no evidence that the interests of consumers are being compromised. According to an analysis in WiK (2013) it appears that overall the user complaint procedures are well used with a meaningful right to review. It can be concluded therefore that in the case of the traditional postal services the consumer protection measures introduced by the Postal Directive (1997) are sufficient, although there is scope for greater harmonization. It should be noted however that issues such as the provision and scope of the universal service may become a problem in the coming years.

Also many of the postal service providers now offer services well beyond the scope of the traditional postal services. The consumer protection measures necessary for these services are considered in the next section.

6 E-Commerce Delivery Services

6.1 Postal Parcels

Parcels were not originally part of postal service. Hearn (2013) noted that the market for the distribution of goods, in parcels or otherwise, was the preserve of transport companies—railways, canals, shipping and "common carriers". But at its second Congress in 1878 the UPU decided to establish an "optional" international parcel post system. But most importantly the parcel service remained outside the scope of the state monopoly and consumers therefore had a few rights.

Although some countries were slow to introduce the new postal parcel services,[6] the new service led to a boom in Mail Order trading with some of London's major department stores, advertising extensively and publishing latest times for dispatch to most countries for Christmas delivery. Books, magazines and small goods could also be sent by LETTERPOST. During World War II and afterwards "Red Cross" and "American" parcels played important role in bringing much needed relief to populations that did not have access to so-called "luxury" goods. As goods became more freely available and postal costs increased volumes inevitably declined, and by the 1970s the postal parcel service was a shadow of its former self.

6.2 The E-Commerce Revolution

On the other hand, e-commerce is driving significant increases in the volume of goods delivered by postal parcel and other home delivery services. But the traditional Postal Operators (universal service providers—USPs) are no longer dominant players in this market. According to TPR (2015) their market share, at the European level and according to the number of packages delivered, is only 10 %.

As noted in Hearn (2016) e-commerce is evolving very rapidly and the boundaries between the various sales channels are becoming blurred. Postal and other home delivery options are no longer the automatic preference of consumers. For many the ability to collect the goods from a local store or from a parcel locker accessible 24/7 is more desirable. Returns, that is the ability to return unwanted[7] or damaged goods, are also a significant feature of the market. GLS,[8] DPD,[9] Fastway and Hermes all have a network of 'post offices' to facilitate returns. Other companies offer to collect from the addressee. And some retailers encourage returns to their own stores. The use of big data to personalize and localize the offers of retailers blurs the distinction between domestic and international markets.

[6]For instance the United Kingdom did not introduce the service until 1882, and in the case of the USA a domestic postal parcel service was not introduced until 1913, the delay being attributed to lobbying by the private express carriers and rural retail merchants.

[7]Perhaps because the size is wrong.

[8]Royal Mail's European parcel delivery company.

[9]France's La Poste's European parcel delivery company.

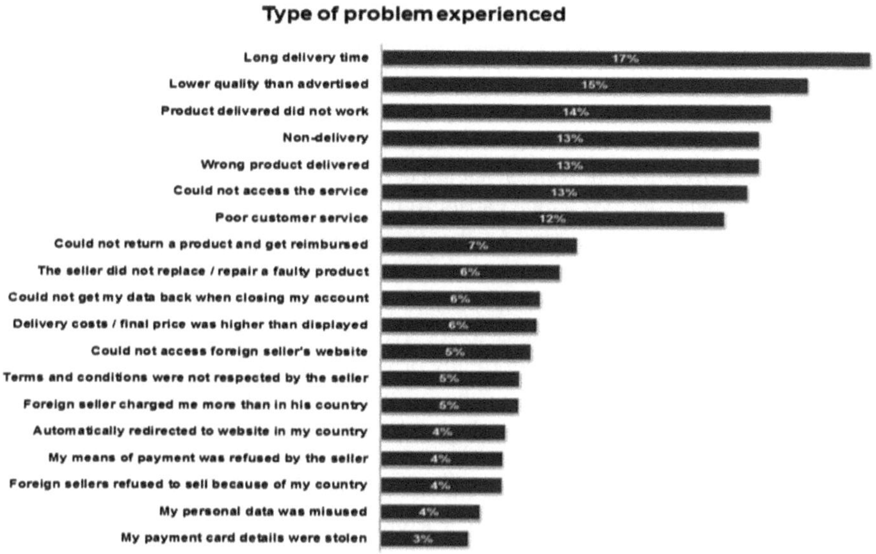

Fig. 1 Consumer concerns about e-commerce. *Source* GfK Belgium (2015)

6.3 European Commission (and Large E-Retailers) Complains About Quality and Price of Parcel Services

The European Commission regularly commissions surveys of consumer concerns about the use of e-commerce. Figure 1 shows the results of a recent survey by GfK Belgium (2015).

The European Commission (and large e-retailers) complains that the quality and price of postal parcel services impacts adversely on the development of e-commerce. But only three of the 19 problems identified by Commission and set out in Fig. 1 could possibly involve postal parcel services. Even these problems identified by consumers, delivery time, non-delivery and difficulty with returns, could equally be due to failure by the retailer and it is simplistic to place the entire blame on the postal services.services.

6.4 Consumer Protection When Goods Are Delivered by Postal and E-Commerce Delivery Services

However consumers have a keen interest in receiving the goods and services they have ordered and in being able to return any goods which are damaged or otherwise not acceptable. Copenhagen Economics (2013) confirms there are a wide variety of players active in B2C delivery (see in particular Table 21). This presents many challenges regarding consumer protection, particularly as most of the delivery companies are subject to the normal law of contract rather than the special position enjoyed by postal service providers.

Under the Consumer Rights Directive (2011) the risk of loss or damage passes to the consumer only when he is in physical possession of the goods. This means that it is the retailer who decides which carrier to use and it is the retailer who negotiates the price and service standards. As the normal rules of contract law apply the liability of the service provider is exclusively to the retailer. In addition, on-line retailers often fail to disclose which service provider is responsible for delivering the goods. As, the consumer wants to receive his goods and the service provider will need some contact in the event of any problem with delivery and presumably it is in the retailer's interest to have the customer contact the delivery company directly. According to TPR (2015) failed delivery rates can vary from 15 to 30 %. Failed deliveries lead to second delivery attempts or being held at a post office or delivery depot pending collection by the addressee.

In essence as a result of the Consumer Rights Directive (2011) the consumer has no contract with the postal service or e-commerce delivery service which delivers any goods ordered from an e-retailer. The only contract is with the seller and it is to the seller that all complaints must be made. However, because of tradition, and the fact that the postal service or e-commerce delivery service may be in contact with the consumer to arrange delivery, consumers may be inclined to make their complaints to the delivery agent. This is undesirable both for legal reasons and because the e-retailer may not become aware of problems which might lead him to change service provider. It is essential therefore to establish an information campaign to inform consumers about the implications of these changes and to inform e-retailers and delivery service providers of their mutual obligations.

Another issue that must be considered is that the "Delivery" charge made by a retailer may not necessarily relate to the cost of delivery to the retailer. The Consumer Rights Directive imposes restrictions on credit card fees that may be charged by e-retailers and it would seem reasonable that similar provisions be enacted to require retailers who show a separate price for delivery to restrict this to the cost involved. A related issue is the need to ensure transparency of the total price charged, as is currently required of airlines. Indeed, the sixth (VAT) Directive requires that VAT inclusive prices be shown in shops and it is the norm for a single price to be displayed. The author would not suggest that a single, delivery inclusive, price be displayed on e-commerce websites but only that there should be transparency as to the total cost.

There is indisputably a need to educate consumers, e-retailers and carriers of these relatively new rules and it should be the role of the European Consumer Centers to help consumers, as Postal NRAs have no expertise in consumer complaints about the sale of goods.

7 Conclusions

Consumer rights concerning the use of postal services been strengthened compared to the time before the Postal Directive was enacted. It is not obvious that more protection is needed for Letters, or postal services generally.

E-Commerce is evolving very rapidly and postal and other home delivery options are no longer the automatic preference of consumers. The Consumer Rights Directive gives consumers real powers but there is a need for education to ensure that consumers, e-retailers and consumers are aware of their rights under the new reality. The Directive needs to be amended to ensure price transparency.

References

Consumer Rights Directive. (2011). Directive 2011/83/EU of the European Parliament and of the Council of 25 October 2011 on consumer rights, amending Council Directive 93/13/EEC and Directive 1999/44/EC of the European Parliament and of the Council and repealing Council Directive 85/577/EEC and Directive 97/7/EC of the European Parliament and of the Council.

Copenhagen Economics. (2013). E-commerce and delivery, a study of the state of play of EU parcel markets with particular emphasis on e-commerce. Copenhagen Economics for the European Commission.

ERGP. (2015). ERGP (15) 26—Report on quality of service, consumer protection and complaint handling European Regulators Group-Posts.

European Commission. (2015). Commission staff working document accompanying the document report from the Commission to the European Parliament and the Council on the application of the Postal Services Directive (Directive 97/67/EC as amended by Directive 2002/39/EC and Directive 2008/6/EC) Brussels, 17.11.2015 SWD (2015) 207 final.

GfK Belgium. (2015, September). Provision of two online consumer surveys as support and evidence base to a commission study: Identifying the main cross-border obstacles to the Digital Single Market and where they matter most, GfK Belgium.

Hearn, J. (2013). Delivering the goods to households—would further regulation help or hinder? In M. A. Crew & T. J. Brennan (Eds.), *The role of the postal and delivery sector in a digital age*. UK and Northampton: Edward Elgar Cheltenham.

Hearn, J. (2016). Implications of recent developments in e-commerce for universal service providers and the USO. In M. A. Crew & T. J. Brennan (Eds.), *The future of the postal sector in a digital world*. Berlin: Springer.

ITA/WiK. (2009, August). The evolution of the European postal market since 1997, ITA Consulting and WiK Consult.

Postal Directive. (1997). Directive 97/67/EC of the European Parliament and of the Council of 15 December 1997 on common rules for the development of the internal market of Community postal services and the improvement of quality of service; as amended by Directive 2002/39/EC of the European Parliament and of the Council of 10 June 2002 and Directive 2008/6/EC of the European Parliament and of the Council of 20 February 2008.

TPR. (2015). Cross-border parcel delivery operations and its cost drivers. Department of Transport and Regional Economics, University of Antwerp, for the European Commission.

WiK. (2013). Main developments in the postal sector (2010–2013). WIK-Consult, Study for the European Commission.

E-Commerce in Europe: Parcel Delivery Prices in a Digital Single Market

J. Scott Marcus and Georgios Petropoulos

1 Introduction

There have been long-standing policy concerns that high retail prices charged for cross-border parcel delivery service may be impeding the growth of e-commerce in Europe, and with it the completion of a Digital Single Market (DSM) in the European Union. The European Commission has just proposed a legislative measure that seeks to increase the transparency of cross-border prices and also to reduce them.

From the perspective of retailers, there is no question that the cost of cross-border parcel delivery is perceived as a problem. Eurostat (2015) conducted a comprehensive survey of businesses in 2015. Among firms already conducting e-commerce on a cross-border basis (or that did so in the past), 51 % said delivery prices were too high when selling to other EU countries, and 27 % said this was a "major problem". Among companies that did not sell online to other EU countries but were trying to at the time of the survey, 62 % said that high delivery costs were a problem, and 41 % considered these costs a major problem. Of firms not selling online, 57 % said that delivery costs were too high, and that this was a major problem. Significantly, for all three groups, high delivery costs were perceived as the most serious single barrier to cross-border e-commerce.

This paper draws heavily on previous work by the authors (Marcus and Petropoulos 2016a and b), and generally draws on experience with the economics of similar challenges in telecommunications in order to shed light on the economic challenges of cross-border parcel delivery.

J. Scott Marcus (✉) · G. Petropoulos
Bruegel, Brussels, Belgium
e-mail: scott.marcus@bruegel.org

G. Petropoulos
e-mail: georgios.petropoulos@bruegel.org

M. Crew et al. (eds.), *The Changing Postal and Delivery Sector*,
Topics in Regulatory Economics and Policy,
DOI 10.1007/978-3-319-46046-8_10

An overview appears in Sect. 2, followed by a discussion of payment flows in Sect. 3. Retail over-pricing is explored in Sect. 4, while wholesale over-pricing is explored in Sect. 5. Section 6 concludes with an assessment of the Commission's new proposed Regulation.[1]

2 Parcel Delivery Prices as a Challenge to E-Commerce in a European Digital Single Market

The growth of e-commerce represents a substantial growth opportunity for Europe. The ability of Europe to fully capitalize on this opportunity appears, however, to be limited by the high prices paid for the shipment of goods across national boundaries within the European Union. In its *Digital Single Market (DSM)* strategy (European Commission 2015) and elsewhere, the European Commission has repeatedly signaled its intent to reduce cross-border parcel delivery prices and to increase the transparency of retail pricing for cross-border delivery services. On 25 May 2016, the Commission put forward a proposed Regulation in order to make these prices more transparent, and also to lower them (see Sect. 6).

The concern here is with basic cross-border delivery services, not with express or courier services; the primary focus is on business-to-consumer (B2C) shipments rather than business-to-business (B2B); and the concern is far greater for shipments by consumers, micro-enterprises, and small and medium enterprises (SMEs) than for large shippers. Further, the focus in this paper is on the national postal operators (NPOs), who continue to play a major role in these cross-border shipments. This has also been the European Commission's central focus in its DSM initiative.

2.1 *Cross-Border E-Commerce Is a Growth Opportunity for the EU*

Online purchasing is growing rapidly within the European Union, as elsewhere, generating benefits for the broader European society. The European Commission (2015) reported that online sale of goods in the EU was increasing "at an average annual growth rate of 22 %, surpassing €200 billion in 2014 and reaching a share of 7 % of total retail sales". Of particular interest are business-to-consumer (B2C) activities. In 2012, B2C e-commerce in the EU28 (reflecting the sum of goods and services purchased online) grew by 18 % to reach €276.5 billion (Brune 2013).

---

[1]Under the *Treaty on the Functioning of the European Union (TFEU)*, a Regulation is binding on the Member States to which it applies. It is thus different from a Directive, which must be transposed into national law before it can take effect.

Cross-border purchasing is also growing in terms of the revenues generated and the number of consumers who order across borders. Eurostat data confirms that 65 % of Internet users shopped online in 2015, and that "... *30 percent of online shoppers bought or ordered goods or services from sellers in other EU countries. ... A rising trend is observed for purchases from sellers in other member states (from 25 percent in 2012 to 30 percent in 2015) and from sellers outside the EU (from 13 percent in 2012 to 18 percent in 2015)*" (Eurostat 2016). FTI Consulting in 2011 had already found that "*distance sales and e–commerce represent 7 percent and 5 percent of [EU] retail turnover [respectively], a mere 1 percent of which is generated cross-border for each activity.*"[2]

Parcel delivery clearly facilitates this e-commerce. Of the €477 billion in e-commerce purchases in Europe in 2015, 53 % was purchases of goods, 47 % was purchases of services (E-commerce Europe 2015). The goods clearly had to be delivered somehow.

The role of micro-, small, and medium enterprise should be of particular interest to Europe, inasmuch as many of the large e-commerce merchants that make these shipments today are headquartered in the United States. There is a clear European interest in ensuring that European e-commerce merchants, which already face an uphill slog in many cases because of small home markets and lack of brand recognition, are not further disadvantaged by incoherent European public policy.[3] Based on Eurostat and other statistics, "15 % of SMEs sell online compared with 35 % of large enterprises; 7 % of SMEs sell across borders compared with 21 % of large enterprises".[4]

2.2 *The Types of Cross-Border Parcel Delivery that Are Subject to High Pricing*

In the case of express or courier services, the presence of multiple vertically integrated providers makes it likely that their prices are competitive. Most e-commerce does not travel this way, however, because these services tend to be too expensive, and because not all shipments require such rapid delivery.[5]

---

[2]FTI (2011); study completed for the European Commission (DG Enterprise).

[3]See FTI (2011): "*[S]mall senders (individuals, micro and small enterprises) ... either pay full price (as published in the publicly available price list of the delivery operator), or obtain small discounts on both domestic and cross-border products ...*".

[4]EurActiv and Digital Europe (2016), "How Digital is the EU in 2015?", at http://www.digitaleurope.org/DesktopModules/Bring2mind/DMX/Download.aspx?Command=Core_Download&entryID=921&PortalId=0&TabId=353, viewed 9 April 2016. See also European Commission (2015), "A Digital Single Market Strategy for Europe – Analysis and Evidence", SWD(2015) 100 Final: "While 17 % of SMEs in the EU sell online (which is already very low), only 7 % sell cross-border to other EU countries.".

[5]See also European Commission (2013).

Large retailers are aware of and able to exploit multiple parcel delivery channels (including self-provision, especially in dense metropolitan areas where their volume of shipments is high enough). Presumably, the largest retailers optimize their use of delivery services so that each shipment is delivered from the most suitable fulfilment center, over the most suitable service. They probably pay less on average for cross-border parcel delivery than do small-scale retailers and individuals; even the largest retailers, however, tend to be dependent on the NPOs to deliver to low density areas.

Small retailers, especially micro-enterprises and SMEs, probably have fewer alternatives to the standard national postal operators (or they may be less aware of them or may not trust them). Consumers and micro-enterprises will tend to pay the NPOs' high published prices (see also Sect. 4.3). Small and medium enterprises may obtain somewhat discounted prices (FTI 2011), but how large the volume of shipments must be to qualify varies between Member States, and what level of discounts might be obtained is, as with most aspects of this very opaque market sector, unknown. Alternative delivery companies exist, but they typically lack the scale economies of the NPOs. Some may provide national coverage, but others might prefer to 'cherry pick' high-density areas where the economics are more favorable.

For low-density areas, a strong analogy to telecommunications economics can be made. It is typically only the historic national operator that has both the obligation and also the scale economies that enable and require it to provide services. In dense urban areas, by contrast, competition can be strong.

2.3 The Impact of Inflated Price

Inflated prices for cross-border delivery impact Europe in many ways. To begin with, if the price of cross-border shipment is inflated for B2C shipments, this price will ultimately paid by the consumer one way or another and is likely to depress demand. Purchases that might have been made but were not because of over-pricing represent a welfare loss to European society.

Second, consumers may look only on domestic websites instead of checking websites in other Member States because they (rightly or wrongly) fear high delivery charges; analogously, small shippers might decline to offer services in other Member States because they lack the knowledge or scale needed to offer services there. In both cases, potential *gains in trade* are foregone if a better or less expensive product that could have been purchased is not in fact purchased.[6]

Third, European competitiveness is lost relative to the EU's global competitors. That SMEs are strongly impacted is particularly worrisome given that Europe is to

[6]The desire to obtain these gains in trade is the reason why countries seek *Free Trade Agreements (FTAs)*.

some extent seeking to catch up with B2C providers elsewhere that were quicker than European firms to capitalize on e-commerce opportunities. European firms seeking to achieve market entry in the face of competition from global giants like Amazon should not be needlessly hobbled by Europe's own postal pricing arrangements.

Finally, shippers might be obliged to warehouse goods at more locations than would have been necessary if prices were more reflective of underlying costs.[7] This again represents a competitive disadvantage in comparison with other regions of the world.

3 Cash Flows in Parcel Delivery

The flow of payments when goods are ordered for physical delivery by the NPOs is as depicted in Fig. 1. The payment typically flows to the retailer or sender of the parcel. The end customer may pay separately for the product and for delivery, or may pay a single price for product and delivery together, which the consumer might typically view as reflecting free domestic delivery.[8] It is however clear that "free" domestic delivery really means that the retailer has covered the average cost of delivery within the price for the goods to be shipped. For most purposes, it is the total payment from customer to retailer that matters, not the manner in which the retailer chooses to package these payments.

Wholesale payments between the NPOs are routine, as shown in Fig. 1. For the most common postal (cross-border) services, payments between postal operators are referred to as terminal dues (TDs). Terminal dues are relevant not only for letters, but also for small parcels (less than 2 kg) delivered as letter post. Inward Land Rates (ILRs) are the wholesale payments between NPOs for heavier parcels of between 2 and 20 kg (up to 31 kg in some countries).

---

[7]It is sometimes argued that goods are not necessarily shipped from the country associated with the website (see Henrik Okholm et al. (2016), "Principles of e-commerce delivery prices", Copenhagen Economics, page 11: "In fact, a large share of online transactions that are perceived as domestic by consumers involve a cross-border element."). This is correct, and reflects a beneficial cost optimisation on the part of the shipper, but is somewhat irrelevant to the concern that fulfilment centres are not necessarily placed where they would be if the delivery were fully reflective of cost.

[8]See for instance Okholm et al. (2016), Copenhagen Economics, Principles of E-Commerce Parcel Prices, pages 21–24.

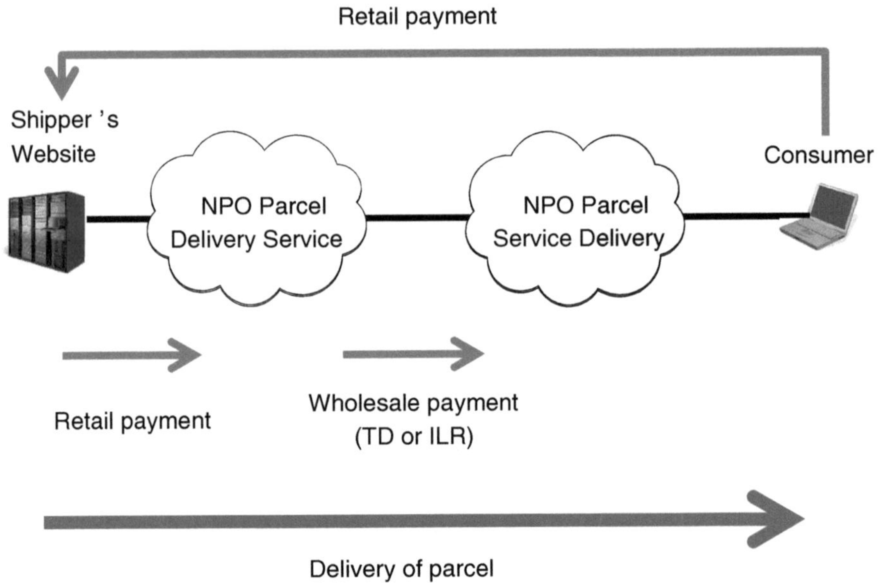

Fig. 1 Cash flows for parcel delivery. *Source* Marcus and Petropoulos

4 Are Cross-Border Parcel Delivery Retail Prices Inflated?

4.1 Domestic Versus Cross-Border Delivery

In assessing the costs of cross-border delivery, it is important to bear in mind that the NPOs have significant additional work to do for cross-border delivery in comparison to domestic delivery. Some of this extra work relates to the distance over which the parcel has to be shipped, but much more of the extra work relates to relabeling and otherwise mapping one NPO's services and processes to those of another. These re-mapping costs are largely unknown, but might be quite substantial.

This extra work means that it is legitimate for cross-border prices to be somewhat higher than domestic. It is clear that cross-border delivery involves a longer chain of operations than domestic delivery, and therefore more cost. For domestic delivery, the chain of operations can be conceptualized as shown in Fig. 2.

For cross-border delivery, the transport operation is more extensive, and additional steps are required (Fig. 3); therefore, the cost to the delivery service is likely to be greater and it should consequently be no surprise if the price is set somewhat higher. Other factors could also contribute to legitimately higher costs than for domestic delivery, including different labour rates or currency exchange fluctuations.

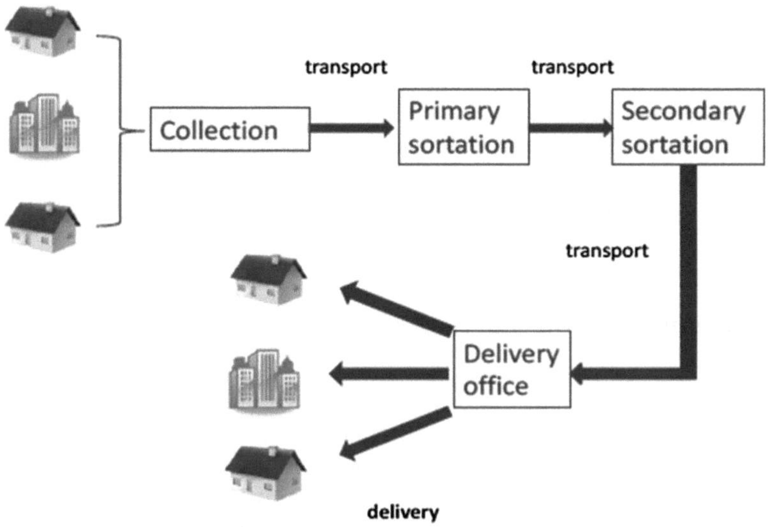

Fig. 2 Steps in domestic postal delivery. *Source* FTI (2011)

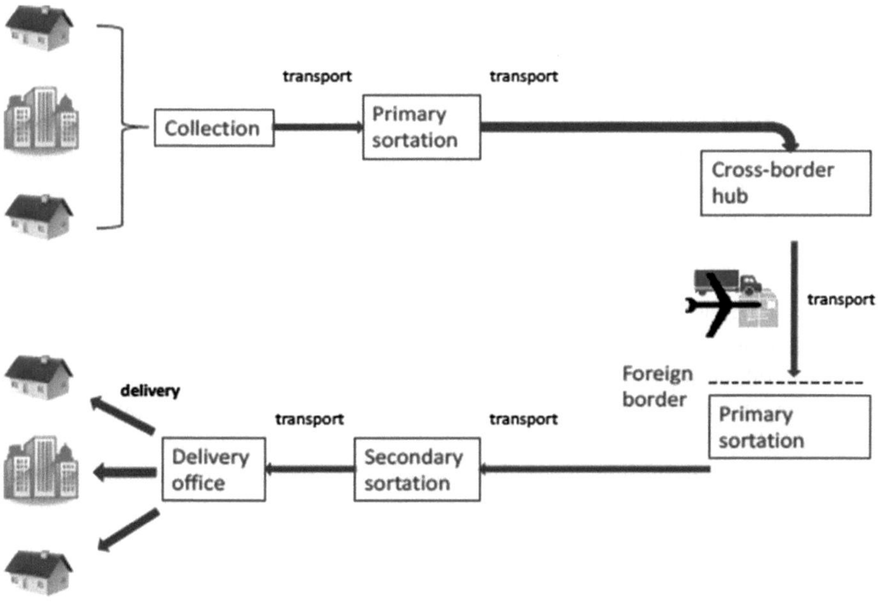

Fig. 3 Steps in cross-border parcel delivery. *Source* FTI (2011)

Most NPOs offer either a single retail price for parcel delivery to most of Europe, or some other aggregation of prices. Consumers generally appreciate the simplicity of these arrangements. In comparing prices, however, this can lead to counter-intuitive *border effects*—the price of shipping a parcel to an adjacent country is often much higher than the price for shipping the same parcel to a more distant location in one's own country. These counterintuitive border-effect price differences do not necessarily constitute a cause for concern in their own right, inasmuch as customers value the simplicity provided by uniform pricing. The more serious concern is that retail prices for cross-border parcel delivery by the NPOs seem to be too high in general (see Sects. 4.2 and 4.3).

4.2 Results from the Literature

FTI Consulting (2011) attempted a comprehensive assessment for the European Commission of whether wholesale and retail parcel delivery prices were inflated. A first key finding was that "… market conditions are very different for large and small senders. Large senders operate in a competitive European cross-border parcels environment, and have much choice and bargaining power vis-a-vis suppliers. The prices they pay are negotiated. By contrast, many small senders tend to use the services of national postal operators, even in cases where they do have alternatives. As a result, they pay higher cross-border prices, as compared to domestic ones. These higher prices could be due to higher cross-border unit costs linked to the smaller scale of cross-border operations; and/or to insufficient competitive pressure, i.e. to the existence of market power."

FTI (2011) concluded, after correcting for factors that make cross-border delivery more costly than domestic, that "… cross-border prices are indeed much higher than domestic benchmark prices and therefore too high. For parcels, they are on average twice as high as domestic benchmark prices, while for packets, which are part of letter mail, they are about 30 % higher." Claes and Vergote (2016) carried out another econometric study for the European Commission in late 2015. They found that "on average, cross-border prices are 324 % higher than their domestic counterpart for letters and 471 % higher for parcels."

It is worth noting that both of these studies, and our own assessment as well (see Sect. 4.3), share the limitation that substantially all research on postal price characteristics has been based mainly or solely on published list prices. Very little is publicly known about how many firms actually pay these prices, how different the published retail list prices are from the discounted prices actually paid by large shippers, and the actual sources and destinations of parcels shipped.

4.3 An Assessment Based on Published Retail Prices

It is clear based on underlying cost considerations that retail prices for cross-border parcel delivery should be higher than domestic, but how much higher? This question has been explored several times by means of econometric analysis, but a

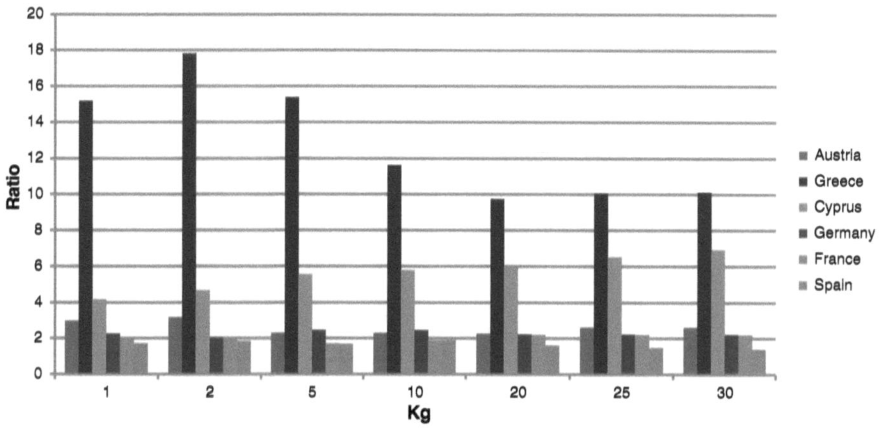

Fig. 4 Ratio of NPO European cross-border parcel delivery prices to equivalent domestic prices in selected member states (by kg). *Source* Marcus and Petropoulos

first order review of retail prices in a range of Member States[9] (even at some risk of over-simplification) can provide a different and complementary view.

The ratio between cross-border delivery prices and the equivalent domestic prices (bearing in mind however that the services are not perfectly equivalent) is far greater in small, peripheral Member States such as Greece and Cyprus than in larger Western European Member States such as France, Germany and Spain (with Austria being closer to Germany than to Greece) (see Fig. 4).[10]

A comparison with parcel delivery prices in the United States is also instructive. The United States is comparable to the European Union as a whole in terms of population, area and GDP per capita, but it is a single federal republic that has had a single national postal service since it was founded.[11] Prices for parcel delivery within the United States thus serve as something of a benchmark of what one might expect if European postal service prices were a true reflection of underlying costs, and in the absence of the *transaction costs* imposed by re-mapping of services from those of the sending NPO to those of the receiving NPO.[12]

US prices for domestic delivery of 'machinable' parcels (i.e. parcels with fairly standard dimensions and falling within prescribed weight limits) show a fairly

[9]All prices are based on a review of NPO websites during the first four months of 2016.

[10]This is consistent with an observation in the FTI (2011) study that economic distortions are less significant in the six largest Member States than in many others. The coefficient of variation in these six countries (i.e. the standard deviation divided by the mean, which provides a normalised measure of variability) ranges as a function of weight from 0.81 to 1.19, which is quite large.

[11]There are also competitors that offer nationwide parcel delivery service, such as UPS.

[12]We acknowledge that there are limitations in these comparisons. First, here are challenges in comparing services that are not quite identical. In addition, US postal prices are low by global standards. Nonetheless, the rough comparison is close enough to enable indicative comparisons.

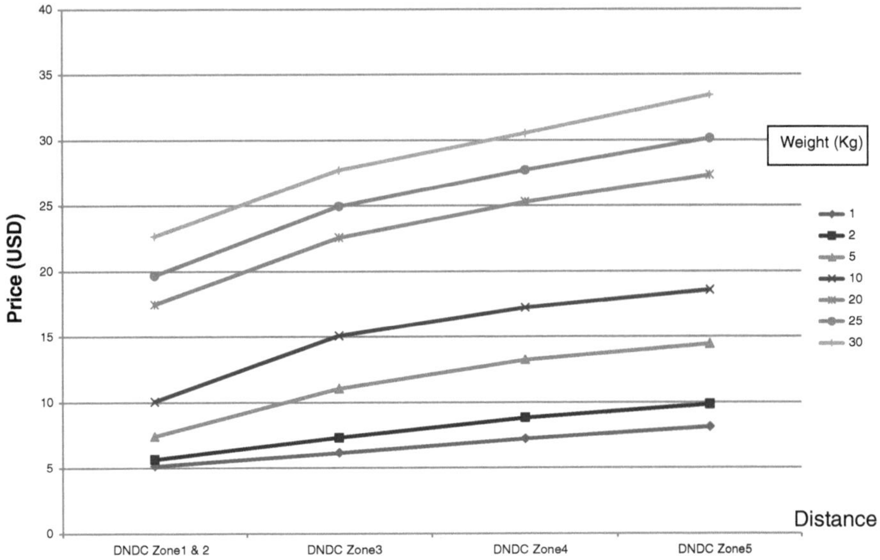

Fig. 5 USPS price (in USD) for domestic parcel delivery to zones *1* (closest) to *5* (furthest), by weight (kg). *Source* Marcus and Petropoulos

smooth curve within each weight category from zone 1 (closest to sender) to zone 5 (furthest from the sender). This is very different from Europe, where prices jump sharply when the first national border is crossed (Fig. 5).

US-EU comparisons are imperfect to the extent that the services are not exactly like for like, and for many other reasons; however, Fig. 6 attempts a rough comparison. Each of the six panels shows selected EU Member States in ascending order by the domestic price for a 1 kg parcel. The left-hand panels show the NPO's published price for domestic delivery within each of the selected Member States for different parcel weight categories; the right-hand panels show each NPO's published cross-border price for delivery to other Member States (either to those that are nearby, or to all EU Member States).[13] For comparison, each panel also depicts the most nearly comparable US Postal Service (USPS) price.[14]

Figure 6 shows that domestic EU prices appear to be somewhat comparable to US prices for short distances, but with a wide range of variation depending on the Member State. For 1 kg parcels (and noting that that parcels of up to 2 kg may

[13]We generally use prices to *Zone 1*, subject however to the caveat that Zone 1 is defined differently in each Member State.

[14]For domestic prices, USPS Zone 1–2 prices (covering distances of up to 150 miles or roughly 241 km) serve as the benchmark. For cross-border prices, USPS Zone 4 prices (covering distances of up to 600 miles or roughly 966 km) serve as the benchmark. Note that Zone 5 prices (up to 1000 miles) are not much different—they are 8–13 % higher than Zone 4, depending on the weight of the parcel.

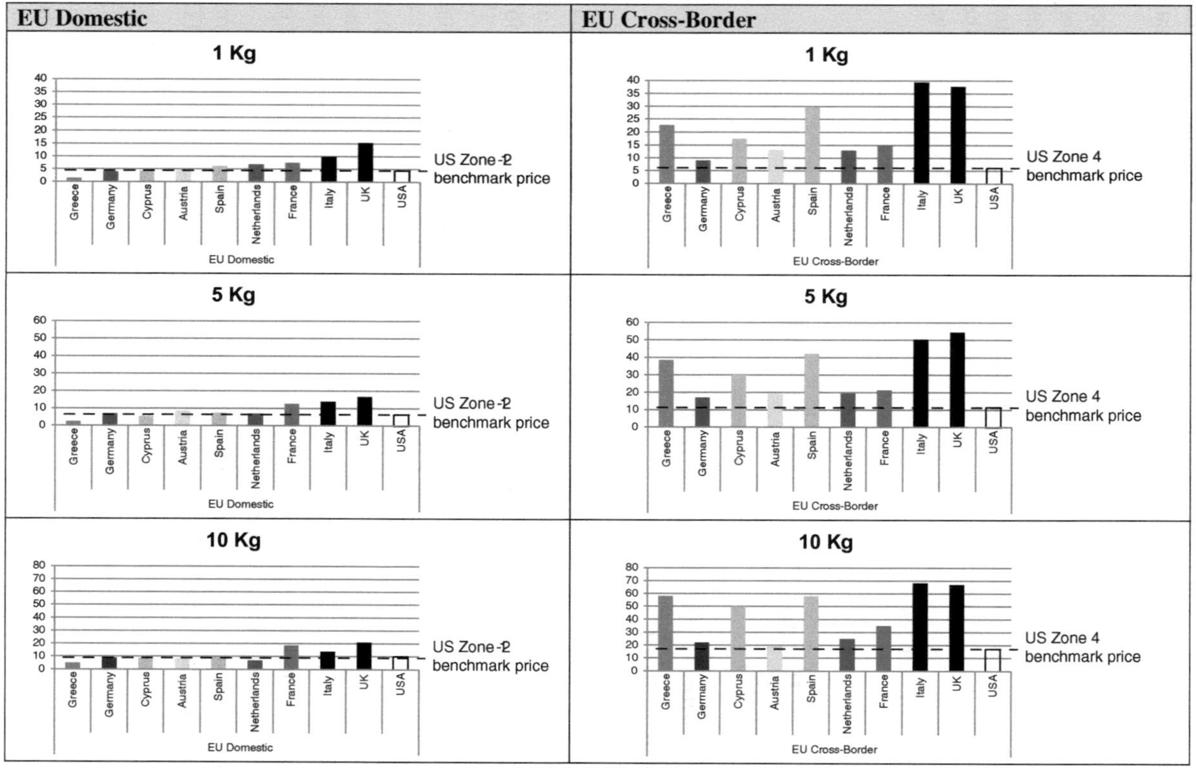

Fig. 6 Comparison of EU domestic and cross-border published retail prices to roughly comparable US postal service published prices (2016, USD). *Source* Marcus and Petropoulos

represent as much as 90 % of all parcels), relatively low domestic parcel delivery prices are found in countries that have low labour costs (such as Greece and Cyprus), and also in some of the larger economies such as Germany (presumably thanks to economies of scale). For 1 kg parcels, the published price for domestic delivery in Greece is 34 % of the comparable USPS price, while prices in Italy and in the UK are 221 and 346 %, respectively, of the US price.[15]

For cross-border prices, the spread is far greater, and all EU prices are higher than the corresponding US benchmark—some are much higher. The published price in Germany for cross-border delivery of a 1 kg parcel is 1.43 times greater than the US benchmark comparison price. Published prices in other Member States are at least twice the US comparison price. Published prices in Spain, Italy and the UK are respectively as much as 4.71, 6.27 and 6.02 times as great. By any measure, these are large differences.

5 Are Cross-Border Parcel Delivery Wholesale Prices Problematic?

5.1 What One Might Have Expected Based on Experience with Roaming

The economics of international mobile roaming (Marcus and Petropoulos 2016a; Philbeck et al. 2012; and Marcus et al. 2015) and the related economics of telecommunications interconnection (Laffont et al. 1998a, b, 2003) provide useful insights relevant to the postal sector. Prior to the Roaming Regulation of 2007,[16] (1) wholesale charges[17] were greatly in excess of real wholesale costs (representing a huge profit for the visited network); (2) these wholesale charges effectively set a floor for the retail price, since they represented a real cost to the network that provided the retail service (i.e. the home network); and (3) retail mark-ups over the wholesale charge that have tended to be in the range of 30 %, both before and after regulation, compounded the problem of high prices because they were effectively in addition to the already high wholesale charge (Fig. 7).

It would be natural to assume that the same should hold for cross-border parcel delivery. For instance, FTI (2011) assumed that excessive wholesale payments (TD

[15]Based on euro/USD exchange rates as of the first week of May 2016.

[16]The original Regulation was "Regulation (EC) No 717/2007 of the European Parliament and of The Council of 27 June 2007 on roaming on public mobile telephone networks within the Community and amending Directive 2002/21/EC". It was subsequently amended in 2009, 2012, and most recently with Regulation 2015/2120. With international mobile roaming, a mobile phone subscriber places or receives calls or SMS messages or uses mobile data services in a country other than the country in which he or she has his subscription.

[17]Prior to regulation in 2007, wholesale charges were roughly €1.00 per minute for calls made, and retail prices roughly €1.30 per minute (Stumpf 2001).

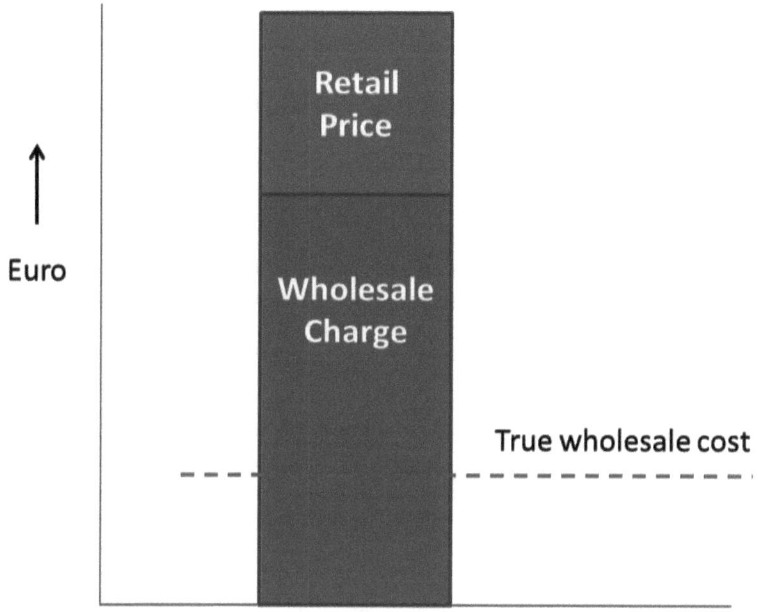

Fig. 7 Relationship between wholesale cost, wholesale charges, and retail price for mobile roaming. *Source* Marcus and Petropoulos

rates) contributed to high retail prices. Surprisingly, this seems not to be the case. Instead, wholesale TD rates seem to be not too high, but rather too low (see Sect. 5.2), with important implications for public policy (see Sect. 5.3).

5.2 *Wholesale TD Prices Appear to Be not Too High, but Rather Too Low*

The structure of TD and ILR wholesale prices is documented by the UPU, but specific rates do not appear to be publicly visible anywhere. Despite the dearth of publicly available information, there is nonetheless good reason to believe that TDs are below a reasonable estimate of NPOs' marginal costs. ILRs have been less studied, and in any case represent a relatively small fraction of total parcel volume.

As a threshold question, one needs to consider what the appropriate price should be. The TD should presumably cover the costs of delivery, but not of collection, in the destination country. (For international traffic, collection is performed in the sending country, not in the destination country). The UPU generally assumes that 70 % of the domestic postal rate is a reasonable proxy for the cost of delivery, which seems fairly reasonable.

There are signposts that TDs are not too high, but rather too low, in (1) the limited literature on this complex topic; (2) the presence of a remailing industry, and the need to use UPU rules to suppress it; and (3) periodic complaints that foreign senders (e.g. from China) can ship goods to Europe for less than European firms.

First, the literature definitely leans in the direction of TDs being too low. Even at the time of the Commission's Postal Green Paper (European Commission 1992), it was already recognised that "most Member States find that their unit costs for delivering [inward cross-border] traffic are not covered." Campbell argues consistently and persuasively that TDs are set well below the nominal cost benchmark of 70 % of the equivalent domestic price (EDP).[18] Two studies by Copenhagen Economics on behalf of the US Postal Regulatory Commission (US PRC) explain the TD system and attempt to estimate the adverse impact on societal welfare that flows from non-cost-based TDs. Copenhagen Economics found that "terminal dues received often are lower than the prices for last-mile handling of domestic (and comparable) letter post items in the receiving country" (Okholm et al. 2014, 2015).

The second clue to below-cost TDs is the presence of a remailing industry, and the need for the UPU to implement rules to hinder it. Remailing has been around for a long time. The European Commission's 1992 Postal Green Paper defined remailing as "a cross-border mail service offered by private operators in competition with the services offered by the postal administration in the country of the customer. … [One] type of remail involves mail being transported from country A to country B for remailing back to country A."

Economic distortions must be present if it is cost-effective to deliver a parcel from country A to country A (in effect a domestic delivery) by shipping it outside the country and then shipping it back. This can only be profitable if the international charge for inward traffic is less than the internal cost. Examples of this kind of arbitrage are well known in the world of telecommunications (where it is known as 'tromboning', and occurs only when international termination rates are less than domestic termination rates and/or on-net termination costs).[19]

Complaints that Chinese senders can ship goods to developed countries at lower cost than merchants within the respective countries are an additional indicator, and a confirmation that this is not merely a historical curiosity.[20] Again, this could only be the case if TDs are artificially depressed.

[18]See for instance Campbell (2014a) and especially Campbell (2014b).

[19]An analogous form of arbitrage came into play in conjunction with the Low Value Consignment Rule (LVCR) exemption from VAT, under which magazines were printed in Denmark, then shipped to the Åland Islands and shipped back to Denmark in order to avoid paying Danish VAT.

[20]See for instance Guo (2014) and Steiner (2016). The issue is by no means confined to the United States.

5.3 *Implications for Retail Services of Low TD Wholesale Payments*

Wholesale payments between network operators for roaming tend to be too high. However, wholesale payments between NPOs for cross-border parcel delivery tend to be too low. Given that the structure of payments is similar for these cross-border services, it might seem surprising that the outcomes should be opposite.

The primary cause[21] appears to be linked to the fact that NPOs are under no obligation (thanks to UPU rules) to make their services available to domestic competitors, nor to foreign competitors who are not NPOs. There is a *de facto* geographic partitioning. This partitioning creates a structure similar in its effects to that of a global cartel, where the NPOs provide favorable prices to one another that they are not obliged to offer to true competitors.

The NPOs do not appear to be under pricing pressure relative to their published retail prices for cross-border parcel delivery (see Sect. 4); however, they are probably subject to substantial competition from alternative parcel delivery platforms for the business of large scale shippers. Keeping TDs artificially low helps the NPOs collectively to compete against alternative cross-border parcel delivery platforms by providing discounted offers to large shippers.

To the extent that these TD wholesale payments might tend to be below relevant marginal costs, the implications for retail prices are profound. If retail prices for cross-border parcel delivery are too high, and wholesale TD payments (a major element of cost) are too low, one can only conclude that the mark-up for those who are obliged to purchase at published prices must be very high indeed. These mark-ups benefit the NPO in the country where the shipment originates, not the NPO that delivers the shipment.

Figure 8 depicts this. The left column represents the published retail price that consumers pay to ship a parcel domestically. The actual cost of delivery is assumed, consistent with UPU assumptions, to be 70 % of the published domestic price. For inward parcels, this same cost is assumed. The lower dashed line can thus be viewed as representing the true cost of delivery, which is the cost that the TDs are presumably meant to cover. Note that this cost is incurred by a different postal service, and in a different country, than the postal service that receives the retail revenue.

The middle column of Fig. 8 depicts both the wholesale payment that the sending postal operator makes to the receiving postal operator (the red rectangle), and the total retail revenue that the sending postal service receives (the total height of the blue column). The retail revenue at published prices is *at least twice as great* (see Sect. 4) as in the case of domestic parcel delivery. On the other hand, the

[21]The difference may also reflect the preferences of developing countries, who represent the majority of UPU members, and may moreover reflect the fact that in the distant past, there were no charges at all.

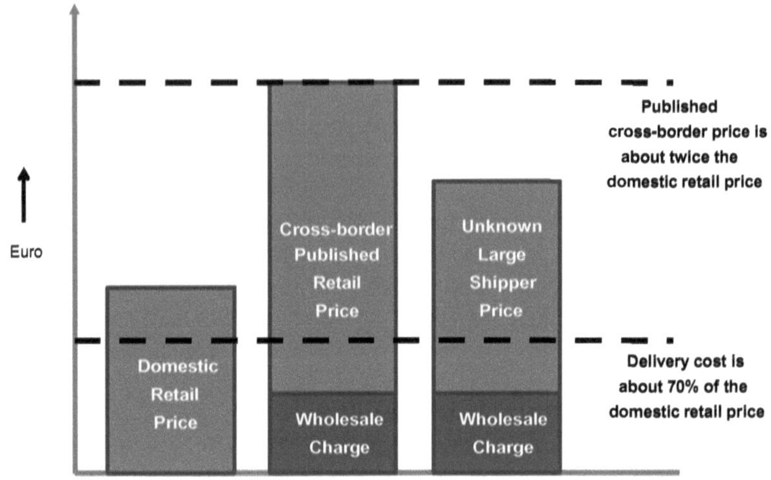

Fig. 8 Relationship between wholesale cost, wholesale charges, and published retail price for parcel delivery by a National Postal Operator (NPO). *Source* Marcus and Petropoulos

height of the red rectangle is actually *even less* than the cost of delivery to the receiving postal service.

The difference between the height of the blue column and that of the red column is then a measure of the NPO's profit (i.e. the gross mark-up of retail over wholesale). One must however bear in mind that the wholesale TD payment is not the only cost that the sending postal service incurs. In addition to the adaptation and labelling costs, there is also the transit of the parcel to the destination country, and probably also an additional sortation step. It is quite unlikely that these costs fully account for the wholesale-retail mark-up, but they should not be ignored. Even so, it would appear that the difference or 'spread' between price and cost must be far greater for cross-border parcel delivery by the NPOs than for domestic parcel delivery.

Again, cross-border parcel delivery differs from mobile roaming in important respects. For mobile roaming, high wholesale charges (both to allies and to competitors) can be viewed as the primary cause of high retail prices. For cross-border parcel delivery services by NPOs, by contrast, low wholesale charges (available only to other NPOs) are not the primary cause of high list prices; rather, they serve as an indication of a market segment where competition is distorted such that low costs do not translate into low published retail prices.

The right column in Fig. 8 depicts the situation for large senders. The wholesale cost to the receiving postal service is presumably largely independent of whether the original sender is large or small, and the TDs paid are likewise unlikely to depend on who the original sender might be; however, the retail price will tend to be lower, and therefore the mark-up of retail over the wholesale TD will also be correspondingly lower. Amazingly little is publicly known about these prices.

6 The Commission's Proposed Approach

On 25 May 2016, the European Commission put forward a proposed Regulation on cross-border parcel delivery services.[22] If enacted by the European Parliament and the Council, would it address the problems identified? It is necessary to consider the key provisions of the proposed Regulation one by one.

Article 3 obliges all parcel delivery service providers[23] to provide key data basic indicators to national postal regulatory authorities. Article 4 requires universal service providers that offer parcel delivery services to provide information on non-discounted retail prices and on terminal rates (terminal dues and inward land rates) to national postal regulatory authorities. The Commission will publish these tariffs, and will attempt to make individuals and small businesses more aware of available delivery options.

Article 5 obliges the national regulatory authority to assess the affordability of the cross-border tariffs obtained under Article 4, and to make its findings available to the national regulatory authorities of the other Member States, to the national competition authority in the same Member State, and to the Commission (which will then publish a non-confidential version). The assessment of affordability would take into account prices for delivery within the Member State, as well as any terminal rates paid.

Article 6 requires universal service providers to meet all reasonable requests to enable parcel delivery services (presumably in other Member states) to use the universal service provider's facilities for the provision of cross-border parcel delivery services. The universal service provider must publish a reference offer; must make specific offers within thirty days of receiving a request; and if no agreement is reached, they are subject to the judgment of the national regulatory authority.

Our sense is the proposed Regulation is generally on target. The information gathering requirements in Articles 3 and 4 address long-standing gaps in the ability of policymakers to understand the functioning of this complex sector (in which government plays a large role in most Member States). The Commission rightly understood that it is necessary to capture data not only about retail prices, but also about wholesale payments between the NPOs; and they rightly reserved for themselves the prerogative to specify the templates of data that parcel delivery services would be obliged to collect.

Article 5 creates for the first time a clear and externally enforceable obligation for national postal regulatory authorities to consider the appropriateness of tariffs not only for domestic delivery (which most if not all were presumably doing in any case), but also the affordability and appropriateness of cross-border services (which appears not to have been done at all). Article 6 attempts, by opening arrangements based on terminal rates to cross-border competitors (and not just to universal service

---

[22]COM(2016) 285 final.

[23]Parcel delivery services that are small (fewer than 50 employees) and that operate only within a single Member State are exempted.

providers), to address long-standing price distortions by introducing basic competition into this part of the postal sector for the first time.

The approach taken in Articles 5 and 6 is logical, but it is different from the approach that was taken for international mobile roaming. For roaming, excessive wholesale prices are a root cause of high retail prices. For cross-border parcel delivery, if wholesale prices are instead too low rather than too high, the problem lies not with the absolute level of wholesale charges, but rather with the very large 'spread' between the retail price charged to individuals and micro-enterprises versus the low level of wholesale payments in the form of terminal rates (see Fig. 8). Making terminal rate wholesale price arrangements available for the first time to delivery services other than NPOs should in principle shrink the spread down to competitive levels.

The obvious risk in any strategy along these lines is that, if done without a simultaneous corresponding adjustment to the (currently below nominal cost) terminal dues rates, it might lead to massive arbitrage. Each NPO's competitors would have access to the NPO's delivery network at a price that is in some sense below the cost of that service to the NPO itself. Competitors could therefore beat the NPO on price even when using the NPO's own network to deliver. It is clear that an upward adjustment to terminal dues rates is needed. If these rates are available to *domestic* competitors—a point on which the proposed Regulation is not entirely clear—then arbitrage seems quite likely. If not, one must still consider whether a resurgence of so-called A-B-A remailing (shipping parcels outside the country in order to ship them back in at rates that are lower than domestic) could raise serious arbitrage concerns.

In order to prevent this, the NPOs will be strongly motivated to raise TDs to levels approximating the true marginal cost of delivery. In a pure free market environment, this would likely happen spontaneously, and would address the long-standing economic distortions in this market.

Cross-border parcel delivery is clearly not a pure free market environment, the nominal liberalization of the postal sector notwithstanding. At global level, these prices are subject to price caps from the Universal Postal Union (UPU); within Europe, to unknown restrictions from the REIMS II agreement. There are also decades of experience with current arrangements that possibly cannot be overcome overnight. The question that we therefore pose is, will these arrangements correct themselves, or will complementary policy measures be needed at European level in order to ensure that prices adapt as they should? The answer to this question is not immediately apparent.

7 Conclusions

Published retail prices for cross-border parcel delivery by the NPOs are indeed high. These high prices represent an impediment to cross-border e-commerce in the EU.

Wholesale payments among the NPOs are not literally the cause of high published retail prices for cross-border delivery, but payments that appear to be depressed relative to real costs serve as a strong indication of a market segment where competition is distorted such that low costs do not translate into low published retail prices. That the low wholesale prices are available only to other NPOs appears to play a crucial role in these distortions.

The European Commission's proposed Regulation is generally on target. Providing price transparency for consumers and empowering national postal regulatory authorities to gather information on wholesale charges and retail prices and to take action against over-pricing are in order.

The proposed Regulation also calls for opening up the apparently below-cost wholesale arrangements to true competitors. This seems to be a very promising way to introduce greater market rationality into this complex space; however, the consequences are difficult to predict. The apparent underpricing of cross-border parcel delivery by the NPOs has been possible only because these arrangements were unavailable to true competitors. If cross-border delivery were available to true competitors at wholesale prices similar to current TD rates, there would likely to be numerous opportunities for competitors to sell services based on NPO networks at prices lower than those at which the NPOs themselves can sell them; moreover, there would seem to be numerous opportunities for arbitrage.

The NPOs should in principle be motivated to raise TDs themselves in order to avoid these problems. This would help address the long-standing economic distortions in this market. In light of price caps at UPU level and the complex intertwined relationships in the sector in general, it is not entirely clear whether this readjustment can happen without further complementary policy interventions. This is an issue that merits close attention going forward.

Acknowledgments The authors would like to express their deep appreciation to James I. Campbell Jr., and would like to thank Robert Clarke and Joost Vantomme for numerous helpful comments. Research assistance by Elena Vaccarino is gratefully acknowledged.

References

Armstrong, M. (1998). Network interconnection in telecommunications. *Economics Journal, 108*, 545–564.

BEREC. (2016). *International roaming: BEREC benchmark data report, April–September 2015*, BoR (16) 28 Rev.1.

Body of European Regulators for Electronic Communications (BEREC), and European Regulators Group for Postal Services (ERGP). (2015). Price transparency and regulatory oversight of cross-border parcels delivery, taking into account possible regulatory insights from the electronic communications sector: Joint BEREC-ERGP opinion. *BoR, 15*, 214.

Brune, D. (2013). E-commerce and opportunities for cross-border parcels in Europe, presentation at the 14th Königswinter seminar on postal economics.

Campbell, J. I Jr. (2014a). *Draft proposals for the UPU Istanbul congress—Terminal dues*, Available at www.state.gov/documents/organization/232813.pdf, Accessed May 14, 2016.

Campbell, J. I Jr. (2014b). Estimating the effects of UPU terminal dues, 2014–2017. In *8th bi-annual postal economics conference on e-commerce, digital economy and delivery services*, Toulouse.

Certain Public Postal Operators. (1997). Agreement for the remuneration of mandatory deliveries of cross border mails (REIMS II).

Claes, A., & Vergote, W. (2016). *Econometric study on parcel list prices*, Available at http://ec.europa.eu/DocsRoom/documents/14647, Accessed May 14, 2016.

E-commerce Europe. (2015). 2014 Key B2C E-commerce Data of Goods & Services at a Glance.

European Commission. (1992). Green paper on the development of the single market for postal services, COM (91) 476 final.

European Commission. (2013). *Mergers: Commission prohibits proposed acquisition of TNT express by UPS—frequently asked questions*, Available at http://europa.eu/rapid/press-release_MEMO-13-48_en.htm, Accessed May 14, 2016.

European Commission. (2015). A digital single market strategy for Europe, SWD (2015) 100 final.

Eurostat. (2015). Companies engaged in online activities: Report, *Flash Eurobarometer 413*.

Eurostat. (2016). *E-commerce statistics for individuals*, Available at http://ec.europa.eu/eurostat/statistics-explained/index.php/E-commerce_statistics_for_individuals, Accessed April 9, 2016.

FTI Consulting. (2011). Community cross-border parcel delivery, study for European Commission, Directorate General Internal Markets and Services.

Guo, J. (2014). The postal service is losing millions a year to help you buy cheap stuff from China, *Washington Post*, Available at https://www.washingtonpost.com/news/storyline/wp/2014/09/12/the-postal-service-is-losing-millions-a-year-to-help-you-buy-cheap-stuff-from-china/

Laffont, J.-J., Rey, P., & Tirole, J. (1998a). Network competition I: Overview and nondiscriminatory pricing. *RAND Journal of Economics, 29*, 1–37.

Laffont, J.-J., Rey, P., & Tirole, J. (1998b). Network competition II: price discrimination. *RAND Journal of Economics, 29*, 38–56.

Laffont, J.-J., Marcus, J. S., Rey, P., & Tirole, J. (2003). Internet interconnection and the off-net-cost pricing principle. *RAND Journal of Economics, 34*, 370–390.

Marcus, J. S., Christin-Isabel, G., & Clarke, R. (2015). International mobile roaming (IMR) across the Gulf Corporation Council (GCC) region, consultation and report prepared for the Gulf Corporation Council roaming working group.

Marcus, J. S., & Petropoulos, G. (2016a). *E-commerce in Europe: Parcel delivery prices in a digital single market*, Bruegel.

Marcus, J. S., & Petropoulos, G. (2016b). *Challenging prospects for roam like at home*, Bruegel.

Okholm, H. B., Boivie, A. M., Russell, N., & Przybyszewski, J. (2014). The economics of terminal dues: Final report, Copenhagen economics, prepared for the U.S. postal regulatory commission, Available at: http://www.prc.gov/sites/default/files/reports/The%20Economics%20of%20Terminal%20Dues_final%20report%20300914.pdf

Okholm, H. B., Boivie, A. M., Edkins, S., & Gårdebrink, J. (2015). Quantification of financial transfers caused by Universal Postal Union terminal dues: Final report, Copenhagen Economics, prepared for the U.S. Postal Regulatory Commission, available at: http://www.prc.gov/sites/default/files/papers/Quantification%20of%20financial%20transfers%20caused%20by%20Universal%20Postal%20Union%20terminal%20dues_final%20report.pdf

Okholm, H. B., Boivie, A. M., Wahl, J. S., Jensen, K., Nygard, A., & Basalisco, B. (2016). "Principles of e-commerce parcel prices" Copenhagen economics, prepared for PostEurop, Available at: https://www.copenhageneconomics.com/publications/publication/principles-of-e-commerce-delivery-prices

Philbeck, I., Marcus, J. S., Mikkelsen, J., & Neu, W. (2012). Trans-Tasman roaming: Service costs, a study for the Australian Department of Broadband, Communications and the Digital Economy and the New Zealand Ministry of Business, Innovation and Employment (MBIE).

Rochet, J-C., & Tirole, J. (2004). *Two sided markets: An overview*, Available at: web.mit.edu/14.271/www/rochet_tirole.pdf

Steiner, I. (2016). Online sellers fume over low epacket postal rates from China, *eCOMMERCE Bytes*, Available at http://www.ecommercebytes.com/C/blog/blog.pl?/pl/2016/1/1453344622.html

Stumpf, U. (2001). Prospects for improving competition in mobile roaming, *WIK Report* Nr. 232, Wissenschaftliches Institut für Infrastruktur und Kommunikationsdienste GmbH.

U.S. Postal Markets and Delivery Liberalization: A Simulation Approach

Margaret M. Cigno and Edward S. Pearsall

1 Introduction

The likely outcomes of liberalizing, or adapting regulations to already liberalized postal markets, are important concerns for many incumbent postal operators. Entry into liberalized postal markets can be analyzed as a simultaneous game with Nash equilibria with the incumbent as price leader if entry occurs. This approach can be extended to encompass multi-product markets, to accept alternative economic objectives, to accommodate various kinds of regulatory controls and to cases where the incumbent is not the price leader.

It is rarely possible to conduct scientific experiments with an actual economic system. Simulation offers a practical alternative by substituting a model intended to mimic the system. However, the rules for setting up controlled experiments, taking observations, and analyzing results all remain about the same. Our simulator mimics the behavior over time of Postal Operators (POs) and Entrant Competitors (ECs) in inter-related postal markets. Our research method sets up these markets as games and solves them numerically using the method of fictitious play as described in a companion paper (Cigno and Pearsall 2016).

We explore critical choices applicable to all posts but focus on the current U.S. postal regulatory regime. The present characteristics of U.S. postal regulation include a vaguely defined Universal Service Obligation (USO), a large and well-protected reserved area, rules that tend to impose a price leadership role on the U.S. Postal Service (USPS), a system of product-specific caps and floors, and, federal ownership with Congressional oversight. The last leaves USPS without a well-defined economic objective. Several end-to-end U.S. postal markets are

M.M. Cigno (✉) · E.S. Pearsall
Postal Regulatory Commission (PRC), Washington, D.C., USA
e-mail: espearsall@verizon.net

M. Crew et al. (eds.), *The Changing Postal and Delivery Sector*,
Topics in Regulatory Economics and Policy,
DOI 10.1007/978-3-319-46046-8_11

already liberalized.[1] However, for most categories of mail, USPS enjoys a monopoly with statutory barriers to entry to any direct competitors. In this paper we explore the economic consequences of liberalizing and partially de-regulating these national markets.

We conduct computer simulations of equilibrium for increased entry and relaxed regulation. The scenarios include variations in USPS's reserved area, less restrictive price controls, a floor on USPS's profits, and arrangements that both do and do not leave USPS as a price leader.

Most important, we treat entry into postal markets as endogenous. Potential entrants are assumed to enter and exit liberalized postal markets in response to profit opportunities. USPS remains in all markets to meet its present USO. Our simulations were conducted with demand and cost functions calibrated to FY 2015 USPS data and elasticity matrices derived from recent econometric research.

Two characteristic properties of many of the equilibria found by the simulator are limit-pricing by USPS and stochastic offerings of different combinations of postal products by potential entrants. At equilibrium limit-pricing leaves a potential entrant with the same profit on each product combination. Then, the potential entrant's probabilistic entries leave USPS unable to improve its objective by altering its prices. An entrant's prices for each product combination are chosen later to maximize the entrant's profit given USPS's prices. (We later include in the model the possibility that the entrant chooses its price without knowing the incumbent's price.) Our model does not make the assumption of standard limit pricing models that the entrant will not enter at the limit price. Unlike those models, our simultaneous game approach treats entry as endogenous with a probability that is not necessarily zero or one.

In Sect. 2 we provide our theoretical approach to understanding a liberalized single-product single-entrant postal market. Our model is unconventional, so in Sect. 3 we digress to explain how the conventional limit pricing approach mischaracterizes decision processes as sequential and requires the auxiliary assumption that no entry occurs at the limit price. In Sect. 4 we set out our data and simulation control settings for a benchmark outcome of postal liberalization in the U.S. under a relaxed regulatory regime. This Base Case is examined in detail in Sect. 5. In Sects. 6–10, we examine sets of simulations designed to exhibit the consequences of pursuing various general alternatives to the current U.S. regulatory system and controlled changes to the parameters of the Base Case. Our numerical results are displayed in five tables accompanying our analysis.

[1]Entrants, including UPS, FedEx and others, have competed with USPS in the delivery markets for Priority mail, Express mail and single-piece Package services since the mid-1970s. In FY 2015 this liberalization applied to only 2.4 % of U.S. domestic mail by volume and 21.7 % by revenue.

Our simulations indicate that USPS can survive liberalization with a smaller reserved area and that effective postal price regulation will be necessary following liberalization. However, effective regulation would require only a few elementary controls. Section 11 concludes by outlining the elements of a reformed regulatory system for USPS based upon our findings.

2 How Liberalized Postal Markets Work

The concepts underlying our simulator apply when an incumbent Postal Operator (PO) remains in a market that has been opened to Entrant Competitors (ECs). Typically, the pre-existing price regulation is relaxed but not eliminated and the PO usually assumes the role of price leader. Any regulation tends to make the prices of the PO sticky by imposing administrative rules or enforcing competition laws that delay the PO's pricing responses to an unregulated EC. Entry and exit by an EC, although we treat it as costless, is also sticky because entry and exit normally require substantial lead times. However, an EC's prices are not ordinarily subject to regulation and can be changed rapidly. Therefore, an EC's prices are not sticky and the EC is in a position to observe the PO's prices before it must set its own (although it does not observe the PO's prices prior to its decision to enter).

Following market opening, the PO may keep some of the advantages it gained as a monopoly. It may actually retain its monopoly over a reserved area of services. The *quid pro quo* for a reserved area is a Universal Service Obligation (USO). The PO is obligated to remain in markets that it might otherwise abandon. A PO may also have advantages that encourage it to remain in postal markets even when not required to do so. A reserved area without the USO may still leave the PO with economies of scope and scale that an EC cannot match. Market opening may also leave the PO in possession of material resources and legal protections that potential EC's cannot command.

Conversely, the role of price leader following a market opening may be a disadvantage since it prevents the PO from setting its prices based upon the product combinations and prices selected by ECs on entry. If a PO can react to an EC's prices in this way, it will act as a Bertrand oligopolist and employ a different set of prices for each combination of products it encounters from ECs.

In the single-good case the market has properties that define a non-cooperative non-zero-sum two-person game between the PO and EC (Pearsall and Trozzo 2008; Pearsall 2011, 2016; Cigno and Pearsall 2016). The PO's pure strategies are the different prices P_I (for "Incumbent") that it may set. P_I is set before the PO learns if the EC is *in* the market and remains unchanged. The EC has only two pure strategies, to be either *in* or *out* of the market. Entry and exit by the EC have no associated fixed costs. However, both require a lead time so the EC does not know P_I with certainty at the time that it chooses to be either *in* or *out*. Equally important, the PO cannot affect the EC's decision to be *in* or *out*. Therefore, the PO's price choice and the EC's decision to be *in* or *out* are made simultaneously.

The payoffs are determined by the player's objective functions. If the EC enters the market, it sets its price to maximize its profits based on P_I, which it observes after entry, producing a reaction function relating P_E to P_I. The PO has two objective functions: an objective function with the EC *in* the market (incorporating that reaction function), and, one with the EC *out*.[2] An incumbent government-owned PO's objective may be to maximize profit, welfare, cost, revenue or some combination of these. To describe the single-good case we treat the PO as maximizing profit.

The EC's strategies may be extended to include stochastic entry by introducing a probability of entry μ in the range [0, 1]. Stochastic entry by the EC becomes relevant if, at the price chosen by the PO, the EC would be indifferent to being *in* or *out* (recognizing that the EC would know P_I when it sets P_E). When the PO sets P_I this way it is engaged in limit-pricing. In the single-product case the EC's profit is limited to zero because the EC always has the option of not entering the market.

We assume that the standard neo-classical conditions regarding demand and cost are respected so that there must exist a Nash equilibrium consisting of a price P_I for the PO and a probability of entry μ for the EC that are simultaneously optimal against each other. The game is solved partly by induction. The EC's reaction function is imported into the PO's profit function with the EC *in*. Then equilibrium is defined by two conditions: P_I maximizes the PO's expected profit given μ, and μ maximizes the EC's profit over the range [0, 1]. Depending on demand and cost, the equilibrium can occur at a limit price that leaves the EC indifferent between being *in* or *out*. When this happens the EC's entries and exits are stochastic. The equilibrium prices P_I and P_E are usually unique.

Equilibrium takes one of three forms:

E1: PO monopoly.

E2: Duopoly with price leadership by the PO.

E3: Limit-pricing by the PO and stochastic entry by the EC.

The equilibria E1 and E2 describe outcomes of the game when it is optimal for the EC to employ a pure strategy. In E1 the EC finds that it is unprofitable to be *in* even when the PO sets a monopoly price. Consequently, $\mu = 0$ and the EC is always *out* and the market becomes a PO monopoly. In E2, $\mu = 1$ and the incumbent PO finds that it is unprofitable to try to drive the EC out of the market.

[2]The PO's objective with the EC *in* the market is $f_I(P_I, P_E)^{in}$, and, with the EC *out* is $f_I(P_I)^{out}$. $f_I(P_I, P_E)^{in}$ becomes $f_I(P_I, P_E(P_i))^{in}$ when we install the EC's reaction function $P_E(P_I) = ArgMax_{P_E}\{f_E(P_I, P_E)\}$ for P_E. The EC's profit function is $f_E(P_I, P_E)$ when the EC is *in* and zero when it is out. A Nash equilibrium consists of a pair of strategies for the two players that are simultaneously optimal against each other. The PO's strategy solves the problem:: $Max_{P_I}\{\mu f_I(P_I, P_E(P_I))^{in} + (1-\mu) f_I(P_I)^{out}\}$ given μ and the EC's strategy solves $Max_\mu\{\mu f_E(P_I, P_E(P_I)) | 0 \leq \mu \leq 1\}$ given P_I. Ordinarily, the EC's solution to this problem is to simply be *in* or *out*. The EC chooses $\mu = 1$ if $f_E(P_I, P_E(P_I)) > 0$ and chooses $\mu = 0$ if $f_E(P_I, P_E(P_I)) < 0$. However, it is necessary to formulate the EC's problem in a way that accommodates ties. Then, the EC's maximization problem may also be solved by a probabilistic mix such that $0 < \mu < 1$.

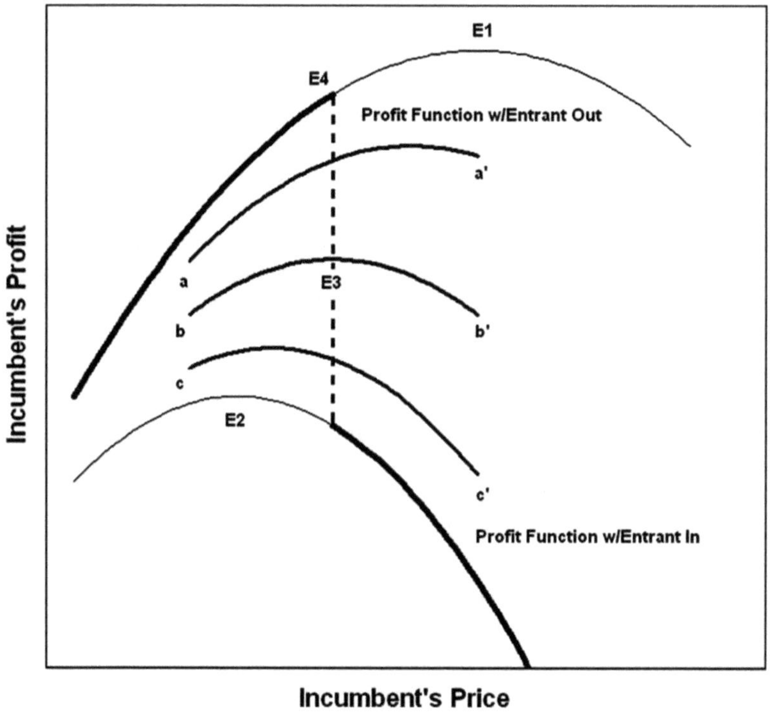

Fig. 1 Forms of Equilibrium

The EC is always *in* and the market becomes a duopoly with the PO acting as the price leader. E3 is a solution consisting of a limit price P_I, which leaves the EC with a zero profit whether *in* or *out*, and a mixed strategy such that $0 < \mu < 1$.[3]

Figure 1 depicts the three forms of equilibrium. The PO's expected profit function with the EC *in* is the parabola at the bottom of the figure. This function is drawn with the EC's reaction function inserted for the EC's price in the PO's profit function. The profit function with the EC *out* is the parabola at the top of the figure. This function is independent of the EC's price. E1 is located at the maximum of the PO's profit function with the EC *out*. It is the equilibrium if the EC always remains out of the market. E2 is at the maximum of the PO's profit function with the EC *in*

[3]To find μ, we differentiate the expected value of the PO's objective function, $E[f_I] = \mu f_I(P_I, P_E)^{in} + (1-\mu) f_I(P_I)^{out}$ with respect to P_I, set the result equal to zero, and solve for: $\mu = \frac{df_I^{out}}{dP_I} / \left[\frac{df_I^{out}}{dP_I} - \frac{df_I^{in}}{dP_I}\right]$, with the derivatives evaluated at equilibrium. The derivative with the EC *in* has two parts $\frac{df_I^{in}}{dP_I} = \frac{\partial f_I^{in}}{\partial P_I} + \frac{\partial f_I^{in}}{\partial P_E}\frac{dP_E(P_I)}{dP_I}$. The first part is the direct effect of the PO's price changes on the PO's profit. The second term is an indirect effect that occurs when the EC sees the change and responds by changing its own price.

and with the EC's price set according to its reaction function. E2 is the equilibrium if the EC is always *in*.

The vertical dashed line connecting the two profit functions is drawn at the PO price that leaves the EC with a zero economic profit. Below the dashed line, the EC takes a loss if it is *in*; above the dashed line the EC gets a positive economic profit if it is *in*. The EC's profits are calculated under the assumption that the EC knows P_I when it sets P_E.

Neither E1 nor E2 can be the equilibrium as Fig. 1 has been drawn. At E1 the EC's profit is positive so it will not remain permanently out of the market as required for the monopoly outcome E1. At E2 the EC takes a loss so it will not remain in the market as required for the duopoly equilibrium E2.

Equilibrium occurs at E3, an intermediate point on the dashed line corresponding to μ. E3 is a stochastic equilibrium because $0 < \mu < 1$. Curves such as a-a′, b-b′ and c-c′ describe the PO's expected profit as a function of P_I for different fixed values of μ. These curves are different weighted averages of the PO's two profit functions. Each of them reaches a maximum at a different price P_I. The equilibrium E3 occurs along the curve b-b' where the price P_I that maximizes the PO's expected profit coincides with the price that leaves the EC with no profit or loss. E3 does not occur where a-a′ or c-c′ reach their maximums because only a PO price corresponding to the vertical dashed line will leave μ unchanged as the game is played. PO prices to the right of the dashed line cause μ to increase because the EC responds to these prices by entering and remaining *in*. Prices to the left cause μ to decrease because the EC exits and remains *out*. The curve b-b′ is the only curve along which the PO can maximize its expected profit without disturbing μ. Therefore, E3 is the Nash equilibrium.

Our simulator extends concepts that apply to the case of a profit maximizing PO offering a single mail service and a single profit-maximizing EC also offering only a single service. It generalizes and applies this single-product model of a liberalized postal market to multiple markets for inter-related postal services. It also generalizes the model with respect to the PO's possible objectives, for various ways that a collection of postal markets might be liberalized, for multiple ECs, and for different kinds of price constraints that might be imposed by a regulator. The simulator is also capable of relaxing the assumption that the PO is the price leader.[4]

The simulator treats liberalized postal markets as a non-zero-sum, non-cooperative, multi-person game and finds the game's Nash equilibrium by our numerical method based on "fictitious play". ECs react to USPS's pricing by choosing combinations of products and prices that maximize their own profit. USPS is assumed to observe the frequencies of entrants' product choices and to set its own

[4]The only difference this makes in the single-product case is that the PO optimizes its choice of P_I against the EC's specific choice of P_E, and not against the EC's reaction function. To calculate μ for this game we just delete the second term of the derivative $\frac{df_I^{in}}{dP_I}$ in footnote 3. This will always result in a higher value for μ because the deleted term is positive.

prices to maximize the expected value of its economic objective subject to constraints imposed under an assumed regulatory regime. The simulator converges iteratively on USPS's prices and frequencies for entrants' product choices and their associated prices that constitute the game's Nash equilibrium.[5]

3 How Liberalized Postal Markets Do Not Work

Our model of liberalized postal markets is unconventional. A conventional model[6] of a single-product liberalized market would place the Nash equilibrium for limit-pricing at the point labeled E4 in Fig. 1. At E4 the PO sets a price that leaves the EC indifferent between being *in* or *out* and the EC always chooses to remain *out*.

The conventional model finds an equilibrium different from E3 by making different assumptions. First, the conventional model treats the strategy choices of P_I and μ for a single play of the game as sequential rather than simultaneous. The PO is assumed to choose P_I before the EC chooses to be *in* or *out* and the EC knows P_I before it must choose. Second, the EC is assumed to always remain *out* if it will be left with a zero profit from entering. This auxiliary assumption makes it unnecessary to consider any values of μ except zero and one.

The first assumption allows the PO to control the EC's choice to be *in* or *out* for a single play of the game. The PO is able to choose any point along the heavily outlined segments of its profit functions in Fig. 1. E4 is the point at which the PO's profit is maximized along these segments. The second assumption effectively erases all of the vertical dashed line except the point E4. When the PO sets the limit price that leaves the EC with no profit, the PO ends up at E4 and not at some lower point on the dashed line.

The conventional model and our model have different equilibria when the PO engages in limit pricing. These equilibria are mutually exclusive. If the

[5]For multiple products the EC's pure strategies consist of product combinations indexed t drawn from a feasible set of such combinations T. μ_t is the probability of use assigned to the combination t. The PO's strategies are price vectors denoted P_I. A Nash equilibrium consists of a pair of strategies for the two players that are simultaneously optimal against each other. The EC's mixed strategy of entry and exit using various product combinations solves the problem: $Max_{\mu_t}\left\{\sum_{t\in T}\mu_t f_E^t\left(P_I, P_E^t(P_I)\right) \middle| 0 \le \mu_t \le 1 \forall t \in T \text{ and } \sum_{t\in T}\mu_t = 1\right\}$ given the prices chosen by the PO. Ordinarily, the solution to this problem takes the form of a single combination. That is, the EC simply sets $\mu_t \equiv 1$ for the pure strategy that yields the largest profit $f_E^t\left(P_I, P_E^t(P_I)\right)$. However, it is necessary to formulate the EC's problem in a way that accommodates ties. Then, the EC's maximization problem is also solved by probabilistic mixes of two or more equally-profitable product combinations. The PO's strategy is a vector of prices for its own products that solves the problem: $Max_{P_I}\left\{\sum_{t\in T}\mu_t f_I^t\left(P_I, P_E^t(P_I)\right) \middle| P_I \in S\right\}$ given the probabilities that describe the EC's entries and exits. The set S embodies the restrictions imposed on the PO's prices by the regulator. In our simulator these restrictions are all linear inequalities.

[6]A conventional model of a liberalized market is the contestable market model of Baumol et al. (1988).

conventional model is correct then E3 cannot be an equilibrium because the EC will never enter. The conventional model moves the limit pricing outcome to E4. If our model is correct then E4 is not an equilibrium because the PO would try to move along the profit function with the entrant *out* to reach the maximum E1. With our model the PO will raise its price above the limit price if it believes that the EC will not enter.

In order to identify the most appropriate model it is necessary to recognize that both the PO's choice of P_I and the EC's choice to be *in* or *out* are decisions that cannot be made instantly effective and thus each has to be made before the other's choice is known. At present, USPS must declare its prices to the U.S. regulator more than 60 days before putting them into effect and must leave the prices in place for at least six months. Although this appears to be advance notice, it is hard to see how an EC could enter or leave a U.S. national postal market any more quickly. We can also expect that the EC will not reveal its decision to be *in* or *out* if it can avoid it since the information may be exploited by the PO. Therefore, the most reasonable assumption is that both the PO and the ECs make their choices simultaneously without knowing what the other player will do.

A PO should know this and would not engage in a futile effort to affect an EC's entry decision *ex-post* by trying to move along the outlined segments of the profit functions in Fig. 1. Instead, a rational PO would form an estimate of μ from whatever information is at hand and maximize its expected profit based upon the estimate. This leads the PO to move along a curve such as aa′, bb′ or cc′ in Fig. 1. Likewise, the EC decides to be *in* or *out* of the market without knowing for certain the PO price that it will face. Thus the PO's choice of P_I and the EC's decision to be *in* or *out* are best depicted as simultaneous decisions, not sequential as is done by the conventional model.

4 Data Inputs and Controls

We simulate the markets for six aggregated categories of domestic mail. These categories correspond to the broadly-defined classes used in current USPS reporting to the Postal Regulatory Commission (PRC). The labels used in our tables are:

1Cls	First-Class Mail
PrOth	Priority Mail and Expedited Packages
2Per	Periodicals
3Std	Standard Mail
4Pkg	Market-Dominant Packages
PclSR	Parcel Select and Return Services

Potential entrants in postal markets offer services that roughly correspond to these six categories. However, we have generally assumed that these services would be somewhat imperfect substitutes for those offered by USPS. At present there are such entrants only in the markets PrOth and PclSR.

The simulator extrapolates from demand models for USPS mail service in existing markets to construct models of postal markets after entry for each possible entrant product combination. The extrapolations are made as described in Cigno and Pearsall (2016) using elasticity tables drawn from recent econometric studies. The demand model is calibrated to USPS volumes, revenues and market shares for FY 2015. USPS's FY 2015 market shares by volume for those markets with entrants were PrOth: 0.494 and PclSR: 0.299.

The simulator employs a highly simplified version of the cost driver model used by USPS for cost attribution. For entrants we assumed generally lower institutional costs than USPS. Weights for the driver calculations are ratios of unit volume-variable costs for each class to the unit volume-variable cost for an average piece of First-Class mail. In effect, the cost driver is the equivalent volume of First-Class mail.

The calibrated demand and cost models were applied to simulate postal markets under existing entry limitations with FY 2015 average revenues per piece installed as USPS's prices. The resulting simulated equilibrium approximated USPS volumes, market shares, revenues and costs in FY 2015. Net costs for an entrant were calculated to leave a zero profit. Consequently, our simulated profits for entrants are profit changes measured from their (unknown) combined profit level in FY 2015.

The demand and cost models are linearized at a point corresponding to an assumed basis solution as described in Cigno and Pearsall (2016). For the basis solution all markets are entered by potential competitors and USPS and its competitors all charge the same prices for similar services. The simulation uses a combination of observed and assumed values for USPS market shares as follows:

1Cls: 0.900, PrOth: 0.494, 2Per: 0.800, 3Std: 0.700, 4Pkg: 0.700, PclSR: 0.299

The marginal diversion rate is the rate at which USPS and an entrant divert mail from each other as demand shifts in response to an unmatched price change. The marginal diversion rates are applied to derive the demand functions for the different product combinations that the entrant may use when entering. The marginal diversion rates for most of our simulations are:

1Cls: 0.900, PrOth: 0.775, 2Per: 0.900, 3Std: 0.900, 4Pkg: 0.900, PclSR: 0.780

The diversion rates for PrOth and PclSR were derived as part of our calibration of the model. The others are assumed values reflecting the belief that the postal services offered by an entrant in these markets would be close substitutes for the services presently offered by USPS.

The parameter settings for a simulation define USPS's economic objective, predetermined market conditions and the controls imposed by the regulator on USPS's choice of prices. The parameter settings also determine several technical features of a simulation. The settings for the Base Case are:

Incumbent Objective: Welfare defined as the sum of the consumers' surplus on just USPS mail services plus USPS's profit subject to a floor on the incumbent's profit.
Incumbent Profit Floor: Imposed at zero (breakeven)
Reserved/Entered Areas: 1Cls is reserved for USPS. PrOth and PclSR are always entered by an entrant. 2Per, 3Std and 4Pkg are open to entry.
Price Caps and Floors: USPS is subject to price floors on all products set at marginal cost plus average product-specific cost.[7] There are no individual price caps.
Global Price Cap. There is no global price cap. The price index is calculated with weights based upon FY 2015 volumes.
Frequency Model: Entry frequencies are estimates using an exponentially weighted average of previously selected product combinations. The estimates truncate the start of the sample and censor frequencies below 0.010.
Iterations: The iteration limit is 200. Simulated results are averages computed for a sample composed of the last 100 iterations.[8]

The Base Case simulates the operation of postal markets when prices are set by a welfare-maximizing postal regulator. Therefore, it is unnecessary to impose any price caps on USPS. The simulator maximizes just the welfare components associated with USPS's own products and profits because these are the only components that are likely to be considered by a postal regulator.[9]

5 Base Case Equilibrium

A summary of the results for equilibrium in the Base Case is displayed in Table 1. The simulator converges upon a solution that exhibits limit-pricing by USPS and stochastic selection of product combinations by a single potential entrant. The "Incumbent" prices shown in Table 1 confront the "Entrant" with three product combinations for which the entrant takes the same added annual loss of about $760 million. The identities of the services in each combination are shown at the bottom left-hand side of Table 1. The entrant alternates its choice among these three combinations at frequencies that leave us with a Nash equilibrium. For the individual products these frequencies translate into the simulated entry frequencies shown in the table. The entrant does not enter the prohibited market for 1Cls.

[7]The added product-specific costs are computed using the basis solution volumes and are very small.

[8]Our experiments with the simulator indicate that convergence is rapid and that there is little to be gained by iterating longer to obtain a larger sample.

[9]The components that are omitted are the consumers' surplus effects for all other products (principally for the products of entrants) and the producers' surplus effects for all other producers (principally the profits of entrants).

Table 1 Base case equilibrium

Set ID:	Base case		4/15/2016 18:6	Simulated ($000)
Demand	Branching AIDS model		Consumers' surplus	73,484,144
Objective	Welfare max. w/zero profit		Producers' surplus	−741,184
Reserved	1Cls Res., PrOth and PclSR Ent.		Social welfare	72,742,959
Price controls	No caps		Welfare benchmark	88,838,076
	Simulated prices ($)		Expected volumes (000)	
Product	Incumbent	Entrant	Incumbent	Entrant
1Cls	0.5318		55,827,631	0
PrOth	5.4106	5.5243	1,898,013	1,670,420
2Per	0.5605	0.5389	4,318,167	550,175
3Std	0.1831	0.1730	55,370,296	41,993,055
4Pkg	3.0020	2.8936	304,893	223,807
PclSR	1.7703	1.9066	3,103,015	3,986,619
	Price constraint	Simulated entry	Market	Price
Product	Multiplier	Frequency	Condition	Control
1Cls	0	0.0000	Reserved	Floor
PrOth	0	1.0000	Always entered	Floor
2Per	0	0.5248	Open to entry	Floor
3Std	0	0.9604	Open to entry	Floor
4Pkg	0	1.0000	Open to entry	Floor
PclSR	0	1.0000	Always entered	Floor
Incumbent	Incumbent	Objective	Global price cap	None
Objective	Value ($000) ($000)	Weight	Price cap index	0.4309
Welfare	29,613,030	0.5954	Last cap multiplier	0
Profit	0	0.4046	Inc. profit floor	0
Adj'd cost	58,921,316	0.0000	Single Ent. profit	−760,513
Revenue	58,921,316	0.0000	No. of entrants	1.0000
	Product	Simulated	Profit from combination ($000)	
Index	Combination	Frequency	Incumbent	Entrant
54	011011	0.0396	1,316,164	−772,619
58	010111	0.4752	59,604	−761,385
62	011111	0.4851	−129,357	−759,041

Otherwise, the entrant is always present in the markets for PrOth, 4Pkg and PclSR, and is a frequent visitor in the markets for 2Per (0.525) and 3Std (0.960).

Neither USPS nor the ECs have an incentive to change the strategies displayed in Table 1. Together the strategies establish the players' prices and the EC's probabilities for offering the three combinations of services. Other combinations are not used either because they violate the assumed regulatory restrictions or because they result in lower profits for the ECs.

USPS's position as the price leader places it at a disadvantage in postal markets where it faces competition. This fact is mostly evident from the "Incumbent" and "Entrant" prices and expected volumes in Table 1. The USPS prices are Ramsey prices given the entrants' probabilities of entry and reaction functions. The entrants' prices maximize an entrant's profit given USPS's prices. USPS gets underpriced in every market where an entrant is present except PclSR. Here the ECs enjoy so much market power (the base case market share for USPS is only 0.299) that they are able to set a price above that of USPS.

The expected volumes in Table 1 are the weighted averages of the volumes for the different product combinations. Opening the markets for 2Per, 3Std and 4Pkg results in substantial losses of market share by USPS in these markets. On the other hand, USPS gains market share in PrOth and PclSR.

Liberalization is unlikely to produce any new entrants in postal markets. The expected profit for the competitors to USPS already present in the markets for PrOth and PclSR drops by about $760 million. More entrants would simply increase this loss.

Price floors were set on all USPS services; however, none of the floors are binding. All of the associated price constraint multipliers are zero.

The assigned objective of the Base Case is to maximize welfare on USPS's products subject to a zero-profit floor. This floor is an effective constraint on USPS pricing. It results in a Lagrangian that positively weights both welfare and profit. These weights are normalized to sum to one and are shown in Table 1. They are welfare: 0.595 and profit: 0.405.

There is no global price cap. A global price cap index computed using USPS FY 2015 volumes as weights is 0.431. The index for USPS prices in FY 2015 is 0.514 so liberalization has the effect of lowering the general level of USPS prices.

The upper right-hand corner of Table 1 shows the calculation of social welfare for the Base Case. Here, social welfare is calculated as the sum of the expected consumers' surpluses for all products offered by both USPS and entrants and the profits of both USPS and all entrants.[10] The welfare benchmark is the maximum social welfare compatible with the data and controls for the Base Case. It is the sum of consumers' and producers' surpluses when USPS prices are set at marginal cost, when entrants' prices are set according to the reaction functions to maximize the entrants' profit, and when the entrants' product combination is selected to maximize social welfare subject to the restrictions on reserved/entered areas. For the base case this product combination is just PrOth and PclSR. The Base Case equilibrium does moderately well against the benchmark, $72.7 million versus $88.8 million, but clearly leaves room for some improvement.

[10]Note that the USPS objective "welfare" shown at the lower left of Table 1 encompasses only the consumers' surplus for products offered by USPS and USPS's profit.

6 The Dark Side of Postal Liberalization

Table 2 displays the results of a series of simulations designed to model incremental openings of postal markets. The table consists of a six-case progression from full opening of all markets (Case 1) to closing all markets (Case 6). The Base Case is Case 2. The other cases are Case 3: 1Cls and 2Per reserved, Case 4: all markets reserved except PrOth and PclSR which are entered, and Case 5: all markets reserved except PrOth and PclSR which are open but not necessarily entered. Otherwise, the data and controls for all of the cases are the same as for the Base Case.

The objective for all of the cases is welfare maximization subject to a zero-profit condition. This choice of objective gives us a set of cases that abstract from the disciplining effects of entry on USPS's prices.

When postal markets are opened there are several conflicting effects on social welfare. On the positive side there are likely to be two somewhat differentiated postal products offered to consumers in postal markets that previously had only the service offered by USPS. On the negative side USPS loses significant economies of scope and scale. The new equilibrium is likely to have multiple suppliers of highly substitutable services. This is inefficient when postal delivery is an activity with declining average costs as in our simulator.

Table 2 shows that it is the latter effect that predominates. The social welfare levels that are achievable without the additional product offerings of potential entrants are higher than the levels that are achievable when entry is permitted. This is the dark side of postal liberalization. Entry leads to less efficient production of an array of highly substitutable products by multiple producers. The added cost from the loss of scale economies by dividing production among several suppliers is more than the consumer's surplus gained from the added selection of products and lower prices.

The lowest level of social welfare in Table 2 occurs in Case 1 with all markets open. In this case, USPS is unable to make a positive profit. The simulator maximizes USPS's profit which turns out to be a loss of $10.3 billion. In all of the other cases the zero-profit condition remains feasible. Reserving 1Cls (Case 2) improves welfare by $6.2 billion. Adding 2Per to the reserved area (Case 3) increases welfare by another $2.0 billion. Adding 3Std and 4Pkg to the reserved area (Case 4) adds another $11.6 billion. Another $3.2 billion is added if we do not assume that entrants will always be present in PrOth and PclSR (Case 5). This improvement occurs because entrants choose not to enter PrOth. Finally, a small retrenchment of around $0.4 billion takes place if entrants are excluded from all postal markets (Case 6).

Perhaps the most important lesson to be drawn is that the economics of the U.S. postal sector create a high bar for successful liberalization. Case 4 is the case that most closely resembles the current situation. If we liberalize all but 1Cls (Case 2) the change creates a large potential welfare loss. In order for the liberalization envisioned in our Base Case to succeed, USPS would have to find production

Table 2 Liberalization simulations

Identification	Case 1		Case 2		Case 3		Case 4		Case 5		Case 6	
Demand	Branching AIDS model		Branching AIDS mode		Branching AIDS model		Branching AIDS model		Branching AIDS mode		Branching AIDS model	
Objective	Welfare max. w/zero profit		Welfare max. w/zero profit		Welfare max. w/zero profit		Welfare max. w/zero profit		Welfare max. w/zero profit		Welfare max. w/zero profit	
Reserved	None, PrOth and PcISR Ent.		ICIs Res., PrOth and PcISR Ent.		1CIs and 2Per Res.		All reserved Ex entered		All reserved Ex open		All reserved	
Price controls	No caps		No caps		No caps		No caps		No caps		No caps	
	Simulated prices ($}		Simulated prices ($)		Simulated prices ($)		Simulated prices ($)		Simulated prices ($)		Simulated prices ($)	
Product	Incumbent	Entrant	Incumbent	Entrant	Incumbent	Entrant	Incumbent	Entrant	Incumbent	Entrant	Incumbent	Entrant
1CIs	0.3710	0.3009	0.5318		0.4996		0.3211		0.3283		0.3068	
PrOth	5.8282	5.6341	5.4106	5.5243	5.2763	5.4443	4.6243	5.1349	4.8774		4.6864	
2Per	1.0089	0.7552	0.5605	0.5389	0.9268		1.4465		1.2494		1.3470	
3Std	0.2025	0.1818	0.1831	0.1730	0.1844	0.1739	0.2410		0.2326		0.2303	
4Pkg	3.9561	3.3111	3.0020	2.8936	3.0097	2.9028	4.9636		4.7014		4.1618	
PcISR	1.9595	1.9813	1.7703	1.9066	1.7768	1.9136	1.6552	1.8709	1.6818	1.8814	1.8569	
	Expected volumes (000)		Expected volumes (000)		Expected volumes (000)		Expected volumes (000)		Expected volumes (000)		Expected volumes (000)	
Product	Incumbent	Entrant	Incumbent	Entrant	Incumbent	Entrant	Incumbent	Entrant	Incumbent	Entrant	Incumbent	Entrant
1cls	37,653,077	33,422,455	55,327,631	0	56,406,789	0	67,333,755	0	68,146,824	0	69,094,053	0
PrOth	1,332,320	1,829,739	1,898,013	1,670,420	1,919,004	1,561,297	2,314,717	1,143,581	3,544,867	0	3,609,004	0
2Per	2,847,920	2,309,865	4,318,167	550,175	4,654,512	0	5,586,087	0	5,708,139	0	5,750,163	0
3Std	38,707,338	54,273,696	55,370,296	41,998,055	55,478,689	44,323,780	83,210,545	0	83,787,271	0	84,935,023	0
4Pkg	214,354	283,801	304,893	223,807	307,728	225,319	483,483	0	488,218	0	501,484	0
PcISR	2,181,696	4,590,473	3,103,015	3,986,619	3,131,208	4,044,707	3,782,427	3,671,443	4,610,722	2,876,188	7,365,960	0
	Price limit	Entry	Price limit	Entry	Price limit	Entry	Price limit	Entry	Price limit	Entry	Price limit	Entry
Product	Multiplier	Frequency	Multiplier	Frequency	Multiplier	Frequency	Multiplier	Frequency	Multiplier	Frequency	Multiplier	Frequency
1CIs	0	1.0000	0	0.0000	0	0.0000	0	0.0000	0	0.0000	0	0.0000
PrOth	0	1.0000	0	1.0000	0	1.0000	0	1.0000	0	0.0000	0	0.0000
2Per	0	1.0000	0	0.5248	0	0.0000	0	0.0000	0	0.0000	0	0.0000
3Std	0	1.0000	0	0.9604	0	1.0000	0	0.0000	0	0.0000	0	0.0000
4Pkg	0	1.0000	0	1.0000	0	1.0000	0	0.0000	0	0.0000	0	0.0000
PcISR	0	1.0000	0	1.0000	0	1.0000	0	1.0000	0	0.7723	0	0.0000

(continued)

Table 2 (continued)

Identification	Case 1		Case 2		Case 3		Case 4		Case 5		Case 6	
Inc. objective	Value ($000)	Last weight	Value ($000)	Last weight	Value ($000)	Last weight	Value ($000)	Last weight	Value ($000)	Last weight	Value ($000)	Last weight
Welfare	−3,825,022	0.0010	29,613,030	0.5954	29,803,036	0.6091	75,702,261	0.8461	80,129,267	0.8524	88,884,764	0.8689
Profit	−10,321,968	0.9990	0	0.4046	0	0.3909	0	0.1539	0	0.1476	0	0.1311
Adj'd cost	47,889,483	0.0000	58,921,316	0.0000	59,339,394	0.0000	69,310,726	0.0000	76,359,126	0.0000	81,180,293	0.0000
Revenue	37,567,515	0.0000	58,921,316	0.0000	59,339,394	0.0000	69,310,726	0.0000	76,359,126	0.0000	81,180,293	0.0000
Ent. prof it/Inc. floor	4,732,749	0	−760,513	0	−881,319	0	−2,361,568	0	3600	0	0	0
Price index/multiplier	0.4027	0	0.4309	0	0.4309	0	0.4052	0	0.3984	0	0.3902	0
Welfare/benchmark	66,563,998	88,838,076	72,742,959	88,838,076	74,743,874	88,838,076	86,102,803	88,838,076	89,322,358	92,082,833	88,884,764	91,536,233

efficiencies, service improvements and other economies outside the scope of our model of about $13.4 billion.

Access pricing may put this target within reach. Most of the economies of scope and scale in postal operations occur in the delivery function. Access pricing provides a means for USPS to partially recover these economies. We did not consider access pricing and workshared services in the model used to simulate postal markets for this paper. However, the large welfare losses shown from liberalization show the importance of exploring access pricing as an option for avoiding them.

7 The Reserved Area

The simulations shown in Table 3 were conducted for the purpose of defining a reserved area that would allow USPS to break even while opening as many postal markets as possible to potential entrants. We changed the simulator's controls to run with profit maximization as the USPS objective and with no caps on USPS prices either individually or globally.

Case 1 simulates equilibrium without any reserved area. The result is that entrants enter every postal market with probability one and USPS's maximum possible profit is a loss of $10.3 billion. Full market opening leaves USPS unable to break even by a large margin.

Case 2 corresponds to the Base Case with a reserved area of only 1Cls, while Case3 adds 2Per. In Case 2 USPS's maximum profit is $4.9 billion and in Case 3 the maximum profit rises modestly to $5.5 billion. In Case 2 USPS could not make a $5.5 billion health fund contribution currently required by U.S. law while in Case 3 this contribution would become feasible—barely.

Case 4 represents the *status quo* with market opening limited to only those markets, PrOth and PclSR, already open. USPS's possible profit in this scenario soars to $27.1 billion. Thus the reserved area that is presently assigned to USPS is far larger than necessary to ensure that USPS can break even.

Cases 5 and 6 have the same reserved area as Cases 2 and 3. USPS is still assumed to maximize profit. However, these cases were run using a somewhat different model of postal markets in which entrants make their pricing decisions and product selections simultaneously. With these changes in the model, USPS is not obliged to be the price leader in postal markets. These cases become interesting if, following liberalization, the US postal regulator is able to compel potential entrants to submit their prices to the regulator at the same time as USPS. We consider this unlikely; in practice potential entrants would probably not be subjected to any price regulation. The change makes it less profitable for potential competitors to enter postal markets but otherwise appears to have little effect on our results. Surprisingly, it decreases rather than increases USPS's potential profits. Nevertheless, social welfare improves modestly when USPS is not obliged to be the price leader in markets where entry is permitted.

Table 3 Reserved area simulations

Identification	Case 1		Case 2		Case 3		Case 4		Case 5		Case 6	
Demand	Branching AIDS model		Branching AIDS model		Branching AIDS model		Branching AIDS model		Branching AIDS mode		Branching AIDS model	
Objective	Profit max.		Profit max.		Profit max.		Profit max.		Profit max.		Profit max.	
Reserved	None		1Cls		1Cls, 2Per		1Cls, 2Per, 3Std, 4Pkg		1Cls		1Cls, 2Per	
Price controls	None		None		None		None		Simultaneous pricing		Simultaneous pricing	
	Simulated prices ($)		Simulated prices {$)		Simulated prices {$)		Simulated prices ($)		Simulated prices ($)		Simulated prices ($)	
Product	Incumbent	Entrant	Incumbent	Entrant	Incumbent	Entrant	Incumbent	Entrant	Incumbent	Entrant	Incumbent	Entrant
1Cls	0.3711	0.3009	0.7697		0.7203		0.6095		0.7618		0.7189	
PrOth	5.8289	5.6344	6.0816	5.7985	5.8523	5.6532	4.8648	5.1339	5.8023	5.6928	5.6628	5.5897
2Per	1.0092	0.7553	0.5995	0.5392	1.3497		2.7221		0.6016	0.5388	1.2514	
3Std	0.2025	0.1818	0.2071	0.1844	0.2132	0.1878	0.4980		0.1919	0.1775	0.1956	0.1797
4Pkg	3.9573	3.3117	4.1320	3.4160	4.2237	3.4704	14.2776		3.4697	3.1210	3.5244	3.1574
PclSR	1.9597	1.9814	1.9604	1.9813	1.9863	2.0007	2.0602	2.0379	1.8707	1.9478	1.8839	1.9609
	Expected volumes (000)		Expected volumes (000)		Expected volumes (000)		Expected volumes (000)		Expected volumes (000)		Expected volumes (000)	
Product	Incumbent	Entrant	Incumbent	Entrant	Incumbent	Entrant	Incumbent	Entrant	Incumbent	Entrant	Incumbent	Entrant
1Cls	37,634,269	33,434,502	39,192,455	0	39,229,458	0	39,194,767	0	39,344,825	0	39,385,213	0
PrOth	1,331,655	1,830,054	1,331,928	2,042,817	1,334,617	1,844,270	1,335,489	1,147,280	1,597,153	1,898,476	1,545,312	1,757,498
2Per	2,846,498	2,310,666	2,928,358	826,752	3,237,092	0	3,222,925	0	3,089,022	642,615	3,250,420	0
3Std	38,688,004	54,290,126	38,654,485	57,731,794	38,583,988	62,162,253	48,008,798	0	51,028,937	48,950,755	52,263,415	51,849,815
4Pkg	214,247	283,883	214,157	299,486	214,017	307,669	278,948	0	273,841	256,885	275,992	262,372
PclSR	2,180,606	4,591,212	2,179,796	4,608,726	2,177,674	4,769,261	2,182,293	5,038,662	2,639,703	4,330,573	2,681,173	4,438,953
	Price limit	Entry	Price limit	Entry	Price limit	Entry	Price limit	Entry	Price limit	Entry	Price limit	Entry
Product	Multiplier	Frequency	Multiplier	Frequency	Multiplier	Frequency	Multiplier	Frequency	Multiplier	Frequency	Multiplier	Frequency
1Cls	0	1.0000	0	0.0000	0	0.0000	0	0.0000	0	0.0000	0	0.0000
PrOth	0	1.0000	0	1.0000	0	1.0000	0	1.0000	0	1.0000	0	1.0000
2Per	0	1.0000	0	0.8020	0	0.0000	0	0.0000	0	0.6139	0	0.0000
3Std	0	1.0000	0	1.0000	0	1.0000	0	0.0000	0	1.0000	0	1.0000
4Pkg	0	1.0000	0	1.0000	0	1.0000	0	0.0000	0	1.0000	0	1.0000
PclSR	0	1.0000	0	1.0000	0	1.0000	0	1.0000	0	1.0000	0	1.0000

(continued)

Table 3 (continued)

Identification	Case 1		Case 2		Case 3		Case 4		Case 5		Case 6	
Inc. objective	Value ($000)	Last weight	Value ($000)	Last weight	Value ($000)	Last weight	Value ($000)	Last weight	Value ($000)	Last weight	Value ($000)	Last weight
Welfare	−3,831,507	0.0000	19,253,517	0.0000	19,942,888	0.0000	52,295,943	0.0000	18,875,739	0.0000	18,377,149	0.0000
Profit	−10,321,965	1.0000	4,945,648	1.0000	5,527,632	1.0000	27,096,335	1.0000	4,636,872	1.0000	5,150,473	1.0000
Adj'd cost	47,877,202	0.0000	48,241,286	0.0000	48,365,341	0.0000	49,847,369	0.0000	52,142,580	0.0000	52,226,370	0.0000
Revenue	37,555,237	0.0000	53,186,934	0.0000	53,892,973	0.0000	76,943,704	0.0000	56,779,452	0.0000	57,376,843	0.0000
Ent. profit/Inc. floor	4,739,086	None	2,322,076	None	2,378,724	None	−908,957	None	710,413	None	690,027	None
Price index/multiplier	0.4028	0	0.5569	0	0.5665	0	0.8130	0	0.5390	0	0.5469	0
Welfare/benchmark	65,550,682	88,838,076	63,502,975	88,838,076	66,513,748	88,838,076	67,211,607	88,838,076	64,890,701	88,838,076	67,160,963	88,838,076

Finally, we note that none of the reserved area simulations is attractive as a model for regulatory reform. In all of the simulations, price regulation is suspended resulting in very high USPS prices in the reserved areas and social welfare levels that range from \$63.5 to \$67.2 billion. The social welfare level for the Base Case (\$72.7 billion) represents a much better performance primarily because maximizing profit is not the assumed objective of USPS.

8 The Case for Postal Price Regulation

Opening postal markets to entrants still leaves USPS with a considerable amount of power in the liberalized markets. Price regulation of some kind is needed to prevent abuses that can occur if USPS fully exploits this residual market power. If USPS acts as a profit maximizer, then the abuses take the form of higher prices, leaving USPS with excessive profits. If USPS acts to maximize cost or revenue following liberalization, then the abuses are likely to partly take the form of cross subsidies enabling USPS to set prices to take excessive shares of postal markets from entrants. Cross subsidies will also be the result of price regulation when a regulator imposes individual price caps that lie below the price floors that we have assumed. Case 2 from Table 3 shows what happens if USPS acts to maximize its profit following liberalization of all markets except 1Cls. Without any kind of price regulation USPS is able to raise its prices not only in 1Cls but in all postal markets to produce an excess profit of \$4.9 billion compared to the Base Case. Another noteworthy feature of this case is that none of USPS's prices fall below the price floors. This is characteristic of our simulations when we assume that the economic objective of USPS is to maximize profit.

This changes if USPS's objective is to maximize cost or revenue subject to a profit constraint. The results in Table 4 show why price floors are needed to avoid cross subsidies when USPS does not behave as a profit maximizer. Case 1 reproduces the Base Case, however, the weights for the global price cap have been changed to the Base Case volumes for USPS. In Case 2 the assumed objective is cost maximization subject to a zero-profit floor. With this change the price floors for PrOth and PclSR become necessary to prevent USPS from pricing these categories below marginal cost. With the price floors preventing cross subsidies, cost maximization results in a substantially higher level of overall welfare than the Base Case.[11] This is the net result of sharply lower prices for PrOth and PclSR by both USPS and entrants, mostly lower prices for all other services except 1Cls, no change in USPS's profit and a loss of about \$2.5 billion by entrants. The result in Case 3 where revenue maximization is the objective is somewhat similar. The price floors prevent USPS from underpricing PrOth and PclSR and welfare improves, but

[11]Recall that in the Base Case only the USPS components of social welfare are maximized subject to a break-even constraint.

Table 4 Relaxed regulation simulations

Identification	Case 1		Case 2		Case 3		Case 4		Case 5		Case 6	
Demand	Branching AIDS model		Branching AIDS model		Branching AIDS model		Branching AIDS model		Branching AIDS model		Branching AIDS mode	
Objective	Welfare max. w/zero Profit		Cost max. w/zero profit		Revenue max. w/zero profit		Welfare max. w/zero profit		Cost Max. w/zero profit		Revenue max. w/zero profit	
Reserved	1CIs Res., PrOth and PclSR Ent.		1CIs Res., PrOth and PclSR Ent.		1CIs Res., PrOth and PclSR Ent.		1CIs Res., PrOth and PclSR Ent.		1CIs Res., PrOth and PclSR Ent.		1CIs Res., PrOth and PclSR Ent.	
Price controls	No caps		No caps		No caps		No caps, simultaneous pricing		No caps, simultaneous pricing		No caps, simultaneous pricing	
	Simulated prices ($)		Simulated prices ($)		Simulated prices ($)		Simulated prices ($)		Simulated prices ($)		Simulated prices ($)	
Product	Incumbent	Entrant	Incumbent	Entrant	Incumbent	Entrant	Incumbent	Entrant	Incumbent	Entrant	Incumbent	Entrant
1CIs	0.5318		0.5839		0.6635		0.5334		0.5976		0.6633	
PrOth	5.4106	5.5243	4.5368	5.1954	4.5368	5.2013	5.2125	5.4491	4.5368	5.1964	4.5368	5.2018
2Per	0.5605	0.5389	0.5629	0.5395	0.5742	0.5420	0.5559	0.5383	0.5528	0.5399	0.5725	0.5405
3Std	0.1831	0.1730	0.1819	0.1729	0.1815	0.1732	0.1830	0.1729	0.1805	0.1729	0.1793	0.1733
4Pkg	3.0020	2.8936	2.5411	2.7083	3.3789	3.0906	2.5240	2.6825	1.8995	2.4040	2.5861	2.7327
PclSR	1.7703	1.9066	1.5078	1.8084	1.5078	1.8085	1.7041	1.8823	1.5078	1.8097	1.5078	1.8097
	Expected volumes (000)		Expected volumes (000)		Expected volumes (000)		Expected volumes (000)		Expected volumes (000)		Expected volumes (000)	
Product	Incumbent	Entrant	Incumbent	Entrant	Incumbent	Entrant	Incumbent	Entrant	Incumbent	Entrant	Incumbent	Entrant
1CIs	55,827,631	0	51,690,576	0	45,543,127	0	55,642,617	0	50,685,447	0	45,857,194	0
PrOth	1,898,013	1,670,420	2,739,656	1,225,210	2,765,799	1,236,485	2,087,538	1,569,407	2,747,220	1,226,883	2,764,838	1,233,964
2Per	4,318,167	550,175	4,468,573	340,978	3,840,562	543,490	4,417,834	491,960	4,429,085	325,868	3,987,650	434,490
3Std	55,370,296	41,998,055	90,297,665	5,962,826	79,242,187	19,679,693	68,344,134	27,834,874	91,943,029	4,742,420	87,404,931	12,297,746
4Pkg	304,893	223,807	354,440	196,088	285,003	250,707	348,785	193,409	411,842	154,805	354,701	199,785
PclSR	3,103,015	3,986,619	4,447,173	3,174,943	4,448,690	3,177,014	3,446,938	3,784,568	4,462,021	3,182,367	4,464,291	3,185,828
	Price limit	Entry	Price limit	Entry	Price limit	Entry	Price limit	Entry	Price limit	Entry	Price limit	Entry
Product	Multiplier	Frequency	Multiplier	Frequency	Multiplier	Frequency	Multiplier	Frequency	Multiplier	Frequency	Multiplier	Frequency
1CIs	0	0.0000	0	0.0000	0	0.0000	0	0.0000	0	0.0000	0	0.0000
PrOth	0	1.0000	−1,951,651	1.0000	−1,481,781	1.0000	0	1.0000	−2,859,029	1.0000	−3,268,411	1.0000
2Per	0	0.5248	0	0.3366	0	0.5347	0	0.4752	0	0.3168	0	0.4158
3Std	0	0.9604	0	0.1386	0	0.4653	0	0.6535	0	0.1188	0	0.2871

(continued)

Table 4 (continued)

Identification	Case 1		Case 2		Case 3		Case 4		Case 5		Case 6	
4Pkg	0	1.0000	0	1.0000	0	1.0000	0	1.0000	0	1.0000	0	1.0000
PcISR	0	1.0000	−3,444,626	1.0000	−2,929,086	1.0000	0	1.0000	−5,444,836	1.0000	−6,639,539	1.0000
Inc. objective	Value ($000)	Last weight	Value ($000	Last weight	Value ($000)	Last weight	Value ($000	Last weight	Value ($000	Last weight	Value ($000)	Last weight
Welfare	29,613,030	0.5954	55,186,905	0.0000	43,784,725	0.0000	36,519,178	0.5877	53,495,250	0.0000	46,765,643	0.0000
Profit	0	0.4046	0	0.3361	1,306,144	0.0001	0	0.4123	0	0.3597	1,269,539	0.0001
Adj'd Cost	58,921,316	0.0000	69,140,971	0.6639	65,965,386	0.0000	62,262,988	0.0000	69,361,107	0.6403	67,327,735	0.0000
Revenue	58,921,316	0.0000	69,140,971	0.0000	67,271,530	0.9999	62,262,988	0.0000	69,361,107	0.0000	68,597,273	0.9999
Ent. profit/Inc. floor	−760,513	0	−2,506,515	0	−2,303,368	0	−1,288,481	0	−2,601,290	0	−2,462,583	0
Price index/multiplier	0.4877	0	0.4900	0	0.5313	0	0.4823	0	0.4922	0	0.5266	0
Welfare/benchmark	72,742,959	88,838,076	78,533,386	83,838,076	72,997,117	88,838,076	75,025,827	88,838,076	78,487,942	88,838,076	74,894,894	88,338,076

only slightly. In Case 3 the profit floor is ineffective and USPS's profit rises to $1.3 billion without additional controls.

Cases 4, 5 and 6 repeat the simulations under the assumption that USPS is not the price leader in liberalized markets. The results follow the same pattern observed with USPS as price leader. However, in Cases 4 and 6 welfare is about $2.0 billion higher than in the comparable Cases 1 and 3. Welfare in Cases 2 and 5 scarcely differs. On the whole it appears best not to impose the role of price leader on USPS if there is a way to avoid it.

9 A Global Price Cap

Table 5 displays the results of several simulations with a global price cap. Currently, USPS price controls consist of individual floors and/or caps on all but PrOth and PclSR. In the simulations in Table 5 the floors remain but the individual price caps are replaced by a single global price cap.

Case 1 is the Base Case. In Case 2 we reproduce a basic theoretical result known to apply to the efficient regulation of monopolies. A profit-maximizing monopolist can be induced to self-select Ramsey prices by imposing an appropriately designed global price cap. The secret to the design of the global cap is that the regulator must select the demand volumes corresponding to Ramsey prices as the weights for the global price index. When the regulator sets the global cap at the welfare-maximizing level of average revenue per piece, the constrained monopolist will respond by choosing the Ramsey prices. This can greatly simplify the design of regulatory systems aimed at efficient price regulation.

In Case 2 we show that the global cap works if USPS maximizes its profit in liberalized postal markets where it is no longer a monopolist. The simulated equilibria in Cases 1 and 2 are virtually identical.[12] They both result in Ramsey prices and corresponding volumes, profits, welfare *et cetera*. However, in Case 2 the prices are chosen by USPS to maximize its profit subject to a global price cap constructed with index weights corresponding to the Base Case volumes and with the cap set at the Base Case average revenue per piece (0.4877).

In Case 3 and Case 4 we test the global price cap under the assumptions that USPS maximizes cost and revenue, respectively, subject to a zero-profit floor. The simulated equilibria for these two cases are very similar to each other but vary somewhat from the equilibrium in Cases 1 and 2. In Cases 3 and 4 USPS raises the price for 1Cls slightly (from 0.532 to 0.555) in order to lower its prices for PrOth (from 5.410 to about 4.960) and PclPR (from 1.770 to about 1.625). These changes allow it to raise its cost (or revenue) from $58.9 to $63.1 billion while maintaining a

[12]The remaining small differences between the two cases can be almost completely eliminated by extending the length of the simulations beyond 200 iterations and using a sample size larger than 100.

Table 5 Global price cap simulations

Identification	Case 1		Case 2		I Case 3		I Case 4		I Case 5		I Case 6	
Demand	Branching AIDS model		Branching AIDS model		Branching AIDS model		Branching AIDS model		Branching AIDS model		Branching AIDS model	
Objective	Welfare max. w/zero Profit		Profit max.		Cost max. w/zero profit		Revenue max. w/zero profit		Profit max.		Profit max., zero profit pricing	
Reserved	1Cls Res., PrOth and PclSR Ent.		1Cls Res., PrOth and PclSR Ent.		1Cls Res., PrOth and PclSR Ent.		lCls Res., PrOth and PclSR Ent.		lCls Res., PrOth and PclSR Ent.		1Cls Res., PrOth and PclSR Ent.	
Price controls	No caps		Global cap		Global cap		Global cap		Global cap w/FY 2015 Wgts		Global Cap w/Fy 2015 Wgts	
	Simulated prices ($)		Simulated prices {$)		Simulated prices ($)		Simulated prices ($)		Simulated prices ($)		Simulated prices ($)	
Product	Incumbent	Entrant	Incumbent	Entrant	Incumbent	Entrant	Incumbent	Entrant	Incumbent	Entrant	Incumbent	Entrant
1Cls	0.5318		0.5317		0.5550		0.5551		0.5334		0.5212	
PrOth	5.4106	5.5243	5.4101	5.5238	4.9726	5.3575	4.9591	5.3573	5.5263	5.5684	5.4952	5.5574
2Per	0.5605	0.5389	0.5626	0.5392	0.5590	0.5391	0.5628	0.5391	0.5521	0.5388	0.5563	0.5388
3Std	0.1831	0.1730	0.1830	0.1731	0.1827	0.1729	0.1829	0.1729	0.1827	0.1730	0.1833	0.1730
4Pkg	3.0020	2.8936	3.0025	2.8930	3.0660	2.9325	3.0669	2.9325	2.3270	2.5834	2.2353	2.5438
PclSR	1.7703	1.9066	1.7704	1.9065	1.6250	1.8513	1.6211	1.8512	1.8547	1.9401	1.8496	1.9382
	Expected volumes (000)		Expected volumes (000)		Expected volumes (000)		Expected volumes (000)		Expected volumes (000)		Expected volumes (000)	
Product	Incumbent	Entrant	Incumbent	Entrant	Incumbent	Entrant	Incumbent	Entrant	Incumbent	Entrant	Incumbent	Entrant
1Cls	55,827,631	0	55,824,496	0	53,989,805	0	53,962,416	0	55,770,539	0	56,627,338	0
PrOth	1,898,013	1,670,420	1,897,915	1,670,933	2,319,506	1,453,329	2,331,346	1,445,860	1,790,871	1,729,809	1,814,639	1,711,455
2Per	4,313,167	550,175	4,320,580	540,985	4,245,220	602,856	4,247,724	600,591	4,711,434	154,578	4,800,209	130,966
3Std	55,370,296	41,998,055	55,347,391	42,041,968	65,802,946	31,335,146	66,026,971	31,058,584	61,252,347	35,713,470	62,857,464	33,610,004
4Pkg	304,893	223,807	304,873	223,829	303,812	228,659	303,894	228,751	362,514	180,080	370,193	174,034
PclSR	3,103,015	3,986,619	3,102,805	3,986,667	3,837,489	3,542,643	3,857,908	3,530,653	2,695,721	4,261,226	2,722,416	4,245,360
	Price Limit	Entry	Price Limit	Entry	Price Limit	Entry	Price Limit	Entry	Price Limit	Entry	Price Limit	Entry
Product	Multiplier	Frequency	Multiplier	Frequency	Multiplier	Frequency	Multiplier	Frequency	Multiplier	Frequency	Multiplier	Frequency
1Cls	0	0.0000	0	0.0000	0	0.0000	0	0.0000	0	0.0000	0	0.0000
PrOth	0	1.0000	0	1.0000	0	1.0000	0	1.0000	0	1.0000	0	1.0000
2Per	0	0.5248	0	0.5248	0	0.5842	0	0.5743	0	0.1584	0	0.1188
3Std	0	0.9604	0	0.9802	0	0.7327	0	0.7228	0	0.8218	0	0.7822

(continued)

Table 5 (continued)

Identification	Case 1		Case 2		1 Case 3		I Case 4		I Case 5		I Case 6	
4Pkg	0	1.0000	0	1.0000	0	1.0000	0	1.0000	0	1.0000	0	1.0000
PclSR	0	1.0000	0	1.0000	0	1.0000	0	1.0000	0	1.0000	0	1.0000
Inc. objective	Value ($000)	Last weight	Value ($000)	Last weight	Value ($000)	Last weight	Value ($000)	Last weight	Value ($000)	La st weight	Value ($000)	Last weight
Welfare	29,613,030	0.5954	30,039,338	0.0000	36,415,088	0.0000	35,434,813	0.0000	35,326,850	0.0000	37,042,565	0.0000
Profit	0	0.4046	10,099	1.0000	0	0.8009	0	0.7511	376,672	1.0000	0	1.0000
Adj'd cost	58,921,316	0.0000	58,949,119	0.0000	63,079,233	0.1991	63,084,257	0.0000	58,951,210	0.0000	59,505,421	0.0000
Revenue	58,921,316	0.0000	58,959,218	0.0000	63,079,233	0.0000	63,084,257	0.2489	59,327,882	0.0000	59,505,421	0.0000
Ent. profit/Inc. floor	−760,513	0	−751,674	None	−1,684,488	0	−1,685,002	0	−463,224	None	−533,396	None
Price index/multiplier	0.4877	0	0.4877	71,937,193	0.4877	45,828,282	0.4877	56,869,788	0.4309	80,548,481	0.4256	84,718,860
Welfare/benchmark	72,742,959	88,838,076	72,608,756	88,838,076	73,449,311	88,838,076	73,463,366	88,838,076	75,431,213	83,838,076	76,311,654	88,838,076

zero profit. The changes also cause entrants' profits to fall by about $1.0 billion. In effect, USPS attempts to exploit its reserved area monopoly (1Cls) to provide the profit cushion needed for incursions into the markets PrOth and PclSR where entrants are always present. However, these incursions are so limited that the price floors for these categories are ineffective.

In general, it appears that the practical advantages of a global price cap are not badly compromised if USPS pursues some economic objective other than profit maximization so long as USPS remains subject to a zero-profit floor. The social welfare that results from Cases 3 and 4, around $73.4 billion, actually exceeds the Base Case level of $72.7 billion.

Global price caps are usually proposed in a different form from the price cap used in Cases 2-4. In practice, the demand volumes for Ramsey prices in liberalized markets are likely to be unknown to a postal regulator. This makes the selection of the weights for the global price index and the choice of a cap value problematic. Under the circumstances, a regulator applying a global price cap would probably attempt to construct the index and set the cap using an observable set of recent volumes. We have done this using FY 2015 USPS volumes in Cases 5 and 6.

In Case 5 USPS is assumed to maximize its profit under a global price cap that prevents USPS from exceeding the index value of the Base Case as shown in Table 2. Recall that this index value (0.431) was computed using FY 2015 volumes for weights. Except for 4Pkg, prices do not change very much from those of the Base Case. Profits for both USPS and an entrant increase by over $0.3 billion. Social welfare improves by about $2.7 billion.

In Case 6 we decrease the price cap value just enough to eliminate the positive USPS profit that occurred in Case 5. This slightly reduces USPS's prices for 1Cls, PrOth and 4Pkg and leaves the prices of the other categories little changed. An entrant's profits would fall slightly as the entrant's prices responded. Finally, social welfare increases by $0.9 billion.

The lessons to be drawn from Cases 5 and 6 are, first, that the advantages of a global price cap as an instrument of regulatory control do not depend too much on the selection of weights for the index. And second, a good rule for setting the cap value is to set the cap to eliminate excess profit.

10 Two Inefficient Practices

We simulate two common practices that can be inefficient in the more competitive environment created by a postal liberalization. These are, first, imposing a lump sum tax on USPS, and second, capping only the prices of services in the reserved area. The first three cases in Table 6 show the results of imposing a required minimum profit level on USPS. So long as USPS is solely owned by the U.S. government this is nominally equivalent to a lump sum tax equal to the required additional profit. Case 1 is the Base Case with USPS breaking even. Case 2 is identical except that the profit floor has been raised to $1.0 billion. Social welfare

Table 6 Inefficient practices simulations

Identification	Case 1		Case 2		Case 3		Case 4		Case 5		Case 6	
Demand	Branching AIDS model		Branching AIDS model		Branching AIDS model		Branching AIDS model		Branching AIDS model		Branching AIDS model	
Objective	Welfare max. w/zero profit		Welfare max. w/1.0M profit		Welfare max.w/1.0M subsidy		Profit max.		Cost or rev. max., w/zero profit		Profit max.	
Reserved	1CIs		1CIs		1CIs		1CIs Res., PrOth and PcISR Ent.		1CIs Res., PrOth and PcISR Ent.		1CIs Res., PrOth and PcISR Ent.	
Price controls	None		None		None		1CIs capped		1CIs capped		1CIs capped for zero profit	
	Simulated prices ($)		Simulated prices ($)		Simulated prices ($}		Simulated prices ($}		Simulated prices ($)		Simulated prices ($)	
Product	Incumbent	Entrant	Incumbent	Entrant	Incumbent	Entrant	Incumbent	Entrant	Incumbent	Entrant	Incumbent	Entrant
1CIs	0.5318		0.5586		0.5049		0.5318		0.5318		0.5021	
PrOth	5.4106	5.5243	5.4872	5.5552	5.3320	5.4914	5.9373	5.7043	5.3009	5.4688	5.9180	5.6917
2Per	0.5605	0.5389	0.5631	0.5390	0.5533	0.5388	0.8242	0.6590	0.7341	0.6178	0.8570	0.6762
3Std	0.1831	0.1730	0.1850	0.1739	0.1831	0.1730	0.2043	0.1828	0.1832	0.1733	0.2039	0.1826
4Pkg	3.0020	2.8936	3.1291	2.9522	2.8706	2.8326	4.0268	3.3527	3.8298	3.2724	4.0144	3.3452
PcISR	1.7703	1.9066	1.7917	1.9150	1.7481	1.8979	1.9594	1.9808	1.7410	1.8964	1.9594	1.9809
	Expected volumeA (000)		Expected volumes (000)		Expected volumes (000)		Expected volumes (000)		Expected volumes (000)		Expected volumes (000)	
Product	Incumbent	Entrant	Incumbent	Entrant	Incumbent	Entrant	Incumbent	Entrant	Incumbent	Entrant	Incumbent	Entrant
1CIs	55,827,631	0	53,947,475	0	57,774,171	0	55,353,536	0	55,110,684	0	57,352,478	0
PrOth	1,898,013	1,670,420	1,833,945	1,713,186	1,964,389	1,627,626	1,331,248	1,922,408	1,359,531	1,603,006	1,331,248	1,906,203
2Per	4,318,167	550,175	4,154,342	583,551	4,463,330	551,467	2,850,246	1,739,025	3,165,851	1,497,676	2,850,246	1,839,561
3Std	55,370,296	41,998,055	53,163,768	44,338,818	58,586,817	37,935,464	38,672,321	55,620,373	55,423,445	43,387,695	33,672,321	55,388,822
4Pkg	304,893	223,807	294,644	232,307	315,538	215,008	214,193	290,169	234,825	277,705	214,193	289,071
PcISR	3,103,015	3,986,619	2,998,749	4,056,225	3,211,338	3,913,765	2,180,333	4,595,383	3,262,470	3,899,331	2,180,333	4,594,802
	Price limit	Entry	Price limit	Entry	Price limit	Entry	Price limit	Entry	Price limit	Entry	Price limit	Entry
Product	Multiplier	Frequency	Multiplier	Frequency	Multiplier	Frequency	Multiplier	Frequency	Multiplier	Frequency	Multiplier	Frequency
1CIs	0	0.0000	0	0.0000	0	0.0000	32,340,862	0.0000	21,814,939	0.0000	36,338,746	0.0000
PrOth	0	1.0000	0	1.0000	0	1.0000	0	1.0000	0	1.0000	0	1.0000
2Per	0	0.5248	0	0.5644	0	0.5347	0	1.0000	0	1.0000	0	1.0000
3Std	0	0.9604	0	1.0000	0	0.8812	0	1.0000	0	1.0000	0	1.0000
4Pkg	0	1.0000	0	1.0000	0	1.0000	0	1.0000	0	1.0000	0	1.0000

(continued)

Table 6 (continued)

Identification	Case 1		Case 2		Case 3		Case 4		Case 5		Case 6	
PcISR	0	1.0000	0	1.0000	0	1.0000	0	1.0000	0	1.0000	0	1.0000
Inc. objective	Value ($000)	Last weight	Value ($000)	Last weight	Value ($000)	Last weight	Value ($000)	La st weight	Value ($000)	Last weight	Value ($000)	Last weight
Welfare	29,613,030	0.5954	28,158,767	0.5467	32,938,113	0.6433	26,063,556	0.0000	27,988,444	0.0000	26,664,790	0.0000
Profit	0	0.4046	1,000,000	0.4533	−1,000,000	0.3567	1,020,782	1.0000	0	0.7755	0	1.0000
Adj'd cost	58,921,316	0.0000	57,672,600	0.0000	60,374,174	0.0000	51,704,768	0.0000	58,755,638	0.2245	52,136,924	0.0000
Revenue	58,921,316	0.0000	58,672,600	0.0000	59,374,174	0.0000	52,725,549	0.0000	58,755,638	0.0000	52,136,924	0.0000
Ent. profit/Inc. floor	−760,513	0	−478,965	1,000,000	−966,623	−1,000,000	2,061,720	None	−607,821	0	2,052,290	None
Price index/multiplier	0.4309	0	0.4446	0	0.4178	0	0.5226	0	0.4936	0	0.5095	0
Welfare/benchmark	72,742,959	88,838,076	71,687,989	88,838,076	73,876,485	88,838,076	69,631,131	88,838,076	70,221,248	88,838,076	70,227,649	88,838,076

declines by slightly less than $1.1 billion. This means that consumers' surplus has fallen by about $2.1 billion. In Case 3 USPS is allowed to run a loss of $1.0 billion. Then, welfare increases by $1.1 billion and consumers' surplus rises by about $2.1 billion.

The welfare loss from a lump sum tax occurs because USPS must convert the tax into a general increase in postal prices. The lump sum tax then becomes a specific tax on postal services. Most taxes are inefficient because the tax erodes the tax base. A specific tax does this by decreasing demand. Our results show that a tax on USPS following liberalization is especially inefficient. The net effect of the tax is to reduce social welfare by more than one dollar for each dollar collected. An ideal tax would cause no loss in social welfare and a reasonably efficient tax would cost far less than one dollar in welfare.

The last three cases in Appendix Table 6 show the results of imposing an individual price cap on only the services in the reserved area (1Cls). In Cases 4 and 5 the cap is set at the price of 1Cls from the Base Case (0.5318). In Case 4 USPS is assumed to maximize profit, in Case 5 USPS is assumed to maximize cost (or revenue, both result in the same equilibrium). The price cap on 1Cls is effective in both cases. In Case 4 social welfare drops to $69.6 billion from the Base Case $72.7 billion. In Case 5 the drop is to $70.2 billion. In Case 6 the price cap on 1Cls has been lowered until USPS breaks even when it maximizes profit. The price cap remains effective and welfare drops to only $70.2 billion. Recall from Sect. 8 that a global price cap that allows USPS to earn a zero profit can be imposed by the regulator to leave social welfare at $72.7 or higher. Cases 4, 5 and 6 indicate that it is impossible to achieve this level of welfare by capping only 1Cls while still allowing USPS to break even. The basic problem with the price cap on just 1Cls is that it must distort postal markets in order to be effective. These distortions cause appreciable welfare losses.

11 Conclusions

This paper employs an unconventional model of liberalized U.S. postal markets to simulate equilibrium under various schemes for liberalizing and de-regulating them. Entrants enter and exit with different combinations of postal services in response to the profit opportunities available in the markets. This behavior and USPS's pricing responses constitute a game that we solve by the method of fictitious play. We simulate the players' choices of strategies as the game is repeatedly played and analyze the results as we would a statistical sample.

The results of our simulations require more investigation before they can serve as a sufficiently reliable guide to the redesign of the U.S. regulatory system. In particular, our simulator should be enlarged and extended to explore delivery access. We also have not considered changes to USPS's USO. However, if confirmed by further research, our simulations show that regulation following liberalization can be achieved over a wide range of conditions with a modest reserved area and a small tool box of simple-but-effective regulatory controls.

USPS can be financially viable following liberalization with a reserved area consisting only of 1Cls. This liberalization would require regulatory controls in order to avoid welfare losses when USPS sets its own prices. It would be desirable (but may be impossible) to avoid making USPS the price leader in the liberalized markets. We have found that it is inefficient for the U.S. postal sector to be exploited as a source for public revenues and that price caps limited to individual postal products tend to create inefficiencies.

Our simulations indicate that an effective regulatory system needs three controls: individual price floors set at or slightly above marginal cost to prevent cross subsidies; a global price cap set on an index of all USPS prices with weights determined by the postal regulator; and, a profit floor set near zero to require USPS to also consider profits when setting prices to maximize any economic objective other than profit. If USPS can be relied upon to maximize its profit following liberalization, then both the individual price floors and the profit floor become unnecessary and only the global price cap is required.

Acknowledgments The views expressed in this paper are those of the authors. The authors wish to thank Michael Crew for his encouragement and assistance with the research reported in this paper. We have also benefited from the comments of Thomas-Olivier Leautier of the Toulouse School of Economics.

References

Baumol, W. J., Panzar, J. C., & Willig, R. D. (1988). *Contestable markets and the theory of industrial structure* (Revised Edition). Orlando, FL: Harcourt Brace Jovanovich.

Cigno, M. M., & Pearsall, E. S. (2016). *A model for simulating equilibrium in multi-product markets following de-regulation and liberalization*. Presented at the 24th Conference on Postal and Delivery Economics, Florence, Italy, May 18–21, 2016, available from the authors at espearsall@verizon.net.

Pearsall, E. S., & Trozzo, C. L. (2008). *A contestable market model of the delivery of commercial mail*. Paper presented at the IDEI 5th bi-annual Postal Economics conference "Regulation, Competition and Universal Service in the Postal Sector", Toulouse, March 13–14, 2008, available from the author at espearsall@verizon.net.

Pearsall, E. S. (2011). *On equilibrium in a liberalized market*. Paper presented at the CRRI Advanced Workshop on Regulation and Competition, 30th Annual Eastern Conference, Skytop PA, USA, May 18–20, 2011, available from the author at espearsall@verizon.net.

Pearsall, E. S. (2016). A game-theoretic model of the market for international mail. In M. A. Crew & T. J. Brennan (Eds.), *The future of the postal sector in a digital world*. Switzerland: Springer.

The Sharing Economy and the "Uberization" Phenomenon: What Impacts on the Economy in General and for the Delivery Operators in Particular?

Claire Borsenberger

1 Introduction

The word "Uberization" comes from a service developed by the firm Uber, founded in San Francisco in 2009, active in 59 countries and more than 200 cities worldwide and valued at $62.5 billion at the end of 2015. The service UberPop allows ordinary people, without any taxi license, to behave as taxi-drivers carrying passengers with their personal car (Griffin 2014; Areblad 2015).

Today "Uberization" has become common language and refers to the substitution of intermediated relationships with direct exchanges between service providers and users who interact on Internet platforms (Oram 2001; Sundararajan 2014). These online platforms provide a peer-to-peer marketplace for regular people to trade directly with each other in many sectors such as accommodation (Airbnb, HomeAway), car rental (RelayRides, Getaround), transportation by car (Uber, Lyft), Do It Yourself (1000tools.com, SnapGoods) and so on.

Postal operators cannot avoid this phenomenon. Many startups are developing an Uber-like business model on the last mile delivery segment. The two giants in the B2C e-commerce sector, Google and Amazon, are also developing their Uber-like delivery services, respectively Google Express and Amazon Flex Service. Uber itself is now targeting the transport of goods in addition to the transport of passengers.

The opinions expressed here do not necessarily reflect the position of La Poste. I sincerely thank Isabelle Carslake, economist at Frontier Economics, for her valuable comments.

C. Borsenberger (✉)
Department of Doctrine et Modélisation, Direction of Regulation, Institutional and European Affairs, Groupe La Poste, Paris, France
e-mail: claire.borsenberger@laposte.fr

C. Borsenberger
University François Rabelais, Tours, France

M. Crew et al. (eds.), *The Changing Postal and Delivery Sector*,
Topics in Regulatory Economics and Policy,
DOI 10.1007/978-3-319-46046-8_12

The aim of this chapter is to better understand the Uberization phenomenon, its impact on the economy in general and on parcel delivery sector in particular. In Sect. 2, the Uberization concept is defined, its link with the sharing economy and its drivers discussed. Then the benefits and the concerns raised by the sharing economy are discussed in Sect. 3 before giving an overview of the current debate over whether the sharing economy needs to be regulated in Sect. 4. Section 5 concludes.

2 The Uberization Phenomenon, Its Link with the Sharing Economy and Its Drivers

2.1 Uber, a Firm Belonging to the "Sharing Economy"?

The Uberization phenomenon has been portrayed by its supporters as an example of the "sharing economy" which encompasses under-used assets such as goods and services that are shared or exchanged for both monetary and nonmonetary benefit. The firm Uber itself defines its offer not as a taxi service but as a car sharing transportation service (Areblad 2015). In the same spirit, Airbnb defines itself as "a social website that connects people who have space to spare with those who are looking for a place to stay".

To its detractors, Uber distorts the original spirit of the sharing economy based on gift, reciprocity, exchanges rather than sales, and non-profit transactions.[1] Belk (2014) talked about "pseudo-sharing" practices, "a wolf-in-sheep's-clothing phenomenon"; Kalamar (2013) denounced practices of "sharewashing" (like "green-washing" practices).

According to Sundararajan (2014), the phrase 'sharing economy' creates a misconception about these platforms and the businesses they enable. Although some may effectively facilitate sharing, they are typically not organized like food cooperatives or farmer collectives and do not fit with the functional economy as defined by Stahel (1997) or the gift economy (Cheal 1988).[2] Rather, they are grounded in simple free enterprise, individual property rights, external financing, trade-for-profit, market-based prices, and new opportunities for exchange. As emphasized by Geron (2013), "the concept of sharing has created new markets from things that were not previously considered as monetizable" and has converted informal peer activities into businesses. Nevertheless, the sharing economy is considered in its broadest sense in the remaining of this chapter.

---

[1]The pioneers of collaborative consumption criticized the wasteful character of consumerism in a world with limited resources and emphasized the social dimension of the sharing economy (Caillé 2013; Botsman and Rogers 2011).

[2]The functional economy seeks to optimize the use of goods and services and thus the management of existing wealth. The gift economy is based on exchanges where valuables are not traded or sold, but rather given without an explicit agreement for immediate or future rewards.

2.2 A Growing Phenomenon Which Spares no Economic Sector

Recent developments in technology and the development of the Internet have made it possible for individuals to do business and exchange content online with other private individuals, instead of having to trade with a traditional company as a middle hand as in traditional 'business-to-consumer' (B2C) commerce (Yu et al. 2004), at a scale without precedent. Placing the capabilities of these new digital technologies in the hands of millions of consumers has created the possibility of digitally intermediated peer-to-peer business. This is reinforced by the parallel development of social networks that have encouraged the development of relationships and interactions between specific communities.

In 2013, 44 percent of US consumers were familiar with the notion of the sharing economy, and 19 percent of the total US adult population had engaged in a sharing economy transaction (PwC 2015). In 2014, 89 percent of French people had already taken part in at least one practice of "collaborative consumption" (DGE 2015).[3] According to the Future of Privacy Forum, a Washington DC based think tank, the total value of the sharing economy in 2013 was estimated to $26 billion worldwide and could reach $110 billion in the coming years. Lilico and Sinclair (2016) estimated that around half of the final consumption of EU 28 households is in markets amenable to sharing-economy business models.[4]

Many traditional sectors and industries are disrupted by sharing practices. According to PwC (2015), the five key sharing sectors are the automotive industry or, more generally, the mobility industry, the retail and consumer goods industry, the accommodation sector, and the entertainment, media and communications sector. Sharing practices in these sectors have the potential to grow from roughly $15 billion in global revenues today to around $335 billion by 2025.

As many other economic activities, "the last mile [delivery sector] is under attack" (Accenture 2015). Many start-ups are entering the market of last-mile delivery of goods with an 'asset-light' business model. Among disruptors in the last-mile delivery sector, one can cite companies such as Postmates, Deliv, LaserShip, OnTrac, Roadie, Kanga who are operating in US cities, EasyVan, GoGoVan in Hong Kong, Delivery in India, Renren Kuaidi in China, Colisweb, Colivoiturage, Colismalin, Stuart, TokTokTok, Deliver.ee, Drivoo and Bring4You in France, PiggyBaggy in Finland and Nimber in Norway. Even Uber with UberRush and UberCargo (recently rebranded UberVan), Google with Google

[3]Rachel Botsman defined the "collaborative consumption" as an economic model based on sharing, swapping, trading, or renting products and services, enabling access over ownership. It is reinventing not just what we consume but how we consume (http://www.collaborativeconsumption.com/2013/11/22/the-sharing-economy-lacks-a-shared-definition/).

[4]They define the sharing economy as "the use of digital platforms or portals to reduce the scale for viable hiring transactions or viable participation in consumer hiring markets (i.e. 'sharing' in the sense of hiring an asset) and thereby reduce the extent to which assets are under-utilized".

Express and Amazon with FlexService are entering the market, a proof of the business opportunities offered by this activity.

A growing segment of on-demand delivery logistics is the Same Day delivery market, a segment until today served by express and courier operators. According to Gonzales (2014), about $100 million of merchandise was ordered via Same Day delivery in 2014 in 20 US cities, generating about $20 million in shipping fees. He predicted that by 2018, $4 billion of merchandise will be ordered via Same Day delivery, generating a little over $1 billion in shipping fees. According to the US Same Day couriers' trade association CLDA (Customised Logistics and Delivery Association) cited by Milt (2015), the Same Day market is worth $8.7 billion. Another specific niche targeted by disruptors is the meal and fresh food delivery service market, valued at $90 billion by 2019 (16 percent of food service global market) according to Rocket Internet (2015). Pioneers on this segment of activity (Foodora, Citycake, Resto-In) are now competing with Uber and its service UberEats already operational in Los Angeles, Chicago, New York, Austin, San Francisco, Seattle, Washington, Toronto, Barcelona and Paris.

2.3 *The Drivers of This Growth*

Along with the development of Internet, Sundararajan (2014) listed three other key factors that have led to the growth of the sharing economy at an unprecedented scale. The emergence of digital technology-based platforms that facilitate economic exchange, and of online or mobile payment systems that allow individuals to achieve peer-to-peer economic transactions, is the first of these factors. Urbanization and globalization is another. Cities have always been a place of interaction between people due to their proximity and a place of exchanges of goods through marketplaces and a place of shared use of infrastructure and services like healthcare, libraries, and public transport. The growth of the world population and the increasing concentration of people in cities both create new needs (for example in terms of mobility) and facilitate production of local services, which are at the heart of the sharing economy. Last but not least, according to Sundararajan, the development of the sharing economy is driven by ecological considerations people's desire to choose 'asset-light' forms of living that utilize fewer resources and lower their ecological footprint.

An additional factor should be added to this list: the current economic crisis. Because of the bad economic context, some individuals have turned to peer-to-peer practices to supplement their revenues by providing some services and monetizing excess or idle resources. According to Robert et al. (2014), peer-to-peer practices "are conditioned by the financial opportunity they represent and the immutable quest of purchasing power."

3 The Pros and the Cons of the Trend of Uberization

These peer-to-peer platforms change the way many people commute, shop, go on vacation, and borrow. They open up new opportunities and generate positive externalities, but also disrupt long-established companies.

3.1 The Sharing Economy: An Engine of Sustainable and Durable Growth

Like many others economists, Sundararajan (2014) argued that the sharing economy generates productivity gains, reduces transaction costs thanks to an increased utilization of shared assets, leading to cost and price decreases, sustaining consumption and economic growth. Koopman et al. (2015) also support this view. The sharing economy creates value for both consumers and producers by giving people an opportunity to exploit on a more productive way underutilized assets or "dead capital". By coordinating buyers and sellers online, marketplaces reduce the transaction costs and the need of intermediated organizations (such as the traditional firms) and by collecting and analyzing a huge amount of data, they are able to monitor exchanges more efficiently and reduce information asymmetries, making both the supply and demand sides of markets more competitive. Moreover, according to Lilico and Sinclair (2016) and contrary to a preconception that sharing increases inequality,[5] the sharing economy is likely to reduce social exclusion by increasing access to goods and services (for instance, increased access to mobility might reduce isolation among the elderly) and to reduce inequality by diminishing the degree to which either wealth or the ability to borrow is necessary to access valuable assets, and by increasing the welfare of low-income consumers.

More globally, according to Gori et al. (2015), "sharing-economy models may constitute one of the primary instruments through which a city becomes smart" (p. 13). This new economic model based on the usage rather than the property of goods, on a shared and more efficient use of resources, is potentially source of positive externalities for the planet (provided that reuse does not slow the diffusion of new, more resource-efficient technologies and that sharing practices do not create a "rebound effect" leading to overconsumption). According to Demailly and Novel (2014), shareable goods account for about a quarter of French households' consumption expenditure and a third of the quantity (in tons) of goods they throw out each year (like clothes, books, DVDs and CDs, household electrical goods, furniture, tools, and so on). If sharing models could be operated under the most favorable conditions, savings of up to 7 percent in the household budget and 20 percent in terms of waste could be achieved.

---

[5]At first glance, the sharing economy might exacerbate inequality: the existing owners of assets will be able to increase the return on those assets by increasing their utilization (homeowners can rent out their homes using Airbnb, for example), but fewer people will own assets.

The impact of sharing practices on the environment will depend on the organization of production and on consumers' behavior. The first empirical studies concluded sharing practices generate positive externalities. For example, Santi et al. (2014) showed that cumulative trip length can be cut by 40 per cent or more thanks to ride sharing practices in New York City, leading to reductions in service cost, price and CO_2 emissions. In the same spirit, Copenhagen Economics (2015) concluded that a well-functioning peer-to-peer transport service in Stockholm is likely to create significant economic benefits by reducing the use of private cars and consequently, congestion and pollution. Under conservative assumptions, this would create a total value for society of up to SEK 870 million per year (around $102 million).

3.2 The Sharing Economy: A Disruptive Change for Traditional Actors that Raises Some Concerns About the Level Playing Field and Labor Conditions

Beside these rather positive points, peer-to-peer practices put competitive pressures on established players. Indeed, established manufacturers of physical goods or traditional service providers could be negatively affected by the growth of the sharing economy, which could induce a decrease in the demand for their products and services (the disruptors proposing both better and cheaper services). Ultimately, the degree of disruption created by sharing platforms will depend on how much customers are willing to switch away from traditional providers, on the level of rents in traditional sectors that can be more or less easily captured and the competitive intensity among disruptors. For example, Zervas et al. (2014) estimated that the entry of Airbnb into the Texas accommodation market has had a negative impact on local hotel revenues: an additional 1 percent increase in the size of the Airbnb market will result in a 0.05 percent decrease in total hotel revenue.

On last-mile delivery markets, previously cited new actors are clearly disrupting established couriers, express and postal operators. But, from now, no empirical study has been done to estimate the impact of this new business model on traditional operators. In all cases, it is clear that not having vehicles, warehouses to maintain and regular salary and benefits to pay helps these start-ups to minimize their costs and creates a new cost-effective logistics network, adding flexibility to the delivery process. For some experts, the competitive threat put on established delivery operators is rather low: the peer-to-peer model could only be applied to specific and local market segments and has some pitfalls. For example, according to an anonymous source cited by Isaac (2016), several delivery start-ups are currently facing difficulties to recruit and keep drivers and are not profitable. On the contrary, some analysts [like David Battersby, Redmayne-Bentley investment manager, or Gary Paulin, co-founder of brokerage Aviate Global, cited by Prakash (2016)] think that new entrants could dent the market share of incumbent courier, express and postal operators.

Current consumer protection regulatory rules may not be appropriate to deal with this new economy. (Regulation based on market dominance is assessed in Sect. 4.) This raises asymmetries and several concerns about the level playing field between the new platform players and traditional service providers. For example, while traditional companies have to comply with strict rules to ensure consumer protection, sharing economy platforms have much freedom in this field; application of rules related to the liability of the intermediary or data protection for example is not always well defined on peer-to-peer markets. In the long run, this lack or inadequacy of consumers' protection rules could be detrimental to the development of the sharing economy based on trust.

Another highlighted concern of the sharing economy is related to the fact that under the current rules, most of the revenues coming from peer-to-peer practices escape taxation. In Spain, it is estimated that in the accommodation sector, such practices would have caused a tax shortfall of €2.5 billion per year. In the USA, States would have lost 3.4 percent of their annual tax revenues on car sales due to the development car sharing practices (DGE 2015). New taxation policies are being developed to ensure the taxation of these activities.[6]

Last but not least, the working conditions of these new self-employed workers have raised important concerns. According to Sundararajan (2015), two opposite forms of employment could emerge. On the one hand, we might see more, what Sundararajan calls "empowered micro-entrepreneurs", i.e. "individuals who take control of their own destinies on an unprecedented scale, working fewer hours with more flexible schedules, striking a better work-life balance and earning money doing work they enjoy". On the other hand, we could see more disenfranchised workers gaining low wages, facing high levels of job insecurity, without or with only a low social safety net.

These self-employed workers acting in the sharing economy do not enjoy the same labor conditions as in large companies. They do not have the same access to regular training, limiting their ability to respond to the changing skills requirements of the economy and to develop their career. In addition, they do not access the supplementary social protection schemes (health insurance and welfare) as developed for employees in large companies under basic welfare schemes. Finally, the chances for them to be granted personal loans by financial institutions is lower, as their revenues are variable and do not match as easily with bank criteria. The same goes for housing, especially in large cities, where the rental deposit asked for is likely to be higher for them, as their revenues tend to be more variable in the sharing economy as in more traditional jobs.

However, according to authors such as Schor (2014) and Hall and Krueger (2015), the way platforms of sharing economy affect wages themselves is actually not clear.

---

[6]To limit fiscal distortions, several countries or cities implement new rules. For example, the French government introduced in December 2015 new rules to tax revenues from collaborative economy: platforms like Airbnb or Drivy will now be obliged to provide their members with a statement of revenues earned during the previous year, an amount that they will have to declare to fiscal authorities (if this obligation is not satisfied, platforms will be subject to a fine of €10,000).

In the current gloomy economic environment, new earning opportunities could be a good thing at least for some workers of the sharing economy. According to an empirical study by Sundararajan and Kokkodis, cited by Sundararajan (2015), wages in the sharing economy were higher than the national averages in "non-offshoreable" occupations like plumbing or electrical work (that could not be made at distance) but significantly lower in "offshoreable" ones (for example, call center operators who could make the job from a foreign country). They explained the observed higher average wage rates by the fact that peer-to-peer platforms give customers a more visible window into labor quality levels of providers (thanks to online feedback and reputation systems) and that these feedback systems motivate providers to do a better job (knowing that bad job could severely impair their ability to find work in the future). Hall and Krueger (2015) obtained a similar result when comparing the after-tax net hourly earnings of Uber's drivers and taxi drivers: according to their study, Uber drivers earn at least as much as taxi drivers, and in many cases even more.

3.3 *An Opportunity for Traditional Providers of Delivery Services?*

In the postal sector, the "Uberization" of delivery could threat the universal postal service provision by reducing the profitability of traditional postal operators in a moment in which they are trying to develop their parcel delivery activity in order to compensate the decrease in mail volume and revenues. On the other hand, these changes offer new business opportunities to traditional providers.

Some operators like DHL are testing their own crowdsourced delivery services to compete with disruptors (the "Bring.Buddy" project). Other operators made the choice to conclude partnerships or to make acquisition of disruptors. For example, in February 2016, UPS participated to the fund raising launched by Deliv. GeoPost (a subsidiary of the French postal operator La Poste) took over a minority share in the capital of Stuart, an on-demand delivery French start-up in October 2015. To win market shares the last-mile delivery market over their rivals, parcel delivery operators are also investing in alternative forms of delivery, in order to offer more choice and flexibility to consumers. Many offer parcel delivery services in relay points, in automatic parcel boxes, or even directly in your car trunk.

4 Is Specific Regulation Needed?

Concerns about the new business models of the sharing economy (related to consumers' protection, working conditions, fiscal issues, and so on) raise a common question among States: should these new business models be regulated in a specific way to minimize risks and maximize benefits to consumers, workers and the whole economy?

4.1 *The Pro-regulation Proponents' Argument of Peer-to-Peer Platforms' Dominant Position*

The pro-regulation proponents expressed concerns about peer-to-peer platforms' market domination and the risk they use their dominant position to engage in anti-competitive behavior that may ultimately reduce consumer welfare. Conversely, the opponents to any form of regulation argue that dominant platforms are already facing competition and new entrants. Even if Uber is currently dominating the ride-sharing sector in many countries, Lyft is a genuine competitor in many US cities. Similarly, Airbnb faces the competition of VRBO and HomeAway among others. On the last mile delivery market, we saw that competition is tough. Thanks to the very low switching costs normally associated with these sectors, it's very easy for consumers to move around and look at competition. Furthermore, as argued by Tapscott and Tapscott cited in the *Wall Street Journal* (2016), blockchain technology could soon disrupt the current disruptors by connecting services providers and users directly without any intermediary, in the same way as cryptocurrencies, such as Bitcoin, had disrupted the payment system and the financial sector (Bach and Jaag 2015).[7] In sum, the dominant position argument to justify regulation is rather thin.

Another argument against the pro-regulation proponents' point of view is that the above dominance issues related to network effects, reputation, lock-in, and so on, are not specific to the sharing economy but common to the whole "digital economy". Competition authorities are already well versed in these issues and well equipped to handle these competition policy issues. So, there is no need for additional law or body of regulation in this area.

4.2 *Arguments Based on New Market Failures*

The pro-regulation camp argues that new market failures appear in the sharing economy such as safety concerns, labor concerns, and so on, and that the mechanisms based on reputation which should discipline agents, are not free from drawbacks (they can be biased or manipulated by interested parties) and raise concerns about privacy (Ranchordas 2015; Dzieza 2015; Dambrine et al. 2015).

[7]La'Zooz and Arcade City are examples of this new sort of cooperative ride-hailing service, connecting directly riders and drivers without any intermediary platform and using the blockchain technology to issue "crypto-equity". The main difference between Uber & Co and La'Zooz or Arcade City is on the pricing decision level: whereas Uber and Lyft manage prices in a centralized way, by decentralizing that decision to the level of the driver and rider, Arcade City frees the driver to be an entrepreneur (he is free to set its own rates) and empowers the rider with control over their entire experience (riders are able to review driver profiles in advance of choosing their ride).

For the anti-regulation camp, reputation effects are a better regulatory mechanism than the law (Koopman et al. 2015). Platforms have a natural incentive to alleviate exchange-deterring forms of information failure and offer efficient feedback mechanisms, since their commercial success is linked to the ability of their participants to engage in exchange and so relies on trust. In this context, Edelman and Geradin (2015) pled for an "updated regulatory framework that is sufficiently flexible to allow software platforms to operate and deliver their services efficiently, while ensuring that service providers, users and third parties are adequately protected from harms that may arise from services provided through these platforms" and denounced what they call "protectionist regulation" whose primary purpose is to protect "incumbents" at the expense of new entrants and which so not seem to be justified by genuine consumer protection concerns.

4.3 The Risk of Over-Regulating the Sharing Economy

It seems obvious that applying outdated rules conceived to compensate market failures in the context of old-fashioned commercial relationships between a professional and a consumer (and not for peer-to-peer transactions) is not appropriate. Laws written to regulate taxicabs, hotels, and other industries fit poorly with the new platforms, providers, and consumers using the sharing economy. Business models are different. The "one size fits all" principle is irrelevant. Imposing the same old-fashioned regulatory rules to new ways to do business could get new companies in trouble and stifle innovation. All the benefits consumers get from the sharing economy would be lost (optimized use of previously under-utilized property or skills, ability to bring together people who might otherwise not be consumers with people who might otherwise not be producers, and so on).

The sharing economy needs a new legal framework based on simplified and flexible rules. Regulators must carefully adapt their regulatory tools to fit the diverse ecosystem of new business models, producers, and platforms. In particular, there is more room for self-regulation in the sharing economy. In many cases, peer-to-peer platforms have the right incentives, an incredible amount of information, and are best able to control those consuming and providing services through their platforms. For that reason, new technological and reputation-based mechanisms of self-regulation could be a key tool for regulating the sharing economy.

Some countries have rightly adopted friendly and smart regulatory rules to peer-to-peer platforms.[8] On the contrary, under the lobby of "traditional" providers, public authorities have sometimes imposed the same old regulation rules (relevant to regulate old-fashioned firms) to peer-to-peers platforms and even prohibit some

[8]In February 2014, Amsterdam became the first city to pass so-called "Airbnb friendly" legislation and in London, 1970s regulations limiting short-term stays were scrapped, making it easier for Airbnb and others to operate in the city. The British government has even launched an initiative to make the UK the "global center for the sharing economy".

sharing services like UberPop.[9] Facing the diversity of situations among EU Member States, the European Commission (2016) presented policy orientations aimed to sustain a balanced development of the sharing economy. The Communication invites EU Member States to review and where appropriate revise existing legislation according to this guidance. The Commission plans to monitor the rapidly changing regulatory environment as well as economic and business developments.

5 Conclusions

The sharing economy is a source of uncontestable benefits for consumers who will tend to benefit from lower prices, an increased quality of services, and the ability to satisfy more diverse preferences over time. From the "peer-to-peer" services providers' point of view, the situation is more mitigated: they may enjoy new economic opportunities and higher aggregate earnings, but may not enjoy access to the other benefits associated with traditional employment (paid holiday, paid sick leave, employment protection, and so on). Traditional good manufacturers and existing service providers could clearly be affected by the reduction of barriers to entry and therefore face more competition in the markets in which they operate.

This complex situation has motivated the call for greater regulatory of the sharing platforms. However, there are a number of reasons why regulation might not need to be the same for the sharing economy as for traditional providers. In particular, the transparency provided by digital technologies reduces transaction cost, asymmetries and the need to regulate sharing economy providers in a world based on trust. Moreover, in the digital economy, things are evolving very, very rapidly and according to some experts, the current disrupters of the sharing economy like Uber and Airbnb could be soon disrupted by blockchain technology.

In the delivery sector, even if the business model of last-mile sharing delivery services is in its infancy and not yet always sustainable, it is undeniable that crowdsourced delivery services put pressure on established courier, express and postal operators, pushing them to innovate and to provide even more reliable and fast delivery, to the benefit of consumers. To compete with new entrants, traditional providers should certainly focus more their efforts in asking for a softer regulation regarding the obligations currently imposed to them rather than trying to call for a stronger regulation of Uber-type providers.

[9]UberPop is currently considered as illegal in Spain, France, Germany, Belgium, the Netherlands, Italy, South Korea, Thailand, and India and in some US cities (Miami, Houston, Portland, Austin, and New Orleans). Other US cities, such as Minneapolis and Detroit, have subjected ride-sharing services to taxicab regulations.

References

Accenture. (2015). *Achieving high performance in the post and parcel industry.*

Areblad, L. (2015). *Marketing manager at Uber Sweden*, Stockholm, April 17, 2015.

Bach, C., & Jaag C. (2015). *Cryptocurrencies: New opportunities for postal financial services.* Paper presented at the 23rd conference on postal and delivery economics, Vouliagmeni, Athens, Greece, June.

Belk, R. (2014). Sharing versus pseudo-sharing in Web 2.0. *The Anthropologist, 18*(1), 7–23.

Botsman, R., & Rogers R. (2011). *What's mine is yours: How collaborative consumption is changing the way we live*, UK: HarperCollins.

Caillé, A. (2013). C'est devenu un outil pour reconstruire du lien. Le Monde.fr., 5 janvier.

Cheal, D. J. (1988). *The Gift Economy*. New York: Routledge.

Copenhagen Economics. (2015), *Economic benefits of peer-to-peer transport services*, report for Uber, August.

Dambrine, B., Jerome, J., & Ambrose, B. (2015, June). User reputation: Building trust and addressing privacy issues in the sharing economy. In *Future of privacy forum.*

Demailly, D., & Novel, A. S. (2014). Economie du partage: enjeux et opportunités pour la transition éconologique. Institut du Développement Durable et des Relations Internationales.

DGE. (2015). *Enjeux et perspectives de la consommation collaborative.* Final report, June.

Dzieza, J. (2015). *The rating game—How Uber and its peers turned us into horrible bosses.* October 28.

Edelman, B. G., & Geradin, D. (2015). *Efficiencies and regulatory shortcuts: How should we regulate companies like Airbnb and Uber*? Harvard Business School Working Paper 16-026.

European Commission. (2016). *Communication from the commission to the European Parliament, the Council, the European economic and social committee and the committee of the regions—A European agenda for the collaborative economy.* SWD (2016) 184 final, June.

Geron, T. (2013). Airbnb and the unstoppable rise of the share economy. *Forbes*, January 23. http://www.forbes.com/sites/tomiogeron/2013/01/23/airbnb-and-the-unstoppable-rise-of-the-share-economy/#7e45087a6790

Gonzales, A. (2014). *How big is the same day delivery market*? September 24.

Gori, P., Parcu P. L., & Stasi M. L. (2015). *Smart cities and sharing economy.* EUI Working Paper 2015/96, Robert Schuman Centre for Advanced Studies, Florence School of Regulation.

Griffin, A. (2014). *Uber's cheap service to be banned in France as Paris taxis block roads.* USA: The Independent.

Hall, J. & Krueger, A. (2015). *An analysis of the labor market for Uber's driver-partners in the United States.* Working paper, January.

Issac, M. (2016). Delivery start-ups face road bumps in quest to capture untapped market. *The Wall Street Journal*, February 11, 2016. http://www.nytimes.com/2016/02/12/technology/delivery-start-ups-face-road-bumps-in-quest-to-capture-untapped-market.html?_r=0

Kalamar, A. (2013). Sharewashing is the new greenwashing. *OpEd News*, May 13.

Koopman, C., Mitchell M., & Thierer A. (2015). *The sharing economy: Issues facing platforms, participants, and regulators.* USA: Mercatus Center, George Mason University.

Lilico, A., & Sinclair M. (2016). *The cost of non-Europe in the sharing economic.* Research paper by Europe Economics.

Milt, D. J. (2015). *The Uberfication of deliveries.* ParcelHero Industry Report.

Oram, A. (2001). *Peer-to-peer: Harnessing the benefits of a disruptive technology.* USA: O'Reilly Media, Inc.

Prakash, A. (2016). *Uber may deliver latest blow to European parcel firms.* Reuters, February 16, 2016. http://uk.reuters.com/article/uk-europe-markets-parcel-idUKKCN0VP1N2

PwC. (2015). *The sharing economy, consumer intelligence series.*

Ranchordas, S. (2015). Does sharing mean caring? Regulating innovation in the sharing economy. *Minnesota Journal of Law, Science and Technology.* Tilburg Law School Legal Studies Research Paper Series no 06/2015.

Robert, I., Binninger, A., & Ourahmoune, N. (2014). La consommation collaborative, le versant encore équivoque de l'économie de la fonctionnalité. *Développement durable et territoires*, vol. 5, no. 1, février, pp. 13–14.

Rocket Internet. (2015). Building out the global leadership in online takeaway. March.

Santi, P., Resta, G., Szell, M., Sobolevsky, S., Strogatz, S. H., & Ratti, C. (2014), Quantifying the benefits of vehicle pooling with shareability networks. In *Proceedings of the National Academy of Sciences of the United States of America* (vol. 111, no. 37, pp. 13290–13294).

Schor, J. (2014). Debating the sharing economy, great transition initiative. October.

Stahel, W. R. (1997). The functional economy: Cultural and organizational change. In D. J. Richards (Ed.), *The industrial green game* (pp. 91–100). Washington DC: National Academy Press.

Sundararajan, A. (2014). Peer-to-Peer businesses and the sharing (collaborative). *Economy: Overview, Economic Effects and Regulatory Issues.*

Sundararajan, A. (2015). Will the on-demand economy raise global living standards? *The Huffington Post*, September 9th. http://www.huffingtonpost.com/arun-sundararajan/will-the-ondemand-economy_b_8113616.html

The Wall Street Journal. (2016). Could blockchain technology disrupt Uber, Airbnb? January 25th. http://www.wsj.com/video/could-blockchain-technology-disrupt-uber-airbnb/859799C6-C953-44F2-AEED-617E7B52164F.html

Yu, B., Singh, M. P., & Sycara, K. (2004). Developing trust in large-scale peer-to-peer systems. In *IEEE First Symposium on Multi-Agent Security and Survivability* (pp. 1–10).

Zervas, G., Proserpio, D., & Byers, J. W. (2014). The Rise of the sharing economy: Estimating the impact of Airbnb on the hotel industry. Boston University School of Management Research Paper Series no. 2013-16, February.

Blockchain Technology and Cryptocurrencies: Opportunities for Postal Financial Services

Christian Jaag and Christian Bach

1 Introduction

This paper explores opportunities arising from blockchain technology for postal operators (POs).[1] Blockchain technology has lately received a lot of interest by the media and the industry, especially in financial services.[2] In the past years an entire ecosystem of new companies has developed, offering hundreds of different blockchain applications. Blockchains are a new kind of decentralized, secure and fast means of record-keeping. The first application of blockchain technology are cryptocurrencies like Bitcoin, which have become an alternative to commodity money and fiat money, but POs may be able to exploit this technology in a number of different ways.

Contrary to traditional currencies, cryptocurrencies neither have physical form nor are they guaranteed or backed by any central authority. They are created by their users and attain value by usage and the confidence of those participating in the respective system. Cryptocurrencies are associated with their own payment systems, which allows for payments between individuals digitally without relying on central institutions, intermediaries or further infrastructure as required for conventional payment systems. Besides Bitcoin, there are over 200 further cryptocurrencies that are essentially copying the Bitcoin protocol with some minor changes or improvements. While their legitimacy as currencies has been questioned due to

[1]National incumbents and their competitors.

[2]See e.g. The Economist (2015). Also POs have become interested in the technology, see e.g. USPS (2016).

C. Jaag
Swiss Economics, Weinbergstrasse 102, 8006 Zurich, Switzerland

C. Bach (✉)
University of Liverpool and Swiss Economics, Zurich, Switzerland

M. Crew et al. (eds.), *The Changing Postal and Delivery Sector*,
Topics in Regulatory Economics and Policy,
DOI 10.1007/978-3-319-46046-8_13

their high exchange rate volatility, the significant potential of blockchain technology for applications far beyond payments is undeniable.

As POs typically have a role as financial intermediaries and act in an international and increasingly digital environment, decentralized blockchain-based payment-systems potentially may be of particular interest to them. In fact, as the post has a wide network of access points and is highly trusted by the general public, it may be well-suited to offer services which counter some disadvantages of decentralized payment systems and cryptocurrencies, while retaining the benefits of their technology. By turning to these new technologies, POs may extend their role as a financial intermediary with new domestic and international services. Furthermore, POs may even issue their own cryptocurrency to protect customers from the high exchange-rate volatility of current cryptocurrencies.

The paper proceeds as follows. Section 2 presents a brief characterization of decentralized payment-systems and cryptocurrencies. Also, an overview of government regulation for cryptocurrencies is provided with focus on the United States. Furthermore, several opportunities and challenges for individuals and companies related to cryptocurrencies are presented. In Sect. 3 it is argued that POs could benefit from including financial blockchain applications in their business model. In Sect. 4 the idea of Postcoin, a novel concept for a postal cryptocurrency, is presented. Section 5 briefly discusses non-financial applications of blockchain technology for POs. Finally, a conclusion is offered in Sect. 6.

2 Blockchain Technology and Cryptocurrencies

Blockchain technology was originally created as a way to transfer value, specifically within the context of the digital currency Bitcoin. As such, uses of blockchain technology include payments and other financial transactions.[3] Blockchains enable peer-to-peer transactions by removing the need for a trusted intermediary to verify the transactions, and to delay the transaction while it is being verified. Hence, there is no bank or other single third party keeping the ledger and verifying the transaction — no one entity controls the ledger. Instead, the network, as a whole, verifies the transactions through a decentralized consensus mechanism.

A blockchain makes this possible by being a decentralized ledger. This public ledger is not so different from the ledger that traditional financial institutions maintain, with a record of who owns what. Blockchain technology combines two ideas: First, defining a digital token (i.e. a coin of a corresponding currency) as a chain of transactions makes it possible to solve the problem of double spending, because ownership is defined as having received a coin in the past and being its latest recipient. In contrast, simple possession of a code would not be suitable, because each code can be duplicated.

[3]Further applications will be outlined in Sect. 5.

Second, by using a validation mechanism like proof of work ("mining"), there is only one accepted transaction history. There are two types of participants in a blockchain network: Nodes and miners. Nodes verify the legitimacy of blocks and keep a copy of the blockchain. They also create transaction records (e.g. transferred quantity of currency, addresses involved, proof that the transaction is valid, time of transaction), verify other nodes' transactions and spread them over the network. Mining is the process of adding transactions to the blockchain. Miners are specialized nodes that pick up transaction records, verify them and generate new blocks by performing cryptographic functions. In the case of Bitcoin, miners find a block every 10 min on average and get awarded with new bitcoins in return.[4] Once a transaction has been added to a block and the block is chained to the previous block, it is settled irrevocably.[5] As all users who operate a node of the network must agree on every legitimate transaction[6] in the past (by passing them on to other nodes), determining who owns a specific currency unit is uncontroversial, and without the need to trust anybody. Essentially, a decentralized register determines the number of currency units belonging to the person who is able to prove that he is entitled to spend them.

Generally, blockchains fall into two groups: public and private. In a public blockchain like Bitcoin's, the right to alter the ledger by participating in the consensus mechanism is open to anyone. Transactions are publicly available for anyone to read. Alternatively, in a consortium or private blockchain, the right to alter the ledger by participating in the consensus mechanism is restricted to pre-selected individuals or institutions. Transactions may be either publicly available or restricted to a select number of participants.

2.1 Characteristics

Decentralized payment-systems enable peer-to-peer transactions, i.e. two individuals can exchange value without relying on a centralized third party. This is a major

[4]In Bitcoin, there are two kinds of incentives for miners: The first is new bitcoins. The reward started at 50 bitcoins per block; this value halves every 210,000 blocks, such that the total supply of bitcoins asymptotically approaches 21 million. Users can also attach fees to their transactions (the fee typically amounts to the equivalent of a few USD cents). Miners use the fees to decide which transactions to include in a block and collect the fees (see Jaag and Haller 2016). Currently, the miners' revenue from fees is much lower than the block reward. Since there is a maximum block size, block capacity becomes scarcer with increased usage. As a result, transaction fees become a more important source of revenue for miners (unless the maximum block size is increased—which would require a change in the consensus protocol).

[5]The settlement time of 10 min on average is much faster than with any non-cash financial transaction which may take days or—in the case of credit cards—even weeks.

[6]By participating in the network, nodes know of all transactions and blocks. Therefore, operators of nodes do not rely on third parties for checking whether a payment to them is legitimate and can be trusted. This is the incentive to run a node.

difference to existing payment solutions, as no financial intermediary is required for a transaction. In comparison, for a bank transfer two banks need to exchange money on behalf of their customers. Moreover, allowing an institution to transfer money, the transacting parties not only give away private information related to the transaction, but also give it access to their funds as well as to personal data.[7] Using a decentralized payment-system—without any intermediary—transaction costs are low, while no access to funds or personal information is given away to any third party.[8]

An important implication, which follows from a decentralized ledger, is the irreversibility of transactions. Once a payment is issued, it cannot be reversed. The only way to recover the claim is by asking the receiver to pay back the same amount in a new transaction. The irreversibility follows from the fact that each transaction is added to the blockchain by miners, which in turn cannot be altered but only extended. Therefore, payment in cryptocurrencies is similar to a cash payment, but does not have to be conducted over-the-counter. However, in contrast to the existing non-cash payment systems such as credit card or bank transfer (which are all reversible), the risk of transaction is shifted from receiver to sender via this irreversibility.[9]

Another distinguishing property of decentralized payment-systems is the pseudo anonymity of the transacting parties. When transferring cryptocurrencies, there is no need to disclose any personal information to the public or any third party whatsoever. This substantially reduces the risk of identity theft and fraud common with other forms of payment such as credit cards. Users can act under one or several pseudonyms without any obvious links to their true person. The pseudo anonymity of cryptocurrencies has given rise to some discussion about illegal usage.[10] This is a valid concern and thus an important topic for regulation.

Moreover, decentralized payment-systems are not bound by any geographical limit: Because of the virtual nature of the payment system, it does not matter whether an individual sends cryptocurrencies to a neighbor or to someone on the other side of the world. In contrast, it is often difficult to use traditional payment systems to transact across borders, since the financial intermediaries are bound by country-specific regulation and differing exchange rates. Decentralized payment-systems transcend state borders: essentially, they form a global payment system instead of several national ones.

[7]Especially with credit card payments, this creates the risk of theft.

[8]The success of blockchain-based transactions systems suggests that the cost of processing a transaction is less than the cost per transaction of the equivalent effort by the banking sector and, if need be, monetary authorities, or that additional costs are outweighed by the benefits in speed, security, and privacy.

[9]Cf. Jaag and Bach (2015) for a microeconomic analysis of the irreversibility characteristics of cryptocurrencies.

[10]A specific concern is ransomware that disables the computer unless a ransom is paid. Ransomware cannot accept PayPal or credit cards since those transactions are traceable. The increasing adoption of cryptocurrencies makes using them worthwhile.

Public blockchain-based payment systems need to provide incentives to their users to assist in securing the system. Consequently, it is not possible to use such systems for payments without using some currency as possible reward for securing the network. This can be accomplished by issuing units of a respective cryptocurrency, which can then by "mined" as a "block reward" by those who prove that they contribute to securing the network.[11]

A key property of cryptocurrencies, which significantly distinguishes it from traditional currencies, is the lack of a central money issuer. Cryptocurrencies are created in a decentralized process without any authority controlling the distribution of new units. Hence, there also exists no institution that could actively conduct monetary policy in the system. Consequently, cryptocurrencies are also not backed by any assets that central banks in a fiat or gold-backed system keep on their balance sheet. Exchangeability separates cryptocurrencies from other virtual concepts like frequent flyer miles or Facebook credits, which are neither freely tradable between people nor exchangeable against services outside the issuing company.

2.2 Regulation

Cryptocurrencies their payment systems are hard for governments to regulate. First, there is no central point of access. Second, decentralized payment-systems allow for international money transmission without any concern for national borders. Therefore, regulation would need to be coordinated across countries.

Decentralized payment-systems do not exhibit any central point of access for governmental interference or law enforcement. For instance, it is difficult for authorities to seize money holdings in cryptocurrencies since the entire system is pseudo anonymous. While a government may freeze bank accounts, it cannot do so with decentralized payment-systems. However, institutions and companies offering services related to decentralized payment-systems can be subjected to regulation, as they provide central access points. For instance, currency exchanges, which present a gateway between traditional currencies and cryptocurrencies, can be forced to abide by government regulation such as anti-money-laundering law. Law enforcement against Mt.Gox, a former exchange platform, is an example for this.

In the United States, the Financial Crimes Enforcement Network (FinCEN) has issued a first guidance relating to the regulation of money service businesses in March 2013 (see FinCEN 2013). Different rules apply to users and exchanges. Individuals who use cryptocurrencies to purchase or sell goods, do not fall under FinCEN's regulation. In contrast, cryptocurrency exchanges are considered to be money service businesses and therefore need to comply with FinCEN regulation. This regulation entails anti-money-laundering law. Subsequent to this first

[11]See the introduction to Sect. 2 above.

guidance, FinCEN (2014a, b) has provided additional clarification for services related to cryptocurrencies: miners and software providers do not fall under its regulation.

The New York State Department of Financial Services issued a so-called BitLicense, i.e. a business license of cryptocurrency activities. After it came into effect in August 2015, several Bitcoin companies announced they were stopping business in New York State because of the new regulations. In September 2015, the first BitLicense was issued to Circle Internet Financial (see NYDFS 2015).

2.3 Opportunities

Cryptocurrencies, such as Bitcoin, have innovative features either as a currency, payment system or, more generally, as a technology. With their unique characteristics, they bear the potential to substantially influence the existing financial system. Several opportunities could unfold for individuals, businesses and the economy as a whole.

By substituting traditional payment methods (which rely on financial intermediaries) by cryptocurrencies, it is possible to decrease transaction fees and therefore reduce the costs from non-cash payments. This especially applies to online businesses. Furthermore, decentralized payment-systems provide a quick low-cost way for sending money directly from person to person. For example, with traditional remittance services, emigrant workers pay an average of 12 % in fees to transfer money back to relatives in Sub-Saharan Africa (see Watkins and Quattri 2014).

The combination of low transaction costs with fast, easy usage can provide new methods of revenue schemes based on microtransactions. For instance, with cryptocurrencies it becomes possible to add a tipping system to online services such as blogs or to crowd-funded projects. Previously, small transactions have not been worthwhile, as the transaction costs outweighed the benefits or even the value of the transactions itself.

For individuals and companies it can be advantageous that transactions with cryptocurrencies are irreversible. For instance, payments by credit cards can be reversed after the purchase. Online merchants are thus exposed to the risk that customers reverse their payments after the respective order has already been shipped. In fact, payment irreversibility may strengthen e-commerce by reducing its overall risk, if merchants have more reputation to lose than customers (see Jaag and Bach 2015). In 2016, there are more than 100,000 merchants accepting Bitcoin, including Microsoft, Overstock, Newegg, DISH and Expedia (Nasdaq 2016).

Cryptocurrencies may also offer an alternative store of value for countries with unstable currencies.[12] For instance, in high-inflation countries, it may be beneficial to hold cryptocurrencies as assets in addition to national currency. Moreover, cryptocurrencies do not fall under the authority of government, and can thus not be devaluated or held back for fiscal or other purposes. A recent example is Argentina where the government devaluated the domestic currency to counter the country's trade deficit (see Coindesk 2014).

2.4 Challenges

In spite of several opportunities and a substantial innovation potential, quite some challenges associated with the nature and the use of cryptocurrencies and decentralized payment-systems remain. They open up new opportunities for business cases by trusted institutions like POs.

One major challenge is that it is hard to find out whether cryptocurrencies are a serious technology or just a large scam. Hence, potential users might want to understand decentralized payment-systems before starting to use them. Even though most of them do not understand the traditional financial system either (beyond an intuition and reasonably favorable experience), individuals and merchants who do not comprehend the mechanics of the underlying technology may hesitate to enter the cryptocurrency system due to a lack of trust in the system. Ignorance about decentralized payment-systems is still rather widespread. For instance, according to a survey by The Street (2014), three fourth of the questioned persons in the United States indicated that they are not familiar with Bitcoin at all.

Regulatory uncertainty also severely restricts widespread adoption of cryptocurrencies. Indeed, lack of clear governmental guidance represents one of the main challenges for cryptocurrencies at the moment. Generally, regulation in the financial sector usually demands high compliance and risk management efforts from financial intermediaries. Regulatory uncertainty is thus especially problematic because handling cryptocurrencies may result in the involuntary provision of financial services, subject to government regulation of financial intermediaries. New businesses acting in the uncharted territory of cryptocurrencies are hence exposed to the risk of being prosecuted.

Security concerns about handling and storing cryptocurrencies are another major challenge for users. Adversaries may gain access to their wallet and steal their money. Currency exchanges and companies that store cryptocurrency for their customers are vulnerable, too. If such companies are attacked, users may lose all money on their account. The most prominent example of cryptocurrency theft happened to the exchange platform Mt. Gox, which lost the equivalent of

[12]Exchange rates of currencies used in industrialized countries are usually more stable than cryptocurrencies. However, in developing countries, local currencies may be more volatile.

approximately USD 365 million in Bitcoin (see Bloomberg 2014b). Following this incident, Mt. Gox declared bankruptcy and it is likely that users will not be able to reclaim their assets.

Limited availability of cryptocurrency as well as the lack of trusted exchanges pose further problems for adoption. Currently, access to cryptocurrencies is provided only by online exchanges or personal trade. Exchange platforms are mostly new start-up firms with little reputation and no representation in the real world. However, people not familiar with online services would prefer to exchange currencies over the counter or use credit or debit cards. The introduction of cryptocurrency teller machines provides a partial solution, but it will take some time for their reach to be at a satisfactory level.

Finally, high exchange rate volatility also poses an issue for cryptocurrencies. For instance, the Bitcoin exchange rate against the USD plunged about 35 % in December 2012 after rumors had come up that Chinese regulators were to ban cryptocurrencies in their country (see Bloomberg 2014a). Users and merchants may not be willing to bear price fluctuation risks, which could adversely affect the value of sales. However, they do not necessarily need to bear the exchange rate fluctuation of cryptocurrencies. They can protect themselves from such risk by using hedge funds or service providers that convert cryptocurrencies into traditional currencies instantly. For instance, merchants who accept cryptocurrencies from their customers can immediately exchange them to a traditional currency. Thereby, these merchants benefit from decentralized payment-systems without being exposed to the volatility of corresponding cryptocurrencies.

As more companies and customers adopt them and their liquidity increases, cryptocurrencies are likely to gain in stability as a currency. Besides, a substantial part of the current fluctuations are due to regulatory and market uncertainties—both of which will decrease as regulatory guidance becomes clearer.

The challenges of cryptocurrencies can be summarized as follows. A lack of trusted and established institutions in the realm of decentralized payment-systems unleashes a feeling of risk and necessitates a high degree of personal responsibility, which users are not used to in conventional payment systems. These key challenges could be tackled by trusted firms, which offer cryptocurrency related assistance and services.

Table 1 provides an overview of the discussed opportunities and challenges of cryptocurrencies and decentralized payment-systems.

Table 1 Opportunities and challenges of cryptocurrencies and decentralized payment-systems

Opportunities	Challenges
• Easy-to-use	• Limited availability
• Privacy	• Security in usage
• Low transaction fees	• Reliable institutions
• Microtransactions	• Regulatory uncertainty
• Irreversibility	• Limited prevalence
• Alternative store of value	• Exchange rate volatility

3 Potential Applications for POs

Blockchains and cryptocurrencies provide new technologies which POs can use to better provide financial and non-financial services. Moreover, the challenges associated with the use of these technologies for individual users open up opportunities for new intermediaries like POs as trusted institutions.

Many POs face legal universal service obligations, requiring them—among other things—to provide access to post offices within reasonable distance. In 2013, with 663,210 post offices globally, the network of postal outlets was the densest retail network in the world (see Universal Postal Union 2014). There currently exist two major challenges for traditional POs: Indirect competition from electronic substitutes in the letter segment and direct competition in the parcel segment.

The first challenge results from the increasing use of email and other Internet based services for communication purposes. Since the end of the 1990s, physical mail volumes have declined in most industrialized countries. Consequently, posts face the challenge of operating dense networks of branches, being able to serve the population in proximity, while suffering from a decreasing letter demand.

The second challenge concerns the continuously growing sector of e-commerce. From the perspective of POs, e-commerce constitutes a unique opportunity and a rare growth area. Indeed, the global domestic postal parcel traffic has doubled during the last 20 years. However, liberalization of the parcel segment has attracted considerable competition.

There seems to be a well-suited match between cryptocurrencies and posts in view of the above-mentioned challenges (see Jaag and Bach 2013). On the one hand, cryptocurrencies and decentralized payment-systems are still lacking a physical interface that is easily as well as generally accessible to the public, while on the other hand POs dispose of nation-wide networks of branches with declining usage in their traditional core business. A natural opportunity for Posts seems to flow from using their network as a bridge between traditional currencies and the virtual world of cryptocurrencies by offering local exchange and transaction services. Also, the technology of decentralized payment-systems could be used to innovate and advance existing financial services. Some domestic and international opportunities for POs that might ensue from an implementation of cryptocurrencies into their business model are now presented.

3.1 Domestic Opportunities

Cryptocurrencies and decentralized payment-systems could extend the financial role of POs by enabling the provision of new services in their respective home markets.

3.1.1 Retail Solutions and E-Commerce

Cryptocurrencies appear to fit well the global rise of e-commerce. In 2012, sales in e-commerce already topped USD 1 trillion and are expected to rise annually by approximately 15 % in the next few years (see EMarketer 2013). On the one hand, this means that electronic payment methods will further gain in importance, as there is a physical separation between merchant and customer. On the other hand, this separation also increases the demand for postal logistic services, as the purchased goods need to be delivered to customers. Since cryptocurrencies, especially Bitcoin, are increasingly used in e-commerce, service provision with regards to cryptocurrencies could attract new customers to the post offices for parcels. In particular, persons owning neither a credit card nor a bank account would thus be enabled to access e-commerce via exchanging traditional currencies for cryptocurrencies. As a single intermediary between merchants and customers providing parcel delivery but also facilitating the financial transaction in e-commerce, POs would be able to reduce coordination needs and to offer more efficient e-commerce solutions. By combining their traditional strength in physical delivery with easy and low-cost payment services, POs may facilitate e-commerce and actually contribute to its further growth.

3.1.2 Services for Individuals

POs could also aim towards becoming a leading service point for remittances in cryptocurrencies and corresponding monetary transfers through decentralized payment-systems. Although it is possible for individuals to send, for example, Bitcoin without intermediary, there is still a role for the post as money transmitter. Combined with a postal account, POs could provide an interface for their clients to easily send money without having to understand decentralized payment-systems in detail.

The adoption of additional financial services also seems to correlate with the growth strategies of the financial branch in the postal sector. Indeed, POs already have considerable financial knowledge, which could be transferred to offer new financial services. Together with their extensive physical network, they are in strong position to not only serve domestic but also international markets.

3.2 International Opportunities

As decentralized payment-systems are not limited by national borders, they could provide the infrastructure for commercial and financial transactions on a global scale and serve as a tool for financial inclusion of the poor.

3.2.1 Financial Inclusion

Cryptocurrencies and decentralized payment-systems could become an important tool for POs to further advance financial inclusion. They enable access to the financial system with almost no financial infrastructure requirements. A single post office would be able to provide various financial services with an internet connection being the only requirement. With this technology posts could provide a savings account, where money could be stored in cryptocurrencies. Individuals without a bank account but a postal outlet in near proximity might particularly benefit from this opportunity. In addition, it would be possible to include a service to use cryptocurrency for payments to other individuals or companies. For those without access to the financial system, POs could represent a reliable and trusted gateway to a payment system based on cryptocurrencies, which might look like a scam at first glance. Widespread use of cryptocurrencies for mobile phone payments reflects the fact that the general demand for additional payment methods is high in developing countries. Moreover, in a number of African countries such services have been introduced and are already used by more than 20 % of all adults (see Lammer 2014).

Exclusion from the financial system is an important issue and a major obstacle for participation in global commerce. According to the World Bank (see Lammer 2014), over 2.5 billion adults in the world do not have a formal bank account. The percentage of so-called unbanked people is particularly high in developing countries, where also approximately 200 million smaller enterprises lack access to financial services and credits. Even developed countries, like the United States, are not immune from this issue. For those excluded from the financial system this means that they lack a secure way to save their money or to transfer it to other individuals. On a macro level, this also hinders economic participation and development, as a well-functioning financial system is one of the key enablers for growth.

POs could offer a partial solution to this problem. With their widespread physical presence, which also extends to rural and poor areas, they are well suited to provide a financial gateway for unbanked people incl. financial services. This especially applies to all areas with no bank in near proximity. In fact, about 20 % of the people without an account state as a reason that banks are too far away to use (see Deminguc-Kunt and Klapper 2012).

In this regard, the Universal Postal Union (2012) has set financial inclusion as an important objective for POs in the coming years. For POs there are different business models ranging from a pure cash merchant to a licensed financial service provider (see Universal Postal Union 2013). There is some evidence that POs already contribute to financial inclusion to a certain extent: vulnerable groups, such as the poor, less educated, and those out of the labour force, are relatively more likely to use an account from POs than from other financial institutions (see Anson et al. 2013).

3.2.2 International Money Transfers

Besides offering a secure way to store wealth, cryptocurrencies also allow for efficient international money transaction. This is especially relevant for financial inclusion as remittances are important in developing countries. According to the World Bank (2014), migrants from developing countries have sent back USD 414 billion in earnings to their relatives in 2013. However, sending remittances through traditional channels is very costly, as such a service demands 9 % of the transaction in fees on average.

With cryptocurrencies, it becomes possible to make international money transfers with only a minor fraction of the transaction fees of existing services. This would particularly help poor people to afford money transfers.

3.2.3 Integration of Financial and Physical Transactions

Besides transmitting value, decentralized payment-systems are potentially capable of adding information and other functionalities to transactions. For instance, payment transaction data has a timestamp through inclusion in the blockchain. This timestamp could be used for reference in a parcel's track-and-trace information. Payment data may also contain shipping information, such that the PO and customs are automatically pre-notified of goods to be expedited as soon as a payment hits the blockchain. In essence, decentralized payment-systems allow for a close link between the financial and the non-financial part of commercial transactions, which could unify payment and delivery in a single process.

Introduction of cryptocurrencies and decentralized payment-systems into postal business does not only enable new financial services by the posts, but it could also influence the logistic process and has the potential of innovating international parcels and mail delivery. Consequently, the Universal Postal Union considers decentralized payment-systems as a potential way to simplify the complex system of international transactions, as they offer the possibility to synchronize financial and physical (logistics) transactions (see Anson 2014).

4 Postcoin—A Postal Cryptocurrency

A considerable drawback for cryptocurrencies is their high exchange rate volatility. Remedy could be provided by fully backing cryptocurrencies with other assets as well as by invoking a trusted party as issuer. Such improvements of cryptocurrencies give rise to the idea of a Postcoin. Postcoins could be issued by a PO by tagging (or "coloring")[13] existing digital tokens on a public blockchain,

[13]Colored coins are a method for associating assets with tokens on a blockchain network.

e.g. Bitcoins, to represent a specific asset. The post would sell each unit of Postcoin for a certain amount of local currency, while holding the equivalent value of a defined unit of this asset (e.g. USD, gold or SDR) as reserve.[14] At the same time it would also guarantee to buy back every Postcoin for local currency at an amount at least equivalent to its value in terms of reserves. Thereby, Postcoins could be injected into the economy via an exchange between the respective PO and its customers. Issuing a Postcoin, posts could make use of the open infrastructure of public blockchains and at the same time be in control of the money supply as well as the access and use of their permissive Postcoin currency. The reputation of POs constitutes a key factor in this regard.

4.1 Advancing Cryptocurrencies

Compared to other cryptocurrencies, Postcoin would exhibit the advantage that it does not suffer from volatility: it would offer a stable store of value by virtue of not only being issued by a reliable source but also being pegged to another asset or currency, while still being fast and cheaply transferable on a public blockchain. In essence, Postcoin would enable customers to benefit from all the advantages of cryptocurrencies, while adding a trusted institution to interact with.

Providing a postal currency could solve another issue related to cryptocurrencies: it may be somewhat difficult to handle the plethora of unsystematic information on cryptocurrencies as well as to fully understand their concept. Where the public largely views a PO as a trusted authority, Postcoin could become an alternative cryptocurrency which is both easy to understand and to use. All necessary information can be provided by the post as a reliable institution. The post could offer Postcoin account services at postal franchises and integrate Postcoin accounts into postal websites. Consequently, customers would need no advanced technical knowledge on cryptocurrencies, but would still be able to use the corresponding services such as payments and money transfers.

4.2 Further Potentials of Postcoin

The concept of Postcoin could also serve as a successful business model for countries with unstable national currencies. If people trust the postal system more than the central money issuer of their country, Postcoin might emerge as an

[14]If a PO issues its own currency, it has full control over its supply and essentially takes the place of a central bank. By coloring digital tokens, it puts a layer on another cryptocurrency and uses it as a payment system. All transactions in Postcoins are at the same time transactions in the other cryptocurrency which are verified in the other cryptocurrency's network (and which have to pay according transaction fees).

important store of wealth relative to the national currencies. This could also assist in stabilizing the economy of the respective country. Moreover, it is conceivable that each national PO would create its own Postcoin with international payments being settled between operators. The Universal Postal Union might then act as an exchange between different postal currencies.

It would be even more efficient if the international postal community (national incumbents and competitors[15]) issued one single postal currency with the Universal Postal Union coordinating the efforts of national POs. Such coordination measures might entail regulations, standards and multilateral agreements (see Anson 2014). In particular, the Universal Postal Union would need to ensure that all POs issuing Postcoin adhere to the same exchange rates and reserve standards in an auditable way. If all POs were to coordinate on a single Postcoin currency, the reputation effects would amplify due to the participation of many trusted parties.

Besides, Postcoin services could be implemented at a smaller scale and act as a bonus feature rather than a core part in the business model. Comparable to frequent flyer miles, Postcoin could reward loyal customers and give rights to additional benefits (e.g. exchange for postal services). A bonus system might also be a safe way to test Postcoin as a payment system before launching it as a full-fledged cryptocurrency.

5 Other Commercial Applications of Blockchain Technology

Blockchain technology offers business opportunities for POs beyond currency and financial services, e.g. in identity services, device management or supply chain management (see USPS 2016).

Identity Services POs could offer identity verification services, both for persons and goods. A verified personal digital identity would allow users to know that the peers they are transacting with are real and have proof of ownership. POs could further link that virtual identity used by the customer to operate within a blockchain system with real-world identifiers, such as a person's postal address. Customers could use these verified identities to login to secure websites, notarize documents, or participate in smart contracts. Likewise, identification of goods would allow linking them to digital tokens and track their ownership on a blockchain.

Device Management Another potential application of blockchain technology would be using it to secure and maintain the Internet of (postal) Things. The blockchain's decentralized control and verification system could allow devices to more securely record and transfer data. This would also help increase the security of the network by removing the risks associated with single points of access. With blockchain technology, networks of devices would be able to transact with other

[15]Provided that they comply with the required regulations.

connected devices to, for example, pay for services, share power resources or contract for maintenance services and part replacement.

Supply Chain Management A final application would be better supply chain management: using blockchain to identify packages and mail. POs have a number of customers, partners, contractors and other stakeholders that it coordinates with. Tracking mailpieces on a blockchain would allow POs to keep an auditable chain of custody and embed additional shipment and tracking information to facilitate customs clearance and faster delivery. If a mailpiece was embedded with a sensor, it could keep track of its own chain of custody while executing smart contracts for payment and customs clearance. Generally, blockchain technology would allow for close linkages between the financial, logistics, and delivery parts of commercial transactions with the power to unify payment and delivery in one seamless experience.[16] POs could become a single intermediary between merchants and customers, allowing them to reduce coordination needs, offer more efficient ecommerce solutions, contribute to the growth of ecommerce (particularly cross-border ecommerce), and increase their market share and revenue.

6 Conclusions

In the past few years, the publicity for blockchain technology and cryptocurrencies has increased. They enable transfer of value across the Internet just as emails transfer information. In particular, this means that people can make peer-to-peer transactions without financial intermediaries in between. Furthermore, blockchain-based payment-systems are completely decentralized and lack central institutions. Instead, they are controlled by the community of their users. With their unique characteristics such as low transaction costs and secure transactions, decentralized payment-systems can offer various benefits for individuals, companies and the society as a whole. Nevertheless, there are still some challenges. Most importantly, the exchange rate of cryptocurrencies is highly volatile and decentralized payment-systems lack any established institution for people to rely on.

POs are well-suited to counter some of the main weaknesses. They combine a widespread physical network with a strong reputation as well as with substantial experience in financial service provision. Financial services such as savings accounts or money transfers could rather easily be extended internationally and thus assist in advancing financial inclusion. Posts could also issue their own postal cryptocurrency, the Postcoin, which could be capable of protecting customers from the high exchange-rate volatility that cryptocurrencies currently bear.

[16]See Sect. 3.2.3.

Looking into the future, the innovative technology of decentralized payment-systems is likely to persist and to transform the existing financial system. Institutions like posts as well as regulators should therefore keep up with any future developments.

References

Anson, J. (2014). Supporting transactions not pegged to national currencies: A role for the UPU. USPS OIG-UPU International Online Forum on Postal Innovation 2014.

Anson, J., Berthaud, A., Klapper, L., & Singer, D. (2013). Financial inclusion and the role of the post office. World Bank Policy Research Working Paper 6025.

Bloomberg. (2014a). *Bitcoin prices plunge on report PBOC orders accounts shut*. Available at http://www.bloomberg.com/news/2014-03-27/pboc-orders-banks-to-shut-bitcoin-exchange-accounts-caixin-says.html

Bloomberg. (2014b). *Mt. Gox Bitcoin exchange down amid $365 million theft claim*. Available at http://www.bloomberg.com/news/2014-02-25/mt-gox-bitcoin-exchange-goes-offline-as-peers-lash-out-at-firm.html

Coindesk. (2014). *Bitcoin vs Argentine Peso: Which is worse off?* Available at http://www.coindesk.com/bitcoin-vs-argentine-peso-worse/

EMarketer. (2013). *B2C ecommerce climbs worldwide, as emerging markets drive sales higher*. Available at http://www.emarketer.com/Article/B2C-Ecommerce-Climbs-Worldwide-Emerging-Markets-Drive-Sales-Higher/1010004

Financial Crimes Enforcement Network. (2013). *Application of FinCEN's regulations to persons administering, exchanging, or using virtual currencies*. Available at http://www.fincen.gov/statutes_regs/guidance/pdf/FIN-2013-G001.pdf

Financial Crimes Enforcement Network. (2014a). *Application of FinCEN's regulations to virtual currency mining operations*. Available at http://www.fincen.gov/news_room/rp/rulings/pdf/FIN-2014-R001.pdf

Financial Crimes Enforcement Network. (2014b). *Application of FinCEN's regulations to virtual currency software development and certain investment activity*. Available at http://www.fincen.gov/news_room/rp/rulings/pdf/FIN-2014-R002.pdf

Jaag, C., & Bach, C. (2013). Virtual currencies and physical posts: A perfect match. *The Postal Industry, 1*(2), 11–12.

Jaag, C., & Bach, C. (2015). The effect of payment reversibility on E-commerce and postal quality (Chapter 6). In: *Handbook of digital currency* (Elsevier, Amsterdam).

Jaag, C., & Haller, A. (2016). Economic mechanism design in Bitcoin: Mining, block formation and transaction fees. Swiss Economics Working Paper 57.

Demirguc-Kunt, A., & Klapper, L. (2012). Measuring financial inclusion : The global findex database. Policy Research Working Paper No. 6025. Washington DC: World Bank.

Lammer, T. (2014). Virtual currencies, payment systems & financial inclusion. USPS OIG-UPU International Online Forum on Postal Innovation 2014.

Nasdaq. (2016). *The halving: Then & now—A Bitcoin magazine infographic*. Available at http://www.nasdaq.com/article/the-halving-then-now-a-bitcoin-magazine-infographic-cm646839#ixzz4EDstlcdw

New York State Department of Financial Services, NYDFS. (2015, September 22). *Press release —NYDFS announces approval of first BitLicense application from a virtual currency firm*.

The Economist. (2015, October 31). *The trust machine*.

The Street. (2014). *Three in four people have never heard of Bitcoin*. Available at http://www.thestreet.com/story/12306983/1/three-in-four-people-have-never-heard-of-bitcoin.html

United States Postal Service, USPS. (2016). *Blockchain technology: Possibilities for the U.S. Postal Service*. RARC Report RARC-WP-16-011.
Universal Postal Union. (2012). *Annual report 2012*. Available at http://news.upu.int/insight/annual-reports/2012/
Universal Postal Union. (2013). *Global panorama on postal financial inclusion: Business models and key issues*. Available at www.upu.int/fileadmin/documentsFiles/activities/financialInclusion/publicationGlobalPanoramaFinancialInclusionEn.pdf
Universal Postal Union. (2014). *Development of postal services in 2013*. Available at http://www.upu.int/fileadmin/documentsFiles/resources/postalStatistics/developmentOfPostalServicesIn2013En.pdf
Watkins, K., & Maria, Q. (2014). *Lost in intermediation—How excessive charges undermine the benefits of remittances for Africa*. Overseas Development Institute Report.
World Bank. (2014). *Migrants from developing countries to send home $414 billion in earnings in 2013*. Available at http://www.worldbank.org/en/news/feature/2013/10/02/Migrants-from-developing-countries-to-send-home-414-billion-in-earnings-in-2013

Digital Identities: A Good Move for Postal Operators

Claire Borsenberger, Olaf Klargaard and Philippe Régnard

1 Introduction

For consumers, citizens, employees or even producers, digital identity is the passport to the vast online world of goods and services. With the growth of digital e-commerce transactions, communications, social networks, and connected objects, needs for both privacy and secure, reliable identification become both more and more crucial. Reliable digital identities provide a means of distinguishing an individual using attributes (age, gender, address, login, password, biometric data, and so on). This makes possible the development of online communities and online transactions.

The downside of navigating online is that we continuously leave traces everywhere that make up our "digital identity". Disclosing information on personal preferences, lifestyles and so on creates both opportunities and risks. The privacy challenge is not only a question about disclosing explicit or implicit data but also of managing who it is disclosed to and how it is managed over time.

At a first sight, the most obvious solution to protect privacy seems to cut the link between the individual and these data by guaranteeing anonymity, unlinkability or unobservability. But this "simple" solution fails at least for two reasons. Firstly, to benefit from personalized transactions or services, identification is needed. Secondly, guaranteeing strict anonymity is impossible in the digital area. This pleads for the establishment of an efficient system to manage digital identities, to

C. Borsenberger (✉)
Regulation, Institutional and European Affairs Division – Groupe La Poste, Paris, France
e-mail: claire.borsenberger@laposte.fr

C. Borsenberger
University François Rabelais, Tours, France

O. Klargaard · P. Régnard
Digital Division – Groupe La Poste, Paris, France

M. Crew et al. (eds.), *The Changing Postal and Delivery Sector*,
Topics in Regulatory Economics and Policy,
DOI 10.1007/978-3-319-46046-8_14

increase trust in digital services while limiting the disclosure of personal data to the bare necessities (protecting in the way privacy), thereby enabling people to enjoy and benefit from their online experiences.

The focus of this paper, following our previous study on the role of Postal Operators (POs) regarding online privacy and data protection (Borsenberger et al. 2016), is specifically on a key digital infrastructure for ensuring both convenience and privacy protection online: the provision of digital identities by various entities and in particular by POs. We study the main European and US developments, with operational trusted framework and regulations, demonstrating notably that postal role in digital identification, advocated in postal economic literature, has become a reality in some European postal markets.

Section 2 defines the current provision and use of digital identities, demonstrating notably the positive impact on economic and social interactions, and questions the associated shortfalls when considering further development of online transactions. Section 3 analyzes the response brought by some governments, establishing trusted frameworks for digital identities. Section 4 explains the role POs could play in this ecosystem. Section 5 concludes.

2 The Limits of the Actual Decentralized and Commercially-Provided Ecosystem of Digital Identities

In the physical world, identity is generally limited to attributes of civil status (name, surname, date and location of birth, nationality) and is established by public authorities by paper documents (passport, driver license, ID cards, etc.). An individual can then authenticate himself with this document when asked to prove his or her identity to a public (ex: border control) or private (ex: car rental company) party.

A digital identity is not fundamentally different. The European Commission (2007) defined it as a means for people to prove electronically that they are who they say they are and thus gain access to services.

There exist nevertheless some differences. In particular, a digital identity can be provided by many entities such as administration, bank, telecom or postal operator. Currently, the main digital identity providers are social networks like Facebook, Google+, LinkedIn or Twitter.[1] It can even be created freely by an individual

[1]Gigya's survey showed that in 2015, 88 % of US internet users claimed to have logged into websites and mobile applications using their existing social media accounts. This was an 11 % increase since 2014 similar survey, and a 35 % increase since 2012. Social login usage has also increased among UK users from 60 % in 2014 to 66 % in 2015. Interestingly, the survey also showed that 75 % of US users and 62 % of UK users aged 55 and more have used a social identity to authenticate on a website or mobile application. The development of social logins can be easily explained by convenience in usage.

himself (self-asserted identities) when he creates an account on a commercial website or a social network.

In consequence, contrary to the unique civil status identity delivered by governments, an individual could have multiple digital identities: one for his family, one for his friends, one for his colleagues, another when he navigates in a merchant website, and so on. His digital identities are often richer than his civil one, including the name of his friends, his professional contacts, his "e-reputation", and his preferences.

The creation of personal accounts on various service providers' websites, from scratch or using social logins, has allowed users to navigate online anonymously, using pseudonyms or self-asserted identities. It has sustained the growth of online transactions and commercial transactions between firms and individuals, and most interestingly between individuals.

Indeed, online markets are considerably more anonymous than traditional markets (Cabral 2012) as online agents know very little about each other. In this context, people identity and reputation (more precisely e-reputation) take a huge significance. Several studies have demonstrated that the identity of an internet user and his "e-reputation" can provide efficient economic signals to develop trust. For example, Resnick et al. (2006), Cabral and Hortacsu (2010) and Bounie et al. (2008) have provided evidence that there exists a reputation premium which allows "good" sellers to set higher prices. The need of a good reputation explains why it is crucial for an individual to actively manage his personal data and identity on online transaction platforms and on review and feedback systems created by online websites.

But, in the era of "big data", the freedom with which individuals build their digital identities (anonymity, pseudonyms or physical but self-asserted attributes) and share their attributes with other individuals or service providers is challenged in several ways. The multiplication of digital identities can help protect privacy by disclosing partial and contextualized information (Nissenbaum 2010) but can also increase risk of privacy failure by expanding pathways for breach. The mass of data and traces available online, coupled with progresses in calculation capacity, makes anonymity nearly impossible to achieve. Whereas at the beginning of the Internet the anonymity of virtual identities was a common belief (Turkle 1996), in the era of "big data", strict anonymity is very difficult to achieve. For example, De Montjoye et al. (2013, 2015) showed that a small number of anonymous pieces of information are enough to re-identify individuals.

Furthermore, more and more people are worried about the amount of personal information about them that is online. According to Turow et al. (2015), a majority of Americans do not believe that 'data for discounts', that is to say information about themselves they disclose in exchange to specific benefits such as free search, personalized services on financial rewards, is a square deal. They consider that the price they pay (in terms of personal data disclosure) is higher that the benefits they withdraw. In this context, some Internet users adopt tools to protect their personal data and blur their identity (practices of anonymity, use of pseudonyms, information withholding, multiplication of mail addresses, false declaration, and so on).

According to Pew Research Center (2013), 86 % of interviewed internet users have taken steps online to remove or mask their digital footprints and 55 % have taken steps to avoid observation by specific people, organizations, or the government.[2] This raises the question of the accuracy of data collected online: to which extent data represent the reality of an individual? Is the self-asserted digital identity representative of his physical-world identity?

In this context, though convenient, rich in attributes and widely used, the current management of digital identities is reaching its limits. Significant innovations have allowed to bypass some initial drawbacks (social logins for convenience in usage, e-reputation tools for trust promotion), but are now too limited for a change of scale in the development of online transactions. E-reputation mechanisms could be manipulated to mislead buyers about the reliance and quality of a seller: a seller with a bad record could choose to exit a marketplace and re-enter under a new "identity"; on social networks false profiles could be built, photos could be made up or diverted, and so on. A "stronger" mechanism of secured and trusted digital identity is a necessity if we want the scope of online transactions to really achieve its optimal level and cover legal, banking or health issues.

3 A Solution: The Development of State-Sponsored Platforms of Federated Digital Identities

Having identified problems with the current management of digital identities, a number of governments have launched initiatives around online authentication. A general model of a trust framework of federated digital identities is emerging, with a consensus on some key principles.

The first one is that the user must be at the center of the new identity ecosystem and be able to control the use of its digital identity: when connecting to a service provider, he decides which identity attributes are needed to share with whom and under what circumstances. So, the information disclosure will be reduced to the bare necessities. Transparency and user control are considered as the best tools to ensure personal data protection.

Secondly, the system must be convenient. In most national initiatives, the user has a choice among multiple identity providers, which can be used to authenticate to all service providers associated with the platform. The user keeps the convenience from the current social logins system, where one account (from one identity provider) is enough to connect to all service providers. And the choice of the identity provider is left to the user, who can decide the identity provider he is more comfortable with.

[2]Remaining people seem resigned to giving up their data facing the growing difficulties (and the costs incurred) to protect them. This explains why some appear to be engaging in tradeoffs despite everything.

Thirdly, the quality of digital identities in terms of verification of attributes must be improved, so that digital transactions can occur in all contexts without risks for the parties. Whereas the current system of social logins is based on self-asserted attributes of identities, the governance of these new models create different levels of assurance, with variable degree of attributes verification (self-asserted, face-to-face, biometric verification).

Fourthly, the system must be secure and trustworthy: the key change from current system of social logins is the involvement of the State, not as a monopolistic provider of civil status identities (as it was the case in the physical world), but as a benevolent provider of a trust framework (seeking to maximize welfare and not its own profit unlike Google, Facebook and other "private" identity providers). The state defines rules and governance around security and privacy enabling both service providers who accept the digital identity to trust the identity provider chosen by the users, digital identity providers to trust the service provider the user is connecting to, and users who connect to a service provider with a given identity provider to trust all the parties (notably the fact that the service provider only collects the chosen identity attributes and uses them for the chosen destination).

This notion of a trust framework of federated digital identities is neither a theoretical innovation nor a first-time implementation, as similar initiatives had been launched in the past.[3] The key differences in recent government initiatives are their involvement in the governance of the ecosystem and engagement to respect the philosophy and principles of federated models.

The UK government has been among the first to launch a public platform of federated digital identities aimed at covering all identities' verifications through public services. Initiated in October 2014 by the government Digital Service (GDS), *Gov.uk Verify* (initially known as *UK identity assurance program*) is an open platform aiming to facilitate British citizens' ability to log on and achieve on-line administrative procedures (e-administration). Limiting its role in setting governance and operating the platform, the government certifies any digital identity provider that respects some rules and technical criteria.[4] Based on a 5-step process to secure the digital identity validity, UK Gov.uk Verify provides a solid cross checking of identity attributes by the digital identity provider. The platform already provides a large access to public services.[5] Fifteen additional services will be available in the 18 forthcoming months dealing with tax credit, income tax estimate, state pension checking, driving license information, and other public services. According to the program director in GDS, over 50 government services are

[3]See for similar models analysis: Open Identity Exchange (2010), "What is a Trust Framework".

[4]In the beginning of 2016, 8 certified companies were recognized by the government to act as digital identity provider on the platform: Barclays, CitizenSafe, Digidentity, Experian, Post Office, Royal Mail, SecureIdentity and Verizon.

[5]Department for Work and Pensions (DWP) to ask for a universal credit, to fill tax assessment notice or electric tax notice, to update his company car tax…, Majesty's Revenue and Customs (HMRC) to ask for a tax credit, to log on his personal tax account, Driver and Vehicle Licensing Agency (DVLA) not share information on his driving License.

planning to adopt *Gov.UK Verify*, and 500,000 identities have been verified in 17 months of existence of the beta service.[6] The goal is to reach 10 million British users and could be extended to access private sector websites and services: Gov.uk Verify could play a significant role in identity assurance for the private sector according the Chair of Open Identity Exchange (OIX), Don Thibeau. When connecting for example with banking, insurance, legal, or health related services, users could then have the choice to rely on a neutral, non-commercial and secure digital identity, limiting the use of social login to transactions with limited impact on data breaches.

In France, a similar universal open public platform called France Connect was developed from the end of 2014, experimented in late 2015 with selected identity providers and (public) service providers and has been launched in live in February 2016. Similarly to *Gov.UK.verify*, France Connect enables citizens to log on public administration websites to access information and achieve on-line administrative procedures. Some differences can be noted on the French model: France Connect is not only a federated identity platform but also connects administrative departments to share personal citizens' data (under control of the citizen, authorizing the data sharing from the France Connect platform) and consequently avoids citizens from providing references and documents already known by the public authorities. France Connect's platform main objective in terms of deployment is to be used by key national public services. On the digital identity providers' side, France Connect is soliciting both public and private identity providers to connect to the platform. Currently, only two identity providers are active: tax department and the French PO (La Poste) identification systems. A third, National Health administration (Ameli—French health department of social Security) should become a digital identity provider by the end of 2016.

In the USA, as soon as 2011, the White House launched a large initiative around secured digital identities called the "National Strategy for Trusted Identities in Cyberspace" (NSTIC).[7] The NSTIC relies on key principles of open and trusted frameworks of federated digital identities. *Connect.gov* is the current implementation of the NSTIC: an "identity ecosystem, a marketplace of digital websites with enhanced security and privacy that would eliminate the need for individuals to manage multiple user names and passwords".[8] As in France and UK, the project is supported and operated by the government and Federal agencies, providing trust and legitimate governance rules to the ecosystem. Digital identity providers connected to the platform (the Connect.Gov «Sign-In Partners») have been certified by a government run program to ensure compliance with privacy and security standards. Current digital providers available through Connect.Gov are Google, ID.me,

[6]UK identity assurance program director, Janet Hugues. Available at https://identityassurance.blog.gov.uk.

[7]National Strategy for Trusted Identities in Cyberspace, Enhancing Online Choice, Efficiency, Security, and Privacy, April 2011, White House.

[8]Source: Connect.gov presentation, available at www.connect.gov.

PayPal, Verizon, and Yahoo. Connect.gov objective is to be widely used by agencies and all federal government online services.

The most recent initiative is the launch by the Italian government via the "Agency for Digital Italy" of the Public System for Digital Identity (SPID).[9] Wider in scope than many examples shown above, this platform enables citizens and companies to log on public administrative services and private companies members within only one digital identity. The agency announced that by June 2016, over 600 services would be available and accessible through SPID.

Many other countries (like Austria or New-Zealand) have developed similar state-sponsored or operated platform, all respecting the principles of convenience for users, privacy, security and trust. These national implementations have been accompanied by international initiatives aimed at establishing an outbound recognition of nationally provided digital identities (like the eIDAS Regulation at the European Union level[10]).

Compared to the current system dominated by the social networks as identity providers, when digital identities are authenticated and guaranteed by the State, private websites will not necessary need any further information on consumers to deliver their service, increasing the degree of privacy protection.

4 The Role of POs in These Trust Frameworks

Whereas the ecosystems of state-sponsored digital identity platforms merely existed, analysts from the USPS Office of Inspector General were visionary when they identified in 2012 the future opportunities for USPS in that field:

> As a highly trusted, venerable government institution with both a legal mandate to protect privacy and the authority to protect users from fraud, the U.S. Postal Service is in a unique position to play a key part in a vital infrastructure for new digital identity creation and authentication services (USPS 2012).

Traditional postal values around data protection, as well as their national physical network coverage, clearly position POs in the digital identity ecosystem.

One should remember that core asset of POs is not, and has never been historically, to deliver mail. Any company or institution, any local courier is able to deliver mail and documents. The value of POs is instead to ensure individuals that their documents and data are handled securely by a trusted organization, that the postman has respected the secrecy of correspondence (old name for personal data protection) and that the registered letter has been delivered to the right (identified)

---

[9] *Sistema Pubblico di Identità Digitale.*

[10] The "regulation on electronic identification and trust services for electronic transactions in the internal market" (eIDAS) adopted by the European legislators on July 2014 and officially entered into force in July 2016, ensures that people and businesses can use their own national electronic identification schemes to access public services in other EU countries where eIDs are available.

person. These values position POs for a critical role in currently developing digital identity ecosystems.

An additional asset for POs in this environment is their capacity to link physical-world attributes and digital identities: through thousands of postmen visiting every address and millions of individuals visiting postal outlets every day, POs benefit from an unbeatable industrial capacity to verify identity attributes in the physical world. They are able to provide identity ecosystems with a high level of assurance verified digital identities, relying on in-person authentication. The national database of change of addresses, covering millions of fresh and secured data on mail addresses is also a major asset which POs can use to deliver verified identity attributes for digital identities.

The role of POs in terms of privacy protection and the ongoing digital transformation of some POs has been studied in the postal economic literature (Borsenberger et al. 2016): the creation of new tools allowing individuals to store, control and share their data is one of the new services now delivered by POs to individuals, leveraging their trusted role and their capacity to manage personal data securely. These "personal data stores" services are notably offered by POs like Post Danmark (E-boks), New-Zealand Post (My vault) or La Poste (Digiposte).

Being user-centric, privacy-by-design in their historical role, capable to manage data and identities at a large scale, POs could naturally manage digital identity registration and verification and are already engaged in these frameworks in various ways. Far from a theoretical statement or an expert recommendation, the engagement of POs in national identities ecosystem is now a reality in many countries. Conscious of their role and legitimacy in the trusted identity space, and supported by governments searching for trusted contributors to their platform, some POs are widely engaged in the state-sponsored identity platforms implemented in the last couple of years.

For instance, in the UK, we observe a double participation of the postal ecosystem to *Gov.uk.verify* since both Royal Mail and Post Office Limited are now recognized "certified companies" (digital identity providers) by the British government. Post office Limited had applied from the beginning of the project whereas Royal Mail's service of digital identity has only been launched in March 2016, to be ready for the industrialization phase of *Gov.uk.verify*. Both postal contributors will be able to provide citizens with free and secured digital identities.

In France, La Poste has historically offered a service of digital identity (IDN, "Identité numérique") since 2011, with a high level of assurance in the verification process, the registration involving in-person authentication in postal outlet or at individuals' residences by the postman. Face-to-face verification of ID cards, passports and physical addresses has ensured a best-in-class status for La Poste digital identity in France, that allowed the French PO to be one of the few digital identity providers accepted on the France Connect platform. Poste Italiane is providing a similar service to the Public system of Digital Identity platform, and Poste ID now belongs to the 3 digital identity providers selected by SPID, with InfoCertID and TimID (Telecom Italia Trust Technology). USPS role in the US Connect.gov program is an interesting one. The USPS has not been primarily considered as a provider of digital identities, nor as a provider of identity attributes (addresses, in-person ID verification, etc.) but as the operator of the technical platform. If the Connect.gov program is implemented by the General Services Administration (GSA) and the National Institute of Standards and Technology (NIST), the USPS serves as the technology manager and is responsible for the "USPS Connect" service that provides the connection point between digital identity providers and online federal government services (service providers).

5 Conclusions

The development of online services has naturally generated the creation of multiple accounts and associated online identities, in silo. At the beginning, the creation of personal accounts on various service providers' websites has allowed users to navigate online anonymously, using pseudonyms or self-asserted multiple identities to safeguard their privacy. But gradually, more and more people are realizing that the mass of data and traces available online, coupled with progresses in calculation capacity ("Big Data"), makes anonymity nearly impossible to achieve.

Moreover, with the growth of services available online, the multiplication of registration processes led many users to opt for easy-to-remember but weak passwords for convenience and/or to reuse them across many services, creating vulnerability and making online fraud and identity theft easier and more and more frequent.

Aware of the fact that the absence of verified identities could lead to a lack of trust and limit the growth of online transactions, digital identity providers have emerged. The first ones were the social networks (Facebook, Google+, LinkedIn or Twitter). But social logins are hardly any more secure than usernames and passwords and brings their own drawbacks. Consequently, more and more individuals distrust the current system of digital identities management. The establishment of a "stronger" mechanism of secured and trusted digital identity appears as a necessity.

In this context, many governments around the world are developing state-sponsored platforms of federated digital identities, providing a solid checking of identity attributes thanks to a secure, convenient and user-centric mechanism generating trust. POs have a key role to play in these trust frameworks. Thanks to their assets (traditional postal values around data protection, national physical network facilitating in-person identity check), POs appear as "natural" digital identity providers and some are already engaged in this way beside Governments.

References

Borsenberger, C., Klargaard, O., & Régnard, P. (2016). Personal data and privacy issues and postal operators stand. In M. A. Crew & T. J. Brennan (Eds.), *The future of the postal sector in a digital world* (pp. 261–270). Berlin: Springer.

Bounie, D., Bourreau, M., Gensollen, M., & Waelbroeck, P. (2008). *Do online customer reviews matter? Evidence from the video game industry*. Working Paper in Economics and Social Sciences ESS-08-02, Telecom Paris, February.

Cabral, L. (2012). Reputation on the internet (Chapter 13). In M. Peitz & J. Waldfogel (Eds.), *The Oxford handbook of the digital economy* (pp. 343–354).

Cabral, L., & Hortacsu, A. (2010). The dynamics of seller reputation: Theory and evidence from eBay. *Journal of Industrial Economics, 58*, 54–78.

De Montjoye, Y.-A., Hidalgo, C. A., Verleysen, M., & Blondel, V. D. (2013). Unique in the crowd: The privacy bounds of human mobility. *Nature.com, Scientific Reports, 3*, Article n° 1376.

De Montjoye, Y.-A., Radaelli, L., Singh, V. K., & Pentland, A. S. (2015). Unique in the shopping mall: On the re-identifiability of credit card metadata. *Science, 347*(6221), 536–539.

European Commission. (2007). *Electronic identities: A brief Introduction*. Working paper. http://ec.europa.eu/information_society/activities/ict_psp/documents/eid_introduction.pdf

Federal Trade Commission. (2016). *Consumer sentinel network data book for January-December 2015*, February.

Gigya Research team. (2015). *State of privacy & personalization survey*. Available at: http://www.gigya.com/blog/new-study-the-2015-state-of-consumer-privacy-personalization

Nissenbaum, H. (2010). *Privacy in context: Technology, policy and the integrity of social life*. Stanford: Stanford University Press.

Open Identity Exchange. (2010, March). *What is a trust framework*. Available at: http://openidentityexchange.org/wp-content/uploads/the-open-identity-trust-framework-model-2010-03.pdf

Pew Research Center. (2013, September). *Anonymity, privacy, and security online*. http://pewinternet.org/Reports/2013/Anonymity-online.aspx

Resnick, P., Zeckhauser, R., Swanson, J., & Lockwood, K. (2006). The value of reputation on eBay: A controlled experiment. *Experimental Economics, 9*, 79–101.

Turkle, (1996). *Life on the screen: Identity in the age of the internet*. London: Weidenfeld & Nicolson.

Turow, J., Hennessy, M., & Draper, N. (2015, June). *The tradeoff fallacy—How marketers are misrepresenting American consumers and opening them up to exploitation*. A Report from the Annenberg School for Communication University of Pennsylvania.

US Department of Commerce. (2014). Connect.gov overview. National Institute of standard and technology, US Department of Commerce, USPA & GSA, October 2014. Available at : http://www.smartcardalliance.org/wp-content/uploads/lamp.pdf

U.S. Postal Service Office of Inspector General. (2012). Digital identity: Opportunities for the postal service, May 29, 2012, RARC-WP-12-011.

White House. (2011, April). *National strategy for trusted identities in cyberspace, enhancing online choice, efficiency, security, and privacy*. Available at https://www.whitehouse.gov/sites/default/files/rss_viewer/NSTICstrategy_041511.pdf

The Digital Future of the Printed Publishing Material and the Impact on the Postal Sector

Simona Romito and Stefano Gori

1 Introduction

Digitization is a rapidly developing phenomenon that is disrupting many industries and activities, including the mailing industry. It is important to understand whether the dramatic drop in letter volumes and revenues, experienced by the overwhelming majority of Postal Operators (POs) in industrial countries, can be linked to the disruptive effects of the digital revolution. In the past two decades there has been extensive research on e-substitution between different communication products going back to Nikali (1995), who modeled the effect of a number of teleservices (for example, telefax) on letter mail (see also Diakova 2005; Jimenez et al. 2006).

Our research focuses on the impact of digitization on the publishing industry and more specifically on the impact of mail volumes generated by this sector in Italy. The objectives of this research are to understand whether the decrease in mail volumes in Italy over the recent decade is the result of e-substitution and not only of the economic crisis and the abolition, in March 2010, of the government's tariff

The views presented are those of the authors and not of the affiliated institutions. We would like to thank the Chair of the session, George Kuehnbaum, the discussant, Michael F. Scanlon, and Michael Crew for the constructive criticism and the comments concerning the trends in first class versus second class mail in the US in the past decade.

S. Romito (✉) · S. Gori
Poste Italiane, Rome, Italy

S. Gori
CeSPI, Rome, Italy

M. Crew et al. (eds.), *The Changing Postal and Delivery Sector*,
Topics in Regulatory Economics and Policy,
DOI 10.1007/978-3-319-46046-8_15

support scheme for publishers (which removed the reduction of their delivery cost). Our research also examines the importance of the impact of access even to basic digital services (the inverse of digital divide) on volumes generated by the publishing industry.

This paper has five subsequent sections. Section 2 of this paper describes the main problems being faced by the Italian publishing industry arising from digitization. Section 3 examines the trend of PO's mail volumes with a focus on volumes generated by publishers. Section 4 discusses the availability of the digital infrastructure and Sect. 5 examines the access to the digital services. Section 6 concludes with a focus on how digitization has affected the postal sector and the way forward for postal operators.

2 Digitalization and the Impact on the Volumes Generated by the Publishing Industry

Digitization has had a significant impact on the publishing industry. One of the main phenomena that has emerged is a different way of reading an editorial publication. Reading from computers and more recently from mobile devices (smartphones and tablets) rather than traditional hardcopy is becoming increasingly popular. The digital revolution has led to globalization that has weakened the link between the place where information is produced and where it is consumed. Moreover, the time between the production and the consumption of information has been reduced dramatically. Consequently, information has become a continuous flow generated, enriched, translated and disseminated through various communication means. The traditional relationship between those, who produce the information (journalists, editors) and those, who consume it has been disrupted, as a result of a global trend of linking consumers to producers and reducing the space for middlemen.

Advertisers are gradually accepting the persuasiveness of advertising employing digital media. As a consequence they are shifting from media with a high per contact cost to what they believe are cheaper and more effective advertising services such as Internet and mobile advertising.[1] As a result, according to McKinsey (2015), this change is so deep that the media industry is facing a "tremendous uncertainty" so that global companies might deeply change their corporate organizations in order to adapt to this new environment. In the future, digital advertising could become the main media channel, exceeding even television, if recent high growth rates continue.

The Italian publishing industry was impacted not only by these changes but also from the economic and financial downturn. Table 1 presents the impact on the industry of these behavioral, technological and economic trends. Table 2 shows some

[1]Bradley and Houck (2016) believe that this is a misconception.

Table 1 Economic trends in the Italian publishing industry

Publishing industry (indicators)	2007	2014	Delta % 2014 versus 2007	CAGR 2014 versus 2007 (%)
Average sales per issue—weekly periodicals (thousand)	12,749	8580	−33	−6
Average sales per issue—monthly periodicals (thousand)	13,144	6184	−53	−10
Average daily newspapers (thousand)	5400	3499	−35	−6
Publishing revenues (thousand)				
Periodicals	4100	2162	−47	−9
Newspapers	3508	2109	−40	−7

Source Figures from la Stampa in Italia (2011–2013 FIEG), (2008–2010 FIEG) and authors' estimations
CAGR Compound annual growth rate

Table 2 GDP in Italy from 2007 versus 2014

Economic indicators—base = 100 2007 and 2014	2007	2014	Delta % 2014 versus 2007
GDP	100	~92.5	−7.5
Of which household consumption	100	~92	−8

Note Figures are estimated by the authors' from the chart provided in Banca d'Italia (2015)

economic indicators, which can measure the reflections of the main phenomena ("digitization" and economic crisis) on the dynamics of publishing industry revenues.

Table 1 indicates that publishing revenues and the average sales of newspapers and periodicals have dropped dramatically between 2007 and 2014.

Changes in gross domestic product, an important driver of household spending in newspapers and periodicals,[2] do not appear to be the main cause. Table 2 shows that the Italian gross domestic product (GDP) decreased by a much smaller percentage in the same period showing that there is another main cause which determines the trend which might be digitization.

3 The Effect of the Publishing Industry Digitization on the Mail Volumes

During the same period, digitization has hit the mailing industry as a whole, as technology and consumer choices have dramatically changed. Trends on postal volumes managed by the Italian Universal service provider (USP) are shown in Table 3.

[2]According to a study carried out by the Association of the Printers of newspapers and magazines (FIEG 2014), there is a strong link between household consumption (as a proxy of GDP) to the consumption of printed material such as newspapers and magazines.

Table 3 Mail volumes in Italy

	Mail volumes (mln)—main categories	2007	2014	Delta % 2014 versus 2007	CAGR 2014 versus 2007	Competitor's market share	GDP—Delta % 2014 versus 2007	Of which household consumption—Delta % 2014 versus 2007
Poste Italiane	Priority mail	1502	702	−53	−10			
	Bulk mail	1729	996	−42	−8			
	Registered mail	250	182	−27	−4			
	Insured mail and legal process	40	31	−23	−4			
	Direct Marketing	1419	811	−43	−8			
	Products for publishers	1017	434	−57	−11			
	Total mail volumes	5957	3157	−47	−9	~10	−7.5	−8

Source Poste Italiane (2009, 2015) Annual Report 2014, 2008, and stock exchange prospectus

The table above shows that the magnitude of the loss of total mail volumes has been significant and the trend for publishers has been even greater. Volumes linked to products for publishers have lost more than bulk mail and direct marketing.[3]

In analyzing the determinants of changes in volumes, relative to newspapers and periodicals, it is important to take into account the fact the government tariff supports were removed in 2010. These supports reduced the tariffs paid by publishers for delivery, with the government compensating Poste Italiane for the difference. In particular, on March 31 2010, through the Ministerial Decree from the Ministry of Economic Development, the government, because of the economic crisis, decided to abolish all subsidies for the delivery of publications. We strongly believe that the decrease in volumes generated by the publishing industry can be explained not only by the decreasing GDP but also by the removal of tariff integrations (a supply side effect) and by e-substitution (a demand effect).

[3]The decrease in volumes of insured mail and legal documents is lower than other categories of mail, as the demand is substantially linked to legal obligations.

4 The Digital Divide: The Availability of Connection

The postal and publishing industries have been affected by digitization. To better understand how digitization, the main driver of change, is effective and pervasive, it is necessary to analyze the level of digital divide. The higher the percentage of the population with access to digital services even at low band width the higher the impact on the traditional publishing services. There are two elements to examine: the availability of connection and the use of this connection. There could be cases where there is a low digital divide (hence a high opportunity to access digital services) but a low use of digital services. Bonfadelli (2002) noticed that this could happen because of lack of computer skills, especially among old and uneducated people, and high cost of the access. He affirmed the importance of the social aspects linked to the usage of Internet as supply and access are only a side of the issue. Dijk and hacker (2003) observed the "multifaceted concept of access" as many other social aspects (such as digital skills), further than the physical availability of connection, are important. Reisdorf and Groselj (2015) analyzed the characteristics and attitudes of low Internet users, pointing out that these aspects have been overlooked.

Digitization requires a physical infrastructure that provides the opportunity to be connected everywhere, with a connection speed to allow a pleasant use of content. As Table 4 shows, a speed over 30 Mbps is necessary for some services such as video conferencing (multiple users) and remote computing, while many others can be provided using a lower speed. Not all industries need the same level of connection speed in order to provide their services in a digital way. The table below shows the relation between the speed and some services, which can be made available at that speed.

The faster the connection, the more there are opportunities for the development of new services. However, not all services need a really high connection speed. For publishing, the connection speed required is quite low. For example, a small video for advertising and a pdf file for content needs only a limited connection speed,

Table 4 Speed and services

Download speed	Activities/services available—examples
768 K–1.5 Mbps	Basic E-Mail, Web Browsing, VOIP
1.5–3 Mbps	Streaming music, standard definition video (SD), remote surveillance, telecommuting
3–6 Mbps	File sharing, internet protocol television
6–10 Mbps	Online gaming, video on demand
10–25 Mbps	Telemedicine, remote education, internet protocol television high definition
25–50 Mbps	HD video surveillance
50–100 Mbps	Video conferencing (multiple users), remote supercomputing
>100 Mbps	Real-time data collection, real-time medical image consultation

Source Salway (2015)

Table 5 Cities and towns in digital divide

Digital divide level	Number of cities and towns	Percentage of population in digital divide[a] who cannot access digitized content of the publishing and mail industry (%)
High	310	75–100
Medium	651	50–75
Low	484	25–50
Inexistent	6612	0–25
Total	8057	

Source Authors' estimations from Infratel's data
[a]Population with no physical connection between 2 mbps and 20 mbps and no wireless access

while television requires a minimum of 3/6 mbps. Thinking about the mailing industry, we can see that it is possible to send digitally many different kinds of communications including newspapers/periodicals using a quite limited connection speed.

The next step is to assess the availability of a physical infrastructure able to ensure the necessary speed in order to digitize the mail and publishing industry products. Infratel, a private company completely owned by the Italian state, provides data, for each category of city/town in Italy, on the level of the digital divide, measured as the percentage of the population without either a physical or wireless connection of 02–20 mbps. Table 5 shows the different levels of digital divide measured in this way.

Only 320 municipalities out of a total of 8 thousand (4 % of the total) have a majority of the local population (between 75 and 100 %) with no access to even minimal broadband. Meanwhile in 82 % of municipalities there is no digital divide at all. Furthermore it is worth emphasizing that 97 % of Italian population (in line with the European average) has access to a connection between 2 and 20 mbps, which is necessary to get access to content previously delivered by the traditional printing industry. This suggests that a digital divide is not limiting e-substitution away from traditional forms of publication delivery.

5 The Digital Divide: The Widespread Use of the Internet

In recent years publishers have made information available through Internet, allowing many readers to easily shift from physical content to digital one. Naturally, the use of the online content requires the widespread use of Internet. Only when both factors affecting the digital divide (the availability of connection in the country and the widespread use of Internet) are overcome, the market becomes fruitful to provide the content in a digital way substituting printed items. As mentioned above, there could be cases where there is a low digital divide (hence a high opportunity to access digital services) but a low use of digital services.

Table 6 Penetration of the internet

		Percentage
People who can access Internet from at least one location or device (population aged between 11 and 74 years)		85.5 %
Cluster	Among these people - lowest cluster scores	Percentage of penetration on the target (%)
Gender	Women	83.6
Age	People aged between 55 and 74 years	62.8
Geographic area	South Italy and islands	81.8
Population	Cities with a population between 30.000 and 100.000 inhabitants	83.8
Education	Primary school	53.2
Working	Unemployed	78.1
Professional status	Workers	88.6
Non professional status	Retired people	58.6

Source Audiweb Trends (2015)

Research from Audiweb (2015) shows that 85.5 % of Italian citizens (about 41 million of inhabitants) between 11 and 74 years of age can access Internet from at least one device or location. Table 6 shows the lowest percentage of people with a specific sociodemographic characteristic that can access the Internet from at least one device or location.

Table 6 shows that Internet access among those with a specific socio-demographic characteristic is, in the overwhelming majority of cases, very high. There are no obstacles concerning the Internet diffusion as also the lowest scores of the clusters are still high resulting in the inclusion of all categories in the digital world. Another group with low percentages, "retired people", may not be accustomed to the Internet and thus have less demand for access compared to university students who can access Internet from at least one location or device.

Many categories have penetration rates on the target of over 95 % such as university and high school graduates, executive, managers, academics, entrepreneurs, free professionals, employees, teachers and high school and university students. Italy has historically been a country with a high mobile penetration. Moreover, the percentage of the population who access Internet from more than one device or from different locations is constantly growing, around 1.6 % in the past year. This will lead to a multimedia strategy from the publishing industry.

Finally, note that access to publishing contents and communication does not require a sophisticated computer. Smart-phones and tablets are sufficient as the important matter is the download speed which is low (the other instrument necessary is a screen). The 95.3 % of the Italian population between 11 and 74 years old, about 46 million people, have their own mobile phone and about 31 million of those can access the Internet with their mobile phone. In the last year, the number of people who can access the Internet via their mobile device has increased by more than 4 million people. Moreover, as the overwhelming majority of these mobile phone owners are quite young (people between 11 and 34 years) it follows, that in the future, older people who do not use the mobile devices to access the Internet will become a smaller fraction of the population. As this leads to more widespread Internet access, demand for printed material delivered by the post will fall.

The progress made by Italian citizens in using towards a digital economy and society is also reflected in the Digital Economy and Society Index 2016 as Italy is "part of catching up cluster of countries"[4] and it has "developed fast over the last year and got closer to EU average". The same report states that people that use Internet regularly has increased by 4 % between 2015 and 2016. Furthermore, it is worth noting that on the other side the broadband is "widely available". Hence, this report confirms that the basic physical infrastructure (the broadband) is available but the main problem relies on the digital skills of the population who is overcoming this issue. Another important phenomenon that the report identifies is the preference of the Italian citizen for the mobile broadband connection. Thinking about all this elements together and their effect on the postal and publishing industry it seems that, also considering the really low band necessary to digitize the printed materials, there might be a further push to e-substitution.

Other evidence comes from AGCOM (2015). The NRA has noticed that Italian people access news online mainly by personal computer, as in other countries (United Kingdom, France, Spain, Germany, United States). But the trend in Italy, as well in other countries, is a decrease of access through personal computers and an increase through smartphones. Relating this evidence to the always increasing number of people (especially young people) who can access to Internet it follows again the same issue of the potential increase of e-substitution of printed publishing materials and mail items.

Other evidences about the increasing access to Internet derives from ISTAT (2014) which found an increase of 4 %, from 2013 to 2014, in the number of families which can access to Internet from their home. The report observes also that the daily use of web increases (about +3 % from 2013 to 2014). About the people who don't access to Internet again there are old people and people with a low level of education. Better results are achieved by the social differences as the number of workers who use Internet has increased of about 10 %. This report also found that the number of people who use the Internet has risen about 3 % in the last year. Usage by older people (between 60 and 64 years old) has increased by about 5 %. Hence also the data in this report show the trend of an unstoppable growth of Internet use which is differentiated among the people but with a clear trend. The more people access to Internet the more the world of printed publishing materials and items will be at risk of another relevant wave of substitution.

[4]The "catching up cluster of countries" refers to countries who has a value of the index below the EU average but whose value grows faster than that of EU as a whole.

According to European Commission (2015), the process of digitization is changing everyday life and will continue in future. It said, "[D]igital was once a niche market for specialists; it has become a general purpose technology which is affecting all sectors and economy and society." In monitoring the Internet use it observes that it is a "success story" as in five years from 2009 to 2014 the regular Internet (at least once a week) users have increased of about 14 % in Europe. To achieve these results Europe has implemented many projects aimed to the digital inclusion in order to decrease the number of people who do not use Internet.

6 Conclusions

Digitization is the main industrial phenomenon of recent years gurus such as Klaus Schwab (2016) through the World Economic Forum have called it "The Fourth Industrial revolution". Among all industries two of them have experienced the disruptive nature of digitization, the publishing industry and the postal sector. The extent of the phenomenon is different between the more developed countries and the developing countries. Digitization started in different times and has developed in different ways all over the world. The publishing industry in Italy has seen a drop in items sold and in revenues, and the number of product postal items generated by publishers and delivered by Poste Italiane has decreased accordingly. Furthermore, and taking into account the economic and financial crisis, the main driver of the overall decrease Poste Italiane, which has seen a major decrease of its total volumes, appears to have been digitization.

The availability of internet connections in Italy is widespread, while there is still a strong opportunity for growth in the use of digital services, hence we can expect further digitization of the publishing industry with an on-going impact on postal volumes. Concerning the use, the growth opportunities are linked to the fact that even if decreasing one third of the Italian population (16–74 years old) still does not use internet regularly (European Commission (2016). As discussed Dutton and Reisdorf (2016), many factors have been linked to inequalities in access to Internet. Furthermore the patterns of Internet use are mainly linked to demographic factors such as age, income, and education. They go a step forward and identify distinct "cultures of internet". We believe that these distinct cultures have a relevant impact on the degree of e-substitution for content generated by the publishing industry and have a spill-over also on postal volumes.

Digitization has had diverse impacts on different industries and countries and the process is still ongoing as the millennial generation ages. What is happening in the publishing industry in countries like Italy is taking place in many industrialized countries is likely to continue and become more widespread. The main finding from our research is that it is sufficient very low band width to generate an e-substitution of mail volumes generated by the Publishing industry. Thus, Postal operators around the world should be concerned, especially those in emerging countries. While POs from industrialized countries can expect the trend to continue as the use of Internet expands but at the same time probably most of the e-substitution in advanced economies has already taken place.

References

AGCOM. (2015). L'indagine conoscitiva su informazione ed internet in Italia.
Audiweb Trends. (2015, June). *Sintesi ed analisi dei risultati della ricerca di base sulla diffusione dell'on line in Italia,* Audiweb.
Banca d'Italia. (2015). L'economia Italiana in breve. Dipartimento di Economia e Statistica, n°102, ottobre 2015.
Bonfadelli, H. (2002, March). The internet and knowledge gaps. *European Journal of Communication.*
Bradley, M., & Houck, A, (2016). *The personalization and volume trade off: A future without saturation mail.* Paper presented at the 24th Conference on Postal and Delivery Economics.
Diakova, E. (2005). Electronic alternatives and direct mail marketing. Pitney Bowes, Background paper n°7.
Dijk, J., & hacker, K. (2003). *The* Digital divide as a complex and dynamic phenomenon. *The Information Society.*
Dutton, W., & Reisdorf, BC. (2016). Cultural divides and digital inequalities: attitudes shaping internet and social media divides.
European Commission. (2015). Digital Agenda Targets Progress Report, Digital Agenda Scoreboard 2015.
European Commission. (2016). Digital Economy and Society Index 2016, Country Profile, Italy, https://ec.europa.eu/digital-single-market/en/scoreboard/italy
FIEG. (2011). La Stampa in Italia—(2008–2010), Marzo 2011.
FIEG. (2014). La Stampa in Italia—(2011–2013), Marzo 2014.
Infratel sito web. http://www.infratelitalia.it/
ISTAT. (2014). Cittadini e nuove tecnologie
Jimenez, L., Diakova, E., & Szeto, C. (2006). Generational analisys of mail users. In M. A. Crew & P. R. Kleindorfer (Eds.), *Progress toward liberalization of the postal and delivery sector.* New York: Springer.
McKinsey. (2015). Global media Report 2015.
Nikali, H. (1995). Replacement of letter mail by electronic communication to the year 2010. In M. A. Crew, & P. Kleindorfer (Eds.) *Commercialization of postal and delivery services: National and international perspectives* (pp. 223–235). Boston Kluwer Academic Publishers.
Poste Italiane. (2015). Annual Report 2014.
Poste Italiane. (2009). Annual Report 2008.
Reisdorf, B. C., & Groselj, D. (2015). Internet (non-) use types and motivational access: Implications for digital inequalities research. *New Media and Society.*
Salway. (2015). How much broadband speed do you need? http://broadband.about.com/b/2011/10/01/broadbandspeedtable.htm
Schwab, K. (2016). *The fourth industrial revolution*, World Economic Forum.

Econometric Benchmarking of Delivery and Processing Costs in the UK Postal Sector

Helen Ferguson, Katie Curry and Nick Convery

1 Introduction

Ofcom took on the regulation of post in 2011 with a primary duty to secure the provision of a universal postal service that would be both financially sustainable and efficient. We have assessed concerns raised by Royal Mail as to the effect of direct delivery competition on the financial sustainability of the universal service. In December 2014, we published a statement on the outcome of our review of direct delivery competition in the postal sector (Ofcom 2014b). This set out our conclusion that it was not necessary, at that point in time, to impose regulatory conditions on direct delivery operators in order to secure the provision of a universal service. In addition, we noted that a range of factors, other than end-to-end competition, were likely to affect Royal Mail's future financial position.

We therefore broadened our review of the factors that could materially affect Royal Mail's ability to continue to provide the universal service in the future (Ofcom 2014a). One such factor is efficiency, and so we have undertaken further analysis of what might represent a reasonable rate of efficiency improvement by

This paper is based on work completed by Deloitte for Ofcom. The authors wish to thank Deloitte for their assistance in preparing this paper. This paper presents the personal views of the authors only and should not be interpreted as the views of Ofcom or Deloitte.

H. Ferguson (✉) · K. Curry · N. Convery
Ofcom, Riverside House, 2a Southwark Bridge Road, London SE1 9HA, UK
e-mail: helen.ferguson@ofcom.org.uk

K. Curry
e-mail: katie.curry@ofcom.org.uk

N. Convery
e-mail: nick.convery@ofcom.org.uk

M. Crew et al. (eds.), *The Changing Postal and Delivery Sector*,
Topics in Regulatory Economics and Policy,
DOI 10.1007/978-3-319-46046-8_16

Royal Mail. This work was subsequently incorporated into a more fundamental review of the regulation of Royal Mail (Ofcom 2016).

Our efficiency analysis drew on a broad range of sources, including an in-depth assessment of Royal Mail's Business Plan, qualitative international comparisons and an assessment of how Royal Mail's costs change in relation to volume changes. The focus of this paper is on an econometric benchmarking analysis used to assess the relative efficiency of Royal Mail's Delivery Offices and Mail Centres. In Sect. 2 we give an overview of the methodology employed. Section 3 describes the data used in the analysis. In Sect. 4, we consider some of the key methodological challenges faced in undertaking the analysis. Section 5 presents the main results of our analysis for Delivery Offices and Mail Centres in turn. Finally, in Sect. 6 we provide some concluding remarks.

2 Methodology

The aim of the analysis was to examine the scope for Royal Mail to make efficiency improvements by raising the performance of its lower performing Delivery Offices and Mail Centres closer to that of its best performing units. We also set out to consider the impact of Royal Mail's recent modernization initiatives on the performance of its Delivery Offices and Mail Centres, and the likely forward looking effect of this on efficiency.

Differences in costs between Delivery Offices or between Mail Centres are likely to be driven not only by relative efficiency but also differences in other factors that drive costs. For example, Delivery Offices cover different geographic areas and so will differ in terms of the total number of delivery points served as well as the distance between these delivery points. Similarly, Mail Centres differ in terms of number of Delivery Offices served as well as their relative proximity to these Delivery Offices.

Econometrics allows us to control for the impact of differences in such factors (where data are available) on cost. In doing so, we are able to estimate the minimum cost needed for a Mail Centre or Delivery Office with a particular set of characteristics to process or deliver mail (respectively). This estimated minimum cost is known as the efficient frontier (shown in Fig. 1). In the simplest econometric benchmarking models (such as Ordinary Least Squares or OLS), any difference between the estimated efficient frontier and the actual observed cost of the unit (known as the error term) is attributed to inefficiency. However, attributing the entire difference between the estimated and actual cost of a unit to inefficiency does not take into account the fact that some proportion of the difference may be attributable to random 'noise' (including one-off events).

In this study, we use a panel Stochastic Frontier Analysis (SFA) approach. SFA is more sophisticated than some other econometric techniques in its approach to using the error term to derive (in)efficiency. Specifically, it allows us to estimate the

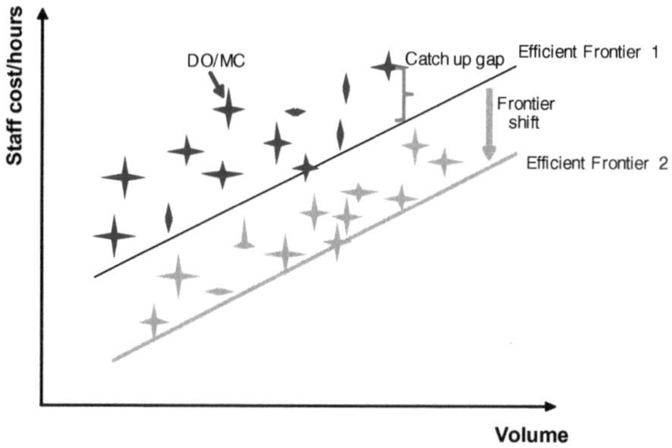

Fig. 1 Efficient frontier. *Source* Deloitte (2016)

proportion of the divergence from the efficient frontier that is due to inefficiency and the proportion that is due to random 'noise'.[1]

We estimate a cost function for a given Delivery Office or Mail Centre *k* in year *j* of the form:

$$\log C_{jk} = a + b \log Q_{jk} + c_i \log \mathbf{X}_{ijk} + \left(u_{jk} + v_{jk}\right) \quad (1)$$

C refers to cost. The analysis was conducted using both people cost and staff hours. However, in interpreting the results and incorporating them into our analysis, we focused largely on the results from the hours models. This abstracts from the inflationary pressures facing Royal Mail, which we assessed separately.

Q refers to output (e.g. delivery points, mail volume) and X is a vector of *i* other control variables that may influence cost (e.g. geography, year, location). The term in brackets is a composite error term, reflecting the fact that SFA attempts to distinguish between deviations of a given Delivery Office or Mail Centre from the estimated efficient frontier that are attributable to inefficiency (u_{jk}) and random 'noise' (v_{jk}).

An alternative method known as Data Envelopment Analysis (DEA) does not rely on specifying a particular form of the cost function as in Eq. 1 (and, in turn, estimating a set of parameters $a, b, c_1, c_2, c_{\ldots}, c_i$). DEA instead uses linear programming to fit an efficient frontier around the data based on the best performing units at different levels of scale. For instance, DEA assumes that if a given Mail Centre is capable of operating at a certain cost, then a Mail Centre with the same characteristics (e.g. scale, geography, location) should also be capable of operating at (or below) that cost. However, like OLS, DEA does not account for the fact that

[1]It should be noted that even with SFA, there is a risk of error which could result in the efficient frontier being overstated. Therefore, rather than using the absolute efficient frontier estimated (based on the most efficient unit), it is more common to use units in the upper decile or upper quartile (i.e. a benchmark against which 10 or 25 % of units are estimated to have higher efficiency scores).

some proportion of the difference between a unit's actual and estimated cost is likely to be due to random 'noise'.

'Panel data' refers to information regarding different entities over a number of time periods. Panel techniques are generally preferable to cross-sectional methods when data are rich enough to support them. They allow researchers to control for variables which are constant across time but vary by individual unit (or vice versa). This is helpful when such variables are difficult to measure and include in the model. A panel dataset is therefore superior to a cross-sectional dataset in controlling for unobserved heterogeneity between Delivery Offices and between Mail Centres.

The use of panel data allowed us to identify changes in efficiency over time through the inclusion of a time trend. This was particularly important to this study given our interest in estimating the impact that Royal Mail's modernization program has had on efficiency to date. It also allowed us to forecast changes in the estimated efficiency frontier over the remaining duration of the program. This provides an additional dimension to understanding Royal Mail's efficiency, in addition to the estimate of the catch-up gap between actual performance of Delivery Offices and Mail Centres and their current efficient frontiers. We discuss this aspect of our analysis in more detail in Sect. 4.

Several other studies have also assessed the relative efficiency of Royal Mail's Delivery Offices and/or Mail Centres. Moriarty et al. (2006) employed both OLS and SFA on a cross-section of data for Delivery Offices and Mail Centres. The study estimated that Royal Mail could save up to £220 m per year in operating Delivery Offices (or roughly 11 % of the relevant costs) and up to £150 m in operating Mail Centres (or roughly 20 % of the relevant costs). The results of the study were used to inform a 3 % per annum efficiency target for Royal Mail during the 2006–10 price control period. Horncastle et al. (2006) employed DEA and SFA on a cross-section of data for Delivery Offices. Using SFA, the study estimated that the average inefficiency factor for Delivery Offices was between 7.7 and 12.7 % depending on the assumptions made regarding the form of the cost function (e.g. Eq. 1), as well as the distribution of the 'inefficiency' error term (e.g. u in Eq. 1). Cazals et al. (2012) reviewed the performance of various panel SFA methods in estimating inefficiency using simulated and real panel data for Delivery Offices and Mail Centres.

3 Data

Delivery Offices and Mail Centres differ considerably from each other across a number of dimensions, many of which may be expected to drive differences in costs. For example, Delivery Offices and Mail Centres differ in terms of the size of the area covered and the volume and type of mail being handled.

To understand the key drivers of cost for Delivery Offices and Mail Centres we had extensive discussions both internally and with Royal Mail. We also looked at previous econometric benchmarking studies of the postal sector both in the UK and abroad (Fenster et al. 2008; Moriarty et al. 2006). We also drew on unpublished studies by Royal Mail, and experience gained by Deloitte in the course of previous work.

We identified mail mix, geography and scale as particularly important drivers of cost. Mail mix refers to differences in the volume and types of mail being processed and delivered. Geography refers to differences in factors such as the number of delivery points per area, the proportion of delivery points which are businesses, and whether the Delivery Office or Mail Centre is in London. For Mail Centres, scale refers to factors such as the number of Delivery Offices served. For Delivery Offices, scale refers to factors such as the number of delivery points served as well as whether or not the Delivery Office also sorts mail for delivery by other offices (known as a Mail Processing Unit).

We gathered data from Royal Mail on Delivery Offices and Mail Centres to account for these differences, as well as information on staff hours and cost. We worked with Royal Mail to identify the appropriate variables to use to capture particular cost drivers, such as quality of service. A summary of the data collected is set out in Table 1.

We included only a subset of the variables from Table 1 in our final baseline model. Table 2 describes the variables included in the final baseline models for Delivery Offices and Mail Centres respectively.

The data collected included information on factors within Royal Mail's control, such as quality of service and staff turnover. However, these factors were not included in the models we used to estimate the efficiency results presented in our main findings. This is because management decisions affecting the level of such variables are part of efficiency and therefore are not independent variables within the model. Instead, they reflect the potential inefficiency to be explained within the error term in our efficiency estimates. We therefore used these variables as part of a second stage analysis to examine the effect of such factors on efficiency, but did not use this in the main part of our analysis to derive the efficiency estimates. For example, we looked at the relationship between staff hours and the proportion of part-time staff, and the level of automation to see whether these factors appeared to have an effect on efficiency.[2] This is, to our knowledge, one of the only studies in regulation that have analyzed the drivers of inefficiency in this way.

One further issue of note is the difference in sample size between the Delivery Office and Mail Centre datasets. This reflects not only the relatively larger number of Delivery Offices, but also the longer period covered by the Delivery Office

[2]We treated quality in this way because we were interested in whether there was any trade-off between unit cost efficiency and quality of service (QoS). On the one hand, a DO/MC targeting a higher quality may incur higher costs to deliver/process the same volume of mail and appear less efficient as a result. On the other, more motivated staff may perform their tasks in less time and also deliver/process mail to a higher QoS, giving rise to a positive association between efficiency and quality. As a result, we did not include QoS in the first stage regression to allow us to test this relationship in the second stage.

Table 1 Data summary

Data category	Delivery offices	Mail centres
Sample period	Financial year 2010/11–2014/15 (5 years)	Financial year 2012/13–2014/15 (3 years)
Sample size	6332 observations (5 years × c.1,266 DOs)	145 observations (3 years × c.50 MCs)
Cost	Staff costs (split by indoor and outdoor operations)[a] Frontline staff costs split by wages, overtime, pension, National Insurance, productivity bonus and temporary resources	Staff costs by grade, split by wages, overtime, pension, National Insurance, productivity bonus and temporary resources
Hours	Staff hours (split by indoor and outdoor operations) Frontline staff hours split by overtime, agency and absence Frontline staff hours split by process (e.g. delivery, collection, other)	Staff hours by MC process (Inward/Outward processing, collection, delivery and distribution) Frontline staff hours split by overtime, agency and absence
Volumes	Weighted and unweighted[b] volume by mail type	Inward/Outward unweighted and weighted volume by mail type
Scale	Number of delivery points served Number of routes covered	Number of collection points served (2014/15 only) MC floor space in square meters
Staff metrics	FTEs Staff turnover (number of leavers and joiners)	FTEs Staff turnover (number of leavers and joiners)
Geography	Size of area covered % area served in rural, suburban, urban areas % business delivery points	Size of area covered
Quality metrics	% special delivery mail delivered on time	% quality of service achieved for 1st and 2nd mail class mail types
Modernization	Start/completion dates of DO modernization and installation of new technologies	Start/completion date of MC modernization and installation of new equipment

[a]Indoor staff costs and hours are the costs incurred and hours spent by each DO in performing indoor tasks, namely the process of sorting mail to walks and other preparation for outdoor delivery. Outdoor delivery represents the journey from the DO to the delivery point, and the delivery of mail to the delivery recipient.
[b]Weights are applied to raw mail volumes in order to account for the different time taken to process and deliver different types of mail and allow aggregation of diverse mail types into one total mail volume metric.

dataset. We used a shorter period for the Mail Centre analysis to mitigate the impact of the significant structural change which has occurred in Mail Centres, which we discuss in detail in the next section.

Table 2 Summary of variables used in baseline model

Delivery offices	Mail centres
Delivery points	Delivery offices per mail centre
Weighted volume per delivery point	Total workload per delivery office
Delivery points per area	Delivery offices per area
Proportion of delivery points that are businesses	London dummy
London dummy	Time of final dispatch
Mail processing unit dummy	Time of final network vehicle
% rural	Year dummies
% suburban	
Year dummies	

4 Modelling Issues

In this section we discuss a number of issues which arose in our analysis which may be of interest to others undertaking SFA modelling in the postal sector. These include: changes in the composition of mail volumes; structural changes in Mail Centres; omitted variable bias; and projecting forward efficiency gains.

4.1 Changes in the Composition of Mail Volumes

Different types of mail require different levels of resource to process and deliver and so, as the composition changes, an operator will face different resource requirements even if the total volume is unchanged. For example, parcels are generally slower to sort than letters, and take longer to deliver as they are less likely to fit through a letterbox. A different product mix represents a different point on the output frontier. If the dataset were rich enough to support it, we could control for the impact of changes in product mix on costs by including volumes of each of the different types of mail as explanatory variables. We therefore experimented with using unweighted volumes by including different categories of mail as explanatory variables. However, this was impractical due to the large number of product types, which meant we would have needed to include an unmanageable number of variables in the analysis.

We therefore used a weighted volume measure (known as workload) that Royal Mail produces for its own internal planning purposes to capture the effect of both changes in volumes and in mail mix. Over the period being analyzed, Royal Mail changed the weightings used in producing workload figures to reflect changes in the time needed to process different types of mail. However, our analysis of efficiency required a consistent set of weights to be used, as changes to the way mail is handled (which would lead to changes in the relative resource requirements for different mail types) are properly to be considered a form of efficiency gain (or loss), and so should not be captured by the explanatory variables in the model. We therefore requested information on weighted volumes based on a consistent set of weights and where these were not available, adjusted the figures based on our understanding of the underlying workload calculations.[3]

4.2 *Structural Changes in Mail Centres*

Another important factor to take into account in our efficiency analysis was the significant amount of change in Royal Mail's processing functions and Mail Centres which had occurred during the period under consideration. Royal Mail has initiated several modernization initiatives since 2007/08, in particular increasing automation and upgrading equipment. At the same time, it has consolidated its Mail Centre estate, significantly reducing the number of Mail Centres it operates from 69 in 2007/08 to 40 at the start of 2014/15. This not only introduces potential technical complexities to the analysis,[4] but also means that Mail Centres which do not close are likely to experience some period of disruption as they absorb mail from closing units.

This presents two challenges. Firstly, the extent of change to the Mail Centre estate means that inferences drawn from data before or during this process may not properly reflect the situation facing Royal Mail in future. Secondly, short term disruption caused by the introduction of new processes or the closure of neighboring Mail Centres does not necessarily reflect a true efficiency gap. Once Mail Centres have adapted to these changes they may return to a higher 'steady state' level of efficiency.

To address these issues, we used a shorter panel for Mail Centres than we did for Delivery Offices. We focused on the most recent three years (2012/13 to 2014/15) to avoid the period during which the most significant disruption was occurring. While Royal Mail continues to undertake continuous transformation within its Mail Centres, including completing the modernization program, the majority of Mail Centres had completed the implementation of the range of modernization initiatives by 2013/14. To allow for temporary disruption from Mail Centre closures, we also excluded observations where the Centre closed within a year, or where it absorbed mail from a closing Centre. This reflected our understanding that a Mail Centre was most likely to experience any temporary adverse effect on efficiency in the year that it was affected by such closure.

---

[3]This implicitly assumes that the original set of weights was correct at the time they were set i.e. represented the efficient processing and delivery times for different types of mail for the initial period.

[4]When the number of cross-sectional units in a panel varies over time, it is referred to as an unbalanced panel and may require a different modelling approach to address potential issues of bias.

4.3 Omitted Variable Bias

A common issue for econometric studies is omitted variable bias. This refers to a bias in model estimates caused by the omission of factors that influence the outcome variable being modelled and are in some way also related to the explanatory variables included in the model. In the context of efficiency studies, this problem arises where the model does not include a particular variable that is important in driving costs. Two undesirable effects can result. First, the effect of the omitted variable could be included in the error term and so incorrectly attributed to inefficiency. Second, its effect could be picked up by an included variable with which the omitted variable is correlated, such that the model results tend to incorrectly state the impact of the included variable on cost.[5]

In the preliminary results, the coefficient on weighted volume per delivery point changed significantly when factors within management control were included in the model for sensitivity tests. Put another way, the relationship between cost/hours and weighted volume per delivery point appeared very different depending on what other variables were included in the model. In looking at relationships between the different variables, we found that weighted volume per delivery point was highly correlated with one particular factor within management control, delivery points per route. As noted above, only factors which are outside management should be controlled for within the econometric model and so we could not include delivery points per route in our main models.

Excluding this variable from our main models made weighted volume per delivery point appear to explain more of the variation in cost/hours than its actual effect, biasing the results. We therefore excluded delivery points per route so as not to include factors within management control, but constrained the coefficient on weighted volume per delivery point in both the costs and hours models to more closely reflect the coefficient value from the models including all factors. Introducing this constraint also had a knock-on effect on the coefficient on delivery points. The coefficient on delivery points was also constrained based on prior literature, which suggests that delivery costs rise in line with the number of delivery points (for example, Cazals et al. 2004). The effect of omitted variable bias on the results was also mitigated by focusing on the gains from catching up to the upper quartile or upper decile rather than the absolute efficient frontier estimated by the model.[6]

---

[5]If the omitted variable is positively correlated with the included variable, then the model results will tend to overstate the impact of the included variable on costs. Alternatively, if the omitted variable is negatively correlated with the included variable, then the model results will under-state the impact of the included variable on costs.

[6]We recognise there may have been other variables omitted from our analysis which also drive costs but consider the impact of these on model estimates is likely to be very limited. Royal Mail identified all important drivers of cost in its discussions with us, so any cost drivers we were not aware of are likely to have a much lesser impact. Moreover, the DO model results were robust to a large number of sensitivity tests, increasing confidence in results.

4.4 Projecting Forward Efficiency Gains Based on the Results

Finally, to use the analysis to inform our view as to Royal Mail's efficiency potential, we needed to be able to project forward what efficiency gains the results suggest Royal Mail should be able to make.

Finding evidence of a catch-up gap between the efficient frontier and less efficient units suggests that there is some gain available from increasing the efficiency of weaker performing units to match that of their more efficient peers. Our model provides an estimate of the size of this gap. A very low estimated gap would indicate that most units are close to the efficient frontier and the remaining gains available may be limited; a very large gap indicates that significant gains could be made by spreading best practice from high performing units to lower performing units.[7] However, the model does not give any insight into how quickly the gap can be closed; this is therefore a matter of judgement.

We also derived estimates of the potential forward looking frontier shifts based on estimates of the efficiency gains made over the sample period. These estimated efficiency improvements in the frontier are likely to be attributable primarily to benefits yielded from the implementation of Royal Mail's modernization program. As the majority of the modernization program had been completed by 2014/15, we recognized it may be possible that most of the frontier shift gains associated with modernization had already been realized and that the historic frontier shifts we had estimated therefore provided limited guide as to the future evolution of the efficient frontier. However, our discussions with Royal Mail as well as our own internal understanding of the time profile of the benefits flowing from modernization initiatives suggested that the impact of modernization is not instantaneous but instead accrued over a number of years. We therefore considered it appropriate to extrapolate estimates of the further scope for efficiencies from the full gains of modernization being realized.

Based on prior work, the impact of modernization felt by Royal Mail Delivery Offices and Mail Centres is calculated with the following assumptions. First, we assumed that modernization had a negative impact on efficiency in the year it was implemented. This may occur as a result of, for example, the disruption to staff having to change their work location following the implementation of new working methods and route optimization. It was further assumed that it takes up to two years following completion for the full impact of modernization initiatives to be realized. The positive impact on efficiency (including making up the lost efficiency in the first year after modernization) was therefore split over the following two years.

[7]Note that this is purely an internal benchmarking model. It does not incorporate the effect of initiatives Royal Mail plans to implement but has not started, or initiatives Royal Mail does not intend to undertake but which have been adopted by other operators. The potential effects of these factors were assessed through other sources of evidence in our review.

The expected frontier shift was estimated by extrapolating the impact of modernization into the following years by considering the proportion of Delivery Offices and Mail Centres that have completed modernization by 2014/15 and the time required for the full impact of modernization to be realized.

It is important to note that these calculations involve a number of assumptions. First, the historical frontier shift is fully attributed to the modernization program. Second, all Delivery Offices and Mail Centres are assumed to complete modernization by the end of 2015/16. Third, the impact of modernization is assumed to be the same regardless of the particular point in time that a given Delivery Office or Mail Centre was modernized. Finally, we assume that no additional efficiency initiatives that drive frontier shifts will be implemented in the years following the sample period.

5 Results

5.1 *Delivery Offices*

Table 3 shows the result of the baseline model using staff hours as the dependent variable. For Delivery Offices, the analysis estimates that average operational efficiency has improved by 5.8 % in terms of gross hours since 2010/11 (indicated by the estimated coefficient for the 2014 dummy).

However, despite these historic efficiency improvements, the econometric results also show that there is considerable difference in the performance of different Delivery Offices, with Delivery Office efficiency scores varying from 60 to 100 % (see Fig. 2). If the catch-up opportunity is assumed to be represented by the upper decile or quartile of the efficient score distribution, the average catch-up gaps (with respect to hours) are 9.8 and 5.0 % respectively. Once the potential frontier shift from realizing the full impact of modernization is factored in, the most conservative estimates produced (based on the upper quartile) suggest that Royal Mail could achieve total efficiency savings in Delivery Offices of 4.3 % to 6.6 % over the following five years. If the upper decile is considered to be the appropriate benchmark, the efficiency savings achievable are estimated to be 6.3–11.5 %. Figure 3 shows the estimated profile of these gains over the period.

5.2 *Mail Centres*

Table 4 shows the result of the baseline model using staff hours as the dependent variable. For Mail Centres, the analysis estimates that average operational efficiency has improved 8.8 % in terms of gross hours since 2012/13 (indicated by the estimated coefficient for the 2014 dummy).

Table 3 Delivery offices—coefficient estimates (baseline model)

Dependent variable	Hours
Log (delivery points)	1
Log (weighted volume per delivery point)	0.80
Log(delivery points per area)	0.0221***
Proportion of delivery points that are businesses	0.802***
London dummy	0.0672***
Mail processing unit dummy	0.0387***
% rural	0.0186
% suburban	0.0370***
2011 dummy	−0.0128***
2012 dummy	−0.0199***
2013 dummy	−0.0429***
2014 dummy	−0.0581***
Intercept	−3.842***
Sample size	6087

Key ***1 % significance **5 % significance *10 % significance
Source Deloitte (2016)

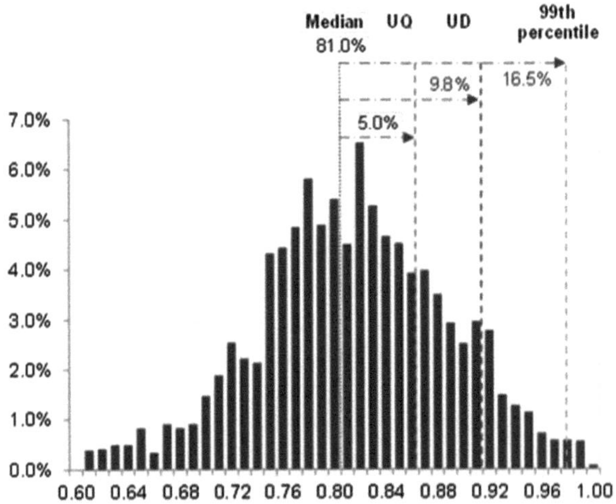

Fig. 2 Catch up efficiency score distribution for the baseline delivery office staff hours model. *Source* Deloitte (2016)

As with Delivery Offices, the results suggest that there remains a difference in performance between Mail Centres (see Fig. 4). Given the extent to which the modernization program has been completed, there is relatively little frontier shift predicted from the analysis. Given the greater methodological challenges with the Mail Centre analysis, we do not attach as much weight to the precise outputs of the model as we do for Delivery Offices. However, we consider the broad scale of potential efficiency savings is sufficiently robust to indicate that there remains potential for Royal Mail to improve the efficiency of its Mail Centres, particularly by reducing the catch up gap between Mail Centres.

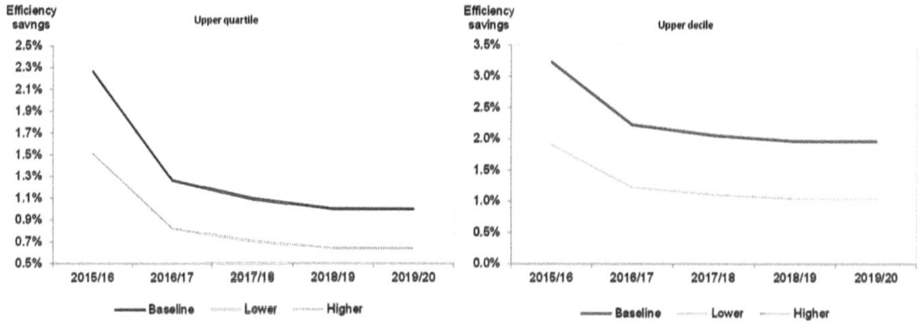

Fig. 3 Range of potential efficiency savings available to Royal Mail DOs. *Source* Deloitte (2016)

Table 4 Mail centres—coefficient estimates (baseline model)

Dependent variable	Hours
Log (delivery offices per mail centre)	1.095***
Log (total workload per delivery office)	0.861***
Log (delivery offices per area)	0.0647**
London dummy	−0.200**
Log (time of final dispatch)	0.0111
Log (time of final network vehicle)	−0.190
2013 dummy	−0.0242**
2014 dummy	−0.0881***
Intercept	−2.541*
Sample size	88

Key ***1 % significance **5 % significance *10 % significance

Fig. 4 Catch-up distributions for the baseline Mail Centre staff hours model. *Source* Deloitte (2016)

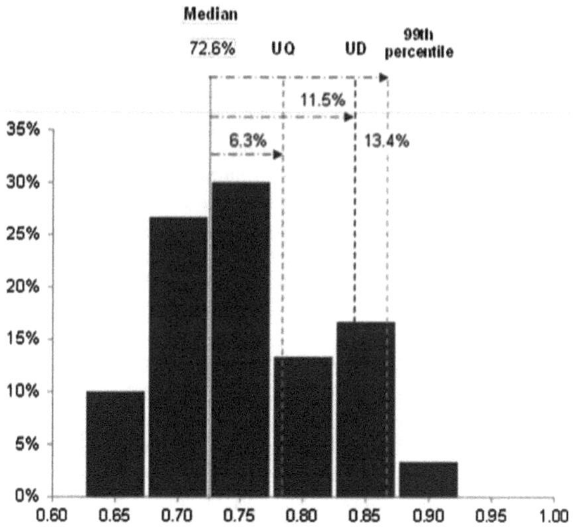

6 Conclusions

Overall, our results show that Royal Mail has achieved efficiency savings over recent years in both its Delivery Offices and Mail Centres. However, despite these historical efficiency improvements, differences in the relative efficiency of Royal Mail's Delivery Offices and Mail Centres still remain. This divergence in performance suggests there is further scope for Royal Mail to increase its overall efficiency by improving the performance of the less efficient Delivery Offices and Mail Centres to catch up with their higher performing peers.

This finding contributed to the evidence supporting our provisional conclusion that Royal Mail has made progress on efficiency in recent years, and that its future plans (if successfully executed) would result in greater efficiency improvements than its historic achievement, but that there remains potential for Royal Mail to make greater efficiency gains than those forecast in its 2015 Business Plan.

References

Cazals, C., Florens, J.-P., & Soteri, S. (2004) Delivery costs for postal services in the UK: Some results on Scale economies with Panel Data'. In M. A. Crew & P. R. Kleindorfer (Eds.), *Regulatory and economic challenges in the postal and delivery sector* (pp. 203–212), Boston, MA: Kluwer Academic.

Cazals, C., Dudley, P., Florens, J.-P., & Jones, M. (2012). 'A panel data analysis of inefficiency and heterogeneity in the postal sector'. In M. A. Crew & P. R. Kleindorfer (Eds.), *Multi-modal competition and the future of mail, Cheltenham, UK and Northampton.* MA, USA: Edward Elgar.

Deloitte. (2016). *Econometric benchmarking in the UK postal sector.* http://stakeholders.ofcom.org.uk/binaries/consultations/royal-mail-review/annexes/benchmarking-report.pdf

Fenster, L., Monaco, D., Pearsall, E., & Xenakis, S. (2008). Are there economies of scale in mail processing? In M. A. Crew & P. R. Kleindorfer (Eds.), *Competition and regulation in the postal and delivery sector* (pp. 315–337). Cheltenham, UK and Northampton, MA, USA: Edward Elgar.

Horncastle, A., Jevons, D., Dudley, P., & Thanassoulis, E. (2006). Efficiency analysis of delivery offices in the postal sector using stochastic frontier and data envelopment analysis. In M. A. Crew & P. R. Kleindorfer (Eds.), *Liberalization of the postal and delivery sector* (pp. 149–164). Cheltenham, UK and Northampton, MA, USA: Edward Elgar.

Moriarty, R., Yorke, S., Harman, G., Cubbin, J., Meschi, M., & Smith, P. (2006). 'Economic analysis of the efficiency of royal mail units and the implications for regulatory policy'. In M. A. Crew & P. R. Kleindorfer (Eds.), *Liberalization of the postal and delivery sector* (pp. 165–182). Cheltenham, UK and Northampton, MA, USA: Edward Elgar.

Ofcom. (2014a). *Postal wider review announcement.* http://stakeholders.ofcom.org.uk/post/postal-wider-review/

Ofcom. (2014b). *Review of end-to-end competition in the postal sector.* http://stakeholders.ofcom.org.uk/binaries/post/end-to-end-statement/end-to-end.pdf

Ofcom. (2015). *Review of the regulation of royal mail.* http://stakeholders.ofcom.org.uk/binaries/consultations/royal-mail-regulation-review/summary/Review_of_RM_regulation.pdf

Ofcom. (2016). *Review of the regulation of royal mail.* http://stakeholders.ofcom.org.uk/consultations/royal-mail-review2016/

Changes to the Universal Service: Influencing Factors, Impacts and Regulatory Implications

Steven Cape and Philip Groves

1 Introduction

The Postal Services Directive 2008/6/EC in Article 3 sets out the obligation on Member States to "ensure that users enjoy the right to a universal service involving the permanent provision of a postal service of specified quality at all points in their territory at affordable prices for all users". In summary, such a service shall normally be provided at least five days a week, except for notified exceptional circumstances or geographical conditions and includes one clearance, one delivery to the home or premises. It also included—both nationally and cross-border—the minimum facilities of clearance, sorting, transport and distribution of postal items up to 2 kg and postal packets up to 10 kg.

Article 5 of the same Directive goes on to specify certain requirements which the universal service must fulfil, such as being made available without any form of discrimination. The last of these requirements which has most relevance to this paper is where it says that universal service provision "shall evolve in response to the technical, economic and social environment and to the needs of users".

The Directive's requirements relating to universal service provision have remained largely unchanged since the first Directive came into effect in 1997 however since that date there were a number of significant developments for the sector which included: the accession to EU Membership of 17 new Member States most of whom have very low mail volumes per capita (i.e. substantially lower than

Ofcom. The views expressed do not necessarily reflect the views of Ofcom

S. Cape (✉) · P. Groves
Ofcom, Riverside House, 2a Southwark Bridge Road, London SE1 9HA, UK
e-mail: stevencape@gmail.com

P. Groves
e-mail: Philip.Groves@ofcom.org.uk

M. Crew et al. (eds.), *The Changing Postal and Delivery Sector*,
Topics in Regulatory Economics and Policy,
DOI 10.1007/978-3-319-46046-8_17

1 item of mail received per household per day); the impact of the decoupling of letter volume growth from GDP in the early 2000s coupled with e-substitution growing and accelerating in pace and scale following the 2008 global financial crisis; the growth in digital communications which has stimulated on-line shopping and provided traditional letter operators with opportunities to grow their parcels businesses as letter volumes further decline; and finally the completion of a process of gradual and controlled market opening which resulted to varying degrees in either end to end competition or network access competition, or a mixture of both, in a number of EU Member States.

However, these extensive changes were not to date accompanied by an evolution in the EU minimum requirements for the universal postal service in the two postal directives that followed the 1997 Directive. This has led to a potential gap in those requirements and the new market realities. Indeed, the intra-EU changes which have taken place in universal service provision since 1997 have only been at the national level and within the constraints of the unchanged minimum framework in the Directive. Accordingly, the changes introduced at national level over the past two decades have tended to focus on reducing the range of products under the USO, for example removing bulk letters, direct mail, non-priority letters or bulk parcels from the USO which are all permitted within the current EU regulatory framework.

The purpose of this paper is to examine changes in the universal service that have been proposed, considered or implemented. Section 2 sets out the significant changes that have been made or trialed, Sect. 3 looks at the impact of these changes, Sect. 4 considers the likely future trends and the finally Sect. 5 discusses the regulatory implications of these and future changes.

2 Significant Changes

In the countries where changes to the universal service have been made or have been considered, the specifications of the universal service have been, or are, typically high. This is not only in terms of the number of days that delivery is required, but also in the range of products included in the universal service, the quality of service targets for these products, and the requirement to maintain a network of post offices and other access points. By way of example, before the recent changes discussed in this paper, the requirement in Denmark, the Netherlands, New Zealand and the US was for 6-day delivery, with D + 1 target above 90 % and requirements to maintain networks, in some cases (Netherlands, New Zealand) to a specific size.

While the requirements for the universal service are high, the volume of letter items being carried over the universal network has been declining. This is the case in almost all developed countries, with some of the most significant declines taking place in Denmark and the US. Between 2005 and 2011, mail volumes in Denmark fell by around 50 % (PwC 2013), and over the same period in the US, single piece First Class mail volumes fell by approximately the same proportion (OIG 2015).

E-substitution is the most common cause of declining mail volumes, as both consumers and businesses switch to faster and cheaper electronic ways to send what they previously would have sent as a physical item. The large decline in Denmark has been influenced by the government decision to move the majority of its communications to electronic methods.

This has put pressure on the finances of universal service providers, who have been attempting to cut costs as volumes have fallen. Although it has been possible in some cases to remove costs from the universal service network, the necessity of maintaining a network capable of providing a universal postal service means that universal service providers are only able to go so far. A particular challenge in some cases is the requirement to maintain geographic coverage. In Finland, 80 % of the country has a population density of 4 people per km^2 (Posti 2015), and in Italy the varied geographic territory has meant that the net cost of the USO has been assessed at a high level, leading to recent notifications of state aid.

It seems that the current universal service in many countries is—to varying degrees—exceeding the needs of residential users of postal services. Although research in Denmark found that 60 % of residential users saw 6-day delivery as necessary, only 15 % had sent a letter in the past week (Thomsen 2015). When the reduction in the number of delivery days was being considered in the Netherlands, a significant majority (85 %) of consumers considered that they would not mind if there was one fewer delivery day (Post and Parcel 2011). Poste Italiane found in its recent research that almost 75 % of residential consumers would be satisfied with a reduction in delivery from 5 to two or three days per week (Gori et al. 2016).

Research commissioned by the Icelandic Ministry of the Interior in 2012 found that 60 % of people would be happy with three day per week delivery, and that 45 % want to receive more mail electronically than physically, with the same proportion happy with the current ratio and just one in ten saying that they would want to receive more physically than electronically (Icelandic Ministry of the Interior 2013). In Finland, following a trial which substituted digital delivery of mail for postal delivery, a majority of users in the trial indicated that they would have been happy to continue this arrangement. In the UK, the regulator's review found that while the needs of users were being served by the postal service, some users indicated that D + 1 delivery of letters was perhaps not required, and some users considered they were less reliant on collection and delivery six days a week (Ofcom 2013).

The most significant changes to the universal service have been to delivery. In the Netherlands, delivery was reduced from six days to five in January 2014, with no collection on a Sunday and no delivery on a Monday. In New Zealand, deliveries in urban areas now take place three days a week instead of five, and in Italy alternate day delivery is to be implemented in three stages over two and a half years across one quarter of the population. For these countries, changes in legislation were required to make these changes. In other countries, changes in delivery have been possible within the requirements of the universal service. The Danish USP has implemented six-day delivery in a more flexible manner, by differentiating between letters sent to businesses and to residential consumers and by implementing an alternate day service for items with a slower delivery speed. For example, letters sent at the weekend to business customers are delivered on a Monday, while those sent to residential consumers are delivered on a Tuesday. And items that do not have to be delivered the next day, such as second class mail, are delivered to households on alternate days. Itella in Finland has also been undertaking trials in delivery to reduce costs, most recently eliminating Tuesday delivery for magazines, bulk and direct mail while delivering USO mail on all weekdays as per the requirement.

A reduction in delivery days or a reduction in the amount of routes taken by delivery postal workers each day is likely to provide most immediate reduction in costs for USPs. However, Itella noted in its trial of delivering only universal service items on Tuesdays had not led to the size of savings that it had anticipated (Posti 2015). It is notable that in the US, USPS had been lobbying for a reduction in delivery days from six to five for a number of years due to declining volumes, but recently stated that it wanted to retain six-day delivery. This is due to increasing volumes of e-commerce parcels being carried over the universal service network and consumers' desire for Saturday delivery.

In its recent response to the European Regulators' Group for Post's (ERGP) (ERGP's) consultation on the implementation of the universal service in the postal sector in view of the market developments, Royal Mail in the UK asserted that it is because of the letters USO that businesses outside of the main cities are able to get affordable parcel delivery services (Royal Mail Group 2014). Although some other European USPs call for reductions in the minimum requirements of the universal service in their responses to the consultation, while supporting the idea of Member States retaining the flexibility to set appropriate national USOs, Royal Mail appears to support keeping the 6-day delivery obligation in the UK.

Changes to delivery points have also been tried or proposed, although these have not yet led to permanent changes. The Finnish USP previously trialed delivery to digital mailboxes in a rural area of the country, with trial members receiving physical items twice a week combined with daily delivery through a digital mailbox. Delivery to community mailboxes has been proposed and discussed in Canada, although this has met with opposition and was only partially implemented, mostly only for new residential apartment developments. The Finnish initiative would require changes to legislation to implement on a permanent basis.

Reducing the number of access points for the universal service network has also been implemented to reduce costs. However, where a minimum number of access points has been specified in legislation this has met with resistance. In the Netherlands, when delivery day reductions were in the process of being determined in 2011, the Dutch Economic Minister at the time considered a reduction in the 18,000 letterbox and 200 post office network "a step too far" (Post and Parcel 2011). But three years later, a further amendment to the Postal Act was proposed, and passed, to allow a reduction in the network, with these changes necessary to keep the universal postal service "accessible and affordable to all" (Post NL 2015). While NZ Post was renegotiating its renewed service standard, it did not propose reducing the total number of post offices, but did want the flexibility to be able to include self-service kiosks in the total. In the agreement, it was required to keep at least one third of the network staffed (Clarke 2014). Other countries, such as Denmark, where the minimum number is not set in legislation, have been able to be more flexible in reducing the access point network. However, despite reducing the number of post offices leading up to 2013, the rise in e-commerce has meant that Post Danmark has been increasing the number of access points to its network, adding 150 in 2014 alone and opening its 1000th post office in 2015 (Post and Parcel 2015).

A far more common change in the universal service is a change in the products included in the universal service. This is because in many European countries, the products included in the USO had gone further than in the Directive and removing them required little legislative change. Bulk mail has been removed from the universal service in Lithuania, Poland and the UK and the maximum weight of universal service parcels has been reduced to 10 kg in Austria, Latvia, Portugal and Slovenia (ERGP 2015b).

3 Impact of These Changes

As the majority of these changes have taken place recently, the impact that they have had on the finances and operations of the USP are too early to fully quantify and are difficult to separate from changes being made as operations are adapted to deal with ongoing volume declines. For example, Post NL has been implementing a strategy of utilizing a more flexible workforce for a number of years and now uses an almost entirely part-time workforce in delivery. This is not as a direct result of it reducing the number of delivery days, but does give it the flexibility in its employment practices to take advantage of cost savings from the elimination of Monday deliveries.

In other countries affected by large letter volume reductions, such changes may have been a catalyst for intensifying operational restructuring to meet the new situation and help ensure the financial viability of the universal service. Prior to the acceleration of mail volume decline post 2008, many incumbent USPs focused on increasing automation of letters sorting and mail center rationalization. Since 2008, many operators were able to implement more innovative and efficient delivery models separating indoor and outdoor work and in some cases resulting in delivery staff undertaking two daily delivery rounds, one in the morning and one in the afternoon.

For example, following the merger of Sweden Post with Post Danmark, to form PostNord, in 2009, Post Danmark's parcels business was transferred to the mail division and over the subsequent years, around one third of its letter mail routes were combined with parcels deliveries. Post Danmark also became a leader in delivery-point sequencing by machine for 90 % of its letter mail volumes. It also made significant investments in flat sorting machines. Post Danmark invested in pre-processing technology, including automatic revenue protection, and between

2007 and 2009 reorganized its delivery processes to adjust its costs and capacity to changing market conditions.

The new PostNord (both the Swedish and Danish branches) made substantial advances in handling unaddressed items, mechanizing and integrating door to door items into a wrapped collection of items per address ready for delivery. PostNord proved particularly adept at reducing operating expenses and other non-staff costs in line with letter volume declines. While for various reasons, Sweden was less affected by e-substitution than Denmark, Sweden had much earlier full market opening than most other Member States resulting in significant level of end to end competition, which forced it to modernize and become more competitive in other ways.

Post NL, which also had similar levels of end to end competition, similarly streamlined its operational practices, including separating indoor and outdoor activities, frequent redesign of routes, outsourcing collection in urban areas to transport companies and measures aimed at increasing the flexibility of existing staff. Including schemes to reduce staff numbers e.g. through early retirement.

As mentioned above, both Post NL and Post Danmark have made changes to delivery, with a change to the universal service legislation in the case of Post NL, that have helped them reorganize and manage the volume of deliveries each day. While lighter delivery days mean that Post NL can take advantage of flexibility in its workforce, on the other hand, the alternate day delivery model implemented by Post Danmark has allowed it to more effectively distribute the delivered mail volume across the week. This means that it has been able to sustain employment for full-time employees without a pressing need to move to a more flexible or part time workforce.

Such operational changes have helped to mitigate profitability reductions due to volume decline, combined with price increases and diversification. Accordingly, in most countries, the EBIT margin from the letter mail segment has either remained stable or showed declines while still remaining positive overall (WIK 2013).

Finally, given that the changes to the USO were in the main not dramatic and have followed and reflected, rather than anticipated, market developments, also taking into account user needs considerations, none of the changes to date has so far been seen as detrimental to consumers.

4 Future Trends

Responses to the ERGP's consultation on the evolution of the universal service obligation provides an indication of the way that USPs, competitors and users of postal services want to see future universal service provision. A key concern is the sustainability of providing the universal service, with flexibility in determining the requirements within member states and reflecting individual national conditions seen in many cases as a way of achieving this in each country.

Reducing the scope and the specificity of the overarching universal service requirement at an EU-level is suggested as a way of achieving by focusing on reliability, affordability and ubiquity, in line with WIK's recommendations to the European Commission (WIK 2013). The ability to reduce delivery days, reduce the speed of basic letter post services, become more flexible in what is considered delivery to the addressee and restrict universal service requirements to residential consumers and small to medium enterprises feature in the responses from a number of USPs and are therefore likely future trends, at least to some extent, regardless of any formal recasting of the USO in EU or national legislation.

A trend that is already occurring to some extent and is expected to continue is the change in the features of products specified as universal services. As noted above, this has already occurred in some European countries, with the removal of bulk mail and the reduction in the maximum weight for parcels considered as universal services. However, this is likely to develop further with a reduction in the speed of delivery for products designated as universal service products. In the long term, this could potentially lead to the loss of next day basic letter services.

The reduction in speed for a universal service product has already taken place in Finland, although this was achieved by increasing the speed and accessibility of the second class letter product. Prior to the passing of the 2011 Postal Act which set out that universal service letters must be delivered with a D + 2 standard, Itella changed the specification of its non-priority letter product from D + 3 to D + 2, and removed the requirement for this to be sent from post offices in minimum shipments of 20 to be able to be sent from pillar boxes and with no minimum requirement. Although Itella stated that it considered the "main principles of the universal service obligation to be the same" following the passing of the 2011 Act (Itella 2011), it is notable that the USP and the regulator are in disagreement about which letter products are included in the universal service.[1]

A more recent change has just been implemented in Australia, where after a period of consultation and engagement, a three speed letters service was implemented in January 2015. This has reduced the speed of the basic letter product and increased the price by 43 %. The standard letter product now has a delivery target of up to 3–6 days depending on the destination, while a premium of $0.50 can be paid to upgrade to a priority service with a delivery target of 1–4 days, again depending on the destination.

During its consultation period, Australia Post explored a number of potential changes to the postal service, including a reduction in delivery days for letters, changes to delivery points and charging for delivery to the home. The introduction of a two-speed service was deemed to be the most acceptable, and Australia Post have noted that it will still be delivering small parcels and express letters five days per week across the same network, so the potential cost savings from a universal

[1]Prior to the Act, Itella considered that non-priority letters were outside of the USO (Copenhagen Economics 2010). Following the Act, Itella considers that priority letters are outside of the USO (WIK 2013).

service product with fewer delivery days would be limited (Australia Post 2015). However, the reduction in speed will reduce costs in transportation, as more mail can be transported by road instead of air, and in sorting, as mail can be sorted throughout the day rather than within a limited timeframe during the night.

Whether the reduction in delivery speed is going to be sufficient to reverse Australia Post's recent losses remains to be seen. A reduction in delivery speed may not bring the greatest savings from delivery changes, particularly where other non-universal service products with faster delivery specifications are being delivered over the universal service network, but it is likely to have a significant impact in countries where it will reduce the amount of expedited long distance transport of mail and allow for greater advantage to be taken of economies of scale in delivery to more remote areas. It also seems to be a reasonable response to e-substitution, as more urgent correspondence is already being sent through electronic means and the user need for next day delivery services of physical items is reduced.

Changes in the access point network of universal service providers are another current trend which is likely to continue. In the majority of European countries, with some exceptions, the number of USP post offices has fallen between 2011 and 2014 (ERGP 2015c). Over the same period, the proportion of post offices offering USP services operated by companies other than the USP (for example, post offices within retail outlets) has increased. Notably, Denmark, where the number of outlets has increased, now has 99.5 % of its post offices managed by third parties, up from 84 % in 2011 (ERGP 2011, 2015a).

A reduction either in the overall number of post offices or the number of post offices directly operated by the USP is a trend that is likely to continue, and in many cases is possible to do within the current restrictions imposed by legislation. In those countries where it is not possible to further reduce the size of the network without legislative change, there is likely to be a greater and more diverse use of the facilities for non-universal service and non-postal products and services as a way of driving increased use and revenue generated from each outlet.

For Poste Italiane, diversification of its business model by utilizing its post office network is likely to have felt like a natural step. It was already offering access to its financial services products through its network, and has started using the facilities for newer business ventures, including working with the government to issue work and residence permits to immigrants, using the post office network as a place to accept and validate documents. Australia Post has also been extending the use of its retail network by increasing the range of non-postal services available at its outlets.

Alongside these shorter term trends, which in many countries would not require extensive legislative change, we expect to see longer term trends in universal service provision which would require legislative change or approval.

So far, New Zealand and Italy are the two leading examples of the implementation in a reduction in the number of delivery days for certain customers in certain areas, albeit the Italian plan is not yet fully rolled out. However it is possible that other countries will follow suite.

For example, discussion is now taking place in Finland over the shape of the future postal USO. This was prompted by a decision by the Ministry of Transport and Communications of Finland to start a project to reform Finland's postal legislation aimed at more flexible services to meet the needs of the changing environment. As one part of a range of reforms to lighten operational and administrative barriers to market entry, access to post codes and the address database will be reviewed together with the scope and extent of the universal service obligation.

The Finnish USP, Posti, made a submission to its Ministry on 24 March 2016 in which it notes that the predicted sharp decline in mail volumes will bring the greatest challenges in rural areas, already running at a loss, it suggests a number of potential solutions including:

1. A reduction in the frequency of required USO deliveries and collections on account of changed recipient needs;
2. Increased use of the exceptions provision in the Postal Services Directive;
3. Supplementing the postal USO with digital distribution;
4. Allowing more flexible delivery in blocks of flats, into bays rather than apartment-specific post boxes.

In parallel, in April 2016 Posti announced changes with effect from 25 April to revise delivery routes and extend mail deliveries towards the evening. Posti announced that it would continue to deliver newspapers seven days a week, parcels six days a week and other mail five days a week. However, at the same time it announced it would extend the timespan of these services to the evening a change it stated was "due to the sharp fall in letters and publication delivery volumes and the increased demand for different types of services delivered to the home". It seems that this change is as much about adapting to the need to provide new services as it is to adapting to the decline in more traditional letter mail and newspaper and magazine subscription services.

It seems likely—given the political sensitivity of postal deliveries - that such decisions will take place gradually, backed up by reliable surveys on customer needs, and in light of the pressures on the ability to finance the USO as well as the need to adapt to new services.

Certain Member States have taken steps to reconfigure access to the postal network by individual consumers and businesses. In the UK this took the form of more flexible collection and delivery times. In the UK, for example, last collection times were extended and the obligation to offer or notify additional collections was removed. Post office outlets were also increasingly located in other retail outlets rather than on a stand-alone basis.

A longer term trend is likely to be to continue the reconfiguration of deliveries so that X/Y delivery models become more prevalent with an assignment of specific days by delivery location for either priority or bulk letters or both. Increasingly, given the growth in electronic communications, for ordinary letter mail the certainty of delivery by a particular day rather than the speed will be of greatest importance.

Similarly, within the current EU framework, there is scope for adjusting the quality of service requirement for 1st class or priority mail which in several countries remains over 90 %. Depending on the geography and transport infrastructure, and the actual level of the target, it may drive additional costs in air transport and associated contingency arrangements which might be out of proportion to the associated consumer benefit. Accordingly, there might be scope to relax high next day delivery targets in the whole national territory depending on whether user needs, including the needs of vulnerable users, are adequately fulfilled by other forms of communication.

In parallel, there is an observable trend for parcels for customers to collect their own parcel deliveries from third party drop off points or directly from retailers (click and collect). Where parcels are delivered alongside letters, this will also affect the cost dynamics and economies of scale and scope of letter deliveries.

The experience of Canada in having to curtail its program of community mail boxes appears to point to the difficulty of replacing delivery to the door or premises.

Unlike e-commerce parcels, which are normally directly ordered by the consumer or for them, letters are normally items such as bills, statements or advertising mail, which fit letter boxes, are easily deliverable and increasingly not time sensitive. Therefore, the recipient would appear to have much less incentive to want to collect such items from a different location instead of getting them delivered directly.

The delivery trials and recent changes in Finland do, however, point to the potential long term for delivery of letter mail to be carried out electronically, for example where households have indicated that this is acceptable to them. This has environmental advantages and has the benefit of fulfilling the communications need identified in the Directive in a flexible way which takes account of social and technological trends.

5 Regulatory Implications and Conclusions

The changes in the way the USO is delivered and reductions in scope of USO products that have taken place in recent years are contributing to the ongoing debate on how universal service providers can remain financially viable, and continue to provide the USO, in the face of declining letter volumes. The Postal Directive makes express provision for the possibility of establishing a compensation fund to meet the net costs of USO provision. While this option was examined in a number of Member States, it was so far only implemented in very limited cases, for example in Poland. Key problems are the issues around how to cost the benefits of USO provision and the fact that the absence of significant competition in most Member States in a declining letter mail market means that the USP is expected to make the bulk of the contributions.

The Directive's provisions allowing for notified geographic exceptions to the minimum USO fulfilment are currently being used as the means by which changes to Italy's USO are being introduced. To some these changes might test the interpretation of the Directive. Nevertheless, should such changes be accepted and become permanent following a reasonable assessment of user needs, this may be a route which other Member States might choose to adopt to bring the USO into line with the reduced importance of daily mail delivery in some instances. Accordingly, there might be no need to redefine the postal USO in the Directive if such an interpretation of the geographic exception clause is accepted.

Another relevant factor for USO provision in Member States is the reduced importance of mail, either sent or received, for younger age groups, meaning that even where overall mail volumes remain high, their importance for the next generation may be reducing. Research from Ofcom shows that six in ten UK citizens aged 16 to 24 had received fewer than 5 items of post in an average week in 2015—and one third had received fewer than 3 items. The same research showed that the average number of letters and cards received per week by those aged 16–24s was 3 (Ofcom 2016). Such data indicates that on average most younger people in the UK, which still retains overall high mail volumes, will not in any case be receiving a daily delivery due to their reduced reliance on letter mail. Policy makers in Member States will need to consider the link between user needs and the specified USO and reach their own conclusions.

The further growth in digital communications might in addition encourage future legislators to adopt a new model by which the Postal Directive would be redefined to ensure delivery of letter items each day but leave open the means by which such items might be delivered, enabling them to be delivered by digital means if judged appropriate.

In practice, given the political sensitivity of USO provision, the flexibility in the current Directive and the limited surveys conducted to date to re-assess user needs, the European Commission has been reluctant to produce proposals to reform the EU framework, preferring to leave the Member States and National Regulatory Authorities to take the initiative depending on who the relevant national postal legislation empowers to make such changes.

In parallel, ERGP, following its review of the changes made to the USO at a national level, which was accompanied by a stakeholder workshop, is now examining relevant studies on user needs in an attempt to identify a common set of such needs and to assess to what extent other means of communication are fulfilling these needs. The ERGP will then assess whether the current EU defined minimum USO scope is sufficient to meet the identified common EU end user needs and whether the EU definition remains appropriate to manage any under or over specification of national USOs taking account of national differences.

To conclude, this paper has outlined the circumstances and the different ways in which national USOs are increasingly being redefined to adapt both to changing user needs and to the financial pressure on USPs arising from low and/or reducing letter mail volumes over a largely fixed network. In addition, analysis of user needs—of households and businesses as senders and recipients of letter mail—is not complete across the EU Member States, which has meant that changes in USO specification have tended to be piecemeal and to lag market developments. In parallel, the EU framework has not so far evolved to reflect the requirement in the Postal Directive for universal service provision “to evolve in response to the technical, economic and social environment and to the needs of users”. For example, daily delivery appears to make little sense from the user or the economic perspective where only a few items per month are received by a household. Another example is how e-substitution, by guaranteeing speed of delivery, appears to have made reliability of delivery, rather than speed reflected in daily delivery, more relevant for letter mail. As more radical USO changes are considered and implemented nationally, such as the large geographic exception to daily delivery in Italy, it will become necessary to examine the limits of the minimum definition in the current Directive to see whether it is sufficiently flexible to cope with such changes or whether a more fundamental USO redefinition is needed.

References

Australia Post. (2015). Your questions. https://conversation.auspost.com.au/yourquestions. Accessed March 30, 2016

Clarke, R. (2014). *Legalizing alternate day delivery: the reshaping of the universal postal service in New Zealand.* Prepared for Comité européen des régulateurs postaux (CERP), for discussion at its 49th plenary meeting, May 29–30, 2014.

Copenhagen Economics. (2010). *Main Developments in the Postal Sector (2008–2010) Part B: Country Fiche Appendix*

ERGP. (2011). *ERGP Report on the Quality of Service and End-User Satisfaction.*

ERGP. (2015a). *ERGP Report on the Quality of Service, Consumer Protection and Complaint Handling—an Analysis of Trends.*

ERGP. (2015b). *ERGP Report on the outcome of the ERGP public consultation on the evolution of the Universal Service Obligation.*

ERGP. (2015c). *ERGP Report on Core Indicators for Monitoring the European Postal Market.*

Gori, S., Martinelli, B., & Scarfiglieri, G. (2016). Using market research to analyze consumer preferences. In M. A. Crew & T. J. Brennan (Eds.), *The future of the postal sector in a digital world.* New York: Springer.

Icelandic Ministry of the Interior. (2013). *Results of a survey on attitudes toward the postal service.*

Itella. (2011). *Interim report for January–June 2011.*

Ofcom. (2013). *Review of postal users' needs.*

Ofcom. (2016). *Ofcom residential consumer postal tracker—2015.* http://stakeholders.ofcom.org.uk/binaries/research/statistics/2016Feb-Apr/Residential_Postal_Tracker_2015_data_tables_tbp.pdf. Accessed April 25, 2016

Post NL. (2015). *Annual Report 2014.*

Post and Parcel. (2011). *Dutch postal reforms to eliminate Monday deliveries.* http://postandparcel.info/44462/news/companies/dutch-postal-reforms-to-eliminate-monday-deliveries/. Accessed April 20, 2016

Post and Parcel. (2015). *Post Danmark opens 1,000th post office, to boost e-commerce access.* http://postandparcel.info/64628/news/markets/post-danmark-opens-1000th-post-office-to-boost-e-commerce-access/. Accessed April 20, 2016

Posti. (2015). *Finnish experiences on a product-specific delivery experiment.* Prepared for the 15th Königswinter Seminar on Postal Economics, 9–11 February 2015.

PwC. (2013). *The Outlook for UK mail volumes to 2023*, Prepared for Royal Mail Group.

Royal Mail Group. (2014). *Royal Mail Group response to the European Regulators Group for Postal Services' public consultation paper on "Implementation of the Universal Service Obligation in the postal sector in view of the market developments".*

Thomsen, T. (2015). *Sustainable USO from a Danish perspective—own reflections*. Prepared for the 15th Königswinter Seminar on Postal Economics, February 9–11, 2015.
U.S. Postal Service Office of Inspector General (OIG). (2015). *Declines in U.S. Postal Service Mail Volume Vary Widely across the United States: Report Number RARC-WP-15-010.*
WIK. (2013). *Main Developments in the Postal Sector (2010–2013).*

Mail Composition and Recipients' Reaction to Direct Mail

Thomas Geissmann, Christian Jaag, Martin Maegli and Urs Trinkner

1 Introduction

Letter mail services have come under pressure from the emergence of electronic communication channels. The development of mail prices and volumes shows that various types of mail evolve quite differently. So far, transactional mail has suffered more from electronic substitution than direct mail. Competition has also evolved differently in the various segments of mail: new postal operators often focus on bulk mail while transactional mail originating from households remains mostly uncontested.

Postal operators (POs) and regulators reconsider their pricing and policy based on the value of mail with electronic competition. Several studies have examined demand for mail and its drivers, most of them from the perspective of senders of mail. However, in order to understand fully the value of mail and its demand it is not only important to consider the sender's but also the recipients' preferences and appreciation of mail because the latter also determine the mail's value for the senders. The recipients' perception of the mail they receive depends on the composition or the mix of mail (further on referred to as "mailmix"): various types of mail interact with each other. Some types of mail are perceived positively and contribute to the attractiveness of the mail channel, thereby increasing the value of

T. Geissmann (✉)
ETH Zürich, Zurich, Switzerland

C. Jaag · U. Trinkner
Swiss Economics, Zurich, Switzerland

M. Maegli
Swiss Post, Bern, Switzerland

M. Crew et al. (eds.), *The Changing Postal and Delivery Sector*,
Topics in Regulatory Economics and Policy,
DOI 10.1007/978-3-319-46046-8_18

other mail. Other types tend to annoy the recipients and degrade the quality of the channel as a means of communication. As a side effect, in many countries "do not mail lists" have emerged. Hence, the mail stream can be interpreted as a platform with multiple market sides: senders of various types of mail and recipients.

To our knowledge, there is no empirical research available on this important topic. This paper is hence a first attempt using data from a recent survey in Switzerland. The paper examines the relevance of interdependencies between various types of mail in analogy to other platform markets. It then empirically analyzes the interdependencies of various mail types based on a Swiss data set of 2016. It shows that a balanced mailmix significantly increases the probability of the recipient reacting positively to addressed advertisement. For example, a higher share of non-advertisement mail in the recipients' mailbox increases response rates to direct advertisement, thereby increasing the advertisers' willingness to pay for postal services. If so, postal services with a high share of advertisement mail might, in particular if they are not restricted by direct competition from competing deliverers, aim to reflect externalities between different mail types in their pricing. More explicitly, such postal services might want to increase the price of advertising mail and decrease the price of mail pieces that recipients like to receive in their mailbox.

The remainder of the paper is structured as follows. Section 2 discusses the related literature. In Sect. 3 the analytical framework is developed. Section 4 presents the empirical analysis and results. Section 5 concludes.

2 Related Literature

There is no empirical research yet on the effect of the mailmix on the recipients' attention and the value of the mail channel for advertisers. For other platforms, e.g. newspapers and TV channels, the interaction between the various types of content and their role in the competition for readers and viewers has been studied extensively.

A platform serves two or multiple distinct groups of agents, where the utilities of the agents in one group depend on the presence of the others. A particularly interesting case is asymmetric interaction of the utilities between the groups on the platform, i.e. one group exerts a negative effect on the other group, while the latter exerts a positive effect on the former. This dissimilar interaction between the groups' utilities complicates the profit-maximizing price setting for the platform provider. A literature on such platforms and two-sided markets has emerged with Rochet and Tirole (2003), Armstrong (2006), as well as Rochet and Tirole (2006) as notable starting points. A standard example for platforms with asymmetric external effects is the media sector, i.e. newspapers, radio, and television channels, where one group consists of the consumers of editorial content and the other group by advertising. The economics of media platforms have been studied extensively. Common to all models is the division of the platform's users in two sides, advertising firms and content consumers. For instance, Anderson and Gabszewicz (2006) model the media sector as a two-sided market in which they take into account the influence of advertising on media usage. The model is applied in the specific context of television by Anderson and Coate (2005). Furthermore, Godes et al. (2009), Crampes et al. (2009), as well as Reisinger (2012) investigate the competition between media companies using a platform model, which also integrates external effects of advertising on the media content consumers. Peitz and Valletti (2008) consider different platform designs for television with subscription fees and for free and compare the resulting advertising intensity and content differentiation. Advertising is both theoretically and empirically found to exert negative externalities on media content consumers, see e.g. Gabszewicz et al. (2004) and Wilbur (2008).

This paper builds on the theoretical framework provided in Jaag and Bach (2016) who model the mail stream as a platform carrying two types of mail (transactional and direct mail) while three groups interact on it: recipients of mail, senders of transactional mail, and advertisers, i.e. senders of direct mail. Both types of senders are interested in the recipients' attention to their items. In particular, the attention for direct mail is affected by the mailmix the recipient receives in his letterbox. Jaag and Bach (2016) conjecture that transactional mail exerts a positive effect on the recipient's attention to his mail. Consequently, the demand for transactional mail and the demand for direct mail are interdependent: Direct mail receives more attention by recipients who receive more transactional mail.

Apart from Jaag and Bach (2016), the postal sector has so far not been studied from a two-sided market perspective in which there is an interdependency between different types of mail. Jaag and Trinkner (2008) model the mail market as a two-sided market, too, but they consider senders and recipients as the two sides of the market. They argue that the subsidization of recipients by senders through the sender-pays-principle is a natural outcome of the two-sidedness of the market. Boldron et al. (2009) make an analogous distinction. They show in a two-sided market model with network externalities that the benefits of senders (per addressee) increase in the size of the high quality delivery network and that such externalities should be considered in the pricing of postal services. Rohr et al. (2011) conclude in their empirical study based on discrete choice experiments that senders do care about the attributes of the postal platform provided on the recipient side, and that the services offered on the sender side are important to recipients. The present paper is also somewhat related to Bradley et al. (2015) who analyze the demand for saturation advertising mail and targeting advertising mail in competition for the recipients' attention. De Donder et al. (2011) study welfare and pricing for bulk mail which comprises two distinct markets, of transactional and advertising mail, for which the price elasticities are different but the cost of providing those services is the same. However, they assume that demands in these markets are independent of each other.

3 The Mail Stream as a Platform

A comparison of the mail stream as a platform to the standard examples from the media sector shows that there are significant similarities. Most importantly, all platforms face advertisers on a first market side, directing advertising to the consumers, and consumers of content mail and editorial content on a second side of the market. Consumers and advertisers are thus two distinct groups on the platform. The most apparent analogies between the television, print media, and mail platforms are presented in Fig. 1.

There are also important differences between the mail stream and media platforms. In the case of the postal mail platform, there are various sender groups in the first market: senders of various mail types, e.g. transactional and direct mail. Furthermore, while senders pay a postage fee to the platform provider, the recipients are not charged any price for the use of the mail stream platform. Media platforms may be free for content consumers, but in many cases they charge a subscription or a price per unit. Naturally, the question arises whether such differences have an effect on the optimal pricing strategy of POs to the two groups of senders. In fact, the media sector can also be modelled with three groups: consumers advertisers and content providers. The structure of the postal platform and the media platform with three customer groups are illustrated in Fig. 2.

Platforms like newspapers and television channels subsidize their editorial content in order to make their platform attractive both for their audience and advertisers. In the case of the postal mail platform, senders in one market can be grouped in two categories: senders of transactional mail and senders of direct mail. Both sender types typically pay a postage fee to the platform provider. Direct mail

		Television Channel	**Print Media Newspaper**	**Mail Mail stream / Mailbox**
Market side1: Marketers	**Demand side**	Advertisers	Advertisers	Senders
	Good	Time slot	Page space	Various mail types
	Price	Price per advert	Price per advert	Postage fee
Market side 2: Consumers	**Demand side**	Viewers	Readers	Recipients
	Good	Televised content	Editorial content	Various mail types
	Price	Subscription or zero fee	Subscription or zero fee	Zero fee

Fig. 1 Analogies between television, newspaper and postal mail platforms. *Source* Jaag and Bach (2016)

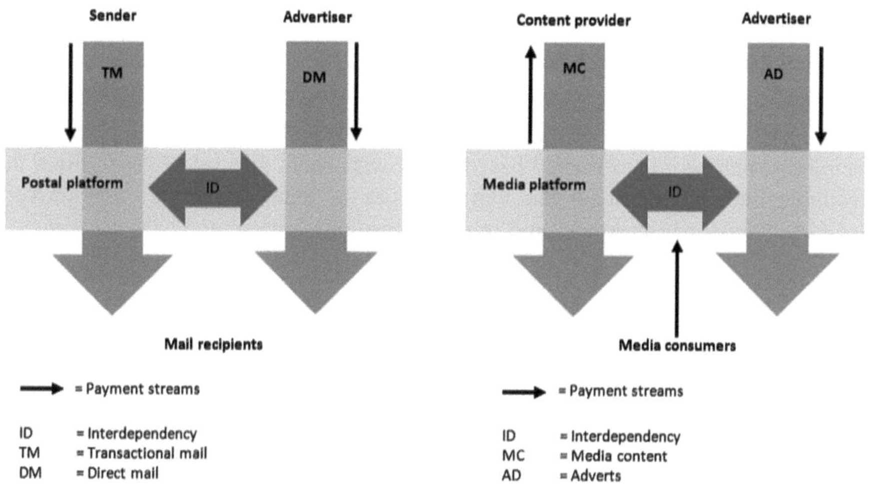

Source: Jaag and Bach (2016)

Fig. 2 Illustration of the structure of the mail stream and media platforms

is usually less expensive than transactional mail, which reflects differences in their direct cost and the competitive environments. Jaag and Bach (2016) argue that it would be beneficial for POs to take into account the positive effect of transactional mail on direct mail reducing the price of the former and thereby increasing the attractiveness of the mail stream as a platform. They show that an improvement of the mailmix by adjusting prices for transactional and advertisement mail in favor of transactional mail is possible for a monopolistic PO, which can thereby fully internalize the interdependency between the mail categories. However, these efforts are thwarted by the decrease of transactional mail due to electronic substitution, which has a long-term adverse indirect effect on direct mail through the degradation of the mailmix. With open postal markets, entrant POs typically focus on bulk and direct mail. Hence, they can freeride on the mailmix provided by the incumbent PO. This reduces the incumbent's incentives to cross-subsidize transactional mail in an effort to make the mail stream an attractive platform for advertising. Hence, besides the adverse effect of electronic substitution, the mailmix also tends to degrade as a result of postal market opening which might indirectly contribute to the substitution of direct mail, too. These considerations, as developed in Jaag and Bach (2016), strongly rely on the assumption that there is indeed an interdependency between various types of mail, i.e. that senders care about the recipient's mailmix. This is certainly the case if the recipients' reaction to their mail depends on their mailmix, too. This assumption will be empirically explored in the following section.

4 Empirical Effect of the Mailmix on the Recipients' Reaction to Direct Mail

In this section, the effect of the mailmix (consisting of various types of mail) on recipients' behavior is estimated based on a Swiss panel data set of 2016. First, the available data is described and various types of mailmix proxies are derived. Second, the estimation model and third the results are presented.

4.1 Data Set and Mailmix Proxies

Over the course of a week in March 2016, a random sample of Swiss recipients were asked daily how many items of different types of mail they received and how they reacted to the direct (advertisement) mail they received. The data set consists of a panel of 11,198 observations (mail items) received by 544 recipients. From the 11,198 mail items, 4,622 were addressed letters, 3,409 newspapers and 2,836 unaddressed items. For every mail item, the recipients reported the type of mail (see Table 1), and what they did with it. For advertising mail, recipients could choose among a series of possible alternatives (for more details cf. next subsection). Some observations contain missing information, especially observations regarding the reaction to addressed advertisement. All observations contained in the sample result from recipients that opened their mailbox. More concretely, all recipients emptied their mailbox daily, which may be an effect of participating in the survey.

In order to investigate the interdependencies between various types of mail items, three mailmix proxies are defined according to Eqs. (1–3).

$$\text{Mailmix 1} = \frac{\text{Non - advertisement mail}}{\text{Total mail}} \tag{1}$$

$$\text{Mailmix 2} = \frac{\text{Private mail}}{\text{Total mail}} \tag{2}$$

$$\text{Mailmix 3} = \frac{\text{Good mail}}{\text{Total mail}} \tag{3}$$

Table 1 summarizes the different mail categories and how they are assigned to three chosen mailmix proxies. Mailmix 1 represents the share of non-advertisement mail items. Mailmix 2 represents the share of private mail received, i.e. mail items sent by private senders. This category excludes mail sent by businesses as well as advertisement. Mailmix 3, share of "good mail", is the share of mail items that are expected to be perceived positively by recipients based on the authors' assessment. Besides all private mail categories in the enumerator of Mailmix 2, the enumerator of Mailmix 3 also contains offers/quotes, payrolls, gifts, and confirmations.

Table 1 Assignment of mail types to mailmix proxies

	Category in data base	Mailmix 1: share of non-advertisement	Mailmix 2: share of private mail	Mailmix 3: share of "good" mail
1	Bill/admonition/credit card statement	X		
2	Advertising mail			
3	Catalog			
4	Notification/contingent	X		
5	Bank statement	X		
6	Appeal for funds			
7	Forms/documents (e.g. for voting or tax)	X		
8	Customer magazine	X		
9	Invitation/reply to invitations	X	X	X
10	Spontaneous writing	X	X	X
11	Mail of clubs or associations	X	X	X
12	Periodic regular mail contact	X	X	X
13	Replies to requests/applications	X	X	X
14	Payrolls	X		X
15	Offers/quotes	X		X
16	Gifts/vouchers			X
17	Greeting cards	X	X	X
18	Picture postcards/holiday greetings	X	X	X
19	Public holiday/season's greetings	X	X	X
20	Announcement of special events (e.g. marriage etc.)	X	X	X
21	Confirmation (e.g. of course enrolment)	X		X
22	Competitions/lotteries etc.			
23	Forwarding of forgotten items	X	X	X
24	Condolences	X	X	X
25	Others			

The descriptive statistics of the mailmix proxies are given in Table 2. The table reveals that the share of received non-advertisement items per recipient in the sample is about 50 % on average over the entire week, and the share of private and good mail is 13 and 18 %, respectively. The entry for "mailmix 2—daily" represents the averages per day (not per week), with a corresponding higher standard deviation.

Table 2 provides descriptive statistics of selected further variables, such as age, gender, whether the recipient receives also unaddressed letters (in Switzerland, about 50 % of households have their mailboxes tagged with “no advertisement”, hence not receiving unaddressed mail), and whether the recipient received newspapers in the respective week/on the respective day (for daily mailmix definitions).

4.2 Model

The effect of different mailmixes on the reaction of recipient i to addressed advertisement mail is estimated by means of an unordered multinomial logit model. It is differentiated between the three reactions R of type j which are “positive”, “neutral”, and “negative”. A reaction to addressed advertisement is considered to be positive if the recipient asked for products or services of the sender, contacted the sender, or searched in the Internet for further information. A reaction is considered to be neutral if the recipient put the mail aside for later action or for other behavior. A reaction is considered to be negative if the recipient discarded the mail immediately. The probability for one of the three reactions j is given in Eq. (4) and depends on several covariates $\mathbf{x}_i$, e.g. age and gender of the recipient or the mailmix. The disturbances are assumed to take on an i.i.d. logit distribution. The log-odd ratios of a positive or negative reaction against the base case of a neutral reaction n then can be given as shown in eq. (5) with the intercept being set to zero. The coefficients of vector $\boldsymbol{\beta}$ are obtained by maximum likelihood technique (Greene 2002).

$$\mathrm{Prob}(R_i = j|\mathbf{x}_i) \equiv P_{ij} = \frac{e^{\boldsymbol{\beta}_j^T \mathbf{x}_i}}{1 + \sum_{s=1}^{3} e^{\boldsymbol{\beta}_s^T \mathbf{x}_i}}, \quad j = 0, 1, 2 \tag{4}$$

Table 2 Descriptive statistics of the variables

	Mean	Std.dev.	Min.	Max.
Mailmix 1—overall	0.495	0.244	0	1
Mailmix 2—overall	0.125	0.143	0	1
Mailmix 3—overall	0.182	0.168	0	1
Mailmix 2—daily	0.125	0.242	0	1
Age category fixed effect	2.849	0.993	1	4
Gender (1 = female)	0.562	0.496	0	1
No ads sticker fixed effect	0.538	0.499	0	1
Also received newspaper fixed effect	0.945	0.229	0	1

Note age category one contains all observations with an age ≤ 30. Category two all with 30 < age ≤ 45. Category three all with 45 < age ≤ 60. Category four all with age > 60

$$\ln\left(\frac{P_{ij}}{P_{in}}\right) = \mathbf{x}_i^T \beta_j \tag{5}$$

4.3 Results

Based on the data described above, the recipients' behavior is analyzed in terms of the reaction to addressed advertisement conditional on mailmix characteristics. Table 3 summarizes the benchmark results of the corresponding multinomial logit models for the effect of different mailmixes on the reaction to addressed advertisement against the base outcome of a neutral reaction (put aside). The upper part shows the complete regression results using the mailmix 2 proxy including a fixed effect of whether or not the recipient also received newspapers. The middle part only presents the estimated coefficient of the mailmix proxy with the models including the same coefficients as shown in the upper part, except the fixed effect of also having received newspapers during the period observed. The lower part presents the estimated coefficient of the mailmix 2 proxy evaluated daily rather than weekly.

All mailmix proxies are highly significant and positive, indicating that a good mailmix increases positive reactions towards addressed mail. For the control

Table 3 Effect of mailmix proxies on the reaction to addressed advertisement [M1]

Multinomial logit model	Positive reaction	
Basis: neutral reaction	Odds ratio	Std.dev.
[M1-1] Mailmix 2—overall	2.763**	(1.100)
30 < Age ≤ 45	0.421	(0.567)
45 < Age ≤ 60	−0.344	(0.591)
Age > 60	0.073	(0.558)
Gender (female)	−0.962***	(0.325)
No ads sticker fixed effects	0.906***	(0.311)
Newspaper fixed effects	−1.066*	(0.598)
Constant	−2.202**	(0.871)
[M1-2] Mailmix 1—overall	1.635***	(0.617)
[M1-3] Mailmix 2—overall	2.889***	(1.095)
[M1-4] Mailmix 3—overall	1.269	(0.873)
[M1-5] Mailmix 2—daily	1.284**	(0.619)

Notes Coefficients other than the estimates of the correlation of mailmix quality with reaction type are shown for M1-1 only. Models M1-2 to M1-4 include all variables of M1-1 except the fixed effect of also having received newspapers during the period observed. M1-5 contains the same explanatory variables as mod-els M1-2 to M1-4. The base variable of the age category is age ≤30. The number of observations is 760

***indicate significance at 1 percent level

**at 0.05 percent level

*at 10 percent level

Table 4 Effect of mailmix proxies on the reaction to addressed advertisement including total mail or unaddressed mail fixed effect [M2]

Additional variable	Total mail		
Multinomial logit model	Positive reaction		
Basis: neutral reaction	Odds ratio		Std.dev.
[M2-1] Mailmix 2—overall	2.985	***	(1.120)
30 < Age ≤ 45	0.502		(0.573)
45 < Age ≤ 60	−0.321		(0.595)
Age > 60	0.130		(0.565)
Gender (female)	−1.019	***	(0.330)
No ads sticker fixed effects	0.961	***	(0.318)
Newspaper fixed effects	−1.023	*	(0.601)
Total mail	−0.016		(0.023)
Constant	−2.189	**	(0.872)
[M2-2] Mailmix 1—overall	1.614	***	(0.619)
[M2-3] Mailmix 2—overall	3.132	***	(1.113)
[M2-4] Mailmix 3—overall	1.306		(0.869)
[M2-5] Mailmix 2—daily	1.275	**	(0.618)

Notes Coefficients other than the estimates of the correlation of mailmix quality with reaction type are shown for M2-1 only. The variables included in models M2-2 to M2-5 are as described in Table 3, except for the additional control variable total mail. The number of observations is 760
***indicate significance at 1 percent level
**at 0.05 percent level
*at 10 percent level

variables, age has no effect on the reaction pattern. Females and newspaper subscriber appear to react less positively to addressed advertisement. Interestingly, "no ads" stickers affect the reaction towards addressed advertisement positively. Postal services are not allowed to deliver unaddressed advertisement to mailboxes with this sticker. Hence, this effect may be related to an increase in attention time for addressed advertisement, assumed that total attention time is constant for addressed and unaddressed mail. Table 4 probes these results with respect to the number of mail items received by the recipient to certify our benchmark results not being primarily driven by the number of total mail items received. The results obtained suggest that the benchmark results are robust in terms of the inclusion of total mail as explanatory variable. The magnitude of the estimates as well as their significance hardly changes.

5 Conclusions

While letter mail services have come under pressure due to the emergence of electronic communication channels, not all mail types are being substituted equally but the mailmix seems to degrade over time. This paper interprets the postal mail stream as a platform with two market sides carrying various types of mail of different value to the recipients which may interact with each other. Jaag and Bach (2016) argue that it would be beneficial for POs to take into account the positive effect of "good" mail by reducing its price and thereby increasing the attractiveness of the mail stream as a platform.

To provide first empirical support for this argument, this paper hypothesizes that the value of direct mail to advertisers depends on the composition of mail. This hypothesis is tested by analyzing data from the Swiss mail market collected in the first quarter of 2016. Three mailmix proxies are defined to investigate the interdependencies between mail types. For all three mailmixes the results suggest that a good mailmix significantly increases the recipients' propensity of reacting positively to addressed advertisement. The paper therefore provides first empirical evidence that a differentiated pricing of mail based on its content might benefit the mail platform as a whole.

References

Anderson, S. P., & Coate, S. (2005). Market provision of broadcasting: A welfare analysis. *Review of Economic Studies, 72*, 947–972.

Anderson, S. P., & Gabszewicz, J. J. (2006). The media and advertising: A tale of two-sided markets. In V. A. Ginsburgh & D. Thorsby (eds.), *Handbook of the economics of art and culture* (Vol. 1, pp. 567–614).

Armstrong, M. (2006). Competition in two-sided markets. *RAND Journal of Economics, 37*, 668–691.

Boldron, F., Cremer, H., De Donder, Ph., Roy, B., & Joram, D. (2009). Network Externalities and the USO: A two-sided market approach. In M. A. Crew & P. R. Kleindorfer (Eds.), *Progress in the competitive agenda in the postal and delivery sector, Chapter 12.*

Bradley, M. D., Colvin, J., & Perkins, M. K. (2015). Targeting versus Saturation: Derived demand for direct mail. In M. Crew & T. Brennan (eds.), *Postal and delivery innovation in the digital economy* (pp. 65–75).

Crampes, C., Haritchabalet, C., & Jullien, B. (2009). Advertising, competition and entry in media industries. *Journal of Industrial Economics, 57*, 7–31.

De Donder, P., Cremer, H., Dudley, P., & Rodriguez, F. (2011). Welfare and pricing of mail in a communications market. *Review of Network Economics, 10*(3).

Gabszewicz, J. J., Laussel, D., & Sonnac, N. (2004). Programming and advertising competition in the broadcasting industry. *Journal of Economics & Management Strategy, 13*, 657–669.

Greene, W. H. (2002). *Econometric analysis*. New Jersey: Pearson Education.

Godes, D., Ofek, E., & Sarvary, M. (2009). Content vs. advertising: The impact of competition on media firm strategy. *Marketing Science, 28*, 20–35.

Jaag, C., & Bach, C. (2016). *The mailstream as a platform, Swiss Economics Working Paper 55.*

Jaag, C., & Trinkner, U. (2008). Pricing in competitive two-sided mail markets. In M. Crew & P. Kleindorfer (eds.), *Competition and regulation in the postal and delivery sector* (pp. 136–149).

Peitz, M., & Valletti, T. M. (2008). Content and advertising in the media: Pay-TV versus free-to-air. *International Journal of Industrial Organization, 26*, 949–965.

Reisinger, M. (2012). Platform competition for advertisers and users in media market. *International Journal of Industrial Organization, 30*, 243–252.

Rochet, J.-C., & Tirole, J. (2003). Platform competition in two-sided markets. *Journal of the European Economic Association, 1*, 990–1029.

Rochet, J.-C., & Tirole, J. (2006). Two-Sided markets: A progress report. *RAND Journal of Economics, 37*, 645–667.

Rohr, Ch., Trinkner, U., Lawrence, A., Hunt, P., Woo Kim, Ch., Potoglou, D., & Sheldon, R. (2011). *Study on appropriate methodologies to better measure consumer preferences for postal services*. Final Report to the European Commission.

Wilbur, K. C. (2008). A two-sided, empirical model of television advertising and viewing markets. *Marketing Science, 27*, 356–378.

The Total Price of Mail: A Consumer Perspective

Benjamin Gough, Kirk Kaneer and Margaret M. Cigno

1 Introduction

Recent postal economics literature typically examines postal costs from the incumbent National Postal Operator (NPO) perspective, often looking at costs of providing the Universal Service Obligation (USO) (Cremer et al. 2008; Bradley et al. 2009) or individual product costing (Robinson and McMurdie 2009). Little attention is given to the costs incurred by consumers of mail. Prices are almost universally considered in monetary terms as the price paid to the service provider to obtain the service. However, total price to obtain the service is the sum of the money price and any costs or disutility incurred by the consumer in obtaining the service. Commuting in Washington, DC or any major city is an example. When driving a car, the total price is the congestion cost plus the money spent on gas, tolls, etc. Depending on an individual consumer's preferences, the total cost of obtaining the service may be much greater than the money price alone.

The opinions expressed in this chapter are exclusively those of the authors. The authors would like to thank the following for their valuable insights: Shoshana Grove; Michael Bradley; John Waller; Larry Buc; and the participants at the CRRI's 23rd Conference on Postal and Delivery Economics and 34th & 35th Annual Eastern Conferences.

B. Gough (✉)
Economic Regulation Adviser, Water UK, London, UK
e-mail: benjamin.gough@cantab.net

K. Kaneer
Risk Analysis Research Center, Office of the Inspector General,
Arlington, Virginia, USA
e-mail: kirk.kaneer@uspsoig.gov

M.M. Cigno
Director of the Office of Accountability and Compliance, Postal Regulatory
Commission, Washington, D.C., USA

M. Crew et al. (eds.), *The Changing Postal and Delivery Sector*,
Topics in Regulatory Economics and Policy,
DOI 10.1007/978-3-319-46046-8_19

In the case of mail, the total price for consumers is the sum of the unit price of postage (the "money price") and the cost to the consumer of getting the mail to the point of posting ("consumer costs"). Individual consumer costs can range from the relatively low (the price paid for envelopes and packaging materials for letters and parcels), to comparatively high (the opportunity cost of traveling to a postal collection point). When expressed in the aggregate, there is the possibility that these consumer costs could be considerably higher than the money price. In the United States, this is particularly true given that American households make approximately 3 million visits to a Post Office (PO) annually (see Appendix B).

Although not generally considered in the calculation of postal price elasticity, these consumer costs aggregate across consumers to determine a product's demand function. In other words, demand for a given consumer product may be highly sensitive to a number of prices and costs that the consumer incurs when consuming a product, in addition to the price of the product itself. Modeling consumer costs, when analyzing demand for postal products, may provide additional insight into consumer behavior, and prove valuable to posts as they set prices across various consumer categories.

These consumer costs may result in differences in the total price of mailing among various users, affecting how fairly the NPO is meeting its USO mandate.

This chapter seeks to identify and model the real price of letters and parcels for the consumer in order to provide insights as to how changes to the U.S. Postal Service may have unintended consequences.[1] Section 2 explains the analytical approach, with Appendix A providing the detailed methodology.

Section 3 presents the findings of the analysis, specifically how the total price of mail compares to the money price. The model is then used to show how efficiency policies could affect these total prices; sensitivity analysis identifies the consumer cost most sensitive to change, and then the effect of a policy specifically relating to that component is assessed.

Section 4 presents the potential policy and regulatory implications of the findings by exploring how the consumer costs of obtaining postal services could be addressed as part of the USO. It also examines the potential business impacts of these total prices, in particular their effect on elasticity estimates.

Section 5 concludes the chapter by offering insights into how this work's important findings could be developed further in future.

---

[1]Large users are outside the scope of the chapter because their internal costs are more complex and driven by profit and loss considerations, and they have a greater ability to take advantage of existing postage discounts. Including large users would expand the chapter considerably; they could however be the topic of a separate chapter.

2 Analytical Approach

2.1 *Total Price Components*

To understand the total price faced by users, this chapter models a number of key factors in the process of sending mail.

The first consumer costs incurred in sending a letter begin with the process of letter preparation; these are the unit price of the envelope and the opportunity cost of the person preparing the letter. The opportunity cost is the hourly federal minimum wage;[2] this provides a standard value for an average mail user's time and avoids us having to complicate the model through seeking to encompass a wide range of wages. The cost of parcel preparation is modelled in the same way, though modified slightly under the assumption that single boxes are purchased, rather than packs.

The second set of consumer costs is incurred in the journey to and from the point of posting (post box or a PO). These are the opportunity costs (again the federal minimum wage) of the user in the travel to and from the postal point and the subsequent parking and queuing. It is assumed that the journey includes the use of a car; further iterations of the model could incorporate a distance function below which a car would not be used. The use of a car results in vehicle costs per mile (including fuel cost and depreciation).

2.2 *Distance Factor*

It is assumed that, in general, consumers do not make a car journey solely to send an item of mail, instead they combine this trip with other tasks. This behavior is reflected using a deviation factor within the model.

There is no readily available information regarding how residential users combine trips to the PO with other shopping stops. The model incorporates the limited information available. This is the national average market radius of POs, developed by Yezer (2010), and the national average shopping trip distance, which includes multiple stops, developed as part of a national transportation survey conducted by the U.S. Department of Transportation (2009). It is assumed the national average shopping trip distance includes stops at POs. As such, the model estimates the increase in the distance of the national average shopping trip, given an increase in the national average market radius of POs. This then provides the basis for the incremental cost of deviating from a shopping trip to send a letter. Full details of this modelling approach, along with all other equations, can be found in Appendix A.

[2]Data on Federal Minimum wage from US Department of Labor website: http://www.dol.gov/dol/topic/wages/minimumwage.htm.

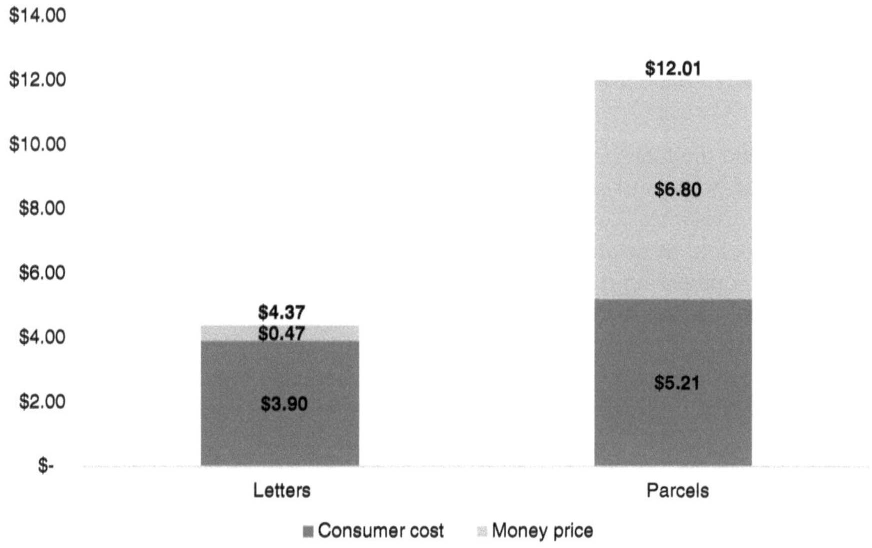

Fig. 1 Total price of mail (letters and parcels)

3 Findings

3.1 Price May Be Significantly Greater Than Postage

Having obtained a series of indicative values for the various cost factors, the data is input into the models, creating a total consumer cost for both letters and parcels. Figure 1 shows the consumer costs combined with money price of postage to create a total price of mailing.[3]

As seen in Fig. 1, the total price is significant when compared to the money price; they represent over eight times the letter postage price and around 75 % of the parcel postage price. In a time when the USPS is facing considerable cost pressures and is seeking to increase efficiency, it is vital to consider how proposed changes could affect the total price of mail for consumers.

3.2 Sensitivity Analysis

In order to understand which of the individual consumer costs has the greatest impact on total consumer costs, and therefore which areas are most sensitive to

[3]The money price (letters) is the stamp for a First Class Letter. The money price (parcels) is the lowest price for 1–3 day Priority small flat rate box. Both prices taken from the USPS website: https://www.usps.com/ship/mail-shipping-services.htm.

changes by policy makers, sensitivity analysis has been conducted through varying each component by 1 %.

Table 1 sets out the sensitivities in the letter model. The analysis shows that distance travelled has the greatest impact on total cost. This result is intuitive, as the distance factor affects both the labor and the vehicle costs. This finding is also true of parcels, as shown in Table 2.

Having identified the cost component most sensitive to change, the model is now used to test the impact of a policy which specifically affects this distance factor.

3.3 *Impact of Network Optimization*

The policy examined is based on optimization scenarios in which there are changes to the location of post boxes and POs. This concept was explicitly referenced in Yezer (2010) as a way to increase the efficiency of the USPS network.

To test the effect of network optimization on consumer costs, the distance model is used to create a number of scenarios. For the purpose of this analysis, the distance costs for parcels and letters are considered to be the same.

The "Base Case" scenario is the current national average shopping trip distance, around 6.4 miles, and that is assumed to include cases for a stop at a PO. Scenario A increases this distance, with a deviation based on Yezer's optimal national average PO market radius, to 4.33 and 5.5 respectively (see Eq. 3.1). Scenarios B, C and D increase the distance by 0.5, 1 and 2 miles respectively. The impact of these scenarios on the travel cost to residential users is displayed in Table 3.

The scenarios in Table 3 show that moving towards the optimal network specification described in Yezer (2010) does not have a significant impact on the costs faced by residential users.

However, the larger distance adjustments in Scenarios B to D do result in a significant additional cost to residential users, almost a dollar per mile.

In the analysis the transaction time (parking and queuing) was held static at 15 min (0.25 h). If network optimization results in faster transaction times the total costs in each of the scenarios may be lower. The analysis shows that in order to offset the cost to the consumer of a 0.5 mile increase in travel distance, the transaction time would have to be reduced by about 15 %, from 15 to 13 min. This reduction is potentially achievable; however, it is possible that closing POs or reducing hours would actually increase the transaction time by causing an upsurge in traffic to the remaining outlets, causing total costs to rise.

Reconfiguring the entire retail network requires considering the overall impact to users, as closing POs could leave gaps in services at some locations. As shown by the analysis, such reconfiguration could cause travel distance and transaction times, and therefore the total price of mailing, to significantly increase for postal customers within the relevant market areas. The implications of these issues for policymakers and the USPS itself are set out below.

Table 1 Letter cost sensitivity analysis

	Letter preparation cost						Trip cost									
Sensitivity	Quantity letters	Price per pack of 500 Envelopes[a]	Minimum wage (per hour)	Earnings per minute	Time spent prepping letter (minutes)	Total letter prep. cost ($)	Distance	Average speed (miles per hour)	Vehicle cost @ $0.581 per mile[b]	Driving time (hours)	Parking and queuing time (hours)	Labor cost per Hour	Labor ($)	Total trip cost	Total letter mailing cost	Letter sensitivity (% Chg. from base line)
Base case	1	$34.49	$7.24	$0.121	2	$0.3103	2.17	30	$1.26	0.07	0.25	$7.24	$2.33	$3.5904	$3.9007	NA
Envelopes	1	$34.83	$7.24	$0.121	2	$0.3110	2.17	30	$1.26	0.07	0.25	$7.24	$2.33	$3.5904	$3.9014	0.02 %
Wage	1	$34.49	$7.31	$0.122	2	$0.3127	2.17	30	$1.26	0.07	0.25	$7.31	$2.36	$3.5904	$3.9031	0.06 %
Distance	1	$34.49	$7.24	$0.121	2	$0.3103	2.19	30	$1.27	0.07	0.25	$7.24	$2.34	$3.6082	$3.9185	0.46 %

[a]Data on envelope price and numbers per pack obtained from here the Staples website: http://www.staples.com/Staples-Gummed-Left-Window-10-Envelope-4-1-8-x-9-1-2-White-500-Box-121632-/product_121632

[b]This is based on the American Automobile Association's estimates for the running cost of an average car

Table 2 Package cost sensitivity analysis

	Package preparation cost						Trip cost									
Scenario	Quantity boxes	Price per pack of 25 boxes[a]	Minimum wage (per hour)	Earnings per minute	Time spent prepping box (min)	Total box prep. cost ($)	Distance	Average speed (miles per hour)	Vehicle cost @ $0.581 per Mile	Driving time (h)	Parking & queuing time (h)	Labor cost per hour	Labor ($)	Total trip cost	Total box mailing cost	Box sensitivity (% Chg. from base line)
Base Case	1	$25.49	$7.24	$0.121	5	$1.6229	2.17	30	$1.26	0.072	0.25	$7.24	$2.33	$3.5904	$5.2133	NA
Boxes	1	$25.74	$7.24	$0.121	5	$1.6331	2.17	30	$1.26	0.072	0.25	$7.24	$2.33	$3.5904	$5.2235	0.20 %
Wage	1	$25.49	$7.31	$0.122	5	$1.6290	2.17	30	$1.26	0.072	0.25	$7.31	$2.36	$3.5904	$5.2193	0.12 %
Distance	1	$25.49	$7.24	$0.121	5	$1.6229	2.19	30	$1.27	0.073	0.25	$7.24	$2.34	$3.6082	$5.2311	0.34 %

[a]Data on price per package box from the Staples website: http://www.staples.com/11-1-4-x8-3-4-x6-Partners-Brand-Heavy-Duty-Boxes-25-Bundle-HD1186R-/product_405839

Table 3 Distance scenarios[a]

Trip costs, including transaction and queuing time								
Scenario	Distance	Average speed (Miles per hour)	Vehicle cost @ $0.581 per Mile	Driving time (h)	Parking and queuing time (h)	Labor cost per hour	Labor ($)	Total trip cost
Base case	2.17	30	$1.26	0.07	0.25	$7.24	$2.33	$3.59
A	2.27	30	$1.32	0.08	0.25	$7.24	$2.36	$3.68
B	2.70	30	$1.57	0.09	0.25	$7.24	$2.46	$4.03
C	3.14	30	$1.83	0.10	0.25	$7.24	$2.57	$4.39
D	4.32	30	$2.51	0.14	0.25	$7.24	$2.85	$5.36

[a]Lacking other data, 1/2 the average national average PO market radius of 4.33 miles is used, i.e. 2.17 trip distance alone for the "Base Case", then the deviations calculated by Eq. 3.1 for the remaining scenarios, A through D, are added

4 Implications

The modelling has shown that the total price of mailing is greater than just the money price of the postage, and is most significantly affected by the distance travelled to the point of posting. This leads to the question of how policy makers and regulators should respond to these findings when seeking to increase the Postal Service's efficiency.

The logical starting point is the legislation that sets out the guiding principles of regulating the USO. Affordability is a key tenet of the USO, as set out in both the 1997 EU Directive on Postal Services (Directive 97/67/EC) and the Postal Regulatory Commission report (2008, p. 20) on universal service. However, in both these cases "affordability" is generally interpreted based on the postage rate charged to consumers not the total price of mailing.

Postage, the monetary component of price, is an inadequate approach to considering "affordability"; as the modelling results show, the money price is only one relatively small part of the total price, and misunderstanding or ignoring total prices could have significant repercussions.

4.1 Regulatory Implications

As noted above, the findings suggest that travel distance is a large consumer cost for residential users. It is also an aspect over which the operator can assert some control. Given that there are affordability and geographic scope requirements for the USO, limiting the maximum distance travelled to access postal products may be necessary to ensure that the USO is ministered fairly. Most European countries have chosen this path, implementing various constraints reflecting density, distance, or a specified number of post offices or agencies. However, there is no evidence that total price to users are included in their calculations of minimum density or maximum distance.

The United States has no requirement related to density or distance for the location of post offices. By law "No small post office shall be closed solely for operating at a deficit, it being the specific intent of the Congress that effective postal services be insured to residents of both urban and rural communities" (39 U.S.C. 101(b), 1970). Evidence suggests that the most unprofitable offices are located in rural or remote areas. In fact, the consumer cost for mail preparation might vary significantly by geographic location as average labor costs likely differ by location, as well as other factors, such as employment status.[4] Currently, the total price of mail is not a consideration in the location of post offices in the United States, although distance between post offices has been a concern. The legal requirement above on PO closure opens to door to the type of approach provide in this chapter.

However, in a report on retail optimization the Postal Service Inspector General stated, "Modernization should not be thought of as solely a cost-saving response to the Postal Service's financial problems. Instead, it should be seen as a way to meet demand more efficiently and equitably in a way that cuts costs, encourages constant reevaluation and improvement, and aligns the Postal Service's retail network to the way people live now" (USPS-OIG 2010, p. 2). Considering consumer costs when evaluating post office consolidations is consistent with both the Office of the Inspector General's finding and the USO.

Many issues would need to be considered if recognition of total prices to residential users were to be considered a requirement of universal service and any subsequent attempts to optimize the PO network. A primary issue is whether the financial impact on the postal operator is greater from subsidizing users or from maintaining set distances between access points and consumers. The answer to this question would allow the operator to fulfil its universal service obligation at the least cost.

A possible approach in addition to the cross subsidy currently would be to provide discounts on postage for rural consumers. This subsidy could take the form of zoned prices that reflect the cost to users based on the distance travelled to access postal services is some degree greater than the average distance travelled. Similar subsidy already exists in the United States for mail sent to remote areas of non-contiguous United States such as Alaska Bypass Service, which is Parcel Post® mail that is prepared so as not to require handling by NPO personnel or in an NPO facility. These services are currently subsidized by all users and were established as a means of ensuring that rural populations received delivery of food and other commodities. However, attempting to extend this kind of subsidy would likely not pass in Congress. Given competition and pressure from declining letter volumes the

[4]Retirees may represent a large proportion of postal customers, who still rely upon access to traditional post office services.

potential for cross subsidy is considerably reduced. It would increase prices for all users, and therefore would be lead to a further decline in volumes.

Maintaining set distances between access points and users could be performed through formulating minimum access requirements related to the location of POs or agencies based on density, distance, or a specified number of access points. This approach is of particular relevance when considering network optimization. For example, the analysis of total prices in this chapter indicate that there are likely to be some POs that are loss-making from an NPO perspective, but from a consumer perspective would actual contribute to lower total mail prices than other POs. This is not to say that loss-making POs should necessarily remain open, but rather that when considering which loss-making POs should be closed there is a need to consider the totality of the effects on consumers. Re-optimizing the network would still be needed to find a balance between lowering costs to the NPO while having minimal effects on the total price for the affected users.

Whilst maintaining loss-making NPOs that nevertheless lower total prices avoids the need for controversial direct subsidies, the loss in revenue to the NPO still needs to be reimbursed. The cost to the NPO of operating postal managed retail facilities is factored into the money price of postage for all users, so the cost of keeping facilities open to reduce consumer costs in affected areas could be considered an indirect subsidy. However, this indirect subsidy is likely to be negligible, given that the cost to the NPO of maintaining rural post offices, where the distance travelled to post offices is greatest, is likely well below the cost of maintaining more urban retail facilities (due to lower lease costs and fewer employees).

In addition to potential subsidy issues, analyzing which POs have the greatest effect on total prices would require actual NPO data as well as locality differences in wage rates and possibly raw materials. These data include: the current distance between POs and the residents they serve; the mailers served by each PO; the volume of mail attributable to each PO; the frequency of visits to each PO; wage rate differences by geographical region; raw material cost differences by geographical region; and actual transaction times. Some data, such as the distance between POs, transaction times while at the PO, and the number of visits and products sold at each PO, are available from NPO data systems. However, there are many issues with the current data systems that would need to be addressed before accurate real costs could be calculated. Data on wage rates are available from the Bureau of Labor Statistics. Population density is available from several sources. The difference in raw material is likely the most difficult data to find. Consumer Reports has much of this data but in a disaggregated format that would take considerable time and effort to convert to usable data for this exercise.

Another issue is whether recognizing the total price for residential users and not the total price for large users is discriminatory. The internal costs of large users are difficult to model because of the nature of their operations and more complex postage prices. So large users are outside the scope of this chapter. Even so, these costs likely vary significantly by type of industry and individual business.

Large users are also likely to have a greater ability to take deeper advantage of existing postage discounts than do smaller businesses. In the United States, there are numerous discounts for mail that is entered into the postal system after undergoing specific preparation requirements. These discounts are known as worksharing discounts. There has been much discussion throughout postal economic literature about the role of Efficient Component Pricing in establishing workshare discounts. It is possible that data on the real costs of large users could improve the development of these discounts. Large users also have access to Negotiated Service Agreements with the NPO. More visibility into the total price of mail may improve the process of negotiating terms for such agreements.

There are also numerous considerations regarding how a subsidy would be implemented, monitored for fraud, and regulated.

4.2 *Operator Impacts*

Whilst the primary focus has been on the importance of understanding the total price of mail by regulators and policy makers, this understanding is also particularly important for the postal operator itself.

Disregarding the total price of mail in favor of a narrow focus on the money price of postage could have significant commercial impacts, as it could lead to inefficient pricing and a subsequent loss of volume to competitors. This is most apparent when applying price elasticity estimates used in many applications of economic theory to postal regulation. For example, reliable estimates of demand elasticity are key parameters in efficient pricing, defining the universal service obligation, and ensuring financial viability.

Looking at the total price of mail for users may explain, at least in part, the recent significant volume losses despite the relatively price inelastic demand for postal products. For example, in the United States the estimated price elasticity of demand for First-Class single-piece mail is quite low. Table 4 shows the estimated price elasticity for fiscal years 2011 to 2015.

Yet as seen in Fig. 2, the volume for First-Class Single Piece Mail has decreased significantly since fiscal year 2011 despite price increases that mirror inflation.

Understanding the impact of the total price of mail on postal demand elasticity may help avert similar volume losses in the parcel market.

Table 4 Price elasticity for first-class single-piece mail[a]

	Letters	Flats	Parcels
2015	−0.140262	−0.140262	−0.258407
	First-class single-piece mail		
2014	−0.157693	−0.157693	−0.467278
2013	−0.089791	−0.265177	−0.213121
2012	−0.189484	−0.189484	−0.189484
2011	−0.182393	−0.182393	−0.182393

[a]Derived from USPS econometric demand equation tables for market dominant products, FY 2011, 2012, 2013, 2014, 2015

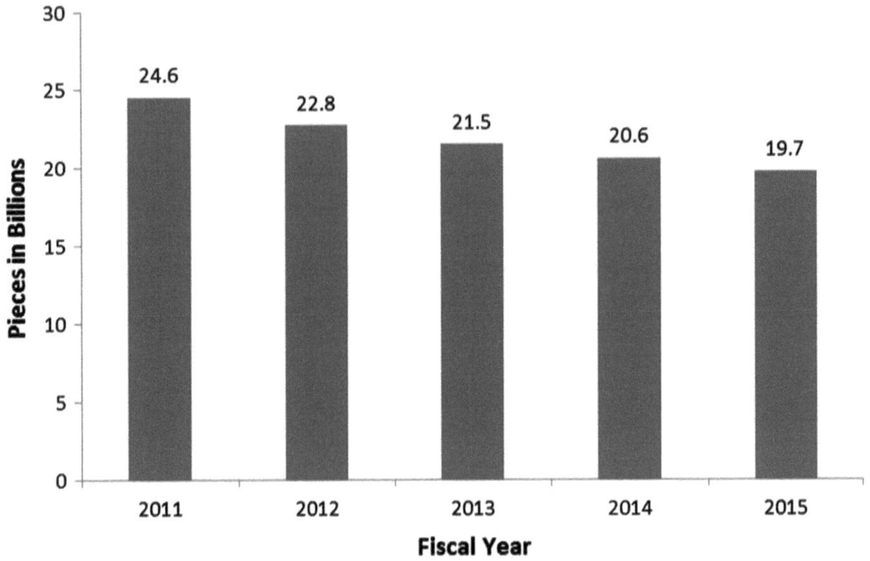

Fig. 2 First class single-piece letter mail volume (developed from USPS revenue piece and weight reports)

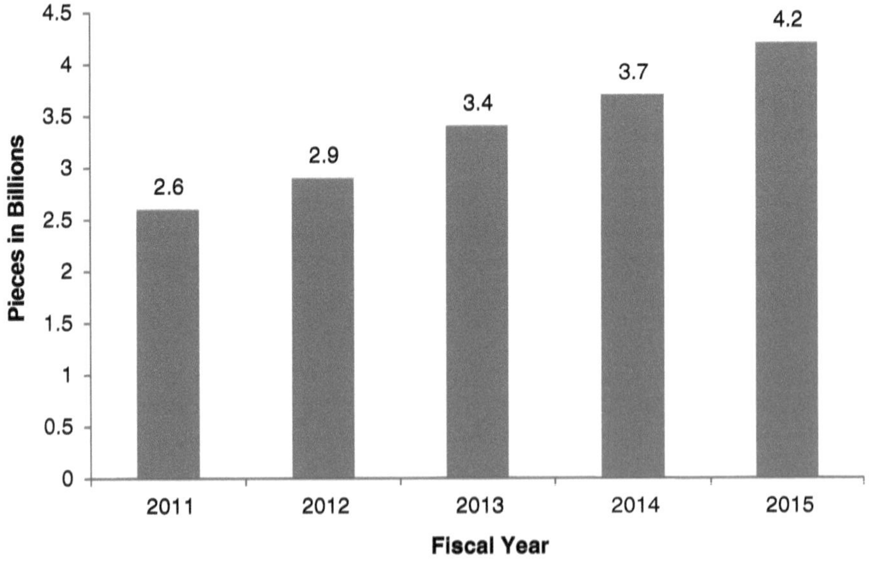

Fig. 3 US postal service parcel volumes (developed from USPS revenue piece and weight reports)

Parcels have recently been a bright spot for USPS; Fig. 3 illustrates the growth in parcel volume over the past 10 years. However, in general, parcel products have much higher price elasticity than letter mail, ranging from −0.5 for Alaska Bypass Mail to −0.9 for Parcel Post. If the total price of parcels increases substantially, consumers may use alternatives to USPS parcel delivery. This could lead to similar volume losses as experienced by letter mail.

If reliable data on the total price for users could be gathered it may be possible to include these as variables in "total price" elasticity estimates. Rather than basing a price elasticity estimate on the change in postage rates, the estimate could be based on change in overall price to the user. However, such an analysis may be difficult given that changes in the price of the variables may not occur in the same timeframe, may be highly correlated, and may generate different user reactions. Further research is required before such an analysis could be performed.

5 Conclusions and Future Research

The analysis in this chapter is a first attempt to identify and model the significant total prices faced by residential users of mail.

Decision makers will need to understand better the total price of postal service, in the near future, as the PO network will need significant adjustments to meet the challenges of declining volumes and revenues. For example, in an effort to lower expenses, in recent years USPS has been closing or severely contracting operating hours at its retail locations. Since fiscal year 2010 the number of post offices has declined from 32,662 (USPS, 2013, p.34) to 31,606 (USPS, 2015, p.26). Operating hours at close to 10,000 post offices have been adjusted (USPS, 2014, p.48). This raises a number of questions deserving more attention than can be given in this chapter. These include post office closures' impact on driving time of consumers, who then need to use alternate posting points. Similarly, the effect of reductions in operating hours on waiting lines as well as additional travel time. Other issues include how post office closure have been offset by the increase in other retail outlets selling postal products.

The modelling also suggests that if postal efficiency efforts such as reductions in retail locations and delivery services only measure cost savings from the NPO perspective and ignore the effect on the total price for users, decision makers risk mistaking such cost reductions for efficiency improvements. Such optimization efforts may actually result in negative net change in the total efficiency of the postal value chain if the total price for large numbers of mail users increase significantly. Similarly, an increase in consumer costs may afford opportunities for new competitors to the NPO to enter the market and offer services (such as more convenient collection locations) that remove some of these costs. In growth sectors such as parcels, this possibility of competitive entry should be of particular concern to the NPO if it wishes to secure financially-viable future.

While limited modelling of consumer costs has been undertaken, the initial analysis has shown the need for much more aggressive data collection and modelling efforts to support data-driven policy making, fairness, and business decisions. This further work could include: Looking at the total price for both large users and small businesses that send greater volumes of mail than residential consumers; looking at different wages for users; and seeking to model rural and urban sender behaviors and network specifications separately. Certain assumptions in the current model around transaction times could also be refined to take account of those users who are simply dropping-off pre-stamped items rather than obtaining services from a postal clerk. Modelling the total price for customers using competing services to the NPO could also be instructive in understanding whether other postal operators are seeking to compete with the NPO on a total price as well as money price basis. Future work may also focus more on parcel users as the NPO seeks to maintain market share in this growing sector while achieving service efficiencies.

Appendix 1: Methodology

The model considers the cost of letter preparation ($\boldsymbol{prep}_{t1}$) to be a function of the money price of the envelope and the opportunity cost of preparation time. This is computed as follows:

$$\boldsymbol{prep}_{t1} = \boldsymbol{Q} \cdot \left(\frac{\boldsymbol{P}_{\mathbf{pack}}}{\boldsymbol{pack}_t} + \frac{w}{t_{letter}} \right) \tag{1.1}$$

The envelope price is calculated by dividing the price of a pack of envelopes, $\boldsymbol{P}_{\mathbf{pack}}$, by the number of envelopes in a pack, $\boldsymbol{pack}_t$. w is the opportunity cost (the hourly federal minimum wage) for the person responsible for preparing the letter; this is divided by the time taken to prepare one letter, t_{letter}. Both these factors are multiplied by the quantity of letters prepared, $\boldsymbol{Q}$.

Parcel preparation cost is modelled in the same way, though modified slightly under the assumption that single boxes are purchased, rather than packs.

$$\boldsymbol{prep}_{t2} = \boldsymbol{Q} \cdot \left(\boldsymbol{P}_{\mathbf{box}} + \frac{w}{t_{box}} \right) \tag{1.2}$$

The cost of distance travelled to and from the point of posting (post box or a PO) is computed as follows:

$$\boldsymbol{trip}_t = \left(\frac{\boldsymbol{d}}{s} + \boldsymbol{t} \right) w (\boldsymbol{C}_{vehicle} \cdot \boldsymbol{d}) \tag{1.3}$$

Where $\boldsymbol{d}$ is distance to and from point of posting, $\boldsymbol{s}$ is average speed travelled, and $\boldsymbol{t}$ is transaction time (e.g. parking, queuing, etc.). w is the driver's hourly wage; this creates the opportunity cost element. It is assumed the user drives to the point of posting; $\boldsymbol{C}_{vehicle}$ constitutes vehicle cost per mile (including fuel price and depreciation). Solving gives total trip cost $\boldsymbol{trip}_t$.

The total price p_{t1} for letters is therefore the above consumer cost factors plus the money price of postage ($p_{postage1}$):

$$P_{t1} = Q\left(\frac{C_{\text{pack}}}{pack_t} + \frac{w}{t_{letter}}\right) + \left(\frac{d}{s} + t\right) w(C_{vehicle} \cdot d) + p_{postage1} \tag{1.4}$$

Simplified:

$$P_{t1} = prep_{t1} + trip_t + p_{postage1} \tag{1.5a}$$

The total price of sending parcels, simplified, is therefore:

$$P_{t2} = prep_{t2} + trip_t + p_{postage2} \tag{1.5b}$$

Distance Modelling

The model estimates the increase in the national average shopping trip, given an increase in the national average market radius of POs, as follows:

$$\Delta d = 2\left(\sqrt{\left(\frac{\bar{x}d}{2}\right)^2 + \left(\frac{\text{r2} - \text{r1}}{2}\right)^2}\right) \tag{3.1}$$

$\bar{x}d$ is the current average distance residential user's drive on a typical multi-stop shopping trip. To calculate how the national average distance of a shopping trip that includes a stop at the PO might increase with an increase in the national average market radius of POs a deviation from the current average multi-stop shopping trip, i.e. $\bar{x}d$ is estimated. A further assumption is the average residential user resides at a distance of $1/2$ the national average postal office market radius. Thus, the deviation due to an increase in the average radius market is $1/2$ the difference between a future postal PO market radius, ***r2*** and the current market radius, ***r1***; this forms the term $\frac{r2-r1}{2}$ in **3.1**.

The model uses this deviation and $\bar{x}d$ to calculate the hypotenuses of two right triangles, where the deviation and ½ $\bar{x}d$ forms the opposite sides. Figure 4 illustrates this method.

Using the estimates in Yezer (2010, p. 33) of the national average PO market radius, both current and optimal, implies: ***r1*** = 4.33 miles; ***r2*** = 5.5 miles. This suggests a typical deviation from the current average shopping trip of 0.55 miles.

This 0.55 mile deviation from the 6.4 mile average shopping trip forms two right triangles, each with a base of 3.2 miles (Fig. 4). These two hypotenuses, 3.245 miles each, implies $\Delta d = 2(3.245) = 6.490$miles, a $^9/_{10}$ mile increase in the national average shopping distance in cases that include a trip to a PO. For

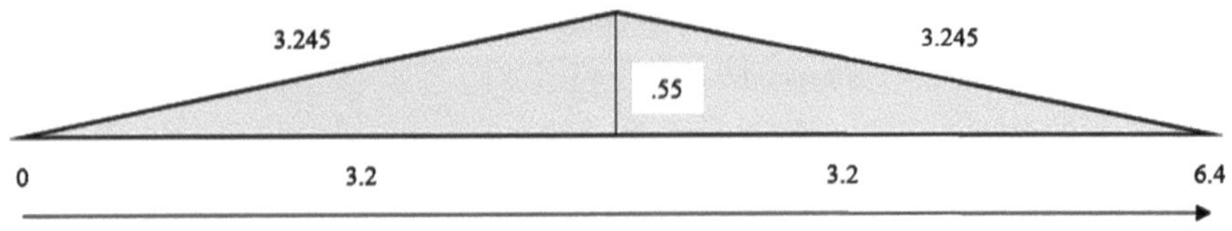

Fig. 4 Change in multi-stop shopping trip distance, before and after change in po market radius change

estimating residential users cost, ***r1/2*** is used to establish a baseline mileage, i.e., 4.33 ÷ 2, in conjunction with deviations calculated by **3.1** to estimate the costs of increasing postal market radii on residential users.

Appendix 2: Number of Trips to POs, Annual Estimate

See Table 5.

Table 5 Number of trips to POs per household

Number of households	Percent of HH visits to PO in past month	Estimated HH visits to PO in past month	Number of times PO visited	Estimated number of trips per month
122,500,000	32 %	39,200,000	1.5	58,800,000
122,500,000	21 %	25,725,000	5	128,625,000
122,500,000	7 %	8,575,000	7	60,025,000
Monthly total				247,450,000
Months per year				12
Annual Estimate				**2,969,400,000**
Number of PO locations thought the U.S., Page 18				35,756
Estimated average number of visits per postal office location per year				**83,046.20**
Average annual number of trips per HH to PO				24.24

Source USPS (2011, p.15 & 18)
Note The average number of trips to PO of 24.24 compares well with 468 annual shopping trips per HH reported by the U.S. Department of Transportation (2009)

References

Bradley, R., Burns, P., & Houpis, G. (2009). Costing elements of the universal service. In M. A. Crew & P. R. Kleindorfer (Eds.), *Progress in the competitive agenda in the postal and delivery sector.*

Cremer, H., De Donder, P., Boldron, F., Joram D., & Roy, B. (2008). Social costs and benefits of the universal service obligation in the postal market. In M. A. Crew & P. R. Kleindorfer (Eds.), *Competition and regulation in the postal and delivery sector.*

Directive 97/67/EC of the European Parliament and of the Council of 15 December 1997 on common rules for the development of the internal market of Community postal services and the improvement of quality of service, OJ L 015 of 21 January 1998.

Postal Regulatory Commission, "*Report on Universal Postal Service and the Postal Monopoly*", 2008.

Postal Reorganization Act of 1970, 39 U.S.C. 101(b).

Robinson, R., & McMurdie, J. (2009). Postal costing beyond ABC: Estimating the economic cost of mails services. In M. A. Crew & P. R. Kleindorfer (Eds.), *Progress in the competitive agenda in the postal and delivery sector.*

United States Postal Service. (2011). "*The Household Diary Study, Mail Use and Attitudes in Full Year 2011*".

United States Postal Service. (2013). "*2013 Annual Report to Congress*".

United States Postal Service. (2014). "*2014 Annual Report to Congress*".

United States Postal Service. (2015). "*2015 Annual Report to Congress*".

U.S. Postal Service Office of Inspector General, "*Analyzing the Postal Service's Retail Network*", 2010.

U.S. Department of Transportation, "*2009 National Household Travel Survey*", 2009.

Yezer, A. M. (2010). *The postal service retail facility location and size problem: A report prepared for the U.S. postal service office of the inspector general*, 2010.

Websites

Staples website. http://www.staples.com/imageRUNNER-1025/cat_CL205106. Accessed July 11, 2015

US Department of Labor website. www.dol.gov. Accessed 07/11/2015

USPS website, https://www.usps.com/ship/mail-shipping-services.htm. Accessed April 26, 2016

The Challenge of Designing Access to the Postal Network: An Economics Perspective

Henrik Ballebye Okholm, Bruno Basalisco, Julia Wahl and Mindaugas Cerpickis

Access to the postal network has figured prominently in the regulatory debate as more and more operators are required to provide access to their postal network. Yet, guidance for operators and regulators on how to design access regimes that withstand a regulatory and competition review has to date been surprisingly limited. A faulty design of the pricing and non-pricing part of access can have negative implications for the postal operator's (PO's) profitability, for competition, for economic efficiency and ultimately the social welfare resulting from market outcomes.

This paper does not attempt to resolve the question of whether access regulation is appropriate for postal markets but instead, it aims at providing recommendations for elements of access design. This should be consistent with a regulated operator's commercial reality and compliant with principles of regulatory and competition economics. Moreover, it outlines a number of tests that a 'compliant' access regime should be able to fulfil.

The first part of this paper introduces the topic of access to the postal network by discussing the regulatory goals and main challenges underlying access. The second section discusses elements of access design from an operator, regulator and competition authority viewpoint. The third section concludes.

1 Regulatory Goals of Access

Network access is one of the key tools used by regulators to stimulate competition in network industries. Access to the postal network (hereafter referred to simply as access) describes a service whereby the incumbent PO gives access to other postal service providers and postal users to its network at selected points of the postal

H.B. Okholm (✉) · B. Basalisco · J. Wahl · M. Cerpickis
Copenhagen Economics, Copenhagen, Denmark

M. Crew et al. (eds.), *The Changing Postal and Delivery Sector*,
Topics in Regulatory Economics and Policy,
DOI 10.1007/978-3-319-46046-8_20

supply chain and then the PO delivers the access mail fed into its network (see also ERGP 2012). From a postal regulatory point of view, access regulation aims at promoting efficiency and effective competition and, thereby, conferring benefits on the users of postal services (Ofcom 2012, p. 142).

In relation to promoting efficiency, according to the OECD (2010, p. 12), three types of efficiency should be taken into account: *allocative, productive, and dynamic efficiency* (see also Cabral 2000, p. 26):

> Allocative efficiency requires that output be at the appropriate level. Productive efficiency requires that such output be produced in the least expensive way given the available set of technologies. Dynamic efficiency refers to the improvement over time of products and production techniques (Cabral 2000, p. 28).

In relation to promoting effective competition, access regulation aims at enhancing competition in two ways. Firstly, access obligations should directly improve competition—where a postal company[1] receives mail from customers, and then accesses the NPO's network for the letter to be delivered to the final recipient.[2] Secondly, it can also enhance end-to-end competition where a postal company not only receives the letter from the customer but also then delivers it to the recipient, bypassing the NPO's network entirely.[3] Access can be a platform for end-to-end competition, if it is (a) allowing a rival operator to establish a customer base from which to begin to offer an end-to-end service and (b) allows a rival operator maintain a national service to customers with a limited delivery network (Ofcom 2012, p. 237).

Ultimately, the goal of any regulatory intervention is focused on benefits to end users, in the form of price savings, improved accessibility and/or quality of services.

From a postal regulatory or a competition policy point of view, the single most important question relating to any aspect of access design is whether an as-efficient competitor can compete. If an as-efficient competitor cannot compete given the choice of access prices and conditions, this qualifies as price-based or non-price exclusionary conduct by the dominant USP or, expressed differently, an abuse of dominant position in the meaning of article 102 of the Treaty on the Functioning of the European Union.[4]

There is much controversy about using access regulation to enhance competition. In particular, there is a risk of promoting less efficient market structures. One possible outcome is to shift senders' not just indirect but also direct demand from bulk mail to access services and vice versa. Depending on the scope of upstream

---

[1]Postal company represents any firm operating in the postal industry, without any regards on where it operates in the value chain.

[2]In this case, the postal company is considered in the value chain as an intermediary.

[3]In this case, the postal company also and/or only operates a postal network.

[4]The recent Post Danmark II judgement has raised the bar for an assessment of exclusionary abuse. According to the European Court of Justice (ECJ), depending on the characteristics of the market, even a less efficient competitor must be able to compete (Recitals 55–62).

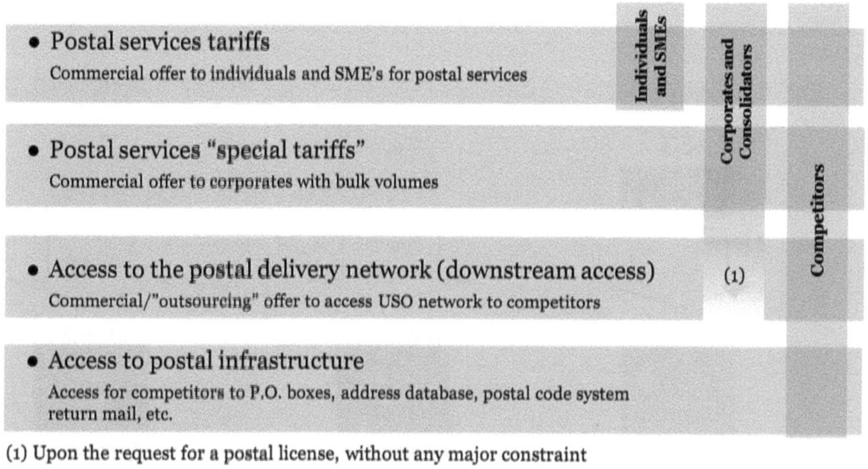

Fig. 1 Availability of postal services to different customers?

activities provided by the bulk mailer (sender) and/or access seeker, the sender may be able to procure directly both alternatives.

In fact, upon the request for a postal license, end users themselves can gain access to the postal delivery network without any major constraint; see Fig. 1.

For instance, if the access price is set below the bulk mail price, then bulk mailers (e.g. business mail senders) find it less expensive to become access seekers or send mail via intermediaries that use access product, compared to buying the PO's bulk mail products. Thus, the PO will be limited in its ability to price its bulk mail product. On the other hand, setting the access price higher than the bulk mail price can amount to a margin squeeze, forcing access seekers or intermediaries to limit what they can charge, Either way, access price regulation affects prices bulk mailers pay for delivery; see Fig. 2.

In addition, notwithstanding the best regulatory intentions and technical expertise, market dynamics decrease the level of predictability. Geradin (2015) argues that the predictability of market outcomes is much lower in mail markets than in many telecommunications markets (see also Panzar 2002). As acknowledged by the OFT (2009, p. 1), this uncertainty exacerbates the effect of regulatory risk in an already risky marketplace.

There are three reasons why regulatory intervention in highly dynamic mail markets with falling volumes may cause regulatory failure and in the end reduce consumer welfare. Firstly, regulatory intervention can add to the uncertainty in the market and reduce incentives to invest leading to a 'ladder of divestment'.[5] Secondly, fast adaptation is needed, yet regulatory intervention delays changes.

[5]The 'ladder of divestment' refers to a situation where favorable access conditions incentivize network operators to compete based on access instead of investing in their own delivery capacity.

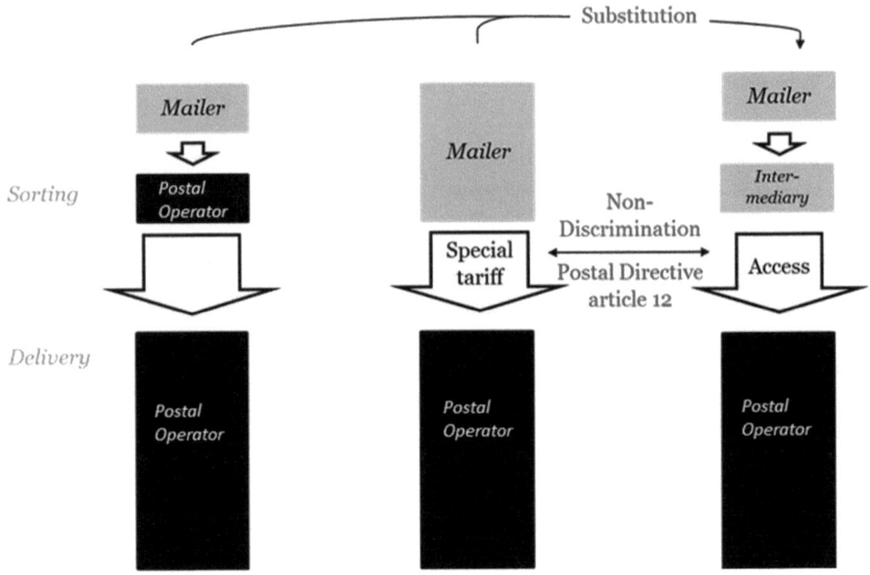

Fig. 2 Different users of access will receive same conditions

Last, but not least, balancing multiple goals is challenging. As a result, regulatory intervention comes at a cost, which puts use of access regulation for increasing end-to-end competition into question.

1.1 Economic Aspects of Access Design

Once access has been mandated by the NRA or requested by a competitor, both the USP and the NRA face a host of challenges concerning the design of the access regime. This can be grouped into three types of questions:

1. **Scope of Access:** Should access be mandated to USO products only or also to non-USO products?
2. **Access prices:** How should access charges be set to allow for efficient pricing and avoid exclusionary pricing?
3. **Access points:** At which point in the delivery chain should access take place?

The solution to each of these questions might thereby crucially depend on the viewpoint of one of the three main 'stakeholders' in the debate around access regimes:

First, the USP, which has to give access to its network, has an overall goal of maintaining its mail business profitable and ensuring the sustainability of the USO.

Second, the national regulatory authority (NRA) who has mandated access pursues the objective of introducing competition to the market by means of access regulation. According to the Third Postal Directive, the NRA should also aim at non-discriminatory and transparent access conditions and prices as well as the cost-orientation of access prices (European Parliament 2008).

Third, once access has been introduced, the national competition authority (NCA) scrutinizes the access conditions and prices to avoid three types of practices that can amount to exclusionary conduct: margin squeeze, predatory pricing or non-price forms of discrimination. We note that the NCA has no *prima facie* stakes in the introduction of access, but any access regime introduced by the USP or NRA should withstand a competition law review.

In this paper, access seekers, i.e. the competitors, are not included as an explicit stakeholder, but it is assumed that their viewpoint will be covered by both the NRA and NCA to the extent that these authorities want to ensure that as-efficient competitors are able to compete with the USP.[6] That notwithstanding, the statutory remit of these agencies is such that the focus is on pursuing what is best for competition, which is not necessarily the same as what the incumbent's competitors want. Moreover, different competitors may be affected in different ways by regulatory or competition enforcement. So it is unavoidably challenging for NRA/NCA to factor in and balance competitors' interests.

The multiplicity of (possibly conflicting) goals that an access regime has to fulfil raises the question of ideal access design. In the following three sections, we discuss each of the five elements of access design from the viewpoint of the USP, NRA and NCA. We thereby attempt to give an insight into the economic aspects of access design to be considered as well as to give guidance on features of access design.

2 Scope of Access

If a decision has been taken to mandate access, the first decision in relation to the design of an access regime is the determination of the scope of products to which access applies. While, in some cases, national postal laws limit access to USO products, the question of whether to include only a subset of these products (or other products) still arises. In other cases, the postal law does not determine a clear product scope of access. This raises questions, such as: should access apply to a sub-set or all USO products? Should access apply to USO products as well as non-USO products?

[6]One might theoretically consider that an access regime may be designed so that also less-efficient competitors can compete (cf. Post Danmark I). In practice, it is unclear under which market structures this would be a justifiable approach for postal markets, in terms of improvements to social welfare.

Table 1 Goals for the scope of access

Stakeholder	Goals
USP	Maintain profitability, USO sustainability
NRA	Efficient access
NCA	None

From the NRA's point of view, the product scope of access should be defined such that it allows for efficient access and a competitive postal market. In other words, access should be extended (or limited) to those postal services for which end-to-end competition cannot profitably arise. In turn, the USP aims to maintain a profitable business and to ensure a sustainable USO. See Table 1 above for a summary of stakeholders' goals for the scope of access.

Notwithstanding the goals of the USP, the question of a minimum product scope for access arises, if sector-regulation does not define it. ERGP (2012, p. 5) states that the essential facilities doctrine may be a useful concept to test and determine the economic fundamentals in this question, even if the legal application of essential facility arguments depends on case law and diverges globally across jurisdictions.

A general definition of essential facilities is "facilities the access to which is essential (and not just cheaper than the alternative) in order to compete on the downstream market, and whose owner is dominant and has no valid reason (lack of capacity, cost of achieving interoperability, protection of IP rights, …) to deny access." (Caillaud and Tirole 2004, p. 3).

Moreover, in the definition of access scope NCA enforcement may not be as valuable as regulatory constraints. As set out by the US Supreme Court (2014) under the late Justice Scalia in Verizon v. Trinko,[7]

> One factor of particular importance is the existence of a regulatory structure designed to deter and remedy anticompetitive harm. Where such a structure exists, the additional benefit to competition provided by antitrust enforcement will tend to be small". In other words, in these circumstances, antitrust enforcement yields "slight benefits", likely outweighed by the costs and risks of antitrust enforcement of "detailed [access] sharing obligations.[8]

In the postal context, an essential facility describes a network or infrastructure, controlled by the incumbent operator, without access to which competitors are unable to provide services to end-customers. A network is 'essential' when replicating the services provided over that network is not feasible or economically not reasonable. The extent to which a postal network can be regarded as an essential facility will be subject to a case-by-case assessment of whether it is indispensable for competitors to rely on the incumbent's postal network in order to build a viable letter business for a certain letter product. The relevant question to ask is, whether competitors need to make prohibitively high investments in order to put competing postal networks into place.[9]

[7] Verizon Communications v. Law Offices of Curtis V. Trinko, LLP, 540 U.S. 398 (2004).

[8] *Id.* at 412.

[9] This debate relates back to the ladder of divestment, see Sect. 1.

While this question has to be answered case-by-case, we observe a number of general features of the postal sector. On the one hand, building a nationwide network requires an extensive postal network with large amounts of capital. On the other hand, the low degree of sunk costs and large share of labor cost in mail delivery provide for relatively low entry barriers. Moreover, evidence from various EU countries shows that entrants do not have to copy the incumbent's business model. Instead they can sustain viable business models without relying on access, either by limiting the geographical coverage to urban areas with high population density or the product scope of their business while operating all along the postal value chain (WIK 2010).[10] At the same time, business models with practically full geographical coverage also exist in Europe.[11] Hence, an end-to-end competitive market situation can arise without access to the incumbent's infrastructure (see Fratini et al. 2009; Copenhagen Economics 2014).

Thus, from the outset, the 'essential facility' argument for granting access beyond the product scope determined in the respective postal law is a weak one. Furthermore, the design and implementation of the scope of access requires detailed supervisory requirements, which antitrust enforcement is unlikely to meet. According to Areeda (1989), "The problem should be deemed irremedia[ble] by antitrust law when compulsory access [involves the antitrust enforcement body] to assume the day-to-day controls characteristic of a regulatory agency" (Areeda 1989 at 853).

3 Access Prices

The effective price charged for access by the USP to a user of access can be lower than the price the USP charges for a standard end-to-end service due to operational or volume-stimulation considerations.

First, from a cost and operational perspective, access to the postal network usually involves a number of preparatory and pre-sorting activities that the access user completes before injecting the mail into the postal network. The fact that the USP avoids these activities and therefore has lower cost is reflected in the access price (typically via a so-called operational discount applied to the price of a standard end-to-end service).

Second, from a demand-stimulation perspective, since access buyers typically deal with large quantities of mail, the question arises as to the most economically efficient way to provide quantity discounts to intermediaries (such as access buyers) that is consistent with the purpose of quantity discounts, that is to foster scale economies within the PO (within the bounds of competition law). The setting of prices for access has been the most contentious question for operators, regulators

[10]See Bring Citymail in Sweden as an example.

[11]For instance, Sandd in the Netherlands.

and competition authorities alike, since they have to strike a fine balance between numbers of potentially conflicting goals, which we discuss in turn.

For the USP, it is most important to maintain a high degree of pricing flexibility under an access regime. When setting prices, POs aim at recovering the costs pertaining to an efficient postal network. For national POs, where a large share of a firm's total costs consists of fixed and common costs, efficient pricing implies market-based pricing and, therefore, price differentiation. This means that POs cannot recover their cost by pricing at marginal cost, as might a firm that faces no fixed or common costs in the production of its products and has non-increasing marginal costs. Allocatively efficient prices with markups above marginal costs to recover fixed and common costs will reflect their customers' price sensitivities for the product or service in question. This so-called market-based pricing (related to yet distinct from Ramsey pricing since the latter concept is associated with monopoly) is necessary for the efficient recovery of fixed costs (Tirole 1988, p. 70).

POs apply various forms of second and third degree price differentiation to stimulate senders' volumes, fostering allocative efficiency. Absent price differentiation, senders (which have much differing preferences) would face all the same price per same type of letter. If the PO had to offer only a single price, then to recover its high fixed and common costs, that price would be much above marginal cost. This would leave out of the market many potential senders (those valuing the service above marginal cost but below the single-price of sale): a loss of allocative efficiency. Price differentiation allows the PO to provide simultaneously multiple price points, to match the different preferences of different senders. The additional transactions made possible by the presence of multiple offers increase allocative efficiency on the market. Thus, the POs' price differentiation increases economic efficiency and social welfare.

Market-based pricing becomes even more crucial in postal markets where volumes are declining and in which customer preferences are changing. In such a context, it is important for POs to have the pricing flexibility that enables them to respond to changes in demand as well as competition and adjust their services and prices in a timely manner.

From the NRA's perspective, access prices must abide by a number of criteria to be in line with the goals of efficient entry and to ensure competition. The Third Postal Directive (Recital 39) requires access prices to be cost-oriented, i.e. for access prices to reflect the costs that the USP avoids with access compared to the costs it incurs when delivering the standard mail service covering the complete range of features offered for the clearance, sorting, transport and distribution of individual postal items (European Parliament 2008). The USP's access prices hence have to be in line with the principle of avoided costs.

Furthermore, article 12(5) of the Third Postal Directive requires the USP to apply access tariffs in a transparent and non-discriminatory manner. This means that access seekers that conduct the same level of preparation and sorting activities need to be rewarded with equivalent access prices including equivalent associated conditions as confirmed by the CJEU Deutsche Post/Vedat Deniz judgement (2008, Recital 28).

Table 2 Goals for access prices

Stakeholder	Goals
USP	Maintain pricing flexibility
NRA	Efficient entry, cost-orientation, non-discrimination, transparency
NCA	Non-discrimination, avoid margin squeeze

In turn, the NCA's goal is to prevent exclusionary pricing. The NCA scrutinizes whether, given the access prices and conditions set by the USP, an as-efficient competitor can compete. If an as-efficient competitor cannot compete, this can amount to competition issues of price-based exclusionary conduct, i.e. an abuse of dominant position in the meaning of article 102 of the Treaty on the Functioning of the European Union (TFEU).[12] See Table 2 below for a summary of stakeholders' goals for access prices.

Exclusionary pricing can take two forms. Either the margin between access tariff and retail price for a given services is too slim for an as-efficient competitor to compete (margin squeeze) or the overall (effective) end-to-end prices are too low for an as-efficient competitor to compete, i.e. it constitutes predatory pricing (European Commission 2009, Recital 23). This raises the question of how and what level access charges should be set maintain the USP's pricing flexibility, to allow for efficient entry and efficient pricing while avoiding exclusionary conduct. The considerations in this section are also summarized in Table 2.

Against the background of these goals for access pricing, several economic issues arise as to the design of the operational, cost-related part of access pricing and the quantity-related part of access pricing. We discuss those in turn.

3.1 Access Prices: Cost-Plus or Retail Minus

The first choice the USP or NRA needs to make is whether to set prices according to a cost-plus or retail minus model. Cost-plus pricing means that access prices reflect the long-run incremental cost (LRIC) of the operator plus a reasonable mark-up. With retail-minus pricing, the access price is set as a discount on the total retail price of the standard end-to-end service, the discount reflecting the PO's avoided cost for those activities that are carried out by the user of access.

The PO's ability to apply market-based pricing crucially hinges on the choice between cost-plus and retail minus pricing. The cost-plus model implies that the operator has to charge a similar price for services for which it incurs similar costs (e.g., domestic bulk mail and international bulk mail, insofar as these are indeed

[12]Recent case law suggests that the bar for assessing exclusionary conduct should be even higher in the sense that the USP's behavior should not even prevent a less efficient competitor from competing, see Post Danmark II, Recitals 55–62.

similar). As long as the "plus" is constant across all consumers and services (as is standard regulatory practice) this approach prevents market-based pricing, since prices do not adapt to customers' price sensitivities. The consequence of this will be higher prices for price sensitive mailers, as well as lower market volumes and therefore higher costs and higher prices for all mailers.

Second, such a model would cause significant bypass by intermediaries that are free to set prices according to customers' price sensitivities and can enable competitors to take over the "best deals" (also called arbitrage). This risks undermining the operator's profitability and USO sustainability. On top of that, it discourages the possible emergence or extension of alternative end-to-end delivery networks, curtailing the incentive for an infrastructure-based business model.

As opposed to cost-plus pricing, the retail-minus approach maintains the PO's flexibility in pricing access. When the PO is able to set the retail price, it is still able to charge different access prices depending on the price-sensitivity of different customers and, via the minus (i.e. operational discount), the PO will still be able to reflect the difference in service between the access and the standard retail service. This however applies only if the access products are defined at a granular level. With insufficient granularity of access products, it is likely that an access product/price corresponds to multiple retail products, each with different customer bases and price sensitivity, thus the access-retail price link is unraveled. If this is the case, retail-minus pricing may have similar (negative) effects as cost-plus pricing.[13]

While the PO would may benefit from a retail-minus approach to access pricing, the NRA has to take into account several different goals when choosing between the two approaches. From a pure cost-orientation perspective, the performance of a retail-minus approach depends upon the extent to which retail prices are in the first place cost-oriented. This ensures that access prices are also consistent with cost orientation.

From the point of view of allocative efficiency, however, the NRA should favor the retail-minus approach. Preventing market-based pricing via the cost-plus pricing model would be detrimental to the postal industry, in the short run (in terms of reduced sustainability of the USO) and in the long run (in terms of endangered survival of all delivery operators). Moreover, declining volumes make it difficult to forecast costs, which makes the cost-plus type of price regulation less adaptable to (sudden) drops or changes in mail demand. On top of that, the retail-minus approach also ensures efficient competition, as work-sharing discounts give a direct incentive to perform work-sharing activities as soon as those can be produced more efficiently.

However, how does the retail-minus perform in relation to the goals of the Postal Directive and competition law, namely non-discrimination and avoidance of exclusionary conduct? The retail-minus approach should ensure non-discrimination,

[13]These effects may include: (i) restraining an operator in differentiating prices based on users' price sensitivities, (ii) encouraging mailers to seek access directly, (iii) encouraging competitors to use access to serve only end-users with low price sensitivity, and (iv) setting retail prices higher can lead to losing customers with high price sensitivity.

as all access users that undertake the same preparatory and pre-sorting activities on their mail are eligible for the same discount levels. More specifically, it ensures non-discriminatory treatment of mailers that pay the same access price independently of whether they buy access directly or whether they go through an intermediary. Furthermore, the application of retail-minus pricing should safeguard the USP against any allegation of margin squeeze or predatory pricing—provided that the minus is at least as large as avoided costs, consistently with the work-sharing operational discount principle, e.g. as mandated by the EU Postal Directive, as clarified by the CJEU Deutsche Post/Vedat Deniz case. It should avoid margin squeeze, because any as-efficient (upstream) competitor should be able to offer prices to the final customer (e.g., big mailers) that is equal to or below the total operational rebate that the USP offers on its retail price for the end-to-end service.

Whereas conceptually, the retail-minus approach seems to fit both the goals of the Postal Directive and competition law, practically whether or not the USP's operational rebates withstands a regulatory and competition policy review hinges on the correct application of the avoidable cost methodology. We suggest for the USP and/or NRA to test the correct application of the avoidable cost methodology in four steps:

First, the avoidable cost calculation needs to build upon reliable cost information, usually from regulatory cost accounts that are approved by the NRA (European Commission 2009, recital 25). In many instances, a challenge arises, when the regulatory accounts are not sufficiently granular. In this case, further cost analysis is needed.

Second, the calculation needs to build upon a relevant comparison between the access product and the corresponding end-to-end products or products.

Third, the USP needs to identify the avoidable activities in a correct manner and considering the correct time horizon.

Finally, the avoidable cost of each individual activity needs to be calculated correctly, using the right approximation of avoidable cost (which is often the variable cost).

3.2 *Quantity Rebates: On Aggregate or a Per-Sender Basis?*

A key decision in the design of access regimes revolves around the way quantity rebates should be applied and calculated for the PO's different customers (intermediaries, competitors or big mailers). More specifically, the question is whether quantity rebates should be granted based on the aggregate mail volume injected by an individual customer over a certain period (typically one year) or based on the volumes injected by each of the senders i.e. end-users.

From the PO's point of view, market-based pricing relies on second degree price differentiation, which allows mailers to self-select the discount level, based on what quantity of services they choose to purchase from the PO. Another classical example of second degree price discrimination is the two-part tariff, which corresponds to a volume discount system (Tirole 1988). Economic theory shows that with 2nd degree price differentiation (volume discounts i.e. non-linear pricing) the market is expanded, more buyers take part in the market and more goods are sold than under simple linear pricing—assuming that buyers are heterogeneous.

This assumption holds in the postal industry, where business customers (mailers) have very different preferences and valuation for the postal service. Willig (1978) proved that non-linear pricing schemes have superior efficiency than pricing based on a single tariff.

Thus, volume discounts increase allocative efficiency, as they facilitate setting the added payment for additional volume closer to marginal cost. When customers vary, the supplier can enable additional sales by reducing the price for the biggest customers, to approach the level of marginal cost. Insofar as additional transactions are thus enabled, social welfare consequently is increased (Varian 1990).

To ensure an effective market-based pricing mechanism, a PO can apply these discounts on a per sender basis, so that the mailers' self-selection mechanism functions without interference. The per-sender model for quantity rebates implies for the quantity rebate level to be calculated based on the volume of mailings generated individually by each sender of mail. Intermediaries (consolidators or any access seeker) still obtain quantity rebates: the latter are not calculated for the total (aggregated) mail quantities they deposit, but by summing the discount level associated to the quantity of mail of each of the senders that provide mail to the access seeker.

POs apply a per-sender model to preserve the quantity-stimulating function that is at the heart of a quantity rebates scheme. More specifically, the per-sender model prevents bypass and arbitrage by intermediaries using access regulation to obtain very large volume discounts.[14] If intermediaries obtain a volume discount based on aggregate volumes they can give small senders the high level of quantity rebates that the USP originally intended for large senders. In particular, mailers with low price sensitivity may be able to buy access directly from the access provider.

Without the possibility to apply rebates on a per-sender basis, the only way for the USP to minimize the room for arbitrage is to increase the lowest prices (i.e. prices paid by segments of consumers with high price sensitivity). This would result in overall higher prices for price sensitive users, leading to lower market volumes, higher unit costs and higher prices for all end-users. In a context of possible e-substitution, this might incentivize mailers to substitute away from postal mail towards electronic mail. Lower volumes and higher costs may also reduce the financial sustainability of the USO.

Instead, under the per-sender model, the quantity-stimulating function of the rebates is preserved and consolidators obtain the same quantity rebates than their own clients (senders) would obtain if they dealt directly with the USP. The

[14]The definition of intermediaries includes any sender X that starts acting as an intermediary (consolidator), e.g. allowing any other company Y to get a PO's quantity discount, "without having increased its volume of mailings".

per-sender model allows for allocative efficiency via a close match between prices and mailers' sensitivity to price via the self-selection mechanism. This form of market-based pricing has thus a demand stimulating purpose and effect; it also constitutes demand stimulation insofar as it prevents or delays e-substitution. From the USP's perspective, it would hence be most efficient and most profitable to implement a per-sender model for quantity rebates.

Concerning its goal of efficient entry, the NRA should consider that only the per-sender model ensures efficient entry. Without the per-sender model it would be possible for intermediaries to build a business model based on the purely administrative consolidation of large quantities of mail without needing to be more efficient in the sorting or preparation activities.

Concerning the goals of non-discrimination for both the NRA and NCA, the per-sender model is not distorting competition in the mail market. While quantity rebates are a form of price discrimination, price discrimination becomes problematic only when customers in comparable situations are treated differently (as defined in the EU law principle of equal treatment, see CJEU bpost case, recital 27).[15] To test whether these quantity rebates create competitive concerns, it needs to be tested whether the quantity rebate via a per-sender model results in a *primary line injury*, i.e. a distortion of competition between the PO and its competitors, or a *secondary line injury*, i.e. a distortion of competition between the PO's customers. For this to occur, the firms the treatment of which is being assessed must first of all be on the same line, i.e. the comparability condition.

The European case law on the per-sender model clarifies that, firstly, quantity rebates used to stimulate demand are not discriminatory—senders of small versus high quantities of mail are not in comparable situations concerning quantity rebates. Secondly, that the application of quantity rebates on a per-sender basis is not discriminatory—senders versus intermediaries are not in comparable situations concerning quantity rebates.[16]

Following the economic reasoning in these decisions, the per-sender model does not induce a secondary line injury. Senders (i.e. mailers) and intermediaries are not in comparable situations as to the objective pursued by quantity rebates, which is to stimulate demand of postal services.[17] Only bulk mailers can be encouraged by quantity rebates to increase the volume of mail handled by the USP. In other words, since intermediaries and senders do not compete with each other, a per-sender model cannot distort the competition between them.

---

[15]"The principle of equal treatment, which is one of the fundamental principles of EU law, requires that comparable situations must not be treated differently, and different situations must not be treated in the same way, unless such treatment is objectively justified" (CJEU bpost case), recital 27.

[16]These cases involved the Belgian USP bpost and the French USP La Poste.

[17]See Case C 340/13, bpost v IBPT [2015], Recital 27, 48, Conseil de la Concurrence, Opinion 07-A-17 of 20 November 2007, Recital 195, 205, 206; Opinion of Advocate General Sharpston, delivered on 16 October 2014, Recital 88–90, 92.

Moreover, the per-sender model does not per se induce a primary line injury, since it does not interfere with the separate application of operational discounts based on avoided costs, which allows intermediaries (including access-based operators) to develop sustainable business models and to compete with the USP.[18] For instance, in France, La Poste's price structure including a per-sender condition was cleared in a market characterized by the presence of alternative end-to-end networks.[19]

On top of that, the per-sender model levels the playing field on the consolidation market. In fact, in absence of a per-sender model larger consolidators would be more attractive for mailers since for achieving higher accumulated discounts. This would create considerable entry barriers for small consolidators. Furthermore, a regulatory decision blocking per-sender could constitute discrimination, by applying comparable treatment to dissimilar situations.[20] In conclusion, applying a per-sender rule in order to preserve the quantity stimulating function of quantity rebates is consistent with economic efficiency and compatible with the relevant case law.

3.3 Quantity Rebates: Avoiding Exclusionary Conduct

The issue of volume discounts has been a major area of analysis in the literature and practice of network industries. Volume discounts (either to originators of mail or to worksharing providers) are an important example of nonlinear pricing in the postal service, though their analysis has only recently begun (Crew and Kleindorfer 2012).

As to volume discounts, competition law constraints imply that the PO's pricing should avoid amounting to exclusionary conduct, which is a concern insofar as a firm is dominant. In fact, quantity rebates can have a loyalty-enhancing effect. Loyalty-enhancing rebates can in the extreme (given shape and intensity of discount structure) lead to market foreclosure. According to European Commission (2009, §23) anti-competitive foreclosure arises when a dominant firm's pricing practices make it unattractive for customers to switch a relevant share of demand away from the dominant firm to an alternative supplier, even if the alternative supplier is an as-efficient competitor.[21]

European case law after the CJEU AKZO case (CJEU 1991) and Commission prioritization guidance (European Commission 2009) guides dominant companies

---

[18]Conseil de la Concurrence, Opinion 07-A-17 of 20 November 2007, Recital 205.

[19]Conseil de la Concurrence, Opinion 07-A-17 of 20 November 2007.

[20]This has been explicitly postulated in the Opinion of Advocate General Sharpston, delivered on 16 October 2014, Recital 88.

[21]One form of loyalty-enhancing rebates are retroactive rebates, whereby customers obtain a discount on all the units purchased, if a certain threshold of purchases is met.

to compare prices against own costs (bright-line test).[22] When the effective price that an as-efficient competitor would have to set to attract part of the purchases from a customer at the dominant PO is below costs, the pricing of a dominant company is exclusionary, because an as-efficient competitor cannot attract customers from the dominant firm and remain profitable. In other words, some customers, which are contestable, are made not contestable by the pricing policy of the dominant company.

An effects-based analysis—as advocated by the European Commission for its prioritization—assesses a quantity rebate case-by-case concerning its effects on competition (European Commission 2009). More specifically, the analysis of a dominant firm's pricing can assess whether the price level and structure has any impact for the relevant quantity that competitors can compete for. This can be a part of a broader examination of "all the circumstances of the case", to be conducted within a competition case (see Post Danmark I 2012).

To check for foreclosing pricing, the NCA carries out a price-cost comparison. As confirmed by the Post Denmark I judgment (see Post Danmark I 2012), the relevant cost benchmark to use for the postal sector (as an approximation of AAC) is the incremental cost benchmark, i.e. the cost attributable to (i.e. incremental to) the product in question.[23] More specifically, the average incremental costs are the costs that would disappear in the short or medium term (three to five years) if the USP were to give up its business activity of distributing a certain mail product (see Post Danmark I 2012).

In a market where access is introduced and used by competitors to the dominant company, the presence of access makes a second business model available to competitors as they contest the dominant firm's customers. Therefore, an as-efficient competitor test should incorporate this additional option when assessing (or forecasting for compliance purposes) the effect of the dominant company's pricing structure. In other words, the presence of access can imply an adaptation of the test for predation and this can have implications in postal markets. However, this exercise requires making assumptions about the extent to which a competitor relies on end-to-end vs an access-based business model.

Consistently with the bright-line approach to compliance requirements for dominant companies, it can be disproportionate to hold dominant companies accountable to comply with competition law if they do not and cannot have the information needed to comply—in the case information on the choice of business model by the competitor. For the same reason, the equivalently efficient operator

[22]Notwithstanding the legal certainty enshrined in the bright line criteria that the dominant company should inform its compliance upon a known quantity, i.e. its own costs, a rival may be excluded by a rebate based on how the rebate relates to the rival's cost, not per se to the cost of the dominant firm (Brennan 2008).

[23]See also Commission Decision of 20 March 2001, Case COMP/35.1 41 Deutsche Post AG, OJ L1 25/27. §10 The Commission stated that Deutsche Post "must earn revenue on [the specific service open to competition] which at least covers the costs attributable to or incremental to producing that particular service".

(EEO) is the cost standard used in ex-post competition enforcement: dominant companies should compare prices against their own costs, since they cannot know their competitors' costs.

A further complication for an access-giving dominant company's pricing compliance effort is that different competitors can have different business models and different scales of operation. An access-giving dominant company, by definition, does not use a business model based on using access. Thus, how can a dominant company apply an equivalently efficient operator approach that encompasses access as part of the business model when its own business model does not? A reasonable effort could be to test and calibrate an as-efficient competitor model based on a set of plausible stylized competitors that match the available information on existing competitors.

4 Access Points

The third question for access design is at which point in the delivery chain access should take place, i.e. at which point the access seeker should drop off its mail in order for it to be fed into the delivery network. While both the USP and the NRA have a common goal of efficiency, the NRA might want to facilitate access for different types of access seekers by providing for several access points along the delivery chain, for instance by mandating access not only to sorting centers but also at local distribution offices. See Table 3 for a summary of stakeholders' goals for access points.

However, any access points further downstream that the inward sorting center are likely both operationally inefficient and incompatible with the cost-orientation requirement for access prices. Access that is provided further downstream, for instance at distribution offices, would lead to a duplication of resources and therefore to an increase in costs. Insofar as mail can only be fed efficiently into the mail stream at sorting centers, the USP would have to redirect the mail from the multiplicity of distribution offices to the sorting center thereby incurring extra transport costs. Moreover, the USP can also not avoid the sorting and transport activities and costs from the sorting center back to the local distribution office. On top of that, distribution offices might not be equipped to handle the large mail volumes that access usually involves. Thus, access should be allowed only where it is efficient for the USP from an operational point of view, i.e. the inbound and/or outbound sorting centers, see Fig. 3.

Table 3 Goals for access points

Stakeholder	Goals
USP	Efficiency
NRA	Efficient and workable access
NCA	None

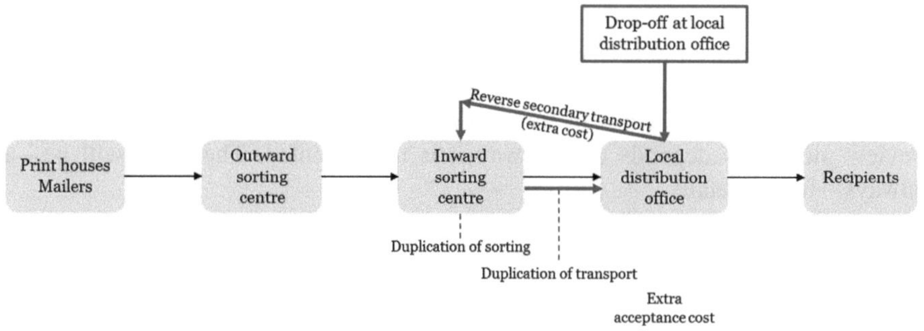

Fig. 3 Access at distribution offices causes a duplication of resources

Finally, any access prices charged would have to reflect the lack of avoided costs. This creates a tension between the cost-orientation requirement and the requirement for access prices to be lower than the standard end-to-end service price.

These elements have been at the basis of the German and Italian NRAs' conclusion not to set out access to local distribution centers (AGCOM 2013a, b; Pohl 2010, p. 26). They are further corroborated by the finding, that in virtually all EU member states with access regulation implemented, access takes place at inward and/or outward sorting centers. Thus, if access is granted at different points in the delivery network there should be different access prices, with the difference reflecting the cost avoided when moving up the delivery chain from one access point to the next.

5 Conclusions

While the aim of the paper was not to resolve the question of whether access regulation is appropriate for postal markets, it has investigated the different questions that arise when designing an access model—when it is mandated. It has also outlined the different possibilities for designing access from the viewpoint of the USP as well as the postal regulator and competition authority.[24]

It is the methodological conclusion of this work that the sometimes seemingly conflicting goals of those three stakeholders can be catered for by the same elements of access design. This finding can help the prior analysis and discussion of whether access is appropriate in the first place.

If it is agreed for access to be mandated, an access model compatible (from a regulatory and competition economics viewpoint) with the goals of all three key stakeholders would: (a) apply to a limited set of products for which it is

[24]A further factor for consideration is the economic effect of geographically differentiated prices (zonal pricing) in access, to which the same principles discussed in this paper should apply.

demonstrated that the PO's network is an essential facility, (b) include a retail-minus approach to access pricing, (c) include a per-sender model for quantity rebates, and (d) allow for access only at sorting centers.

In the end, whether or not an access regime withstands regulatory or competition review ultimately depends on the way it is implemented. The devil will be—as always—in the detail.

References

AGCOM. (2013a). Allegato B alla Delibera n. 384/13/CONS.

AGCOM. (2013b). DELIBERA N. 728/13/CONS.

Areeda, P. (1989). Essential facilities: an epithet in need of limiting principles. *Antitrust Law Journal, 58*, 841.

Brennan, T. J. (2008). Bundled rebates as exclusion rather than predation. *Journal of Competition Law and Economics, 4*(2), 335–374.

Cabral, L. M. B. (2000). *Introduction to industrial organization*. Cambridge, MA: MIT press.

Caillaud, B., & Tirole, J. (2004). Essential facility financing and market structure. *Journal of Public Economics, 88*(3–4), 667–694.

CJEU. (1991). Case C-62/86, AKZO Chemie BV v Commission.

CJEU. (2008). Joined Cases C-287/06 to C-292/06, Deutsche Post AG and Others v. Bundesrepublik Deutschland.

CJEU. (2012). Case C-209/10, Post Danmark I.

CJEU. (2015a). Case C 340/13, bpost SA v. IBPT.

CJEU. (2015b). Case C-23/14, Post Danmark II.

Conseil de la Concurrence. (2007). *Avis no 07-A-17 du 20 décembre 2007 relatif à une demande d'avis de l'ARCEP sur le dispositif de remises commerciales de La Poste*.

Copenhagen Economics. (2014). Regulatory developments in post and telecommunications: A tale of two industries. In M. A. Crew & T. J. Brennan (Eds.), *Postal and delivery innovation in the digital economy*. NY: Springer.

Crew, M. A., & Kleindorfer, P. R. (2012). Nonlinear pricing, volume discounts and the USO under entry. In M. A. Crew & P. R. Kleindorfer (Eds.), *Multi-modal competition and the future of mail*. Northampton: Edward Elgar Publishing.

ERGP. (2012). Report on "access" to the postal network and elements of postal infrastructure.

European Commission. (2001). Commission Decision of 20 March 2001, Case COMP/35.1 41 Deutsche Post AG, O.J.L. 125/27.

European Commission. (2009). Guidance on the commission's enforcement priorities in applying Article 82 of the EC Treaty to abusive exclusionary conduct by dominant undertakings, O.J.C. 45/7.

European Parliament and the Council of the EU. (2008). Directive 2008/6/EC amending Directive 97/67/EC. (Third Postal Directive).

Fratini, A., et al. (2009). Access to postal infrastructure and service elements in the postal sector. In M. A. Crew & P. R. Kleindorfer (Eds.), *Heightening competition in the postal and delivery sector*. Northampton: Edward Elgar Publishing.

Geradin, D. (2015). Is mandatory access to the postal network desirable and if so at what terms? *European Competition Journal, 11*(2–3), 520–556.

OECD. (2010). Regulatory policy and the road to sustainable growth.

Ofcom. (2012). Securing the universal postal service.

OFT. (2009). Government in markets: Why competition matters—A guide for policy makers.

Opinion of Advocate General Sharpston, bpost SA v. IBPT, Case C-340/13, [2014] E.C.R.

Panzar, J. (2002). Reconciling competition, downstream access, and universal service in postal markets. In M. A. Crew & P. R. Kleindorfer (Eds.), *Postal and delivery services: Delivering on competition*. Boston, MA: Kluwer Academic Publishers.
Pohl, M. (2010). *Der Netzzugang bei Briefdiensten in Deutschland und Groábritannien*. Hamburg: Diplomica Verlag.
Tirole, J. (1988). *The theory of industrial organization*. Cambridge, MA: MIT press.
Varian, H. R. (1990). *Intermediate microeconomics—A modern approach*. NY: W.W. Norton & Company.
WIK. (2010). Netzzugang und Zustellwettbewerb im Briefmarkt.
Willig, R. D. (1978). Pareto-superior nonlinear outlay schedules. *Bell Journal of Economics, 9*(1), 56–69.

Should the Postal Sector Change Its Social Model to Succeed in Its Transformation?

Dominique Bailly and Margaux Meidinger

1 Introduction

The digital revolution and the fear of a possible collapse of mail activity, require national postal operators (NPOs) to carry out greater transformation of their economic model. Changes to this economic model could be viewed as bringing about a comparable change in the social model historically based on employment stability. Aside from the labor motivations, this principle of employment security answered a strong economic need. It favored a relationship of trust between employees and consumers and guaranteed higher-quality services. This traditional model has already been challenged, there has been a significant decrease in employment, and (NPOs) have implemented a social optimization[1] through different levers, with a mix depending on their strategic orientations. Nevertheless, compared to some other industries the postal sector has not, so far, been faced with a radical social transformation. But, what about tomorrow? The sector could in the future undergo faster, more profound and more complex change both in economic and social terms. In the light of more cost-based competition and the continued decrease in mail volumes triggered in particular by always faster digital evolutions, POs have to reconsider their economic model. In a labor-intensive industry, namely, the postal sector, can a shift in economic model take place without a profound reconsideration of the social model?

[1]Social optimization covers all measures put in place to optimize the labor structure and its costs. These measures encompass in particular the evolution of status (part-time, short term contracts), the evolutions of wages, increased flexibility of the work organization as well as employees' mobility.

D. Bailly · M. Meidinger (✉)
La Poste Group, Paris, France
e-mail: margaux.meidinger@laposte.fr

M. Crew et al. (eds.), *The Changing Postal and Delivery Sector*,
Topics in Regulatory Economics and Policy,
DOI 10.1007/978-3-319-46046-8_21

This paper aims to analyze the impact of the economic transformation on POs' social model. Section 2 explores the different social levers and transformation strategies put in place by incumbents to enable a balanced social optimization. Section 3 underlines how in the future, the postal sector could face a more intense but also more complex social transformation. Section 4 explains how, despite this necessary transformation, the postal sector should preserve its unique asset of proximity. The paper will largely rely on the results of the ongoing EU-funded project conducted by the European Social Dialogue Committee for the postal sector (SDC) which consists of an analysis of the collective labor agreements (CLAs) signed within national incumbents in Europe to manage the change process.

2 A Variable but Moderated Social Transformation

Since the beginning of the 90s, faced with the combined threats of market opening and e-substitution, the European NPOs have carried out significant optimization and modernization of their activities. Every part of the postal activity has been concerned by this process. The mail production chain has been strongly mechanized, the mail distribution network has been partly or totally in some cases transformed into contact points managed by external providers, and the mail distribution organization has been continuously adapted to meet changing volumes (Bailly and Meidinger 2011).

2.1 Different Social Transformation Levers

This operational transformation has been supported by a social adaptation. Of the different levers, the most largely used is the decrease in employment which concerns the large majority of incumbents but has varied in terms of intensity. It appears that, on average, European NPOs saw a decrease of 2.5 % between 2010 and 2011(WIK 2010–2013 2013). In the selection of countries studied this change ranges from a reduction of 29 % in PostNL from 2011 to 2014 to a slightly increase in Deutsche Post AG of 1.7 % from 2010 to 2014 as shown in Table 1. In most cases, the decrease of employment has been managed by natural attrition enabled by the high average age of postal employees. It has been sometimes supported by organized voluntary departure programs but very rarely by forced departures.

Other social transformation levers which can be used by companies involve changing employment forms and status. However, the research conducted by the SDC, in particular in the framework the 2015–2016 EU-funded project "Mobilizing social partners in a new context", has shown that the forms of employment have not changed significantly. As shown by Figs. 1 and 2, in general, the use of part-time or temporary contracts has remained stable and in some cases it has even decreased.

Table 1 Postal operators' social transformation levers

	Mail evolution 2009/2014 (%)	Employment evolution 2009/2014 (%)	Turn over (departures) (%)	Part-time rate (%)	Short-term rate (%)	Voluntary departure programs	New wage grids
Poste Italiane	−32	−6.2	5	9.8	1.6	Yes	No
PostNL	−29	−14 (2011/2014)	35	79	0.2	Yes	Yes (with part-time deliverers)
Royal Mail	−22	−14	7.5	26.4	2.9	Yes	No
La Poste	−21	−10.2	4.1	6.6	9.7	No	No
Bpost	−20	−16 (2010/2014)	10	25.6	1.9	No	Yes (auxiliary employees with limited wage progression)
Swiss Post	−14	+0.3	4.2	49.1	6.1	Yes	No
Deutsche Post DHL	−10	+1.7 (2010/2014)	12.8	36.1 (Deutsche Post AG)	18 (estimation)	No	Yes (for newly recruited employees)

Postal operators' 2010 and 2015 Annual Reports, IPC 2015 Global Monitoring report

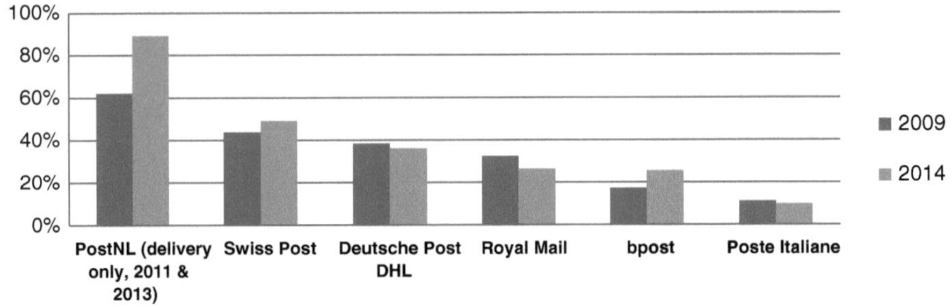

Fig. 1 Part-time employment rate (NPOs' 2010 and 2015 Annual Reports)

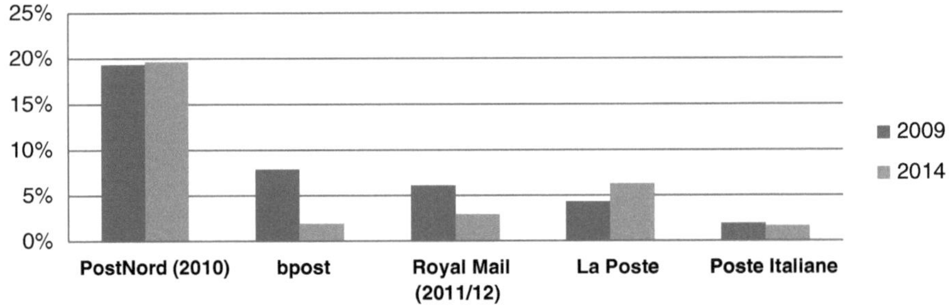

Fig. 2 Short-term employment rate [NPOs' 2010 and 2015 Annual Reports (no data available for PostNL)]

Figure 1 shows that use of part-time employment varies greatly among European postal operators ranging from more than 80 % to less than 10 %. This is directly linked to the national social regulation framework. Moreover, with the exception of PostNL, there is general stability both in countries where this rate was higher or lower.

In general, the rate of short-term contracts is rather low among the postal operators studied. It has remained stable over recent years, with companies like bpost and Royal Mail even seeing a decrease.

(a) Balanced social transformations linked to the mail volumes' evolution and the NPOs' strategies

Table 1 provides data on the decrease of mail volumes and employment. In Germany and Switzerland where the mail reduction over five years has been below 15 %, employment has increased slightly with no voluntary departure programs put in place. In general, we can observe that the use of optimization levers has been moderated in all incumbents with the exception of PostNL which, however, has clearly shown a change in its social strategy since 2013. Even if initially, it had foreseen a fully part-time structure in delivery, the Dutch operator chose to maintain a number of traditional postmen/postwomen.

The social transformation had indeed been managed within the framework of constant dialogue with the national trade unions and, in general, has been supported through the signing of collective labor agreements between social partners. For instance, within Deutsche Post DHL, since 1994, the management of change has been supported by several agreements aimed at protecting employment and working conditions (SDC report 2016). The successive agreements have confirmed the Employment Guarantee Pact (lay-offs due to restructuring are forbidden). The October 2011 CLA shows a trade-off between social partners on the one hand as it ensures the freeze of externalization of mail delivery activities till end of 2015 and on the other hand establishes a wage differentiation between new and old employees with 4 % wage decrease for newly recruited ones.

The balanced social transformation is also shown in Royal Mail in the case of the agreements of 2010[2] and 2014.[3] These agreements recognize the urgent need to transform with key measures to support change management through the modernization of the organization while ensuring employees' job protection. They also encompass a commitment to predominantly full-time workforce (¾ of employees), open-ended contracts as the rule, no additional outsourcing and the objective to manage change without compulsory redundancy but with a program of voluntary departures.

The European Commission implementation report on the Postal Directives confirms that even if there has been a social adaptation to support the modernization, the postal sector has not for the moment been faced with a radical transformation. It underlines in particular that « in many instances, modernization has been managed in a socially responsible way together with the trade unions ».[4]

Postal operators' social transformations are also strongly linked to their business strategies which vary in their orientations from more industry-focused strategies to those favoring services. Indeed, the adaptation of postal operators has not only relied on optimization and modernization of traditional activities. It has also been conducted through the diversification of their portfolio of activities enabling them to find new growth levers as already analyzed in Bailly and Meidinger (2013). Among these strategies, four models can be identified. The industrial model aims to optimize domestic mail and parcels activity through a cost/volume approach. The logistics model aims to extend traditional activity to parcels, express and logistics with, in particular, an international dimension. The financial and insurance services model relies on a dense and extended network of post offices. The multi-activities model combines these different approaches and aims at finding a balance between a diversified portfolio of activities.

Social transformation strategies are closely linked to these diversification strategies. The industrial approach requires an optimization of networks and social

[2]« Business Transformation 2010 and Beyond », 2010.

[3]« Agenda for growth, industrial stability, pay and protections », January 2014.

[4]Report from the Commission to the European Parliament and the Council on the application of the Postal Services Directive, 17 November 2015.

costs. Likewise, the logistics model does not require an extended domestic network. Postal operators which have adopted these strategies tend, therefore, to have put in place a more significant social optimization. On the other hand, the services and multi-activity models rely on a large network as well as trained and stable staff to ensure good quality for customers' services.

2.2 The Moderated Social Transformation Relies on Structural Causes

In general, it appears that the social transformation has been different among countries but that it has remained relatively cautious and managed in a socially responsible manner. The use of different optimization levers has allowed most postal operators to gain additional margins of maneuver. There has however been neither a disruption of the traditional social model nor major restructurings comparable to what has happened in other sectors like the steel or mining industry.

This relative stability can be explained by three main structural reasons. Firstly, most postal operators, there is still have sufficient demographic potential for natural attrition resulting from the high average age of employees and voluntary departure programs, which are able to complement it efficiently. Secondly, for the moment, mail activity remains the main activity for most postal operators and the volume of this activity is still such that delivery can be managed at a marginal cost. In this sense, parcel activity can still be conducted by incumbents without putting too much pressure on costs and competitiveness. At the same time, competition on the mail market remains limited in most countries with therefore little threat of social dumping. Finally, diversification towards new activities which are furthest from traditional activities has mainly taken place through external acquisitions and has therefore had a lesser impact on the historical model. All of this has occurred within a framework of constant universal service obligations (USOs), which require that all contact points be served every day despite the decrease in volumes.

3 Towards an Acceleration of Social Transformation

The last years have enabled social challenges to be increasingly taken into account. The fact that the European Commission application report includes a paragraph specifically on the matter shows that the ongoing changes in the sector are scrutinized more closely regarding this aspect. In the forthcoming years, this interest could further increase as it appears that social evolutions could become stronger, more complex and more heterogeneous. The impact of the digital economy on postal operators will trigger a faster pace of change and require more agile solutions.

This therefore raises the question of how to make a success of this transformation in employment terms, in particular through internal redeployment (Bailly and Meidinger 2014) in a more complex but also rapidly evolving environment. On the one hand, NPOs need to develop new solutions with in particular proximity services. These services could put opposite requirements on the social model in the sense that urban logistics requires high flexibility while services to individuals relies on a stable workforce. On the other hand, growing parcel activity will have increasing weight in postal operators' organization and therefore progressively impose its own constraints in terms of flexibility to all activities. All this will take place in a context of disappearance of mail at a stronger pace; a decrease which is not fully compensated by the increase of parcels' activities (Bailly and Meidinger 2014).

3.1 Developing New Adapted Solutions

Faced with rapid changes and changing consumers' needs, postal operators need to offer ever more innovative and adapted solutions. Indeed, while the need for fast delivery is declining within the mail market, the growth of e-commerce supported by relevant digital applications has kick-started consumers' interest in fast delivery. Incumbents that have specific know-how and experience in last-mile delivery are therefore among the companies which are best positioned to meet this growing need. Based on their unique network throughout the country, they also have the organizational and logistical capabilities for providing many innovative proximity services.

The development of these services is in particular based on two emerging trends: urban logistics and the silver economy, based on the ageing population, with its own specific requirements, which can be diverging. The fast and reliable delivery of goods within urban zones is one of the areas of development of incumbents' proximity services. Generally speaking, in order to develop these services, which offer highly flexible solutions of delivery at any time of the day NPOs tend to invest in new companies which often rely on a flexible workforce largely composed of independent workers. As a consequence, we are seeing the development of multiple employees' statuses under the umbrella of the same company.

On the other hand, the development of proximity services to individuals, in particular to the elderly population, requires a stable, qualified and reliable workforce. Indeed, many incumbents are developing higher quality services like the delivery of goods at precise timeslots, the hand-delivery of parcels as well as the delivery of food but also medical check-ups for old people or delivery of official documents. Delivery is now even more customer-centric as there is a higher focus on the receiver experience and expectations.

The possibility to offer value-added services to consumers relies heavily on the historic relationship of trust that postal companies have built over centuries with the customers and the society as well as a good knowledge of consumers' preferences and habits acquired by the postmen/postwomen. The role of the postal employees itself has evolved. Indeed, while formerly their main mission was to ensure mail delivery, they are now offering a much wider range of services with track and trace solutions, value-added services as well as possibilities to provide digital payments. Postal employees need to have a contact with customers during the delivery taking care for what is inside the packet with an adapted offer accordingly; they have thus become an important part of the customers' journey. All these elements contribute to reinforce the position of postal incumbents as service companies.

The development of proximity services could therefore trigger a two-tier evolution of employees' statuses due to diverging nature and requirements of these activities. At the same time, the growing parcels' activities require further flexibility and place cost pressures on incumbents.

3.2 Increased Flexibility Requirements Imposed by Parcels

The development of parcel activities is a common trend among all incumbents and is expected to continue in the coming years enabling a partial internal redeployment of employees. Indeed, in order to take advantage of their wide delivery network and large workforce on the competitive parcels' market, postal operators tend to increasingly combine mail and parcel delivery. However, in terms of delivery, parcel activity has flexibility requirements which are much greater than mail activity. As a consequence, some incumbents have already clearly initiated measures to increase the flexibility of their work organization to include parcel delivery.

The example of bpost shows how the new model of organization with a greater focus on flexibility aims to better face competition on the growing parcel market. The collective labor agreement approved on October 2015 over Mail Service Operations "MSO Plan" has installed a new model. Some of the most innovative measures introduced by this plan include the enlargement of working time to Saturday and even Sunday. Concretely this leads to the abolition of additional compensation for working on Saturdays in order to make it a normal working day as well as the introduction of a compensation for working on Sundays. Moreover, it foresees the creation of agile teams to better deal with volume fluctuation in parcels.

Parcel delivery requires products to be delivered when people are at home. In Poste Italiane, the measures negotiated in the collective labor agreement of June 2010 also aimed at developing a new organizational delivery model. This new model foresees, in particular, an extension of the delivery services to cover the entire day (from 08.00 to 20.00) from Monday to Friday and also Saturday morning for a limited number of specialized workers.

The need to extend delivery hours to make them more compatible with consumers' demands has also been taken into consideration within Le Groupe La Poste. It has put in place an experiment in the town of Angers with the aim of redeveloping its parcel activity while anticipating the emergence of new alternative delivery models. Increased competitiveness of its parcels' offerings relies on two levers: the inclusion of small size parcels within mail delivery during the day and an improvement in delivery efficiency for larger parcels which are distributed to private customers in the evening. By relying on evening rounds, La Poste can develop new same-day and next-day delivery services and drastically decrease the number of pending parcels. The customers' satisfaction for this new offer is high. In addition to this trial, the organization of delivery rounds will change with a view at national level to having 10,000 rounds with a midday break until end of 2016 and foreseen deliveries for parcels only on Sundays.[5] These changes with an important impact on work organization will have to be supported by negotiations with social partners. All these measures represent important social evolutions which contribute to ensure the competitive position of the incumbent in the parcels' market.

Fierce competition on the parcels' market can also have an impact on wages as competitors have a lower cost-structure. As an example, in order to become more flexible and more competitive, Deutsche Post DHL has created 49 regional low-cost parcels' delivery companies which a much more flexible structure. These subsidiaries recruit new employees in open-ended contracts but with wages which are 20 % lower than the parent company and aligned with the agreements in the logistics sector. As underlined by the Deutsche Post DHL Board member Juergen Gerdes "In light of the significant discrepancy in wage costs with our competitors, we are, however, not able to realize this with the existing wage structure [...] these new companies afford us the opportunity to create new, attractive and above all permanent jobs with competitive wages…".[6] We are thus seeing different wage structures within the same company. Besides the main "traditional" competitors in the parcel market, new actors from the e-commerce are developing their activities in delivery and seem to appear as the new competitors with a much more flexible business model. The risk of an "Uberization" of the parcel delivery is becoming a reality.

3.3 Towards a Fragmentation of Postal Activities?

In most postal companies the development of innovative, flexible and reliable delivery offers is therefore witnessed. At the same time, the cost-based competition will put further pressure on incumbents to implement stronger social optimization with potentially more radical measures in the future. It appears that the development of different statuses and pay scales within some postal companies according to the requirements of the different activities could continue. These combined trends suggest a more diversified social model within the postal sector. Rather than a

[5]La Poste Group, Presentation, SDC Training seminar on e-commerce and new services, 18 November 2015.

[6]Deutsche Post DHL, « Deutsche Post plans to create up to 10,000 new jobs by 2020 ».

unique model, the work organization and the forms of employment will be more adapted to the specific needs of each activity. This pressure on costs and diverging trends trigger the risk of a fragmentation of the postal sector into diverse activities having their own economic and social model and belonging to different professional branches. Moreover, these economic and social transformations could lead postal activities to become more mainstream economic activities losing their specificities but also to the end of a historic social model.

4 The Postal Sector Has to Maintain Its Unique Identity

4.1 Maintaining a Quality Service

Faced with this increasing competition, postal operators have two different options. Either, on the one hand, to optimize costs in order to have a cost structure closer to their competitors or, on the other hand, to guarantee more quality services for customers. The example of PostNL can be a good illustration of the limits of the first option. Indeed, some years ago, the company made the choice to convert its delivery workforce into a fully part-time structure in order to lower its labor costs as much as possible. The objective was to replace all traditional postmen/postwomen by part-time delivers in order to increase the flexibility of the work organization and lower costs.

This strategy seems, however, to have had limited success. Firstly, in 2010, the company, which was faced with criticism from customers, especially business ones, due to decreased quality of service, has decided to keep a better balance between experienced traditional full-time postmen/postwomen and part-time deliverers. More recently in 2016, PostNL announced that it will offer open-ended contracts to all new staff in parcels' delivery while it was until now largely relying on independent workers for this activity.[7] This change in its strategy is, in particular, justified by customers' new demand in terms of quality of parcel delivery as well as the company's increased diversification into proximity services. Indeed, as stated by its CEO Herna Verhagen these types of services rely on stronger quality requirements and on experienced employees in particular as delivery workers are increasingly entering people's home. She stated however that this will trigger millions of euros of additional costs for the company[8] but it can be assumed that this is a necessary investment to ensure its longer term sustainable development. This change will therefore enable PostNL to recruit better-qualified staff, encourage this staff to remain longer in the company and as a consequence enhance the quality of its services.

---

[7]de Volkskrant « The always cheaper and always faster does not work anymore », 15 April 2016.
[8]DutchNews.nl, « PostNL to offer all new parcel staff a permanent contract », 15 April 2016.

4.2 Proximity as a Unique Asset

Today proximity has regained importance for two main reasons. First of all, the digital age has triggered increasingly dematerialized relations between people with potentially a threat on the quality of physical interpersonal relations. In this context, proximity is a value that people are re-discovering. Secondly, environmental pressure has imposed more local consumption practices. In this context, the proximity with customers and society that incumbents have built over years as a unique asset can represent an essential comparative advantage in a more competitive environment.

Over the centuries, postal operators have built a unique proximity with all customers. This proximity is both physical and relational; it relies on their unique extended network but also on the relationship of trust which has been built with the customers. The value of proximity represents an essential reason to conduct a cautious and balanced social transformation. It is the founding principle of all postal activities and should remain a common link between them justifying the maintenance of core common characteristics. It will also have to be taken into consideration when the future European debate on the USO will open. The optimization of networks, of the USO as well as the social optimization will have to find the right balance in order not to put this essential asset of proximity at risk.

5 Conclusions

The postal sector seems to be facing two sequential phases of social transformation. For the moment, changes to social models have remained limited with no radical change mainly due to structural reasons. However, in the future, the shift of the economic model away from traditional activities and towards an increasingly diversified portfolio of activities could trigger more complex social changes.

In this increasingly evolving context, the unique identity of the postal sector which is proximity should remain the core common characteristic across all the activities. This helps put the sector in a strategic position as a solid link between digital and physical services. Indeed, digital technologies have helped develop new activities, which often have to be materialized in a physical manner. The digital and physical channels are complementary and increasingly interdependent which is why using a multichannel approach is more effective than a single channel one. The key priority of incumbents will be to bring added value by the increasing combination of digital and physical services both within traditional and new postal services.

References

Annual reports from bpost, Deutsche Post DHL, La Poste, Poste Italiane, PostNL, Swiss Post (2010, 2015).

Bailly, D., & Meidinger, M. (2011). The dual trend towards operational efficiencies and social regulation in European postal services. In M. A. Crew & P. R. Kleindorfer (Eds.), *Reinventing the postal sector in an electronic age* (pp. 336–350). Cheltenham, UK and Northampton, MA, USA: Edward Elgar.

Bailly, D., & Meidinger, M. (2013). Human capital and diversification choices for postal operators. In M. A. Crew & P. R. Kleindorfer (Eds.), *Reforming the postal sector in the face of electronic competition* (pp. 350–360). Cheltenham, UK and Northampton, MA, USA: Edward Elgar.

Bailly, D., & Meidinger, M. (2014). Finding the conditions for a successful social redeployment combined with diversification of activities. In M. A. Crew & T. J. Brennan (Eds.), *The role of the postal and delivery sector in a digital age* (pp. 305–316). Cheltenham, UK and Northampton, MA, USA: Edward Elgar.

Deutsche Post DHL, Press release, « Deutsche Post plans to create up to 10,000 new jobs by 2020 », January 22, 2015.

De Volkskrant « The always cheaper and always faster does not work anymore », 15 April 2016.

DutchNews.nl, « PostNL to offer all new parcel staff a permanent contract », 15 April 2016.

European Commission, report from the Commission to the European Parliament and the Council on the application of the Postal Services Directive, 17 November 2015.

European Social Dialogue Committee for the postal sector (SDC), Project « Mobilizing social partners in a new context » report, 2016.

International Postal Corporation, Global Monitoring Report 2015.

Royal Mail & CWU, « Business Transformation 2010 and Beyond », 8 March 2010.

Royal Mail & CWU, « Agenda for growth, industrial stability, pay and protections », January 2014.

WIK, Main Developments in the Postal Sector (2010–2013), 2013.

Is the Universal Postal Union Still Relevant?

Emmanuel Vivet and Roland Leray

1 Introduction

The Universal Postal Union (UPU) will soon be holding its quadrennial world Congress, scheduled to take place in Istanbul in September 2016. One of the outstanding issues will be reform of the UPU. A fierce yet diplomatic battle will no doubt take place between the 192 members on the new formats of the Council of Administration and Postal Operations Council (POC), its two governing bodies.

However, traditional postal operators (POs) are being challenged both by world integrators and web operators, losing market share in the small packet segment. This raises the question of the relevance of the UPU. How relevant can a "single postal territory" (Art. 1 of UPU Constitution) be today where the Internet is open to everyone?

The UPU has been, ever since the 1874 founding treaty and subsequent adjustments, an important arena for world postal coordination. Its *raison d'être* has been to ensure consensus worldwide on a variety of international postal standards, definitions, import and export rules, tariffs, related to money transfer, mail (correspondence), parcel and express.

Our chapter discusses the ability of the 142-year-old world organization to meet the challenges of international postal regulation in an environment that profoundly changed over the last decades. Although terminal dues are a large part of that question, we do not limit the analysis to them and enlarge the scope to other aspects of the UPU: Are the standards produced by the UPU relevant? Are the negotiation

E. Vivet (✉)
Institute for Research and Education on Negotiation (IRENE), Cergy, France
e-mail: e_vivet@yahoo.fr
URL: http://www.essec-irene.com

R. Leray
Le Groupe La Poste, Paris, France
e-mail: roland.leray@laposte.fr

M. Crew et al. (eds.), *The Changing Postal and Delivery Sector*,
Topics in Regulatory Economics and Policy,
DOI 10.1007/978-3-319-46046-8_22

outcomes legitimate? We question whether the "single postal territory" concept, and its practice, can be maintained in an environment where posts are challenged by other operators. Would a reform of the UPU internal negotiation mechanisms improve the situation?

Section 2 of our analysis begins with assessing the economic coverage of the UPU, showing that it only covers a decreasing portion of what can be defined, more broadly, as international delivery. Section 3 argues that posts still play an important role in international delivery and gives some microeconomic reasons for the role for the UPU. Section 4 recalls, however, what the main weaknesses of POs in the management of international flows are. Section 5 explains why the UPU needs reform nonetheless. Section 6 concludes, saying that the upcoming reform might not save the organization from its growing irrelevance in regulating international deliveries unless a broader approach is decided.

2 Proportion of International Flows Covered by UPU Rules

One indicator of the relevance of the UPU is to estimate the percentage of international delivery is still governed by UPU rules.

A first way of estimating the postal sector's percentage is to compare postal revenues with the revenues of other players involved in single-piece shipments. In terms of value, the percentage of the postal sector, both for domestic and international shipments, represents between 10 and 20 % of the single-piece shipment sector. On the whole, postal revenues have been stable in recent years, despite a decline in mail volumes (Allaz 2013).

In Table 1, the share of POs seems to be 59 % in 2014. However, this method has three main limitations. Firstly, it relies on revenues: whereas the value of a piece is smaller in postal networks than it is in the express world. Secondly, it mixes domestic and international shipments, thus blurring the issue of international delivery. The generally accepted proportion of international mail in postal revenues is 5 % (1–1.4 % in volumes)—this proportion is higher for integrators. Finally, it puts aside the issue of bulk shipments delivered directly in the country of destination. We come back on the bulk mail further down in this section. But Table 1 clearly shows that POs' market share is declining.

In order to assess their market share more in detail, it necessary to focus on the size of the market for international delivery. A estimate for outbound international mail is

Table 1 POs' revenues versus integrators' revenues

	1980	1985	1990	1995	2000	2005	2010	2014
Postal revenues	46	67	92	122	145	171	178	178
Integrators revenues	na	na	na	na	64	82	99	121

Operating revenues (in billions SDR)—high income countries (Word bank): *Source* UPU
Integrators revenues (in billions SDR): annual reports (FedEX, UPS, DHL, TNT, etc.)

DPDHL's report in 2015, with €6.6 billion (annual report, p. 26). Another study released in 2015 assesses the size of the world letter mail market at $320 billion in 2015, its cross-border component being just less than 4 % (Adrenale 2015). On top of this, the parcel market is estimated by the study at $260 billion (2015), with its cross-border "lighter weight" share (i.e. below 5 kg) at 12 % and that of cross-border "heavier weight" at 12 % as well. All in all, this would amount to:

International letter mail market + cross-border lighter weight parcel + cross--border heavier parcel = $12 billion + $31.2 billion + $31.2 billion = $ 74 billion (in 2015).

The size of international mail, lighter and heavier parcels would then be above $70 billion. However one may also look at the international delivery from a different angle.

In Table 2, the market size ($34.4 billion) is smaller than in DPDHL's figure, which is $74 billion. The difference can be explained and stems from the cross-border heavier parcel segment, which for DHPDHL represents $31 billion. What is more, the volumes in Table 2 can be checked consistently with UPU figures: for international letters, a 3406 billion pieces figure is very close to 2014 UPU data, while 191 million pieces for DO express and parcels is consistent with 105 million (2015 UPU international parcels data) + 65 million (2015 international EMS). On the non DOs' (integrators) side, we have not verified the data. In sum, the market for international mail and parcels, excluding the "heavier" ones, can be estimated between $34 and $41 billion.

Table 2 Evolution of the competitive cross-border letter and parcel market

Cross-border demand data (millions)		1998	2008	2015
DO revenues		$9172	$11,482	$11,648
	Letters	$6976	$7899	$7649
	Express and parcels	$2196	$3583	$3999
DO volumes		5396	4845	3597
	Letters	5301	4721	3406
	Express and parcels	95	124	191
Other postal and competing operator		1998	2008	2015
Other operator revenues		$9771	$19,541	$22,841
	Letters	$533	$1399	$1402
	Express and parcels	$9237	$18,142	$21,439
Other volumes		619	1193	1259
	Letters	399	839	841
	Express and parcels	220	354	418
DO's share of lighter		1998	2008	2015
	Revenue %	48	37	34
	Volume %	90	80	74

DO Designated operators. DOs are POs, as chosen by governments to implement the obligations of the UPU convention (accept and deliver inbound mail and inbound parcels, pay the terminal dues)

Source Adrenale study, Feb. 2015, Fig. 4, p. 11 ("analysis based on UPU, Colography, Boeing, and competitor, proprietary and other research data")

Beyond market size, Table 2 gives an assessment of the market share of POs: 34 % of revenues for the world competitive market for {cross-border letter + cross border parcel below 5 kg}, and 74 % of volumes thereof. The difference between 34 and 74 % comes from the fact that posts carry lower revenue, lower weight letters and parcels, whereas competitors carry and deliver higher-value and higher-yield packages. The 74 % proportion does not contradict assertions of the UPU, for which "80 % of the mail items generated by ecommerce are sent in the letter post stream to which the UPU terminal dues applies" (Okholm et al. 2015, p. 1).

However, the proportion may be a little lower as it may be the case that the *Adrenale* study has left out some elements of bulk mail. For the B2C segment, bulk shipments are either dropped off by the sender as close as possible to their destinations or picked up from sender's premises. For international destinations, bulk shipments can be dropped off in the country of destination (direct access) or else picked up directly by the postal operator in the destination country as close as possible to the sender (Extraterritorial Office of Exchange). In both cases, international bulk shipments are, in principal, shipped under trade regulations as opposed to UPU regulations. The same goes for parcel, for which a large proportion seems to escape the postal network: more than one UPU international postal parcel in two (or one EMS shipment in two) was dropped off at a post office, which seems to indicate that some B2C shipments were channeled otherwise.

Nevertheless, for mail and small packets weighing less than 2 kg, even after the disappearance of the postal monopoly, the international postal network continues until today to dominate B2C shipments due to the very low remuneration of terminal dues. This system, which does not cover costs incurred by the postal service in the country of destination, eliminates competition and is characteristic of an import subsidy (Campbell et al. 2011; Campbell 2014; Okholm et al. 2015).

While carrying out this analysis, we should keep in mind that despite the importance of B2C shipments, international flows remain marginal. The postal business is mainly a domestic business (about 95 %). This is why international shipments can be supported, even under the cost price, by revenues taken from domestic mail. All in all, the proportion of international flows which are covered by UPU rules is likely to be a maximum of one-third of revenues and less than three quarters of volumes. More research is needed on this. We can also tell that it is declining in comparison to that of integrators'.

3 The Assets of POs and the UPU in the International Delivery Business

Economic literature on the UPU is generally focused on the issue of terminal dues (for mail) and inland rates (for parcels). Copenhagen Economics (2014) laid out clearly the six distortive effects of terminal dues on the market, while Campbell makes regular estimations of the "losers" and "winners" of the current system: the total amount of transfers was assessed between 299 and 618 million SDR, based on 2007 UPU data (Campbell et al. 2011), with other estimations at 418 million SDR for the industrialized countries (Campbell 2014). Bilateral transfers are also analyzed. At a microeconomic scale, Okholm et al. (2015) confirmed in their "mystery shopping experiment" that these distortions do occur in practice, based on the analysis of 50 items bought on internet Asian platforms and carried from Asia to Europe, with a very clear threshold effect at 2 kg. Others (Wojtek 2015) have pointed out the incompatibility of UPU inland rates with EU competition rules. All agree that the growth of cross-border e-commerce will make these distortions more and more obvious.

These studies point out, with an increasing accuracy over the years, the economic inefficiency of some major UPU negotiations and their distortive effects on the market. Yet in the meantime, governments continue to use the UPU as a regulatory tool, imperfect as it may be. The fact that governments continue to use the UPU to regulate—even poorly—the international mail and parcels market can mean that the organization and its network of POs also generate some benefits. If one is to study the relevance of the UPU, a look should be taken at other, perhaps less visible, aspects of the UPU negotiations, not just terminal dues and inland rates. A glance at the list of the 40 working groups of the UPU shows that regulatory work is done on other issues such as the Addressing System, the Quality of Service standards, bags' and dispatches' Labeling, Barcodes, Operational Accounting standards, Security and Air Transport rules, among others, not to mention the Development Funds.

The UPU is therefore a place where POs and their states work on common rules and standards. Most of these standards belong to the category of Public Goods: their use by one member does not reduce the benefit of the other members. If we look at the UPU from a neoliberal institutionalist approach, where states decide to build international organizations (Keohane 1989) because they have some converging goals to pursue, postal rules and standards are typical of these goals. The UPU is instrumental at developing common rules and standards for postal flows worldwide.

In working at the UPU, states try to build on POs assets. What are these assets? Among the postal sector's greatest strengths is in the density of access points, which surpasses that of integrators'. In many countries, postal services have been able to maintain and grow a retail outlet network comprising of, mainly, post offices run fully by POs or in partnership with other stakeholders. This single network has, for over a century, provided a simple, secure and affordable means for citizens to drop off their shipments bound for destinations worldwide (Table 3).

Table 3 Number of post offices worldwide (in thousands)

1980	1985	1990	1995	2000	2005	2010	2014
513	540	580	720	690	640	680	680

Source UPU online database (on www.upu.int), 2016

Table 4 Postal staff (in millions)

1980	1985	1990	1995	2000	2005	2010	2014
4.7	5.0	5.2	6.0	5.3	5.3	5.4	5.3

Source UPU online database (on www.upu.int), 2016

A postal sector's other great strength is its ability to adapt delivery systems to local constraints. As such, in countries that do not have sufficient address or security infrastructures, POs have introduced post-office boxes or depots into the post office network. In other countries, POs have developed secured building access systems for postmen, or fitted out all handover points with infrastructures connecting the postal network (standardized post boxes, parcel pick-up points, etc.). This strength is based on the universal trust and confidence of postal employees, whose number is significant and stable (Table 4).

One could say that the Universal Postal Convention and the UPU are assets as such. Established in 1874, the UPU is officially tasked *to stimulate the lasting development of efficient and accessible universal postal services of quality in order to facilitate communication between the inhabitants of the world* (Preamble of the Constitution). Therefore, the UPU's aim was, first and foremost, to care for shipments between citizens, that is, C2C shipments. Today, more broadly, the Convention governs exchanges between POs on a daily basis, including the remuneration of services between operators. The Convention and its regulations provide, as defined above, a valuable set of technical standards that serve the general interest. The re-negotiation of those standards on a regular basis keeps them up-to-date, indispensable to the work between posts, and explains why the Convention is a binding one; its amendments enter into force upon adoption, as opposed to some other UN texts, that normally require a minimum number of ratifications in the member countries.

The Convention is so clear that disputes between POs and citizens are few and far between: in particular, there is no issue of international pricing, which has been a matter of great concern for telecommunications operators (International Telecommunication Union 2015). Whilst there is an arbitration procedure at the UPU, it is only enforced on rare occasions, a fact which in itself attests to the reliability and exhaustive nature of its regulations. Outstanding payments remain the only issue that has yet to be fully resolved, despite implementing clearing houses managed by the UPU.

Finally, the very existence of the Convention is one of the reasons why the criticism about the anti-competitive nature of terminal dues, or inland rates (Wojtek 2015) can be questioned. Truly, terminal dues represent the setting of prices at world level, with operators being more or less part of the decision-making process, which is not consistent with generally accepted competition rules. But from a financial point of view, it should be noted that more than one of the negotiation actors, some very significant, belongs to the losers (Campbell et al. 2011): this does not normally signal a cartel. From a law point of view, some will argue that terminal dues are negotiated under the security umbrella of a UN-based treaty. From a negotiation viewpoint, finally, we see that terminal dues and inland rates are part of a broader regulatory package that includes obligations put on posts, such as: the obligation to accept inbound flows without a contract (and whatever the quality of the addressing), taxes on export flows, which feed the development funds, and the Universal Service Obligations, at national level.

From a political viewpoint, we note that the European Commission has not attempted, so far, to tackle this complex issue. The anti-competitive nature of the UPU is there, but is part of a broader UN-based general arrangement. This legal feature adds to the flaws of the UPU but will not, in our opinion, be its main drawback in the near future. The sustainability of the UPU and its aim, the "single postal territory", will depend on other, more operational, elements.

4 Weaknesses of Posts and of the Single Postal Territory

One of the weaknesses of the single postal network is disparities in the quality of service and productivity achieved by each postal operator. This reduces the relevance of the UPU (Table 5).

Due to the disparate quality of service and productivity of import procedures, it is very difficult to establish fair remuneration models between designated operators. The UPU remuneration systems tend to benefit low performing countries. In industrialized countries, incoming international mail represents small quantities compared to domestic mail and is incorporated in the much larger national flow. The poor remuneration of the inbound items, which are of lesser value than domestic mail, is hidden by its smaller importance.

International postal shipments do not benefit as much from technological advances as domestic shipments. International shipments are subject to security and customs regulations that are conducted with no automation. C2C flows do not benefit from as comprehensive customs declaration forms as B2C flows. In general, imported items must be re-labelled in order to be seamlessly processed for delivery, which has an adverse impact of end-to-end tracking for customers.

This is also why the international postal network, which was founded on the freedom of transit (Art. 4 of the Postal Convention), is not competitive compared to integrated networks. In Europe in particular, "deferred" parcels are shipped internationally by road, a more reliable and less costly means than the UPU network.

Table 5 Number of letter-post items posted per capita in 2014

Africa and middle East	Asia Pacific	Latin America	Eastern Europe and ICS	Industrialized countries
2	6	18	27	300

Source UPU website, postal statistics: *Development of Postal services* (p. 8)

Increases in the level of UPU exchanges are mainly due to the increase in small packet volumes (in B2C).[1] So, paradoxically, the UPU was created for shipments between citizens (C2C shipments) but now relies on B2C in order to continue to exist. This B2C growth is due to subsidies-like terminal dues (see Sect. 3) and this increase can be taken as artificial (Campbell 2014). The main paradox of the UPU is here: should the organization address the terminal dues anomaly, it would, at the same time, lose a large part of its relevance.

5 Reforming the UPU Is a Necessity

In addition to the inefficiency of some of its major negotiations, the UPU's relevance and existence is also in question. Firstly, its financial position calls for a reform.

There is concern over stable financing sources that continue to decrease. Governments allocate, on a voluntary basis, a number of contribution units to the UPU annual budget (Table 6).

Furthermore, the budget is drawn up based on modified accrual accounting, whereas the statement of the financial position is drawn up based on full accrual accounting. This means that future pension benefits still need to be figured out. The implementation of budgets excluding all of the benefits for employees has accumulated a deficit estimated to be in excess of 70 million Swiss francs. The UPU is not sure to be able to meet its financial commitments from 2020 onwards. There is little hope that UPU member states or their designated operators would increase their contributions.

It is true that straightforward measures such as invoicing registration for UPU conferences, reducing the number of members of the Board of Directors, deciding to make the Convention permanent (which should reduce the duration of the Congress to one week), reducing the number of executive positions and some benefits granted to employees would make it possible to deal with the big expenses that are expected over the coming decade. But this will not put an end to the question of financing the UPU.

Secondly, the question of whether it would be possible to negotiate international delivery rules, or just tariffs, outside the UPU can be asked. While economic

Table 6 Number of contribution units by member States at the UPU

1994	1996	2000	2002	2008	2013	2017
951.5	922	907	878	867,5	852	832.5 (est.)

Source UPU working documents

[1]The annual growth of Chinese small packets to Europe is above 20 %.

literature is thorough about the flaws of terminal dues, hardly any paper explores alternative options. Okholm et al. (2015) considers a way "towards a Non-distortive UPU system" (Sect. 5, p. 10), but contains few considerations on how difficult it would be to achieve this goal, and no considerations on where and how to negotiate them on the world scene. A notable exception is Campbell et al. (2011), who suggests a difficult, yet possible "path to reform" for terminal dues, including through negotiations that would take place outside the UPU—i.e. in an OECD context.

A way of assessing the relevance of the UPU is to take the issue from a microeconomic viewpoint, looking at how an individual member country sees its benefit. For example, France makes an estimated annual contribution of 3 million CHF, which breaks down as follows (source: International Department, La Poste): Contribution to the ordinary budget of 50 units: 1.6 million CHF; tax on shipments to developing countries (QSF): 0.9 million CHF; experts involved in negotiations in Bern: 0.5 million CHF.

Without a Universal Postal Union, its postal operator would incur bilateral transaction costs in negotiating bilateral agreements with fifteen or so other major operators, and just as many bilateral agreements with small satellite operators. Taken globally, a set of negotiations between N partners requires $N(N - 1)/2$ bilateral negotiations, instead of a unique multilateral negotiation system.

However, for a country of the size of France, it is estimated that ten people would suffice to cover all of the legal, operational and financial aspects of the 30 bilateral remuneration agreements, representing a cost of probably less than 3 million CHF. In this perspective, the bilateral path is a valid one, at least for remuneration issues. In practice, some POs may decide to entrust a private operator with delivery, which would cost less than using the designated operator in the country of destination. The POs could even take part of the ownership in these private operators, which would result in tax optimization that would be beneficial for the company.

Another argument for the bilateral path for remunerations is the complexity of UPU terminal dues negotiations: the 192 countries are split in 6 groups, and several mail weights are considered; some posts pay taxes on mail export flows, some do not, depending on the type of bilateral pair; delays and exceptions add to the complexity; on top of this, bonus-malus rules are applied to some of the groups, based on the quality of service—and the quality of service calculation is subject to another sensitive negotiation. As pointed out in the case of the World Trade Organization, international organizations are meant to manage complexity, but complexity can sometimes reach a point where it reduces drastically the negotiation space (or zone of possible agreement). In such a context, too rigid or structured a process can lead to a point where the agreement becomes difficult or impossible (Siroën 2011).

The aviation sector may provide food for thought on the possible evolution towards bilateral negotiations. While the multilateral system of the International Civil Aviation Organization (ICAO) is responsible for safety and security rules, major economic aspects, such as traffic rights, have been governed, ever since 1944, by bilateral agreements. Nowadays, a flexible web of some 4000–5000 bilateral air services agreements continues to regulate the aviation sector worldwide, despite the increasing technicality of aviation talks. These agreements are made by governments, yet the airlines are associated to the talks, as active observers. Every country may designate one or several airlines, depending on the agreement.

The aviation sector thus epitomizes a governance architecture that differs from the postal business under two aspects: first, it puts the emphasis on bilateral negotiations rather than multilateral; second, it associates more than one company per country, thereby enlarging the legitimacy of governmental negotiation outcomes.

But some believe that the UPU has the means to maintain a situation where all postal decisions are made at world level, through UN multilateral negotiations. They count on Article 8 of the Constitution, which stipulates that *designated operators may make Special Agreements concerning the international postal service, provided always that they do not introduce provisions less favorable to the public than those provided for by the Acts*. Article 135.2 of the General Regulations stipulates that *the International Bureau shall see that the Special Agreements do not include conditions less favorable to the public than those which are provided for in the Acts of the Union.*

In practice however, the International Bureau does not have the competence to undertake such checks (especially for agreements between a designated operator and a private operator). It is, rather, the regulator of the destination member country who could check whether the conditions are no less favorable for customers, including with the help of UPU quality of service measures and surveys.

If the designated operator of the country of destination is less efficient than its private competitors, an avenue for reform would be to include those non-designated operators in the work of the UPU. As in the case of the International Organization for Standardization, the cooperation with the private sector is useful when it comes to standards (Murphy and Yates 2009). It is even argued that on the whole, the opening of international organizations to private operators is on the rise (Devin and Smouts 2011, p. 142). In the UPU, the current POC could open itself to more operators on technical matters. Such opening would pay tribute to the variety of delivery service providers of our time. Traditional POs would sit next to integrators, or even web operators, together to work on "international delivery", taken from a broad, not just postal point of view.[2] They could discuss on important standards related to Quality of Service, Insurance, Returns, Compensation for damages, or cooperation between posts and integrators. In this possible way for UPU reform, the POC would simply forgo influencing the Postal Convention (which deals with

[2]«Delivery service providers» is the title used in recent WTO negotiations documents such as the *Trade in Services Agreement* (TISA) currently under negotiation. The WTO approach chooses to no longer separate postal and express operations, but attempts to encompass both of them under the same chapter. Here, we do not mean that the WTO approach is fully consistent, notably because it does not take fully into account the burden of USOs on posts; but we value the attempt to use the term "delivery" and to put everyone under the same regulatory umbrella.

regulations and States), and focus on operational regulations, standards, technologies, not to mention capacity building in developing countries.

6 Reform of the Existing UPU Will not Necessarily Make the UPU More Relevant

If the UPU does not reform, or if the reform is a flawed one, the single postal territory will have endured. The international shipment service provided to retail customers will continue to exist through private networks. Accessible and affordable service providers like of times past, at the time where Thurn and Taxis, the Middle-Age private operator that used to reign over European deliveries, might circumvent the 1874 organization. Morris (2015) will have been right to think that "*the international postal system is profoundly broken and nobody is paying attention*".

If the UPU is to succeed in its reform at the Istanbul congress, and if the diplomatic compromise coming out of the negotiation is fair, the UPU will be more efficient. Improved institutions and more efficient negotiations should normally lead traditional POs to adjusting terminal dues to the cost of delivery. The massive B2C export/import system that flows through the UPU channels and rules, which subsidies POs from some low income/high exporting profile countries, sending packets to higher income countries, would then be revised. A proper revision of terminal dues would make such exports less attractive, paving the way for the massive B2C flows to use alternative international distribution channels.

We can therefore see that a change is in some respects already under way: without reform, the current terminal dues system will be circumvented. With a proper reform, the increase of terminal dues to the level of the true costs will derive most B2C flows outside the UPU. Without these B2C flows, the UPU would empty itself. Paradoxically, a large part of the relevance of the current UPU relies on a terminal dues system that might be down if the reform is a success.

The remaining yet useful part of the UPU is the standardization one, i.e. the setting up of postal rules and standards. Here, what needs to be changed is not just the way the UPU operates, but which stakeholders are members of the UPU. Making sure that all participants in the "delivery business", be them POs or integrators, work together on rules and standards, in order to improve the service to customers worldwide, can be the future of the UPU. Opening the UPU, not just reforming its existing bodies, is the way forward.

References

Adrenale, adrenale.com (2015, February 2). *Research on postal markets: Trends and drivers for international letter mail, parcels, and express mail services.*

Allaz, C. (2013, September). France, *Histoire de la Poste dans le monde*, édition Pygmalion.

Campbell, J. I., Jr. (2014, September 29). *Draft proposals for the UPU Istanbul congress—Reform of the union*. Report for the Advisory Committee on International Postal and Delivery Services, Department of State. https://www.uspsoig.gov/document/terminal-dues-age-ecommerce

Campbell, J. I., Dieke, A. K., & Zauner, M. (2011). *Terminal dues: Winners, losers, and the path to reform*. Presentation at the 19th conference on postal and delivery economics, CRRI, St. Helier, Jersey, final paper 17 June 2011.

Copenhagen Economics. (2014). *The economics of terminal dues*. Report for the US Postal Regulatory Commission.

Devin, G., & Smouts, M.-C. (2011). *Les organisations internationales*. Paris: Armand Colin.

International Telecommunication Union. (2015, September 16). *Report on the LET'S ROAM THE WORLD: The ITU global dialogue on international mobile roaming (IMR)*. ITU Headquarters, Geneva, Switzerland, 18 September 2015.

Keohane, R. O. (1989). Neoliberal institutionalism: A perspective on world politics. In Keohane (Ed.), *International institutions and state power: Essays in international relations*. Boulder, Co: Westwiew.

Morris, D. Z. (2015, December 15). The international postal system is profoundly broken and nobody is paying attention. *Pacific standard*. http://www.psmag.com/business-economics/the-international-postal-system-is-profoundly-brokenand-nobody-is-paying-attention

Murphy, C. N., & Yates, J. (2009). *The International Organization for Standardization (ISO)*. London and New York: Routledge.

Okholm, H. B., Boivie, A. M., Basalisco, B., & Wahl, J. (2015). An economist's perspective on terminal dues. In M. A. Crew & T. J. Brennan (Eds.), *The future of the postal sector in a digital world* (pp. 283–293).

Siroën, J.-M. (2011). Négociations commerciales multilatérales et cycle de Doha: les leçons d'un échec annoncé. *Négociations, 2011*(2), 9–21.

Wojtek. R. (2015). UPU compensation rates for packages under EU competition law—Are there lessons to be learned from other international fee arrangements? In M. A. Crew & T. J. Brennan (Eds.), *The future of the postal sector in a digital world* (pp. 331–345)./ Bibliography>

MIX
Papier aus verantwortungsvollen Quellen
Paper from responsible sources
FSC® C105338

If you have any concerns about our products,
you can contact us on
ProductSafety@springernature.com

In case Publisher is established outside the EU,
the EU authorized representative is:
Springer Nature Customer Service Center GmbH
Europaplatz 3, 69115 Heidelberg, Germany

Printed by Libri Plureos GmbH
in Hamburg, Germany